Small Business Kit

FOR DUMMIES®

2ND EDITION

by Richard D. Harroch

WILEY

Wiley Publishing, Inc.

Small Business Kit For Dummies®, 2nd Edition

Published by
Wiley Publishing, Inc.
111 River St.
Hoboken, NJ 07030-5774
www.wiley.com

Copyright © 2004 Text and any other Author Created Materials Copyright, Richard D. Harroch

Published by Wiley Publishing, Inc., Indianapolis, Indiana

Published simultaneously in Canada

For general information on our other products and services or to obtain technical support, please contact our Customer Care Department within the U.S. at 877-762-2974, outside the U.S. at 317-572-3993, or fax 317-572-4002.

Wiley also publishes its books in a variety of electronic formats. Some content that appears in print may not be available in electronic books.

Library of Congress Control Number: 2004103168

ISBN: 978-0-7645-5984-6

Manufactured in the United States of America

10   9

2O/SR/QW/QU/IN

WILEY

About the Author

Richard D. Harroch is an attorney with over 20 years of experience in representing start-up and emerging companies, entrepreneurs, and venture capitalists. He is listed in *Who's Who in American Law* and is a corporate partner in a major law firm in San Francisco. He is a Phi Beta Kappa graduate of U.C. Berkeley and graduated from UCLA Law School, where he was managing editor of the *Law Review*. He has edited or co-authored a number of legal/business books, including *Start-Up and Emerging Companies: Planning, Financing and Operating the Successful Business* and *Partnership and Joint Venture Agreements*.

Richard was the chairman and co-founder of AllBusiness.com, one of the premier Web sites for small businesses. He was also the founder, CEO, and chairman of LawCommerce, Inc., an Internet company dedicated to providing products and sources to the legal profession.

He has lectured extensively before various legal and business organizations, including the American Electronics Association, the Venture Capital Institute, the California Continuing Education of the Bar, Law Journal Seminars-Press, the California State Bar Business Section, the Corporate Counsel Institute, the San Francisco Bar, and the Practicing Law Institute (PLI).

Richard has served as the chairman of the California State Bar Committee on Partnerships, the co-chairman of the Corporations Committee of the San Francisco Bar (Barristers), a member of the Executive Committee of the Business Law Section of the California State Bar, and co-chair of the *Law Journal* seminar in New York on "Joint Ventures and Strategic Alliances."

Richard has experience in the following areas: start-up and emerging companies, corporate financings, joint ventures, strategic alliances, venture capital financings, employment agreements, IPOs, leases, loans, online and Internet matters, license agreements, partnerships, preferred stock, confidentiality agreements, stock options, sales contracts, securities laws, and mergers and acquisitions.

Publisher's Acknowledgments

We're proud of this book; please send us your comments through our Dummies online registration form located at www.dummies.com/register/.

Some of the people who helped bring this book to market include the following:

Acquisitions, Editorial, and Media Development

Project Editor: Traci Cumbay

(Previous Edition: Kyle Looper)

Acquisitions Editor: Kathy Cox

Copy Editors: Laura K. Miller, Elizabeth Rea

Technical Editor: Tova L. Zeff

Media Development Specialist: Laura Moss

Editorial Manager: Jennifer Ehrlich

Media Development Manager: Laura VanWinkle

Editorial Assistant: Courtney Allen

Cartoons: Rich Tennant, www.the5thwave.com

Composition

Project Coordinator: Courtney MacIntyre

Layout and Graphics: Andrea Dahl, Denny Hager, Michael Kruzil, Kristin McMullan, Lynsey Osborn, Heather Ryan, Melanee Wolven

Proofreader: Aptara

Indexer: Aptara

Special Help Angela Denny

Publishing and Editorial for Consumer Dummies

Diane Graves Steele, Vice President and Publisher, Consumer Dummies

Joyce Pepple, Acquisitions Director, Consumer Dummies

Kristin A. Cocks, Product Development Director, Consumer Dummies

Michael Spring, Vice President and Publisher, Travel

Brice Gosnell, Associate Publisher, Travel

Kelly Regan, Editorial Director, Travel

Publishing for Technology Dummies

Andy Cummings, Vice President and Publisher, Dummies Technology/General User

Composition Services

Gerry Fahey, Vice President of Production Services

Debbie Stailey, Director of Composition Services

Contents at a Glance

Foreword..*xv*

Introduction *1*

Part 1: Starting Up Your Business *7*
Chapter 1: Choosing Your Business Entity..9
Chapter 2: Business Plans 23
Chapter 3: Organizing a Corporation 41

Part 11: Money Matters.................................. *61*
Chapter 4: Raising Capital for Your Business 63
Chapter 5: Bookkeeping and Accounting Basics......................................85
Chapter 6: Small Business Tax Basics..105

Part 111: Employee and Consultant Issues..................... *119*
Chapter 7: Employee Hiring Tools...121
Chapter 8: Motivating and Retaining Employees 149
Chapter 9. Avoiding Employee Problems 165
Chapter 10: Independent Contractor and Consultant Agreements 187

Part 1V: Bulletproofing Your Business............... *205*
Chapter 11: Key Contracts 207
Chapter 12: Legal Issues 233
Chapter 13: Protecting Your Ideas and Inventions................................247
Chapter 14: Avoiding Customer Problems 263
Chapter 15: Real Estate Leases for Your Business 279

Part V: Spreading the Word............................ *297*
Chapter 16: Web Sites, Your Business, and You 299
Chapter 17: Press Releases and Dealing with the Press........................315

Part V1: The Part of Tens *325*
Chapter 18: Ten Ideas to Make Your Business More Successful 327
Chapter 19: Ten Great Web Sites for Small Businesses 331
Chapter 20: (Almost) Ten Great Publications for Small Businesses 337

Appendix: What's on the CD-ROM 341

Index 367

End-User License Agreement 383

Table of Contents

Foreword ....*xv*

Introduction *1*

About This Book...1
Foolish Assumptions 2
What You're Not to Read 2
How This Book Is Organized...2
    Part I: Starting Up Your Business 3
    Part II: Money Matters 3
    Part III: Employee and Consultant Issues...................3
    Part IV: Bulletproofing Your Business........................3
    Part V: Spreading the Word 4
    Part VI: The Part of Tens 4
Icons Used in This Book...4
Where to Go from Here...5

Part 1: Starting Up Your Business 7

Chapter 1: Choosing Your Business Entity 9

Setting Up Sole Proprietorships 12
Creating a Partnership 12
    General partnerships 13
    Limited partnerships 14
    Limited Liability Partnerships 15
Corps Is Short for Corporation, Not Corpses 16
    C corporations 16
    S corporations 18
Helpful Hybrids: Limited Liability Companies 19
Forms on the CD-ROM 21

Chapter 2: Business Plans 23

Writing Your Business Plan 23
The Key Sections of the Business Plan...........................25
    Following the standard format 25
    Reality check..34
Writing a Mini Business Plan 36
Forms on the CD-ROM 36

Chapter 3: Organizing a Corporation 41

A Corp Is Born 41
Playing the name game 41
Choosing a state of incorporation...............................43
Creating the Articles of Incorporation.......................43
(Lights . . . camera . . .) Action of Incorporator 44
Let bylaws be bylaws...46
Maintaining an (up-to-the) minute book 47
Pricing out the cost of incorporation 47
Completing the establishment of the corporation........48
Corporate Actions...48
The board of directors..49
The shareholders 50
Capitalizing the Corporation 51
Issuing stock 52
Keeping a stock ledger..52
Entering into a Right of First Refusal Agreement 52
Forms on the CD-ROM 53

Part II: Money Matters *61*

Chapter 4: Raising Capital for Your Business 63

Borrowing from Peter to Pay Paul 64
Negotiating good loan terms..64
Producing proper promissory notes 66
Sleuthing out SBA loans...66
Putting Your Equipment on a Tight Lease 68
Placing Your Stock on the Auction Block.........................69
Different stocks for different folks...............................71
Securities laws 101 71
Bolstering support with your business plan 75
Preparing a Private Placement Memorandum.............75
Selling stock with a Subscription Agreement 76
Romancing a Venture Capitalist 77
Preparing to meet a venture capitalist 78
Getting to know you 79
The beginning of a beautiful relationship 81
Forms on the CD-ROM 83

Chapter 5: Bookkeeping and Accounting Basics 85

Choosing Your Accounting Method: Cash or Accrual............85
Keeping Records and Books 86
Supporting documents 87
Recording business transactions 88

The Accounting Toolkit 90
    The Income Statement 90
    The Balance Sheet 94
    The Cash Flow Statement 97
    Computing profit margins 100
    Budgets and projections..100
    Auditing financial statements 101
The Forms on the CD-ROM 103

Chapter 6: Small Business Tax Basics **105**
Thinking about Taxes from the Ground Up 105
    Choosing the right business entity 106
    S corporations 106
The Tax Tool Kit 106
    Application for a taxpayer identification number..................107
    Employee forms 107
    Tax deposit coupons 108
A Tax for All Reasons 110
    Income tax 110
    Self-employment tax...110
    Employment taxes 111
    Excise taxes 112
    Sales taxes 112
Elementary, My Dear: Deductions for Your Business.....................113
    Business expenses 113
    Special tax benefits for shareholders of a
        qualified small business..114
Where to Go for More Help 115
Forms on the CD-ROM 116

Part III: Employee and Consultant Issues **119**

Chapter 7: Employee Hiring Tools **121**
Finding the Cream of the Crop 121
    Tried-and-true resources..122
    A tangled Web of resources..122
Parlez-Vous Interview? 124
    Questions to ask 124
    Questions not to ask 124
Checking 'Em Out..128
Hiring Tool Kit 129
    Employment applications 129
    Offer letters 134
    Job offer mistakes to avoid 134

Employment agreements..137
Confidentiality and Invention Assignment Agreements.............137
New employee paperwork 145
Forms on the CD-ROM 146

Chapter 8: Motivating and Retaining Employees 149

Motivating Employees in Good Form 149
Formal and informal appreciation devices 150
Employee Satisfaction Surveys...152
Digging through the Employee Incentive Tool Kit 156
Stock Option Plans 156
Profit sharing 160
Bonuses 160
Cafeteria Plans 161
401(k) plans...161
Unusual perks 162
Forms on the CD-ROM 163

Chapter 9: Avoiding Employee Problems 165

Going by the Handbook..165
Discrimination policy...168
Sexual harassment policy.....................................168
E-Mail policy..171
Drug-free work policy 171
Appraising Can Be Up-Raising 174
Firing Employees...175
Take aim . . . fire!...175
Cease fire 176
Settling up at the end...177
Conducting Exit Interviews...178
Forms on the CD-ROM 185

Chapter 10: Independent Contractor and
Consultant Agreements 187

Forming Relationships with Independent Contractors
and Consultants..187
Independent Contractor Agreements 188
Confidentiality and Invention Assignment Agreements.............194
Tiptoe through the Tax Forms...199
Using a contractor takes determination..............................200
Tax forms of the rich and famous (not poor and nameless) 202
Forms on the CD-ROM 202

Part IV: Bulletproofing Your Business 205

Chapter 11: Key Contracts 207
Understanding Contracts...207
Writing and Negotiating Good Contracts.............................208
    Letters of Intent...212
    Services Contracts..213
    Sales Contracts..218
    Purchase Orders...219
License Agreements...220
Joint Venture Adventures..221
Distribution Agreements...223
The Skinny on Boilerplate Text..225
Amending a Contract...226
Forms on the CD-ROM...232

Chapter 12: Legal Issues 233
Avoiding Legal Wrangles 233
    Keeping good records......................................234
    Taking the corporate quiz: Are you legal?................236
Going Down with the Ship (Not!) 236
    Avoiding personal liability 236
    Negotiating guaranties 240
Checking into State and Local Laws 242
    Getting state and local business licenses 242
    Registering fictitious business names 243
    Filing information with the state 243
    Qualifying to do business in other states................244
Forms on the CD-ROM...245

Chapter 13: Protecting Your Ideas and Inventions 247
Pondering Patents..248
Copyrights and Copycats..250
Tricks of the Trademark...252
    The great mark hunt 252
    Want a mark? . . . get set . . . file!........................254
    Bulletproofing your marks 255
Can You Keep a Trade Secret?...255
Speaking Confidentially 256
Forms on the CD-ROM...260

Chapter 14: Avoiding Customer Problems 263

    Doing Preventative Maintenance 263
        Setting up a customer payment policy 263
        Giving an early payment discount 264
        Handing out warranties 264
    Giving Credit Where Credit's Due 265
        Preparing to extend credit 265
        Reducing the risk of nonpayment 269
    Getting Your Money the Hard Way 273
        Mailing out collection letters 273
        Getting your attorney to send letters 273
        Relying on collection agencies 273
    Forms on the CD-ROM 278

Chapter 15: Real Estate Leases for Your Business 279

    Negotiating an Office Lease 279
        Rent 285
        Negotiating permitted uses 285
        Working out the term of the lease 286
        Escalating rent 286
        Operating costs 287
        Allowing for tenant improvements and alterations 288
        Setting up rules about assignment and subletting 289
        Figuring out renewal options 290
        Option to expand 291
        Looking into security deposits 291
        Reviewing the rules and regulations of the building 292
    Offering an Offer Letter 292
    Forms on the CD-ROM 295

Part V: Spreading the Word 297

Chapter 16: Web Sites, Your Business, and You 299

    Determining a Domain Name 299
        Running a check on an e-brilliant name 300
        Registering a domain name 301
        Buying a domain name from an existing holder 301
        Of domains and trademarks 302
    The Web Site Development Contract 303
    The Web Site Legal Kit 309
        Online Contract 309
        Terms of Use Agreement references 310
        Copyright notices 311

Web site information disclaimers......................................311
Hyperlink disclaimers 311
Forms on the CD-ROM 313

Chapter 17: Press Releases and Dealing with the Press 315

Drafting Good Press Releases..315
Getting the keys to a press release 316
Delivering press releases...317
Checking Out Some Sample Press Releases 318
Meeting the Press...321
Knowing the key players 321
Getting the reporter's attention 321
Establishing a media relations policy...........................322
Forms on the CD-ROM 324

Part VI: The Part of Tens.................................325

Chapter 18: Ten Ideas to Make Your Business More Successful 327

Team Up with Another Company...327
Get Advice..328
Send Gifts to Your Key Customers 328
Seek Financing When You Don't Need It 328
Try Different Ideas 329
Motivate and Reward Employees..329
Research Your Competition..329
Get Favorable Publicity 330
Ask Your Employees 330
Build a Great Company Web Site...330

Chapter 19: Ten Great Web Sites for Small Businesses 331

AllBusiness...331
Business Week 332
The Small Business Administration......................................332
The Internal Revenue Service...333
Entrepreneur...333
CBS Marketwatch 334
American Express — Small Business....................................334
Newspaper Web Sites 335
Wells Fargo 335
Yahoo!..336

**Chapter 20: (Almost) Ten Great Publications
for Small Businesses** **337**
     The Wall Street Journal 337
     Inc. 337
     Business Week 338
     Entrepreneur 338
     Fortune 338
     Fast Company 339
     Forbes 339
     Built to Last: Successful Habits of Visionary Companies 339
     Business Contracts Kit For Dummies 340

Appendix: What's on the CD-ROM *341*
     System Requirements 341
     Using the CD 342
     Adobe Reader 342
     Forms, Forms, and More Forms 342
     Troubleshooting CD Problems 365

Index *367*

End-User License Agreement *383*

Foreword

*W*hen Richard Harroch asked me to write the foreword for his new book, *Small Business Kit For Dummies,* 2nd Edition, I was thrilled. I have known Richard for many years, and I have seen him in action as a lawyer and advisor to start-up and emerging businesses. I knew this would be a great volume.

Why do you need a business kit like this one? Starting a business can be a daunting process. As the Executive Director of the Lester Center for Entrepreneurship at the University of California, Berkeley, I get plenty of proof. Many would-be entrepreneurs with great ideas just never get to first base. They may have the most important and seemingly most difficult part done: They have identified a market opportunity and a profitable way to fill it. They stumble, however, over the "easy stuff," like raising funding, getting properly organized, and, moreover, running the business in a "businesslike" manner. Lawyers and accountants are important resources, but unless you do your own homework and learn the "basics," they can be expensive teachers. This volume gives every entrepreneur quick, straightforward advice and tools to use when approaching a new area of business development.

In my work, I have the privilege to teach the MBA candidates at the Haas School of Business at UC Berkeley. These are undeniably some of the best and brightest young business minds, many of whom are committed to founding their own businesses after graduation. One of the most common complaints I hear about their MBA education is that the faculty don't teach them the fundamentals of organizing and running a small business. That's true. But this book can give you what an MBA education cannot: straightforward guidance on the basics of many of the legal, financial, employment, and management hurdles of starting and running your own business. Topics cover the full spectrum, from the basics of business formation, organization, accounting, and tax and financing to tips for putting your business on the Web and tools for dealing with the press. Chock full with sample forms and templates, *Small Business Kit For Dummies,* 2nd Edition is a treasure chest. The CD-ROM makes everything in the book more directly accessible and customizable for your use.

Starting a business can be the event of a lifetime. The drive of individuals to create new businesses is one of the fundamental engines of our new economy. The oft-quoted statistics are overwhelming: "two-thirds of the net new jobs over the last 25 years have been created by small business. Overall, small business employs one-half of the private workforce."*

Every new business has to start somewhere, and it's a good idea to take things one step at a time (the first customer, the first employee, the first bank loan, the first contract, the first financial statement, and so on). But every "first" entails much for the entrepreneur to learn. This book can be both a guide and a shortcut to getting on with the job!

I have had the good fortune to wear a lot of hats in my career, and for the last twenty years, I've been immersed in starting and running new ventures. In the '80s as the Director of the Entrepreneurial Services practice for Ernst & Young in the Bay Area, in the '90s as Executive Director of the Lester Center for Entrepreneurship and Innovation, and, more recently, as a founding partner in a venture capital firm, I've had the privilege to work with literally hundreds of entrepreneurs starting their own businesses (and yes, I've founded a few of my own along the way). I can honestly say that in every case, this little volume for us "Dummies" would have come in very handy indeed. I will be referring many of my students to this "Kit" for years to come.

— Jerome S. Engel, Executive Director, Lester Center
for Entrepreneurship and Innovation, Haas School of
Business, University of California, Berkeley

Small Business Job Creation: The Findings and Their Critics by William Dennis Jr., Bruce D. Phillips, and Edward Starr.

Introduction

Wouldn't it be great if all it took to run a business was a great idea or service? You'd just need to satisfy your customers. Wouldn't it be wonderful not to have to worry about things like contracts, taxes, employees, bookkeeping, and liability issues? Sure, it'd be terrific, right up to the time that you woke up.

In the real world, if you want to be the captain of your own ship rather than the first mate on someone else's freighter, you have to remember a ton of legal and financial obligations, filings, and issues. With so much to keep in mind, however, you may have trouble figuring out where to start. Often, the problem boils down to not knowing how much you don't know. And don't try to plead ignorance as an excuse, either. If you fail to do the things the law requires of you, it's your problem.

Well, now you can rest a little easier. *Small Business Kit For Dummies,* 2nd Edition, gives you the practical advice that you need to start a business and find a path through a maze of business laws. It also provides you with the sample forms, agreements, policies, checklists, and letters that you need to turn the legal and business jungle to your advantage.

About This Book

Whether you expect your business to operate on a small scale or plan for your business to be the next Microsoft, this book is for you. *Small Business Kit For Dummies,* 2nd Edition, and its accompanying CD-ROM provide advice and sample forms to businesses ranging from raw start-ups to rapidly-growing companies.

This book is not a murder mystery. You don't have to start at page one, and if you turn to the last chapter, you don't necessarily find out whether the butler did it. This book is set up more like an encyclopedia. In an encyclopedia, you don't have to read through all the *A's* before you can read the *B's*. When you need a certain bit of information, you find what you're looking for, use the information, put the book back on a shelf, and go back to growing your business.

Suppose that you want to find a piece of information that allows you to take an extra business deduction, meaning you and the kids get to go to Disney World. You can use a couple of strategies to find the information that you want. First, you can go to the table of contents and locate the topic. In this case, Chapter 6 — "Small Business Tax Basics." Then you can scan the headings until you find where the information you want is hiding. Second, if you know exactly what kind of information you're looking for, you can go directly to the index and find it there.

Inside the back cover of this book, you can find a CD-ROM chock-full of sample forms and agreements that you can modify for use with your business. If you ask an attorney to draft these forms, you may spend many thousands of dollars.

Remember, however, that the law is a funny thing. An agreement or a discussion about an agreement that applies to most businesses may not apply in your particular case or location. Always check with your attorney in cases dealing with a large sum of money or potential exposure. (In fact, it never hurts to check with your attorney about any business form or agreement.)

Foolish Assumptions

This book assumes a basic understanding of business practices and concepts. Because this book is primarily focused on providing a wide variety of tools for businesses, I give as much coverage as possible to the forms and their uses. I provide only a limited amount of coverage of general business concepts (though I do my best to explain the background to each topic briefly). If you feel like you need more background business information, check out www.All Business.com, one of the premier small business sites on the Web.

What You're Not to Read

Some of the topics that you have to be familiar with as a business owner are, by their very nature, technical (for example, taxes, accounting, and contracts). But from time to time, I mark technical explanations that you generally don't need to understand to get the big picture with a Technical Stuff icon (check out the section "Icons Used in This Book" later in the Introduction to find out more about icons). Feel free to skip these discussions — no one's going to get mad.

How This Book Is Organized

This book is organized roughly along the pattern of first things first. Part I covers starting your business, Part II talks about money, Part III moves into getting people to work for you, Part IV gives you information about avoiding legal hassles, and Part V moves into methods for increasing the exposure of your business. The final two parts are the Part of Tens, which appear in any *For Dummies* book, and the Appendix.

Part I: Starting Up Your Business

Every business has to start somewhere. In Part I, you can find information that you have to think about as you get your business off the ground. Chapter 1 gives you information on choosing the business entity for your business (such as corporation, partnership, or limited liability company). Chapter 2 gives you pointers on writing an effective business plan to use as a tool to gauge your business's success and to attract capital. Chapter 3 covers essential information for setting up a corporation to protect yourself from the business's financial and legal liabilities.

Part II: Money Matters

Money makes businesses go 'round, and Part II puts you right in orbit with the big boys. Chapter 4 is an important one, providing tools for infusing capital into your business, including loans agreements, filings necessary to sell stock, and venture capital financing. In Chapter 5, you can find forms and strategies for keeping your books, including accounting methods, cash flow comparisons, and methods of figuring balances and budgets. The tax laws are another set of issues that really affect your business, and Chapter 6 provides tax basics for your business, including discussions of business deductions and IRS filings.

Part III: Employee and Consultant Issues

As your business grows, at some point, you need to hire people to help you meet your goals. Chapter 7 provides advice and tools for hiring employees, such as employment agreements, applications, and questions to ask and not to ask in interviews. Chapter 8 tells you how to retain and motivate employees after you hire them. Look in this chapter for discussions of employee incentive plans, stock options, and benefit packages. Chapter 9 concentrates on employee problems, including strategies for avoiding them and how and when to fire employees. Finally, Chapter 10 deals with hiring independent contractors and consultants, including forms for backing up the nonemployee status of these workers for the IRS.

Part IV: Bulletproofing Your Business

When you're in business, bad stuff can be lurking around every corner. Some bad stuff just eats away at your money. Other bad stuff can land you in court or in jail. Chapter 11 opens up this part with a discussion of your key contracts, including sample forms and agreements that you can modify for your own use. Chapter 12 runs down legal issues that you should be aware of as a businessperson. Chapter 13 contains tools for protecting your patents, trademarks, and other intellectual property, which can be the lifeblood of your company. And Chapter 14 gives you some tools for avoiding customer problems (such as nonpayment) and provides tools to solve the problems when they do occur. Finally, Chapter 15 gives you advice on negotiating a lease for your business.

Part V: Spreading the Word

When your business is going well, you want to publicize it as much as possible. Part V gives you two low-cost methods that are available to just about every business. Chapter 16 gives you tools to exploit the World Wide Web for your business, including things to include in contracts for hiring a Web site designer and online contracts for selling your goods on the Web. Chapter 17 tells you how to get great free publicity from the press by simply using press releases.

Part VI: The Part of Tens

No *For Dummies* book is complete without a Part of Tens. Check out Chapter 18 for ten great tips for making your business more successful. For those readers with Internet access, Chapter 19 provides ten Web sites that apply to small businesses. Chapter 20 provides some publications that small business owners may find useful.

You can also find a useful appendix in this part. The appendix tells you all about the valuable CD-ROM on the inside back cover of this book. Check out the appendix to find an extensive table that outlines the various forms in this book.

Icons Used in This Book

Watch for the following icons that tell where to find particular types of information at a glance:

This icon points out a revenue-generating or cost-cutting measure that directly affects your business's bottom line.

This icon points out a valuable form, agreement, checklist, or letter that you can find on the CD-ROM.

This icon points out an important issue that you don't want to forget about.

This icon signals a point of law that you should check at your state or local level.

This icon flags techie legal jargon and technical discussions that you can skip if you want to.

This icon gives you a hint to save time or trouble.

This icon uncovers a trap that can have grave consequences.

Where to Go from Here

You can start this book wherever you want. If you don't currently have a business, then Chapter 1 is a logical place to start. If you have a small business that you want to grow, check out Chapter 2 on business plans and Chapter 4 on raising capital. If you have a successful business, you may want to start at Chapter 18, where I discuss strategies to make your business even more successful, and work from there.

Part I
Starting Up Your Business

The 5th Wave   By Rich Tennant

"Our business is doing very well. We manufacture the hand carts the whole world is going to hell in."

In this part . . .

The decision to start up a business is not to be taken lightly. To give your business the best chance of success, you need to do a good bit of up-front work.

Your first order of business is to decide what form you want your business to take. Do you want a sole proprietorship? A partnership? A corporation? Chapter 1 outlines the pros and cons of each business entity.

After you figure out which business entity best fits your business, you should sit down and write out a sound business plan. Planning is absolutely necessary to keep your business on the right track and to capture the interest of investors. Chapter 2 gives you some hints on creating solid business plans.

Finally, if you decide to set up a corporation to limit your personal liability, you must jump through some hoops to get the job done. Chapter 3 tells you about the filings and formalities you'll encounter as you incorporate your business.

Chapter 1

Choosing Your Business Entity

. . . .

In This Chapter

▶ Flying solo: Sole proprietorships

▶ Getting a grip on partnerships

▶ Checking out corporations

▶ Looking into LLCs

. . . .

When starting a business, you need to decide early on what legal form the business should take. The common choices are sole proprietorships, general partnerships, limited partnerships, C corporations, S corporations, and LLCs (Limited Liability Companies). Each entity has advantages and disadvantages, and the right choice depends on the nature of your proposed business and various tax and liability issues. In this chapter, I outline the key points that you need to know about choosing the right entity for your business.

Form 1-1 on the CD-ROM (and shown later in this chapter) summarizes the key differences between various types of business entities. You need to pay special attention to tax and liability issues.

Characteristic	C Corporations	S Corporations	Sole Proprietorship	General Partnership	Limited Partnership	LLC
Ownership Rules	Unlimited number of shareholders allowed; no limit on stock classes	Up to 75 shareholders allowed; only one basic class of stock allowed	One owner	Unlimited number of general partners allowed	Unlimited number of general and limited partners allowed	Unlimited number of "members" allowed
Personal Liability of the Owners	Generally no personal liability of the shareholders for the obligations of the corporation	Generally no personal liability of the shareholders for the obligations of the corporation	Unlimited personal liability for the obligations of the business	Unlimited personal liability of the general partners for the obligations of the business	Unlimited personal liability of the general partners for the obligations of the business; limited partners generally have no personal liability	Generally no personal liability of the members for obligations of the business
Key Documents Needed For Formation	• Articles of Incorporation • Bylaws • Organizational Board Resolutions • Stock Certificates • Stock Ledger	• Articles of Incorporation • Bylaws • Organizational Board Resolutions • Stock Certificates • Stock Ledger • IRS & State S Corporation election	• DBA filing	• General Partnership Agreement • Local filings if partnership holds real estate	• Limited Partnership Certificate • Limited Partnership Agreement	• Articles of Organization • Operating Agreement

Form 1-1: Comparison Chart for Different Business Entities, page 1 of 2.

Characteristic	C Corporations	S Corporations	Sole Proprietorship	General Partnership	Limited Partnership	LLC
Tax Treatment	Corporation taxed on its earnings at the corporate level and the shareholders may have a further tax on any dividends distributed ("double taxation")	Entity generally not taxed as the profits and losses are passed through to the shareholders ("pass-through" taxation)	Entity not taxed, as the profits and losses are passed through to the sole proprietor	Entity not taxed, as the profits and losses are passed through to the general partners	Entity not taxed, as the profits and losses are passed through to the general and limited partners	Entity not taxed (unless chosen to be taxed), as the profits and losses are passed through to the members
Management of the Business	Board of Directors has overall management responsibility and officers have day-to-day responsibility	Board of Directors has overall management responsibility and officers have day-to-day responsibility	Sole proprietor manages the business	The general partners have equal management rights, unless they agree otherwise	The general partner manages the business, subject to any limitations of the Limited Partnership Agreement	The Operating Agreement sets forth how the business is to be managed – a Manager can be designated to manage the business
Capital Contributions	Shareholders typically purchase stock in the corporation, either common or preferred	Shareholders typically purchase stock in the corporation, but only one class of stock is allowed	Sole proprietor contributes whatever capital needed	The general partners typically contribute money or services to the partnership, and receive an interest in profits and losses	The general and limited partners typically contribute money or services to the limited partnership, and receive an interest in profits and losses	The members typically contribute money or services to the LLC, and receive an interest in profits and losses

Form 1-1: Comparison Chart for Different Business Entities, page 2 of 2.

Setting Up Sole Proprietorships

Some businesses are formed as *sole proprietorships.* In this case, the business has only one owner — you. Sole proprietorships are easier to set up than corporations or other entities.

To establish a sole proprietorship, you typically need to file a *fictitious name certificate* at a local or state governmental office if you're doing business under a name different than your own. This certificate, in essence, notifies the world who the business's true owner is, such as "John Smith, d.b.a. Blue Vision Flowers." The *d.b.a.* abbreviation stands for "doing business as."

Sole proprietorships are not advisable if you plan to do any significant business because you face unlimited liability for the business's debts — a real disadvantage. Plus, you can have a difficult time growing the business and attracting investors to a sole proprietorship.

The following key points characterize a sole proprietorship:

- **Business transferability:** Selling your business involves selling the business assets and may be more complicated than selling a corporation.
- **Existence:** After you die or become disabled, the business may have difficulty continuing on, both legally and business-wise.
- **Expenses:** You must keep careful records of your personal expenses versus your business-related expenses. The IRS may challenge your handling of certain expenses if it thinks that those expenses may not be legitimate, deductible business costs.
- **Licenses:** You may need various business licenses, sales tax licenses, or permits.
- **Personal liability:** You have personal liability for all of the business's debts and obligations. If something goes wrong with the business, your personal assets (home, car, and bank savings) may be at risk.
- **Tax:** The IRS taxes you and your business as one for income tax purposes. Tax rates for corporations may be more advantageous than tax rates for individuals. (Check out the tax discussion in Chapter 6.)

Creating a Partnership

You can set up your business as a partnership consisting of two or more partners. Partnerships come in three types: general, limited, and limited liability. Limited Liability Companies (LLCs) are similar in some ways to partnerships. I describe LLCs in the section "Helpful Hybrids: Limited Liability Companies" later in this chapter.

General partnerships

General partnerships consist of two or more partners. You can create general partnerships with little or no statutory formalities, although you probably want to have a Partnership Agreement that sets forth the partners' rights and obligations.

Avoid general partnerships like the plague! Each partner in a general partnership may be liable for the debts and obligations of the partnership — not a good situation to be in if things go bad. If you insist on having a partnership, make sure that you have a well-drafted Partnership Agreement and a lot of insurance.

General partnerships tend to be easy to establish and can be more informal than business entities like corporations. But the disadvantage of the partners' horrendous unlimited personal liability more than offsets this advantage.

The following key points typically characterize general partnerships:

- **Personal liability:** The general partners have potential personal liability for the partnership's debts and obligations. If something goes wrong, your personal assets, not just the partnership assets, are at risk.

- **Control and management:** Unless limited by the Partnership Agreement, each general partner has an equal right to share in the management and control of the partnership.

- **Authority:** Unless limited by the Partnership Agreement, any partner can take actions and sign contracts that bind the partnership.

- **Owners and profits:** The owners of the business are partners and split profits and losses as they agree upon.

- **Number of owners:** You can have an unlimited number of general partners.

- **Formation:** General partnerships can be more expensive to form than corporations because you want a lawyer to prepare a detailed Partnership Agreement. Typically, you don't need to have any state filings to form a general partnership. Some local filings may be necessary if the partnership holds real estate.

  Partnership Agreements can be very complicated. This area is one where working with a lawyer is definitely to your advantage.

- **Fiduciary relationship:** General partners stand in a *fiduciary relationship* with each other, meaning that partners generally must act with undivided loyalty, good faith, fairness, and honesty in dealing with each other.

- **Existence:** A general partnership doesn't last forever, and you can dissolve it at the end of a specified term, on the death of a partner, or on other events.

- ✔ **Transferability of interests:** You face real problems trying to transfer general partnership interests, and unless the Partnership Agreement provides otherwise, a person generally can't become a member of the partnership without the consent of all or most of the partners.

- ✔ **Tax:** The IRS taxes the partners, not the partnership, on partnership income (called *pass-through taxation*), thus avoiding the potential double taxation present in regular corporations. (For more tax details, see the tax discussion in Chapter 6.)

Form 1-2 on the CD-ROM includes a checklist of issues that you should consider when drafting a Partnership Agreement.

Limited partnerships

A limited partnership consists of one or more general partners and one or more limited partners. The general partners typically get to make all business decisions, and the limited partners are typically passive investors.

Many businesses have used limited partnerships for owning real estate, restaurants, oil- and gas-related activities, and venture capital funds.

A limited partnership requires you to file an organizational form certificate with the Secretary of State. A Limited Partnership Agreement, setting out the rights and obligations of the general and limited partners, is also important.

Limited partnerships can raise money from passive investors while allowing the general partner to retain near total control of how the business is run. Limited partnerships can be good business structures, especially for real estate holdings, but LLCs (which you can find in the section "Helpful Hybrids: Limited Liability Companies" later in this chapter) or corporations are typically better for operating businesses.

The following key points typically characterize limited partnerships:

- ✔ **Limited liability:** Limited partners aren't personally liable for the partnership's debts and obligations, although their investment in the limited partnership is, of course, at risk for the payment of partnership obligations. The general partners have unlimited liability for the partnership's debts and obligations, and for that reason, the general partner shouldn't be an individual. Instead, consider having the general partner be a corporation or LLC.

- ✔ **Control and management:** Typically, the general partner has the say in all management decisions. However, the Limited Partnership Agreement can give the limited partners various voting rights, such as the right to approve the sale of the business or the right to remove and replace the general partner.

- ✔ **Fiduciary relationship:** The general partner has a fiduciary (trust) relationship to the limited partners and therefore has a legal obligation to look out for their interests.

- ✔ **Securities laws:** A limited partnership interest is usually considered a "*security*" under federal and state securities laws, requiring that you be in compliance with those laws. (See Chapter 4 for a discussion of securities laws.)

- ✔ **Number of owners:** You can have an unlimited number of owners.

- ✔ **Transferability of interests:** Transfer of interests typically requires the general partner's approval.

- ✔ **Profits and losses:** The Limited Partnership Agreement sets forth the partners' rights to profits and losses. You can split up profits and losses in any number of ways.

- ✔ **Tax:** The partners, and not the limited partnership, are taxed on partnership income *(pass-through taxation),* thus avoiding the potential double taxation that regular corporations may face.

If you're going to have a limited partnership, review Form 1-3 on the CD-ROM for a checklist of the items that you should consider including in a Limited Partnership Agreement.

Limited Liability Partnerships

Limited Liability Partnerships (LLPs) are a new entity authorized by certain state laws. LLPs are basically general partnerships with a liability shield for partners. Liability shields come in two basic types: one for tort matters (like negligence claims), and the other to insulate the partners from the partnership's tort and contract obligations.

In many jurisdictions, the law allows only professionals to use LLPs. For example, California LLPs typically are formed only by lawyers and accountants.

LLPs are typically taxed as *pass-through entities,* with the partners, not the entity, paying taxes on the business's earnings.

LLPs are useful in one primary sense — if you have an existing general partnership, and you can qualify for LLP status, you should absolutely convert to LLP status. Such a conversion has little downside, and you can start to protect the partners from the business's various liabilities.

For the most part, however, you should form new businesses as corporations or LLCs, rather than LLPs. (See the section "Helpful Hybrids: Limited Liability Companies" later in this chapter for a discussion of LLCs.)

Corps Is Short for Corporation, Not Corpses

A *corporation* is a separate legal entity formed under a state corporation law. The corporation has shareholders who own stock in the company, a board of directors who have responsibility for overall management of the company, and officers who run its day-to-day affairs.

A key advantage of a corporation is that if it is properly formed and operated, the shareholders are shielded from the corporation's debts and liabilities. Should something go wrong, you only risk the amount that you have invested in the corporation. And, if someone sues the corporation, you're not personally responsible for any damages that a court may award (unless you fail to follow the rules for forming and operating the corporation, as I explain in Chapter 12).

The corporate business entity doesn't protect professionals, such as accountants, doctors, or lawyers, from personal liability for their negligence or malpractice, but it can shield them from personal liability for the acts of their co-owners.

The two main kinds of corporations are C corporations and S corporations. The difference between the two is in the type of tax treatment on the business's earnings. In a C corporation, the government taxes the business's income at the corporate level, and if the corporation distributes any dividends to the shareholders, the shareholders can also pay a tax on that income. This practice is sometimes referred to as *double taxation.* In an S corporation, the government considers that the business income has passed through to the shareholders who are then taxed on their *pro rata share* (the percentage that they own) of the corporation's income.

C corporations

The word "corporation" usually refers to a C corporation. *C corporations* have limited liability and are well-understood entities that can accommodate many businesses. On the downside, corporations require that you follow a fair number of formalities and make several governmental filings. For C corporations, the double tax can be a real expense.

Form 1-4 on the CD-ROM contains a checklist of issues to consider when you decide to form a corporation. I tell you how to correctly form a corporation in Chapter 3.

Corporations make a lot of sense for new businesses — especially if you plan to grow the business and attract investors. Also, you can sell a corporation more easily than almost any other entity. And, if you have hopes of taking the company public, you almost surely have to make the business a corporation.

The following key points characterize C corporations:

- **Limited liability:** Generally, the shareholders, officers, and directors of the corporation aren't personally liable for the corporation's debts and liabilities. Of course, if a shareholder signs a guaranty for a corporate debt, personal liability can be a factor.

- **Perpetual existence:** In contrast to partnerships and sole proprietorships, corporations generally can last forever. However, a corporation may be dissolved by voluntary action.

- **Control and management:** A corporation's overall management is vested in the *board of directors,* a group of men and women whom the shareholders choose. The board of directors, in turn, elects the corporation's officers, who handle the business's day-to-day affairs under the board's general direction.

- **Shareholders' rights:** Shareholders typically have various rights, including the right to elect directors, receive information, inspect corporate records, vote on fundamental business decisions (such as mergers and liquidations), and share in distributions.

- **Owners and profits:** The owners of the corporation are the shareholders who have received stock in the corporation. Such stock is typically common stock, but it can sometimes be *preferred stock* (which grants the holders certain senior rights over the holders of common stock). When the company pays dividends, the common stock holders are entitled to a *pro rata* share of all dividends made to the common shareholders. The dividend rights for preferred shareholders depend on negotiations made in connection with the purchase of the preferred stock. (Chapter 4 discusses the differences between common stock and preferred stock.)

- **Corporate formalities:** You should observe various corporate formalities, such as maintenance of separate books, records, and accounts; completion of various governmental filings; and periodic meetings or written consents of directors and shareholders.

- **Stock transferability:** Shareholders' interests in a corporation are normally evidenced by stock certificates. You can impose reasonable restrictions on the transfer of stock (such as a right of first refusal on transfer) by contract or corporate charter documents. And federal or state securities laws can limit stock transfers.

- **Capital formation:** The corporate entity accommodates a wide variety of forms of capitalization, such as common stock, preferred stock, stock options, warrants, and convertible securities.

✔ **Employee stock ownership:** Corporations provide the best vehicle to give employees equity interests in the business. For example, stock option plans and common stock issuances are quite common in Silicon Valley–based corporations. Corporations allow tax-advantaged stock option grants, which aren't available for other entities.

✔ **Tax:** C corporations are taxed at the corporate level. The government taxes most dividends as income to the stockholders. (This practice is the *double tax.*)

S corporations

S corporations are corporations that can meet certain requirements and that affirmatively elect to be taxed as an S corporation. An S corporation is a regular corporation, but the business's income passes through to the shareholders, and the shareholders pay income taxes based on their portion of the corporate income. This fact holds true whether or not the income has actually been distributed to the shareholders.

For federal tax purposes, if the S corporation has an operating loss, the corporation can pass these losses through to the shareholders to offset other income (subject to some limitations). However, you can deduct S corporation losses on your personal return only to the extent of your *basis* (generally, the amount you invested or have at risk).

S corporations are especially desirable for start-up small businesses. And the decision to be an S corporation isn't permanent; you can later revoke the election.

Depending on your anticipated business operations and income, an S corporation may benefit you. Some states, however, don't allow for S corporation treatment or impose some special tax on S corporations for state tax purposes (although you can still be an S corporation for federal income tax purposes). Discuss this possibility carefully with your accountant or tax adviser before deciding on an S corporation.

In order to become an S corporation, you must follow a number of key rules, including

✔ **IRS election:** All shareholders must sign and file IRS Form 2553 with the IRS. You may also need to make an election with your state of incorporation. New corporations must file the IRS form by the 15th day of the third month of your tax year (basically, a 2½ month window).

✔ **Number of shareholders:** An S corporation can have no more than 75 shareholders.

> ✔ **One class of stock:** An S corporation can only have one class of stock, although certain differences can exist in voting rights among the shareholders.
>
> ✔ **Restrictions on the type of shareholders:** Generally, corporations, various trusts, and nonresident aliens may not be shareholders in an S corporation.

IRS Form 2553 — Form 1-5 on the CD-ROM — must be signed by all shareholders in an S corporation and filed with the IRS. Form 1-6 on the CD-ROM is a transmittal form to accompany the filing.

Helpful Hybrids: Limited Liability Companies

A *Limited Liability Company* (LLC) combines many of the attractive features of partnerships and corporations.

You can form an LLC under a state *LLC statute,* which typically requires that you file an Articles of Organization with the Secretary of State and that the LLC's owners (referred to as *members*) enter into an Operating Agreement. The Operating Agreement functions in many ways like a partnership agreement and can cover many of the issues addressed by a corporation's bylaws.

The principal advantages of an LLC include the ability to limit the member's liability and to obtain pass-through tax treatment. Also, you don't have a limit on the number of investors in an LLC, as you do with an S corporation. The disadvantages of an LLC are that you can face more complications in the Operating Agreement and tax issues than you would for a corporation, plus investors (including venture capitalists) typically prefer to invest in a regular C corporation.

LLCs can be great vehicles for a new entity, but they can also get a little complicated, so make sure to consult with a competent attorney. Also, make sure that you have a good Operating Agreement.

The cost of forming an LLC varies with the circumstances and the state of organization. Some states, such as California, require an $800 minimum annual franchise tax, plus an annual, graduated fee based on the business's income. Legal fees for forming simple LLCs cost $1,000 or more.

The following key points characterize LLCs:

- ✔ **Limited liability:** The members of the LLC are generally not liable for the LLC's debts, obligations, liabilities, or the other members of the LLC. Investors in an LLC generally only have their share of the LLC's capital at risk.

- ✔ **Management:** An LLC may operate under whatever management arrangement the members want. For example, the members may decide to share management responsibilities or to elect one or more managers to handle the management.

- ✔ **Profits and losses:** The members of the LLC have more flexibility than they would in a corporation and are free to decide how to split up the LLC profits and losses. So, for example, they can allocate one member 40 percent of the profits, even though she may have only contributed 10 percent of the capital (subject to some tax rules).

- ✔ **Statutory requirements for formation:** To form the LLC, you must follow a number of state law requirements. For example, the LLC's name typically has to include the words *Limited Liability Company* or *LLC*.

- ✔ **Tax:** An LLC can choose from two taxation options:

  - • **Pass-through taxation:** As they would a partnership, the government taxes the members, not the LLC, on business income.

  - • **Taxed as a separate entity:** This form of taxation is like a regular corporation's tax procedures.

  In most cases, you should elect to be taxed like a partnership, thereby eliminating the potential double tax. The IRS has made this whole process easier with its "check-the-box" rules and forms for election.

- ✔ **Number of owners:** The number or types of members in an LLC is unlimited (unlike an S corporation). Some states require at least two members, but some states (such as Delaware) allow a one-member LLC.

- ✔ **Transferability of interests:** The terms of the Operating Agreement govern the right to transfer member interests. The transfer rights can be subject to various limitations.

Form 1-7 on the CD-ROM contains a checklist of items that you should review before drafting your Operating Agreement.

Forms on the CD-ROM

Check out the following business entity forms on the CD-ROM:

Form 1-1	**Comparison Chart for Different Business Entities**	A chart showing the key features of partnerships, corporations, and other business entities
Form 1-2	**Checklist for Drafting General Partnership Agreements**	A checklist of items to consider when drafting a General Partnership Agreement
Form 1-3	**Checklist for Drafting Limited Partnership Agreements**	A checklist of items to consider when drafting a Limited Partnership Agreement
Form 1-4	**Checklist for Formation of a Corporation**	A checklist of items to consider when forming a corporation
Form 1-5	**S Corporation Election Form (Form 2553)**	The IRS Form to elect S corporation status
Form 1-6	**Transmittal Letter to IRS Enclosing S Corporations**	A sample letter to the IRS for use when sending the S corporation election
Form 1-7	**Checklist for Drafting LLC Operating Agreements**	A checklist of items to consider when drafting an LLC Operating Agreement

Chapter 2

Business Plans

In This Chapter
▶ Writing a business plan
▶ Understanding key sections of the plan
▶ Drafting a mini plan

*P*lanning is essential to your business. Your business probably can't go far without a solid *business plan,* a document that meaningfully describes your business. Investors or venture capitalists want to look at this document before they even think about investing any money in a business. Think of your business plan as both your business's résumé and its growth strategy. A company without a plan is like a poker player who doesn't know how to bluff — clueless.

Preparing a business plan that outlines the plans, strategies, and goals for your business is useful for a start-up or early stage business. This chapter discusses how a business plan functions and how you prepare key sections of the business plan.

Writing Your Business Plan

The soundness of your business plan can make the difference between a company that flounders and a company that prospers. As you settle down to the task of writing your business plan, keep in mind that you can't expect to foresee everything that will happen to your company: No plan provides an absolute roadmap to success. Just give it your best try and be prepared to revise your business plan as the conditions of your company change and as you get your hands on more accurate information.

According to Dun & Bradstreet statistics, poor planning is a prime cause for small business failure.

A business plan serves three key functions:

✔ A planning tool for the growth of the business

✔ A document to convey information to prospective investors

✔ A base to measure and monitor the company's performance over time

Without a plan, you will have a hard time getting investors and lenders interested in reviewing the prospects for your business. Likewise, without a plan, you may have only a haphazard strategy for growing your business.

You can find sample business plans at the following Web sites:

✔ www.AllBusiness.com

✔ www.Bplans.com

✔ www.Inc.com

A well-written business plan conveys a great deal about you and your business. Your business plan communicates your accuracy and credibility while it simultaneously generates enthusiasm in your business. You can expect that your readers will form an opinion of you and your management skills based on the business plan that you submit. Your business plan should be thorough, professional, and realistic.

Business plan don'ts

Here are some tips on what *not* to do when formulating your business plan:

✔ Don't make unrealistic assumptions.

✔ Don't underestimate the difficulties in growing a business.

✔ Don't underestimate competitors.

✔ Don't assume that the reader knows industry technical jargon.

✔ Don't include long, tedious, or overly technical information.

✔ Don't include highly confidential or proprietary information.

✔ Don't avoid discussing the risks to the business because this omission may detract from the plan's credibility.

✔ Don't say that you'll be bigger than Microsoft within 12 months.

The following list gives you some important pointers to remember when writing your business plan:

- ✔ Your business plan should be concise (no one wants to read a long-winded document). In total, your business plan should be 30 to 40 single-spaced pages at most (not counting the appendices).

- ✔ Your business plan should be easy to read and comprehend, and it shouldn't have any typos or grammatical errors.

- ✔ Your business plan should convey the large and profitable market opportunities for the business.

- ✔ Your business plan should convey the strength and depth of your management team.

The Key Sections of the Business Plan

The format of every good business plan, although not set in stone, tends to run along the same basic lines. Remember, a good business plan should have nothing in it that surprises investors.

Following the standard format

The business plan format is fairly standardized, typically containing the following key sections:

- ✔ **Cover page:** Contains contact information and a statement that the plan is deemed confidential

- ✔ **Table of contents:** Enables your readers to quickly find the exact information they're looking for

- ✔ **Executive summary:** Explains, briefly, your business's prospects, needs, and situation

- ✔ **Company description:** Contains a historical account of the company, as well as its future prospects

- ✔ **The product or service:** Explains what is unique about the products or services that your business plans to deliver

- ✔ **The market:** Creates a picture of the market in which your business competes

- ✔ **Marketing:** Informs your reader of how you plan to capture your business's potential market (packaging, distribution, advertising, Web marketing, and so on)

- ✔ **Management/ownership:** Introduces the people holding leadership positions in the business
- ✔ **Competition:** Focuses on your competitors' strengths and weaknesses
- ✔ **Financial statements and projections:** Includes a lot of numbers (hopefully black), like your balance sheet, income statement, cash flow statement, and financial forecasts
- ✔ **Appendices:** Contains résumés of key personnel, an organizational chart with positions and responsibilities, extended market information, and other data to back up the claims in your business plan

The following sections walk you through the important parts of each of these elements.

The cover page

Your business plan's *cover page* should be professional-looking and informative, and it should contain an appropriate confidentiality legend. Form 2-1 later in this chapter shows a sample cover page. Although the confidentiality legend may not be legally binding, you want to let the readers know that you expect them to keep the information confidential.

The executive summary

The *executive summary* introduces the reader to your business plan, and it's the most vital section. Although it comes first, you generally write it last because it summarizes the entire plan.

Effective summaries cover these key points:

- ✔ The company's origins.
- ✔ The product or service and its uniqueness or competitive advantage.
- ✔ The company's goals.
- ✔ The market potential for the product or service.
- ✔ A three- to five-year summary of key financial forecasts, especially sales and profit/loss. (If you're a brand new business, you have to do some research on your market and your competitors and then make some realistic assumptions about how your business can compete.)
- ✔ The management team and its track record.
- ✔ The financing required to grow the business.
- ✔ The exit strategy for investors (how investors will profit, such as from a sale of the company).

Form 2-2 later in this chapter shows a sample executive summary for a software company.

CONFIDENTIAL BUSINESS PLAN

OF

CATCHY SOFTWARE, INC.

November 2004

This Business Plan contains confidential and proprietary information and may not be copied or distributed without the written permission of Catchy Software, Inc.

Catchy Software, Inc.
24 Main Street
San Francisco, CA 94111
Phone: (415) 771-8200
Fax: (415) 771-8201
E-mail: rsmith@catchy.com

Contact: Richard Smith

Form 2-1: A sample business plan cover page.

Executive Summary

Gives general description of the company

Catchy Software, Inc. (the "Company") is a Silicon Valley based start-up company dedicated to developing a suite of software products that will be useful to small businesses, entrepreneurs and business professionals. The Company has already developed Small Biz-Advisor™, a Windows-based software product that provides advice to start-up businesses in connection with organization, marketing and financing.

The Company was formed in 2002 and currently has 10 employees. The Company's management team consists of experienced marketing, software development, and finance personnel who have worked together in the past. The Company's founder and CEO was the Executive Vice President of Marketing at Multimedia Software, Inc., and has over 15 years experience in the software industry. The Company's development team consists of experienced programmers and software designers who have worked at Microsoft, Intuit, and Intel.

Gives management background

In its first full year of operations, the Company reached $750,000 of sales. The Company projects that sales will grow to $7,000,000 a year within the next three years, with a gross profit margin of 42%.

Gives summary projection

The Company's products are high quality, user friendly and innovative. The Company intends to become a leading software provider to small businesses, by expanding and adding to its product line.

States the company's mission

The market for software to small businesses is estimated at $35 billion per year. While the market includes some large competitors (such as Intuit, Inc. and Microsoft), the Company believes that it can compete effectively because of its high quality development team, extensive contacts with distribution partners and innovative product ideas.

Describes the market

The Company is seeking $2 million of equity capital to expand its development and marketing efforts. This capital should enable the Company to finish development on three additional related software products and add key distribution capability. The Company's goal is to grow quickly, in anticipation of an initial public opening.

****

Describes the capital needed and its intended uses

Form 2-2: A sample executive summary for a software company.

In evaluating drafts of your executive summary, check to see whether you have clearly answered the following questions:

✔ Who is the audience for this summary?

✔ Have you clearly introduced your company and its business?

✔ Have you stated both short- and long-term objectives?

✔ Have you addressed the market opportunity for your product or service?

✔ Have you anticipated potential investor concerns and addressed them?

✔ How have you established that your company is unique?

✔ What are the major strengths of your product or service?

✔ What are the main marketplace attractions of this business, and how will your business address the opportunities?

✔ How can new capital help grow your business?

✔ How will investors be rewarded by investing in the company?

The company description

The company section of the business plan should convey a sense of the history and origins of the company, as well as its goals.

Relevant information that you may want to have in this section includes answers to the following questions:

✔ When was the company founded and by whom?

✔ What is the company's form of business organization?

✔ How did the concept for the company's product or service originate?

✔ Is the company's product or service protected by patent, copyright, or trademark?

✔ Why is the product or service worthwhile and viable?

✔ What sales have been recorded to date, and what markets has the product or service penetrated?

✔ How much money has been invested in the company to date?

You should also include a summary of the company's principal objectives — both its long-term statement of purpose and its specific, obtainable, interim goals.

The product

If the company is selling a product, the product section of the business plan not only describes the product in relation to competitive products, but also highlights reasons the product has the potential to penetrate the existing or developing market.

Note: The guidelines in this section apply whether you're selling a product or providing a service. Use this part of your business plan to describe either.

For example, if you're selling a new type of back-support belt, you want to discuss how this belt may be useful to delivery men, dock workers, and even ballerinas!

The product description should detail your product's use and function, along with the needs that it serves. You should address the distinctive features of the product and the advantages and drawbacks of those features. In addition to the product's attributes, you should mention other significant factors, such as cost, quality, reliability, and price.

If the product is still in the development stage, discuss in detail where the project stands and what you need to complete development. Completed milestones and projections for future milestones are helpful road signs. Such milestones include: an early prototype, a working prototype, widespread product testing, and product readiness for manufacture in volume.

If your competitive advantage stems from a unique product, you should include your strategy to protect the product from being copied by competitors. For example, you should discuss patents, trade secrets, or other proprietary protection for the product, along with any proposed strategy for extending such protection.

Investors typically aren't interested in a one-product company. Therefore, you should also discuss logical extensions of the company's product line and future enhancements in the product section.

When a company produces a product, manufacturing accounts for a large percentage of the product's cost, so be sure to include your plan to manufacture the product, the key equipment and materials that you need for manufacture, and the projected manufacturing costs. If you plan to have a third party manufacture the product, identify the party, alternative sources, and the anticipated contractual arrangement.

Management

The management section of the business plan identifies the key members of the company's management team, describes their responsibilities, and documents the relevant experience and accomplishments of each. Focus the discussion on each person's unique abilities and the synergy created by the combination of talent. Include complete résumés that stress accomplishments and relevant track records in an appendix.

Don't overstate the abilities of the existing team in the management discussion. If the group lacks particular skills or experience that your business needs to achieve success, point out such gaps. For example, if your chief financial officer isn't good at adding numbers, this may be a good time to consider a replacement.

 Make sure to convey a commitment to the business on the part of key personnel and a realistic assessment of what the existing personnel can and can't accomplish. Investors look for a balance in marketing, technical, operations, and financial skills, as well as the amount of experience within the management team. Discuss the types of people and skills that you need to add to the team.

This section should also identify members of the board of directors or any advisory board, together with a brief statement of each member's background.

An organizational chart outlining the responsibilities and relationships of the current team members, as well as the positions to be filled, can be included in an appendix.

The market

The market section of the business plan describes the relevant market for the company's products or services. You should discuss the market's size, its projected growth rate, and any of its important subcomponents.

 When a prospective investor reviews the business plan, you must convince her that the market is large, growing, and receptive to the company's products or services. If the market is small or stagnating, investors are less likely to invest in the company.

The market section can also discuss the following:

- ✔ Trends in the market
- ✔ Market receptivity to new products
- ✔ Characteristics of typical customers
- ✔ Market share held by competitors
- ✔ The significance of price, quantity, performance, service, and warranty to the market
- ✔ Feedback about the product from potential customers
- ✔ Independent market studies or statistics

The appendices can include more detailed supporting information.

Marketing

The marketing section of the business plan describes the company's marketing plan and marketing strategy. This section of the business plan should convey to the reader a well-thought-out, multipronged approach to marketing.

Here are some key questions that this section should answer:

- How do you plan to sell or distribute the product?
- What Web and e-mail marketing will you employ?
- What types of advertising will you use? Why did you choose them? What do they cost? How frequently do you plan to use them?
- Will you use an internal sales force and sales representatives, or do you plan to rely on distributors?
- What compensation and incentives will you use to entice distributors and sales representatives?
- If you plan to use a direct sales force, how will you organize them, and what compensation and commission structure will you establish?
- What are the plans for public relations?
- What direct marketing and trade magazine advertisements, product sheets, or promotional materials do you plan to prepare?
- What strategies will you employ to develop brand recognition for the product?

The competition

The competition section of the business plan identifies competing products and technology. You also use this section to identify the following information about competitors:

- Identity
- Resources
- Market share
- Strengths
- Weaknesses
- Recent trends
- Profitability

Compare your product or service with the competition's. How will your price or quality be different? What about performance, service, or other pertinent features? Make sure to address whether your market penetration will come at the expense of competitors, and consider the reactions to your product by competitors. Explain why your business has the potential to capture business from competitors.

Financial statements and projections

The financial forecasts that you put in the business plan appendices should include Balance Sheets, Income Statements, and Cash Flow Projections. The forecasts are typically for a 3 to 5 year period, with the information presented monthly for the first year and then quarterly in following years.

The following list details the ingredients for a well-formed financial section:

- ✔ **Projected sources and applications of funding**
  - Equity, debt, and lease financing you expect to obtain
  - Use of proceeds
- ✔ **Balance Sheet**
  - Three-year projected summary
  - Detail by month for first year
  - Detail by quarter for second and third years
- ✔ **Break-even Analysis**
  - When the company will break even and become profitable
  - Key assumptions to get to profitability
- ✔ **Income projections (profit and loss statements)**
  - Three-year projected summary
  - Detail by month for first year
  - Detail by quarter for second and third years
  - Key assumptions
- ✔ **Cash Flow Projection**
  - Detail by month for first year
  - Detail by quarter for second and third years
  - Notes of explanation
- ✔ **Historical financial reports for existing business**
  - Balance Sheets for past three years
  - Income Statements for past three years

What if you're not a financial statement guru? Get help! Credible financial forecasts are so important that if you're not familiar with financial statements, you should seek help in getting them prepared from an accountant or other source familiar with the process. If you're a diehard do-it-yourselfer who wants this financial mumbo-jumbo in language that you can understand, check out the bestselling *Business Plans For Dummies* by Paul Tiffany and Steven Peterson (Wiley).

Within the main part of the business plan itself, you should include a summary of the key aspects of the financial forecasts. These aspects may include the total cash requirements, when you expect to obtain positive cash flow, and the growth in sales and profit margins that you expect to realize.

If appropriate, the financial summary can also contain alternate forecasts, showing the results that would occur if major assumptions underlying the forecasts change.

The most significant aspect of the forecasts is the underlying assumptions from which you derive the numbers. Make sure that your discussion sufficiently communicates to the reader the basis of your assumptions. For credibility purposes, you should make your financial forecast assumptions realistic, logical, and attainable.

At a minimum, include logic for determining the following key assumptions:

- ✔ Sales
- ✔ Market share
- ✔ Prices
- ✔ Expenses
- ✔ Major capital expenditures
- ✔ Major operational expenses
- ✔ Profit margins

Your Projected Income Statement is probably your most key projection — Form 2-3 later in this chapter shows you a sample.

Reality check

After you complete your business plan draft, circulate it for comment to friends, attorneys, business professionals, and accountants. Ask for their blunt assessments. Even better, ask them to give you a markup of the plan with specific changes.

Ask your reviewers whether your expectations and goals are realistic. Are you too optimistic? Overly optimistic sales projections are common. Have you made some unreasonable assumptions? Underestimating expenses is also common. Do your reviewers disagree with any of your statements?

And I can sum up the ultimate reality check as to the business plan's viability in one sentence: Would the reader consider investing in your company?

Projected Income
Statement
of
Catchy Software, Inc.

Item	2004	2005	2006
Revenues			
Existing Products	$400,000	$625,000	$1,500,000
New Products	50,000	1,000,000	1,500,000
Total Revenues	450,000	1,625,000	3,000,000
Cost of Sales			
Existing Products	200,000	300,000	500,000
New Products	25,000	400,000	600,000
Gross Profit	225,000	925,000	1,900,000
Expenses			
Salaries & Wages	150,000	250,000	500,000
Consultants	25,000	25,000	40,000
Benefits	25,000	35,000	50,000
Payroll Taxes	15,000	20,000	35,000
Research & Development	75,000	80,000	100,000
Insurance	15,000	20,000	25,000
Rent	25,000	27,000	30,000
Utilities	7,000	10,000	15,000
Advertising & Marketing	40,000	60,000	75,000
Web Site	10,000	15,000	15,000
Office Supplies	5,000	15,000	15,000
Legal	15,000	20,000	25,000
Entertainment	5,000	10,000	10,000
Bad Debt Reserve	10,000	20,000	35,000
California Sales Tax	30,000	100,000	240,000
Total Operating Expenses	452,000	707,000	1,210,000
Net Income (Losses) Before Taxes	(277,000)	218,000	690,000
Taxes Paid (Federal)	0	50,000	200,000
Net Income (Loss)	(277,000)	168,000	490,000

Form 2-3: Your Projected Income Statement must be realistic.

Writing a Mini Business Plan

You may also find a two- or three-page business plan useful at times. You can use this condensed plan as a way to introduce the company to prospective investors, lenders, or employees. And, if the party is interested, you can follow up with the complete business plan. Form 2-4, which you can find later in this chapter, is a sample condensed business plan for a consumer products company.

Forms on the CD-ROM

Check out these documents related to business plans on the CD-ROM:

Form 2-1	**Sample Business Plan Cover Page**	A sample cover page for a business plan (includes a confidentiality blurb)
Form 2-2	**Sample Executive Summary for Business Plan**	A sample business plan executive summary for a software company
Form 2-3	**Sample Projections for a Business Plan**	Several sample financial forecasts for a business plan
Form 2-4	**Sample Short Form Business Plan**	A sample condensed business plan for a consumer product company

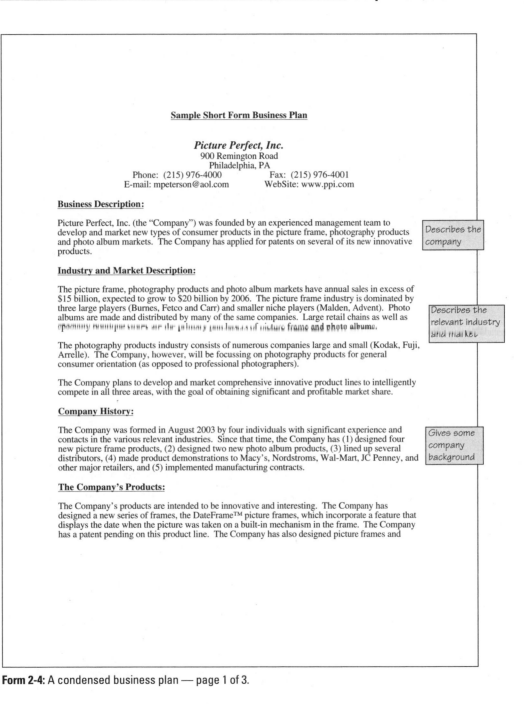

Sample Short Form Business Plan

Picture Perfect, Inc.
900 Remington Road
Philadelphia, PA
Phone: (215) 976-4000   Fax: (215) 976-4001
E-mail: mpeterson@aol.com   WebSite: www.ppi.com

Business Description:

Picture Perfect, Inc. (the "Company") was founded by an experienced management team to develop and market new types of consumer products in the picture frame, photography products and photo album markets. The Company has applied for patents on several of its new innovative products.

Describes the company

Industry and Market Description:

The picture frame, photography products and photo album markets have annual sales in excess of $15 billion, expected to grow to $20 billion by 2006. The picture frame industry is dominated by three large players (Burnes, Fetco and Carr) and smaller niche players (Malden, Advent). Photo albums are made and distributed by many of the same companies. Large retail chains as well as operating multiple stores are the primary purchasers of picture frame and photo albums.

Describes the relevant industry and market

The photography products industry consists of numerous companies large and small (Kodak, Fuji, Arrelle). The Company, however, will be focussing on photography products for general consumer orientation (as opposed to professional photographers).

The Company plans to develop and market comprehensive innovative product lines to intelligently compete in all three areas, with the goal of obtaining significant and profitable market share.

Company History:

The Company was formed in August 2003 by four individuals with significant experience and contacts in the various relevant industries. Since that time, the Company has (1) designed four new picture frame products, (2) designed two new photo album products, (3) lined up several distributors, (4) made product demonstrations to Macy's, Nordstroms, Wal-Mart, JC Penney, and other major retailers, and (5) implemented manufacturing contracts.

Gives some company background

The Company's Products:

The Company's products are intended to be innovative and interesting. The Company has designed a new series of frames, the DateFrame™ picture frames, which incorporate a feature that displays the date when the picture was taken on a built-in mechanism in the frame. The Company has a patent pending on this product line. The Company has also designed picture frames and

Form 2-4: A condensed business plan — page 1 of 3.

photo albums, samples of which are available on request. The Company plans to develop a broad based product line to penetrate the market.

Marketing:

The Company intends to use a combination of employees and distributors for marketing its products. The Company founders have extensive relationships with major prospective chain stores and distributors, which should facilitate marketing. The Company has also been developing distinctive packaging and logos to achieve brand recognition for its products.

Projections:

The Company projects that sales and profits will be as follows, all as further detailed in more extensive projections and underlying assumptions available upon request:

	2004	2005	2006
Revenues	$450,000	$1,625,000	$3,000,000
Cost of Sales	225,000	700,000	1,100,000
Gross Profit	225,000	925,000	1,900,000
Operating Expenses	452,000	707,000	1,210,000
New Income (loss) Before Taxes	(277,000)	218,000	690,000

Gives some summary projections

Management Team:

President:	Barry Sanders: Previously Head of Product Development at Burnes of Boston (the largest picture frame company in the United States); formerly Marketing Manager at Eastman Kodak. 20 years of industry experience.
Vice President of Operations:	Terry Davis: Previously Office Manager at PhotoExpress, Inc.; 10 years of operations experience with Carr Frames, Inc. and Fetco International. 15 years of industry experience.
Vice President of Development:	Joe Bledsoe: Previously Chief Product Designer of Arrelle (consumer photography products) and Product Manager at Macy's; 10 years of industry experience.

Sets out key information on the management team

Form 2-4: A condensed business plan — page 2 of 3.

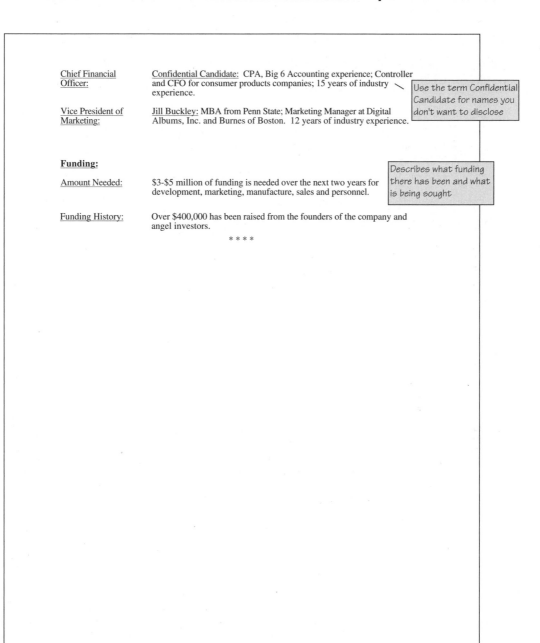

Chief Financial Officer:

Confidential Candidate: CPA, Big 6 Accounting experience; Controller and CFO for consumer products companies; 15 years of industry experience.

> Use the term Confidential Candidate for names you don't want to disclose

Vice President of Marketing:

Jill Buckley: MBA from Penn State; Marketing Manager at Digital Albums, Inc. and Burnes of Boston. 12 years of industry experience.

Funding:

> Describes what funding there has been and what is being sought

Amount Needed:

$3-$5 million of funding is needed over the next two years for development, marketing, manufacture, sales and personnel.

Funding History:

Over $400,000 has been raised from the founders of the company and angel investors.

* * * *

Form 2-4: A condensed business plan — page 3 of 3.

Chapter 3

Organizing a Corporation

- -

In This Chapter

▶ Incorporating your business

▶ Understanding the roles of shareholders and directors

▶ Selling your very own corporate stock

- -

Many owners establish businesses today as corporations. *Corporations* are separate legal entities that you can use to operate a business. Corporations give you the advantage of *limited liability* — meaning that you only risk the amount you invest in the company, provided that you properly operate the corporation.

Corporations aren't that complicated to set up. However, you do have to follow some important steps and create a number of documents. In this chapter, I provide you with the guidelines for properly organizing a corporation.

A Corp Is Born

Forming a corporation requires some basic steps. Corporations are subject to state statutes, and the rules and procedures for creating corporations vary from state to state. Make sure that you consult your state's laws for the precise rules. In this chapter, I often discuss California and Delaware corporations, because those two states have the most incorporations.

Playing the name game

Choosing a name for your corporation isn't something you should do during a commercial break in *Friends* (or even *Law and Order*). Your company's name is a serious decision that impacts your ability to create the documents that you need to properly form the corporation. Not only does the name you choose affect your customers' impression of your company, but the uniqueness of your name can also affect future trademarks, service marks, and your ability to conduct business in your own state and in other states. (I cover the forms associated with trademarks and service marks in Chapter 13.)

Try to select a name for the corporation as distinctive and unique as possible to avoid confusion with the names of other companies. The corporate name can (but doesn't have to) serve as a trademark or service mark for the company's products or services. If possible, pick a name that describes or indicates the company's business. Some names can be very descriptive, but beware of picking a name that may be limiting if your business expands. For example, Joe's TV Repair, Inc. works very well until Joe's business expands to include vacuum cleaner repair.

Before you decide on a name for your corporation, you should conduct the following searches:

- ✔ Has another company filed a conflicting trademark or service mark with the U.S. Patent and Trademark Office? (A variety of companies can check this for you; check out Chapter 13.)

- ✔ Is your proposed name available in key states in which you intend to do business? A conflict in another state generally prevents the company from qualifying to do business in that state under that corporate name. (You can check for conflicts by calling the Secretary of State in the state that you're concerned about.)

- ✔ Is another company using your name? Do a search on various search engines, such as www.google.com, www.askjeeves.com, and www.yahoo.com.

After you select your name, you have to check it with the Secretary of State in the state where you plan to form your corporation. (You can check it by calling the Secretary of State's office or checking its Web site.) The Secretary of State typically refuses to register a name that is "confusingly similar" to an existing registered name. Unfortunately, many names are already taken, so be prepared to check several names at once. The state corporation statute typically requires that your name include the word "Corporation," "Company," "Inc.," or "Incorporated." And many laws prohibit the use of certain words, such as "Bank" or "Insurance," in the corporate name unless the corporation qualifies as such an entity.

After you receive a clearance on the name, you can either incorporate right away with the name or reserve it for a period of time by filing for a *Name Reservation.* The Secretary of State's office can provide you with the procedure.

Choosing a state of incorporation

Because the laws that affect corporations vary from state to state, many people ask in which state they should incorporate their businesses. As a practical matter, you should incorporate under the laws of the state in which the corporation intends to conduct its principal business most of the time. Thus, if you're a California-based business, a California incorporation probably makes sense.

Most states have pamphlets on how to incorporate with sample forms, which you can order by calling up the Secretary of State's office. Or check out www.AllBusiness.com, which contains comprehensive articles, forms, agreements, questions and answers, business guides, business directives, and more — all applicable to entrepreneurs and growing businesses.

If you intend to incorporate in California, check out Forms 3-1 and 3-2 on the CD-ROM. Form 3-1 gives you a checklist for incorporating in the state of California. Form 3-2 guides you through operating a California corporation. If you incorporate in a state other than California, familiarize yourself with this checklist and guide anyway! Understanding the general issues can help you when you consult your corporate attorney.

Delaware, which has a well-developed body of corporate law, is also a favorite haven of incorporation. However, if you're doing business in another state and incorporate under Delaware law, you face extra filings and costs. Delaware may make sense if the company is backed by a venture capitalist with a clear goal of going public.

Creating the Articles of Incorporation

After you select the corporate name and state of incorporation, you must file the official document creating the corporation with the Secretary of State. This document is called the *Articles of Incorporation* or the *Certificate of Incorporation,* depending on the state.

The Articles are typically short — around two pages long. You need to include these key sections in the Articles:

- ✔ **The Corporate Name.** This section of the Articles identifies the formal name of the corporation, following the procedures I describe in the section "Playing the name game" earlier in this chapter.

- ✔ **The Purpose of the Corporation.** Many states, including California and Delaware, allow this section to simply state that you want to create a corporation to engage in any lawful activity for which you can organize corporations in that state. You usually fare better when you make this clause more general because you then have flexibility to expand your business into almost any area.

✔ **Duration.** Most state statutes provide that the corporation can last forever. You generally don't want the Articles to provide for a fixed term of existence.

✔ **The Authorized Capital.** This section must set forth the total number of shares that the corporation can issue, the par value per share, and the different classes of stock. Typically, you have only one class of Common Stock, but sometimes you can issue both Common Stock and Preferred Stock. This section should authorize a sufficient number of shares to cover the founders' shares plus shares that you may issue to future employees and investors. If the state doesn't charge you extra, think about authorizing 10,000,000 shares or more. Chapter 4 discusses issues dealing with raising capital and stock.

✔ **Name and Address of Registered Agent.** Most states require the corporation to designate the name and address of a registered agent for service of process in the state. The *registered agent* is the person who gets the notice of lawsuits filed against your company. If you're incorporating in a state other than where you maintain your principal office, you can, for a fee, designate various professional registered agent companies, such as CSC (`www.corporate.com`) or CT Corporation (`www.ctcorporation.com`).

✔ **Other Required Provisions.** Depending on the state law, you have to put some provisions, such as the preemptive right to purchase future shares, in the Articles to make those provisions effective.

Form 3-3C (shown later in this chapter) shows a sample Articles of Incorporation for a California corporation (you can also find the form on the CD-ROM accompanying this book). Form 3-3D, which you can also find later in this chapter, is a similar document but for a Delaware corporation. Forms 3-4C and 3-4D (on the CD-ROM) are transmittal letters to send to the Secretary of States of California and Delaware, respectively.

(Lights . . . camera . . .) Action of Incorporator

The *incorporator* (usually the founder of the company) is the person who initially organizes the corporation. The incorporator uses a document called an Action of Incorporator to perform important functions, like adopting bylaws, electing directors (if the Articles of Incorporation doesn't name them), and signing the Articles of Incorporation. The incorporator can be a lawyer, a prospective shareholder, or another interested individual.

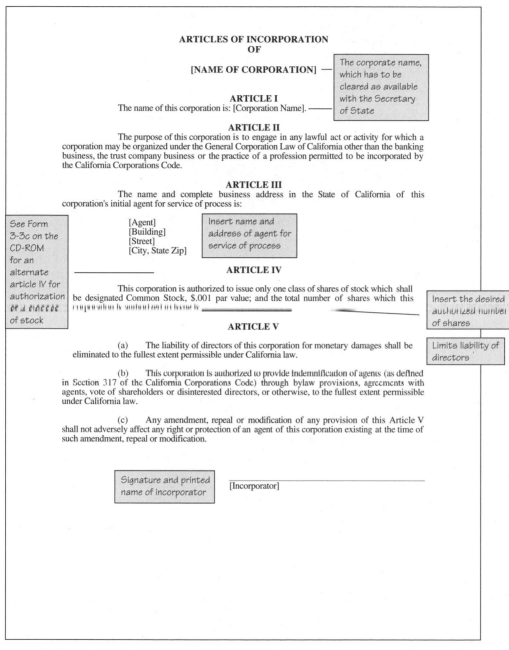

ARTICLES OF INCORPORATION
OF

[NAME OF CORPORATION] ——

| The corporate name, which has to be cleared as available with the Secretary of State |

ARTICLE I
The name of this corporation is: [Corporation Name]. ——

ARTICLE II
The purpose of this corporation is to engage in any lawful act or activity for which a corporation may be organized under the General Corporation Law of California other than the banking business, the trust company business or the practice of a profession permitted to be incorporated by the California Corporations Code.

ARTICLE III
The name and complete business address in the State of California of this corporation's initial agent for service of process is:

| See Form 3-3c on the CD-ROM for an alternate article IV for authorization of a class of stock |

[Agent]
[Building]
[Street]
[City, State Zip]

| Insert name and address of agent for service of process |

ARTICLE IV
_____ This corporation is authorized to issue only one class of shares of stock which shall be designated Common Stock, $.001 par value; and the total number of shares which this corporation is authorized to issue is _____

| Insert the desired authorized number of shares |

ARTICLE V

(a)   The liability of directors of this corporation for monetary damages shall be eliminated to the fullest extent permissible under California law.

| Limits liability of directors |

(b)   This corporation is authorized to provide indemnification of agents (as defined in Section 317 of the California Corporations Code) through bylaw provisions, agreements with agents, vote of shareholders or disinterested directors, or otherwise, to the fullest extent permissible under California law.

(c)   Any amendment, repeal or modification of any provision of this Article V shall not adversely affect any right or protection of an agent of this corporation existing at the time of such amendment, repeal or modification.

| Signature and printed name of incorporator |

[Incorporator]
_____

Form 3-3C: Articles of Incorporation for a California corporation.

Unless the Articles of Incorporation name the initial directors, you *must* create an Action of Incorporator to name the corporation's first board of directors and permit the corporation to transact business lawfully. Make sure that the document is dated or effective on or after the date of incorporation and insert the document in the corporation's minute book.

You can find a sample Action of Incorporator form for a California corporation (Form 3-5C) and for a Delaware corporation (Form 3-5D) on the CD-ROM.

Let bylaws be bylaws

The bylaws of a corporation contain the rules and procedures that govern the rights and powers of shareholders, directors, and officers. Most lawyers have a prepared, standard set of template bylaws, which may need modification in a particular case.

The incorporator or the board of directors typically adopts the bylaws in the organizational meeting or the written consent in place of the organizational meeting. This organizational meeting or written consent is the first action that the board of directors takes in connection with the formation of the corporation (described in the section "The board of directors" later in this chapter).

The bylaws often cover the following:

- ✔ When and how shareholder meetings are called
- ✔ The size of the board of directors
- ✔ When and how board meetings are called
- ✔ Procedures for exercising voting rights
- ✔ Duties and responsibilities of officers
- ✔ Procedures for dividends
- ✔ *Indemnification* (or protection from lawsuits and claims) obligations for officers, directors, and agents
- ✔ The company fiscal year

Form 3-6C on the CD-ROM accompanying this book shows sample bylaws for a California corporation. Form 3-6D on the CD-ROM shows sample bylaws for a Delaware corporation.

Maintaining an (up-to-the) minute book

You keep various important corporate records in the corporation's minute book. This book should contain the company's Articles of Incorporation, bylaws, and minutes or written consents covering all meetings and actions of the directors, committees of the board of directors, and shareholders. You should keep the minute book current and include all necessary documentation in it.

Counsel for investors or underwriters in connection with an initial public offering (IPO) often review the minute book carefully prior to transactions involving sale of stock in the company. Furthermore, up-to-date minute books help you follow proper corporate formalities, which helps keep shareholder liability problems at bay (see Chapter 12).

Typical problems to avoid include the following:

- Minutes that the secretary or other appropriate officer hasn't signed
- Written consents that don't have all required signatures
- Lack of minutes for regularly scheduled shareholder or board meetings
- Written consents that authorize execution of certain documents in the form attached to the written consent but with no copies of the documents attached
- Lack of documentation recording calls or notices of meetings
- Notices or calls of meetings that don't meet legal requirements
- Shareholder minutes that don't reflect the number of shares represented and how they voted
- Resolutions showing board approval but not the shareholder approval for transactions requiring both approvals
- Lack of authorization for issuing stock shares

Pricing out the cost of incorporation

Incorporating your business comes with a variety of costs, depending on the bells and whistles you choose and the complications involved. Table 3-1 shows a rough breakdown for a simple incorporation (which varies by state).

Table 3-1	Incorporation Costs
Activity	*Fees*
Filing fees with Secretary of State	$100-$250
First year franchise tax prepayment	$800-$1000
Various governmental filings	$50-$200
Attorneys' fees	$500-$5000

The biggest variable in the price of forming a corporation is the attorneys' fees. If the incorporation is straightforward, you shouldn't have to pay all that much (most good corporate lawyers already have form documents ready for incorporation). But if you require some complicated agreements (such as a shareholders agreement among multiple founding shareholders), you may have to dig deep to meet the cost.

Completing the establishment of the corporation

You may need to take the following additional steps to complete the establishment of your corporation:

- ✔ Apply for a federal and state employee I.D. number (see Chapter 6)
- ✔ Make any filings to obtain exemptions from securities law registration requirements when selling stock (see Chapter 4)
- ✔ Finalize and approve any important agreements (see Chapter 11)
- ✔ File any fictitious business name statements (see Chapter 12)
- ✔ Make required governmental filings in states where you intend to do significant business (Check with the Secretary of State in the appropriate states)
- ✔ Obtain any needed local licenses and permits (see Chapter 12)

Corporate Actions

The *shareholders* of the corporation are the investors who receive ownership in the corporation in return for money or assets that they invest. The shareholders elect a *board of directors,* which has the overall responsibility for the business. The board in turn elects the officers of the corporation (typically a chief executive officer, vice president, secretary, and chief financial officer). The officers handle the day-to-day affairs of the corporation.

The board of directors

The directors must act in connection with the best interests of the corporation and its shareholders. Board members can provide valuable wisdom and experience in guiding a company to success.

The board members maintain a *fiduciary* relationship with the company (a relationship founded in trust and confidence).

The shareholders get to decide the size of the board. Generally, you want to avoid an unwieldy number of directors or an even number of directors (to avoid deadlock). The board should meet on a regular basis. After filing the incorporation papers with the Secretary of State, the board needs to adopt organizational resolutions (either at a meeting or by unanimous written consent). These organizational resolutions concern preliminary matters for properly establishing the corporation, as I describe in the following sections.

Initial actions by the board of directors

The board of directors can accomplish the organizational resolutions of the corporation by adopting them in a meeting that they call in accordance with the corporation's bylaws or by unanimous written consent. Generally, the directors should authorize

- ✔ Adoption or ratification of the bylaws
- ✔ Designation of principal office
- ✔ The election of the initial officers
- ✔ The selection of the fiscal year
- ✔ The selection of a specimen stock certificate for the corporation's common stock
- ✔ The designation of the corporation's bank or banks
- ✔ The issuance of the stock to initial shareholders
- ✔ The election of S Corporation status, if desirable
- ✔ The payment of organizational expenses
- ✔ The authorization of any Buy-Sell Agreement, leases, or other material contracts

Form 3-7C on the CD-ROM shows sample organizational board resolutions for California corporations; Form 3-7D on the CD-ROM shows sample organizational board resolutions for Delaware corporations.

Ongoing actions by the board of directors

The board has to hold annual meetings, but it typically meets more often than that. Some of the actions that the board may need or want to approve include the following:

- Issuing securities and granting warrants, options, or other rights to purchase securities
- Adopting a stock option plan
- Amending the Articles of Incorporation or bylaws
- Entering into major contracts, leases, or other obligations
- Declaring distributions, dividends, or stock splits
- Borrowing significant sums and providing the security for the loans
- Entering into Employment Agreements with key employees
- Electing officers of the company and setting or changing their compensation and terms of employment
- Adopting or amending employee benefit plans
- Calling shareholders' meetings
- Buying or selling significant assets
- Adopting company policies

The CD-ROM offers an extensive array of forms (Forms 3-8 to 3-32) that you can adjust for your board minutes or consents.

The shareholders

The founders of the business typically buy stock in the company and are its first shareholders. Later on, investors can contribute money or other assets and also become shareholders.

Various actions of the corporation require action by the shareholders, and these actions must be reflected in minutes of meetings or by appropriate written consents. A corporation typically has to hold annual meetings of shareholders, the principal purpose of which is to elect the members of the board of directors.

Some of the actions for which the corporation may need or want shareholder approval include the following:

- Merger or reorganization of the corporation

- Amendment to the Articles of Incorporation

- Amendment of the bylaws (other than an amendment setting the exact number of directors within the range established by the bylaws or Articles of Incorporation)

- Sale or transfer of all or substantially all of the corporation's assets

- Approval of contracts with interested directors

- Authorization of indemnity of a corporate agent for liability incurred when acting on behalf of the company

- Issuance of certain securities

- Adoption of stock option plans

- Dissolution or winding up of the corporation

Form 3-33C is a form for Action by Written Consent of Stockholders of a California corporation that you would use for the shareholders' part of the initial formation of the corporation. Form 3-33D is a similar form for Delaware. For ongoing shareholders resolution in the forms of minutes, consents, and resolutions, see Forms 3-34 through 3-49 on the CD-ROM.

Capitalizing the Corporation

The corporation needs to sell stock to its founding shareholders as part of properly organizing the corporation. This stock sale is sometimes referred to as *capitalizing the corporation,* and the purpose of the sale is to inject start-up funds into the corporation to get it going. Although you don't need to contribute a minimum amount of money to properly form a corporation, you should consider capitalizing the company with sufficient funds to meet its anticipated early needs in order to avoid potential personal liability of the shareholders to creditors of the corporation (see Chapter 4 for more information).

Forms 3-50 through 3-55 on the CD-ROM deal with securities and tax issues for a California corporation. Chapter 4 should make you feel more secure about securities issues. Chapter 6 covers tax issues.

Issuing stock

In issuing shares to its initial shareholders, the corporation must ensure that it complies with both state and federal securities laws. These laws apply whenever you issue a *security,* such as common or preferred stock. Typically, issuing shares to a small number of founding shareholders qualifies for a private placement type of exception from the registration requirements of securities laws. But double-check with your lawyer.

When you sell the stock, you need to issue a stock certificate. Form 3-56 on the CD-ROM is a sample common stock certificate. Form 3-57 on the CD-ROM is a sample preferred stock certificate.

Keeping a stock ledger

The company must keep good records of stock issuances, showing the amount of stock issued, dates issued, and funds received. A stock ledger can help the company organize this information. You should probably keep copies of all the stock certificates the company issues, at least while the company is privately held.

Form 3-58 is a sample Stock Ledger.

Entering into a Right of First Refusal Agreement

Shareholders of start-up companies often enter into a *Right of First Refusal Agreement,* requiring shareholders to offer shares to the company before selling them to a third party. You probably want such an agreement so that you can try to keep stock in friendly hands.

You may also expand the Right of First Refusal Agreement to provide the option for the company to buy back shares of a shareholder who has died, becomes permanently disabled, or is no longer involved as an employee or director of the company.

You can find a sample Right of First Refusal Agreement for a California corporation as Form 3-59C on the CD-ROM. Form 3-59D on the CD-ROM gives you a similar sample agreement for Delaware.

This is the stock
certificate number

This is how much was
paid for the shares

This is a brief summary
of the sale

ABC, Inc.

A Delaware Corporation

Common Stock Ledger

Certificate #	Number of Shares	Shareholder and Address	Original Date of Issuance	Consideration Paid Per Share	Comments/ History/ Transfers
1	1,000	Mona Lessing 3200 Jackson St. San Francisco, Ca 94117	6/30/03	$10.00	Issuance to cofounder
2	1,000	Sue Grisson 14 Hawthorne Lane San Jose, Ca 94297	6/30/03	$10.00	Issuance to cofounder
3	200	Angel Investor, Inc. 300 Sansome St. San Francisco, Ca 94111	9/30/03	$20.00	Seed investment
4	100	Alex Smith 900 Montgomery St. San Francisco, Ca 94523	10/15/03	$20.00	Sale to employee
5	50	Bobby Stewart 1112 Washington Ave. Oakland, Ca 94119	11/15/03	$20.00	Angel seed investment

Form 3-58: A sample Stock Ledger.

Forms on the CD-ROM

The following list contains forms on the CD-ROM pertaining to corporate formalities. (**Note:** Forms ending in a *C* or *D* are the form for use in California or Delaware, respectively):

Form 3-1	**Checklist for Formation of a California Corporation**	A checklist of issues to consider when forming a California corporation
Form 3-2	**Guide to Operation of Newly formed California Corporation**	A comprehensive guide for and discussion of forming a California corporation

(continued)

(continued)

Form 3-3C	**Articles of Incorporation (California corp.)**	Sample Articles for forming the corporation that you need to file with the California Secretary of State
Form 3-3D	**Certificate of Incorporation (Delaware corp.)**	Sample Certificate of Incorporation for forming the corporation that you need to file with the Delaware Secretary of State
Form 3-4C	**Transmittal Letter Enclosing Articles of Incorporation to the California Secretary of State**	A sample letter to send to the California Secretary of State enclosing the Articles of Incorporation
Form 3-4D	**Transmittal Letter Enclosing Certificate of Incorporation to the Delaware Secretary**	A sample letter forwarding the Certificate of Incorporation for filing with the Delaware Secretary of State's office
Form 3-5C	**Action of Incorporator (California corp.)**	A form where the incorporator appoints initial directors for a California corporation
Form 3-5D	**Action of Incorporator (Delaware corp.)**	A form where the incorporator appoints initial directors for a Delaware corporation
Form 3-6C	**Bylaws (California corp.)**	Sample form bylaws for a California corporation
Form 3-6D	**Bylaws (Delaware corp.)**	Sample bylaws for a Delaware corporation
Form 3-7C	**Action by Unanimous Written Consent of Board of Directors in Lieu of Organizational Meeting (California corp.)**	A form of written consent of the board of directors of a California corporation adopting various important organizational resolutions
Form 3-7D	**Action by Unanimous Consent of the Board of Directors in Lieu of Organizational Meeting (Delaware corp.)**	A form of written consent of the board of directors of a Delaware corporation adopting various important organizational resolutions
Form 3-8	**Notice of Meeting of Board of Directors**	A form of written notification of a board of directors meeting

Form 3-9	**Declaration of Mailing Notice of Board Meeting**	A sample form for the corporate records showing that the corporation gave proper notice for a board of directors meeting
Form 3-10	**Waiver of Notice and Consent to Holding Meeting of Board of Directors**	A form for the board of directors to sign waiving requirement of a written notice for a meeting
Form 3-11	**Action by Unanimous Written Consent of Board of Directors**	Template for actions by unanimous written consent rather than at a meeting
Form 3-12	**Minutes of Meeting of the Board of Directors**	Template for recording the actions taken at a board of directors meeting
Form 3-13	**Board Resolution Approving Agreement**	Sample resolution that the board of directors needs to approve, allowing the corporation to enter into an agreement
Form 3-14	**Board Resolution Approving Borrowing**	Sample resolution that the board of directors needs to approve, allowing the corporation to make a certain borrowing
Form 3-15	**Board Resolution Approving Sale of Common Stock**	Sample resolution that the board of directors needs to approve, allowing the corporation to sell stock
Form 3-16	**Board Resolution Approving a Stock Option Plan**	Sample resolution that the board of directors needs to approve, allowing a Stock Option Plan
Form 3-17	**Board Resolution Approving Grant of Stock Options**	Sample resolution that the board of directors needs to approve, allowing the grant of designated stock options to particular individuals
Form 3-18	**Board Resolution Approving Amendment of Bylaws**	Sample resolution that the board of directors needs to approve, allowing amendment of the corporate bylaws

(continued)

(continued)

Form 3-19	**Board Resolution Approving Amendment to Articles of Incorporation**	Sample resolution that the board of directors needs to approve, allowing amendment of the Articles of Incorporation
Form 3-20	**Board Resolution Approving an Employment Agreement**	Sample resolution that the board of directors needs to approve, allowing execution of an employment agreement with a senior-level employee
Form 3-21	**Board Resolution Appointing Officers**	Sample resolution that the board of directors needs to approve, appointing officers for the corporation
Form 3-22	**Board Resolution Approving an Acquisition**	Sample resolution that the board of directors needs to approve, allowing the acquisition of a business
Form 3-23	**Board Resolution Approving Dividends**	Sample resolution that the board of directors needs to approve, declaring dividends that the corporation can distribute to the shareholders
Form 3-24	**Board Resolution Approving Establishing a Committee of the Board**	Sample resolution that the board of directors needs to approve, establishing a precisely-named committee of the board
Form 3-25	**Board Resolution Approving Accountants**	Sample resolution that the board of directors needs to approve, appointing accountants for the corporation
Form 3-26	**Board Resolution Approving a Stock Split**	Sample resolution that the board of directors needs to approve, allowing a stock split
Form 3-27	**Board Resolution Approving a Lease**	Sample resolution that the board of directors needs to approve, allowing the corporation to enter into a lease
Form 3-28	**Board Resolution Approving Property**	Sample resolution that the board of directors needs to approve, allowing the purchase of a particular property

Form 3-29	**Board Resolution Approving Sale of Series A Preferred Stock**	Sample resolution that the board of directors needs to approve, allowing the offer and sale of Series A preferred stock of the corporation
Form 3-30	**Board Resolution Approving S Corporation Election**	Sample resolution that the board of directors needs to approve, allowing the corporation to be taxed as an S corporation
Form 3-31	**Board Resolution Regarding Annual Shareholders Meeting**	Sample resolution that the board of directors needs to approve, establishing the date of the annual meeting of the shareholders and other related matters
Form 3-32	**Board Resolution Regarding Qualification to Do Business**	Sample resolution that the board of directors needs to approve, authorizing the corporation to qualify to do business in appropriate states
Form 3-33C	**Action by Written Consent of Shareholders (California corp.)**	A form of written consent for initial actions or documents that needs to be approved by the shareholders
Form 3-33D	**Action by Written Consent of Stockholders (Delaware corp.)**	A form of written consent for initial actions or documents that needs to be approved by the stockholders
Form 3-34	**Notice of Annual Meeting of Shareholders**	A notice sent to shareholders of a corporation informing them of the date and place of the Annual Meeting of Shareholders
Form 3-35	**Declaration of Mailing Notice of Shareholder Meeting**	A form for the Secretary or Assistant Secretary of a corporation to complete and sign, declaring that a form of Notice of Shareholders Meeting in the form was attached and sent to all shareholders
Form 3-36	**Notice of Special Meeting of Shareholders**	A form sent to the shareholders notifying them of the date, place, and purpose of a special meeting of the shareholders

(continued)

(continued)

Form 3-37	**Waiver of Notice and Consent to Holding Meeting of Shareholders**	A form of waiver, which shareholders need to sign, consenting to a meeting of the shareholders without notice required by the corporation's bylaws
Form 3-38	**Action by Written Consent of the Shareholders**	A template for action that the corporation can take by the written consent of the shareholders, in place of action taken at a meeting
Form 3-39	**Minutes of Meeting of Shareholders**	A template for minutes of a corporation's shareholders meeting
Form 3-40	**Shareholder Resolution Appointing Directors**	A sample shareholder resolution for appointing the directors of the corporation
Form 3-41	**Shareholder Resolution Confirming Accountants**	A sample shareholder resolution confirming and approving the designation of accountants of the corporation
Form 3-42	**Shareholder Resolution Approving Amendment of Bylaws**	A sample shareholder resolution for approval of an amendment to the corporate bylaws
Form 3-43	**Shareholder Resolution Approving Amendment of Articles of Incorporation**	A sample shareholder resolution for approval of an amendment to the Articles of Incorporation
Form 3-44	**Shareholder Resolution Approving an Acquisition**	A sample shareholder resolution for approving the acquisition of a business
Form 3-45	**Shareholder Resolution Approving a Stock Option Plan**	A sample shareholder resolution for approving a stock option plan
Form 3-46	**Shareholder Resolution Approving an Agreement**	A sample shareholder resolution for approving the corporation entering into an agreement
Form 3-47	**Shareholder Resolution Approving Sale of Stock**	A sample shareholder resolution for approving the sale of Common Stock by the corporation

Form 3-48	**Shareholder Resolution Approving Increasing the Size of the Board**	A sample shareholder resolution for approving an amendment to the corporate bylaws to increase the size of the board of directors and to elect new directors for the new seats
Form 3-49	**Shareholder Resolution Appointing Director to Fill Vacancy**	A sample shareholder resolution for appointing a new director to fill a vacant seat on the corporation's board of directors
Form 3-50	**California Form 1502 (Statement by Domestic Stock Corporation)**	The form that the California Secretary of State requires new California corporations to fill out
Form 3-51	**Transmittal Letter to California Secretary of State Enclosing Form 1502**	A transmittal letter enclosing Form 1502
Form 3-52	**California Form 25102(f) (Notice to California Department of Corporations)**	The form that you can file with the California Department of Corporations in connection with the issue of private placement stock
Form 3-53	**Transmittal Letter to California Department of Corporations Enclosing Form 25102(f)**	A sample letter forwarding Form 25102(f) to the California Department of Corporations
Form 3-54	**California S Corp Election form**	The form that you need to file with the California Franchise Tax Board to elect to be taxed as an S corporation
Form 3-55	**Transmittal Letter to Franchise Tax Board Enclosing S Corporation Election Form**	A sample letter forwarding the California S corporation election form to the California Franchise Tax Board
Form 3-56	**Stock Certificate — Common Stock**	Sample Common Stock certificate for a privately held company
Form 3-57	**Stock Certificate — Preferred Stock**	Sample Preferred Stock certificate for a privately held company

(continued)

(continued)

Form 3-58	**Stock Ledger and Capitalization Summary**	A sample form that you can use to keep track of the issue of stock, preferred stock, options, and warrants
Form 3-59C	**Right of First Refusal Agreement (California corp.)**	A sample agreement where the shareholders have to offer a California corporation a right of first refusal on any transfer of their shares
Form 3-59D	**Right of First Refusal Agreement (Delaware corp.)**	A sample agreement where the shareholders have to offer a Delaware corporation a right of first refusal on any transfer of their shares

Part II
Money Matters

The 5th Wave   By Rich Tennant

"So... how did our first stage financing go today?"

In this part . . .

The title of this part is "Money Matters," and it does. Even if you enjoy the work and love being in charge, the success of your business ultimately depends on money. In this part, I take you through some of the financial stuff that you need to know to have a successful business: raising capital, bookkeeping and accounting, and taxes.

Chapter 4

Raising Capital for Your Business

· ·

In This Chapter

▶ Knowing the ins and outs of loans

▶ Leasing equipment

▶ Making stock sales

▶ Working with venture capitalists

· ·

Raising capital can be difficult, time-consuming, and frustrating. You can generally choose from three routes of financing for your company. Use your own money, borrow money, or give investors equity in your company in exchange for money. If you decide to go the first route and use your own money, credit, or equity (such as in your home), the best advice I can give you is not to overextend yourself. If your business fails, you can find yourself up to your elbows in debt.

However, if you're interested in borrowing money, selling *equity* (stock) in your company, or striking a deal with a venture capitalist, this chapter outlines some of the key documents that you need to legally raise capital for your business, as well as ways that you can avoid problems associated with stock offerings.

First, remember two fundamental principles about raising money:

✔ Raising money is always harder than you expect.

✔ Raising money always takes longer than you expect.

If you keep these two principles in mind, you can plan accordingly.

Borrowing from Peter to Pay Paul

Loans are a well-known method of raising capital. A major disadvantage to a loan is that the bank requires you to pay back the loan whether or not the business succeeds; that's not the case with equity securities, which I discuss in the upcoming section "Placing Your Stock on the Auction Block." One advantage of a typical loan is that it entitles the lender to only an interest return on its loan rather than a percentage of the business's profits or a share in the company (either of which an investor expects). This fact means that you don't have to give up a whole lot more than you anticipated if your business does well.

Start-up companies may want to look at individual lenders or the Small Business Administration (SBA) to find attractive terms for loans. (See the section "Sleuthing out SBA loans" later in this chapter.) Pure start-up companies have a hard time getting bank loans, and when banks do make such loans available, they make the terms generally unattractive, including the requirement that the borrower personally guarantee the loan. Bank financing becomes much easier as the company generates significant revenues and profits (particularly if the company has a regular source of accounts receivable that it can use to secure the loan).

Negotiating good loan terms

Whether you obtain your loan from a bank, individual, or other lender, a number of variables that go into the loan document can affect how good or bad a loan is for your business. You can negotiate virtually all the terms in a loan agreement; no such thing as a "standard loan" exists. The key issues to negotiate when contemplating getting a loan for your business include the following:

✔ **Due date:** You need to set a date when you plan to repay the loan's principal. You can formulate this date as a lump sum payment at the end of the term of the loan or as a periodic payment of principal with a final payment. For example, you can agree to borrow $50,000 with the entire principal due in two years. Or you can say that you'll repay the principal in 20 equal monthly installments of $2,500. In any event, make sure that the payment schedule (interest and principal) is reasonable, given your anticipated cash flow.

✔ **Interest payments:** You need to establish the interest rate, which should be in compliance with applicable state *usury laws* — laws that govern how much interest the lender can charge on a loan. You should clearly set forth the loan payment dates (the most common method requires monthly payments by the first day of each month). If your cash flow situation is such that a great deal of cash comes in after the first day of the month, try to adjust the timing of required loan payments.

Often, state usury laws don't apply to banks, and state laws often allow lenders to charge a higher interest rate for business purposes than for personal reasons.

✔ **Loan fees:** The lender may charge upfront loan or processing fees. Be careful on the amount and try to get an estimate as soon as possible so that you can evaluate how attractive the loan is, as a package.

✔ **Prepayment:** Ideally, you want to be free to pay off the loan at any time, even earlier than its due date. Make sure that your loan agreement or promissory note (see the section "Producing proper promissory notes" later in this chapter for details) gives you this flexibility. Try to avoid a prepayment penalty for paying off the loan early.

✔ **Defaults:** The lender is likely to insist that a variety of events can cause a default under the loan, including failure to make payment on time, bankruptcy, and breaches of any obligations in the loan documents. Try to negotiate advance written notice of any alleged default, with a reasonable amount of time to cure the default.

✔ **Grace period:** Try to get a grace period for any payments. For example, the monthly payments may come due on the first day of each month but aren't deemed late until the tenth day of the month.

✔ **Late charge:** If the loan includes a fee for late payment, try to make sure that the charge is reasonable.

✔ **Collateral:** The lender may insist on a pledge or mortgage of some asset as security to protect the loan. Under a mortgage (for real property) or a Security Agreement (for personal property), if you default on the loan, the lender can foreclose upon the asset and sell it to repay the money you owe. If the lender requires you to provide security, try to limit the amount that you have to give to secure the loan. Make sure that when you've repaid the loan, the lender has to release its mortgage or security interest and make any governmental filings to acknowledge this release.

✔ **Cosigners and guarantors:** A lender may ask for a cosigner or guarantor as a way to further insure that you will repay the loan. A cosigner or guarantor runs the risk that his personal assets will be liable for repayment of the loan. Check out Chapter 12 for more talk of guarantees.

✔ **Attorneys' fees:** The lender is likely to insist on a clause saying that you have to reimburse the lender's fees and costs in enforcing or collecting on the loan if you fail to make loan payments. Just try to insert a qualifier that the reimbursement only covers "reasonable" attorneys' fees.

Producing proper promissory notes

Unless the lender is a bank with its own form of loan agreement, a good promissory note is usually sufficient to evidence a loan or borrowing. Promissory notes do not have to be notarized to be legally valid. Promissory notes usually contain the following key points:

- ✔ The date of the note
- ✔ The borrower's name
- ✔ The lender's name
- ✔ The address where you send payments
- ✔ The interest rate
- ✔ The due dates for payment of interest and principal
- ✔ Whether you can prepay the note
- ✔ Any late charges
- ✔ An attorneys' fee clause
- ✔ The borrower's proper signature

Forms 4-1 and 4-2 on the CD-ROM show sample promissory notes. Form 4-1 is a *demand note,* where the lender can call for payment of the note at any time. Form 4-2, which you can see later in this chapter, is a note that provides that payment will be due on an agreed upon date in the future. You draft these notes to protect the lender.

Sleuthing out SBA loans

The Small Business Administration has a variety of programs to assist small businesses. The SBA works with banks and other lending institutions and middlemen to provide loans and financing to small businesses that may not otherwise be able to obtain loans.

You can generally apply for these loans through one of many participating lenders.

One of the more useful SBA programs is the Low Doc program, designed to increase the availability of loans under $100,000 to the small business community and streamline and expedite the SBA loan review process. This program offers a simple, one-page application form and rapid turnaround on loans of up to $100,000. The SBA quickly processes completed applications upon receipt from the lender, usually within a few days.

PROMISSORY NOTE -
PAYABLE ON A DESIGNATED DATE

$_____   [City], [State]

Insert amount owed

For value received, the undersigned ("Maker") promises   to pay to _____ ("Payee"),   or
order, at its offices at [address], the principal sum of _____ Dollars —
($_____), together with interest at the rate hereinafter provided for on the unpaid principal balance of this note
from time to time outstanding until paid in full.

Interest shall accrue on the unpaid and outstanding principal balance of this note commencing on the
date hereof and continuing until repayment of this note in full at a rate per annum equal to ___%. Interest only
payments shall be made by Maker to Payee on or before the [1st] day of each [month]. The principal shall be due and
payable in full on _____, 20__.

Says that principal is payable on a designated date

Maker shall make all payments hereunder to Payee in lawful money of the United States and in
immediately available funds.

The maturity of this note may be accelerated by Payee in the event Maker is in breach or default of
any of the terms, conditions or covenants of any other agreement with Payee or its affiliates. Should default be made in
payment of any installment when due hereunder the whole sum of principal and interest shall become immediately due
and payable at the option of the holder of this note.

In the event any installment provided for herein is not paid on or before two (2) days following its
due date, Maker promises to pay to the holder of this promissory note an amount equal to two percent (2%) of the
amount of such installment. In addition, Maker promises to pay interest on any such unpaid installment from the date
due until such installment is paid in full at a per annum rate equal to the lesser of eighteen percent (18%) or the highest
rate permitted by law. Time is of the essence.

Provides for a late charge

Maker waives presentment, demand, notice of demand, protest, notice of protest or notice of
nonpayment in connection with the delivery, acceptance, performance, default or enforcement of this note or of any
document or instrument evidencing any security for payment of this note.

Failure at any time to exercise any of the rights of Payee hereunder shall not constitute a waiver of
such rights and shall not be a bar to exercise of any of such rights at a later date. In the event of commencement of suit
to enforce payment of this note, the prevailing party shall be entitled to receive the costs of collection including
reasonable attorneys' fees and court costs.

Provides for payment of attorney's fees in the event of default

Nothing contained in this note shall be deemed to require the payment of interest or other charges by
Maker or any other person in excess of the amount which the Payee may lawfully charge under the applicable usury
laws. In the event that Payee shall collect moneys which are deemed to constitute interest which would increase the
effective interest rate to a rate in excess of that permitted to be charged by applicable law, all such sums deemed to
constitute interest in excess of the legal rate shall be credited against the principal balance of this note then outstanding,
and any excess shall be returned to Maker.
                    IN WITNESS WHEREOF, the undersigned has caused this promissory note to be duly executed as of
the date first written below.

Dated: _____   [Maker]_____

                                                          By: _____
                                                          Title: _____

Form 4-2: A promissory note payable on a specific date.

You can find the SBA programs, as well as forms, advice, a list of participating lenders, training services, management counseling, and other valuable information on the SBA's Web site at www.sba.gov.

Form 4-3 on the CD-ROM shows a summary of the SBA's various loan programs.

Putting Your Equipment on a Tight Lease

Equipment lease financing may look attractive to cash-starved businesses. Equipment leases allow you access to many types of equipment — computers, copy machines, fax machines, trucks, and more. The structure of the lease document affects how beneficial the lease is to your company.

Leasing equipment can give you the following benefits:

- ✔ Payments can be a tax-deductible business expense
- ✔ Quicker approval than loans
- ✔ Less paperwork and looser credit requirements than loans
- ✔ Reduced risk of your equipment becoming obsolete

Although equipment leasing doesn't bring cash in the door, it does reduce the amount of cash that you otherwise have to raise for your business. Ultimately, leasing equipment can prove more costly than buying the equipment, but if cash flow considerations are an important issue, then leasing gives you an attractive alternative.

When leasing, make sure to consider the following points:

- ✔ **Lease term:** How long is the lease?
- ✔ **Upfront payment:** What is the size of any upfront payment? Can you lower and spread out the upfront payment over the life of the lease?
- ✔ **Monthly payments:** Are the monthly payments reasonable?
- ✔ **Return rights:** For vendor-leased equipment, under what circumstances can you return the equipment if problems arise with it?
- ✔ **Early termination:** Can you get the right to terminate the lease early? Most lessors are reluctant to do so, but you may be able to negotiate an early termination right in exchange for a fee.
- ✔ **Option to purchase:** Make sure to negotiate a right to buy the equipment. Equipment lessors often give you this right at the end of the lease term, usually for a fixed price (for example, 10 percent of the purchase price) or at fair market value.

Many equipment vendors provide lease financing, as do a number of banks. For early-stage businesses, you can more readily get equipment lease financing from a vendor than from a bank. You can also negotiate better leasing deals with vendors than banks because vendors often want to push their products.

Placing Your Stock on the Auction Block

Raising funding through the sale of *stock* (or other equity interest) means selling ownership in your business in exchange for capital. The upside of stock sales is that you typically don't have to pay back the capital that you raise in the same way that you do with a loan. The downside is that you may have to relinquish some of the control over your company to the investor.

Regardless of whom you intend to sell your stock to, you should run through the items on the checklist that I show you in Form 4-4 later in this chapter to make sure that you remember the key points.

Taking a look at types of investors

Some investors who typically look for an equity stake in your company are as follows:

✔ **Angel investors.** Individuals who want to fund start-up or early stage companies in exchange for equity in the company are called *angel investors* (for obvious reasons). These investors often don't take an active role in running of the company.

✔ **Venture capitalists.** Professional investment groups that invest primarily in high-growth companies, *venture capitalists* can provide significant amounts of funding, management advice, business strategy, contacts, and introductions to other companies. Venture capitalists expect to share in the company's equity and typically insist on a significant say or veto power in the running of the business. For more on

venture capital financing, check out the discussion later in this chapter.

✔ **Strategic partners.** A *strategic partnership*, or joint venture with another company, can provide financing, resources, technology, or information. A *strategic alliance* can involve an investment in your company, which can add both cash and credibility (if the partner is well-known). Strategic partner financings are typically on better terms than venture capital financings.

✔ **Private placements through placement agents.** As your company grows, you may consider hiring a *placement agent* or broker-dealer to help raise money. The placement agent finds suitable investors for the company through its contacts and receives a commission for the sale of the company's securities.

Checklist for Issuing Stock

If you are planning to issue stock, there are a number of important steps that should be undertaken, including the following:

1. Board Approval. The Board of Directors of the company should approve the offer and sale of the stock, any agreements for the sale, and the filing of any needed governmental documents. This can be accomplished through resolutions adopted at a Board meeting (Forms 3-12 and 3-15 on the CD-ROM) or by written unanimous consent (Forms 3-11 and 3-15 on the CD-ROM).

2. Shareholder Approval. Approval of the shareholders may also be necessary, especially if the Articles of Incorporation of the company are being amended. Amendment of the Articles will typically require approval by the holders of the majority of the outstanding shares, either by resolutions adopted at a meeting (Forms 3-37 and 3-48 on the CD-ROM) or by written consent (Forms 3-38 and 3-48 on the CD-ROM).

3. Review the Company Charter. The company's charter (Articles of Incorporation or Certificate of Incorporation) should be reviewed to ensure that you have enough shares authorized to allow the new issuance.

4. Review Compliance With Securities Laws. Before an offer or sale of stock can be made, you need to ensure that the proper steps have been taken to comply with the federal securities laws and the securities laws of the states where the offers or sales of stock are made. Typically, you will want to find a private placement type of exemption to avoid the costly procedures of conducting a registered offering.

5. Prepare Appropriate Agreements. The sale of the stock should be documented by appropriate agreements. When the transaction is not really negotiated, such as the sale of Common Stock to friends and family, a Subscription Agreement may be appropriate (Form 4-13 on the CD-ROM). If the transaction involves venture capitalists or strategic investors, then a more detailed negotiated Stock Purchase Agreement will be necessary.

6. Review How the Sale Will Affect Future Action. The company should review how this stock offering might affect future financings. Ideally, the stock issuance should not unduly restrict the ability of the company to issue additional stock in the future.

7. Price and Number of Shares. The appropriate price for the shares and the number of shares to be issued need to be established. The dilution to the existing shareholders resulting from the new issuance must be reviewed and determined acceptable.

8. Make Securities Law Filings. Make sure to make the required filings with the SEC and any state securities administrators, generally within 15 days of the stock sale. The SEC form for a Regulation D offering is included as Form 4-8 on the CD-ROM, with the cover letter to the SEC on Form 4-9.

9. Stock Certificate. After the sale, the company should issue a stock certificate, signed by the appropriately authorized officers of the company. It will be useful to keep a copy of the stock certificate in the company records. Each stock certificate should be dated and numbered. A sample Common Stock and Preferred Stock certificate are included as Forms 4-5 and 4-6 on the CD-ROM. The certificate should include any appropriate legends, such as those included in Form 4-25 of the CD-ROM.

10. Stock Ledger. The issuance of stock should be recorded on the company's Stock Ledger, showing the date issued, consideration paid, name and address of each shareholder, certificate number and other relevant information. A sample Stock Ledger is included as Form 4-18 on the CD-ROM.

Form 4-4: Ten steps to take when issuing stock.

Different stocks for different folks

You can provide many types of securities to investors in exchange for the capital that they make available. Two of the most common securities are *common stock* and *preferred stock,* and you need to know the differences between these two types of securities:

- ✔ **Common stock:** Shares in a corporation that have no preferences or priorities over other classes of stock. The rights to distributions, number of votes per share, liquidation rights, and other rights are the same for all shareholders on a share-by-share basis. Form 4-5 on the CD-ROM shows a stock certificate for common stock.

- ✔ **Preferred stock:** Shares that give the holders various benefits over the common stock holders. Many professional investors, including venture capitalists, prefer preferred stock to common stock. Form 4-6 on the CD-ROM shows a stock certificate for preferred stock. Preferred stock often comes with the following rights:

  - A priority on the business's assets upon liquidation

  - A priority on any dividends

  - Special voting or veto rights

  - A right to force the company to buy back the shares at some point in the future (known as *redemption rights*)

  - A right to convert to common stock based on a formula

  - Protection against certain stock splits, stock dividends, and future cheap issuances of stock (known as *anti-dilution rights*)

  - A possible separate right to elect a designated number of directors

Securities laws 101

If you plan to sell shares of stock, limited partnership interests, LLC interests, promissory notes, or other interests that may constitute a security, you have to know the requirements of federal and state securities laws.

Federal securities laws

The federal securities laws generally provide that you need to register the offering of any securities with the *Securities and Exchange Commission* (SEC), the government body that monitors compliance with the federal securities laws. Registering a security can be a time-consuming and expensive process, requiring that you file a complete document with the SEC (containing your company's financial statements and other information).

A security by any other name . . .

Although stocks are the most typical types of securities, the following can also be securities and thus also subject to securities laws:

✔ **Warrants:** A warrant is a right, exercisable for a stated period of time, that allows the holder to purchase a stated amount of shares for a designated price. For example, a warrant may state that the holder has the right to purchase 10,000 shares of common stock at $1 per share for up to 2 years. This agreement is, in essence, an option to purchase shares. And if the value of the company's stock later goes up (say to $10), the warrant becomes very valuable because the investor can buy the stock for the $1 price. Companies sometimes give warrants to investors as an "equity kicker" or "equity sweetener" to make the investment more attractive to those investors.

✔ **Promissory notes:** Promissory notes provide evidence of a loan made to the business and relate more to debt financing than equity financing. The key terms of promissory notes are the due date, interest payments, interest rate, and whether the loan recipient pledges any security for repayment of the promissory note.

✔ **Convertible notes:** A *convertible note* is a debt instrument (essentially a loan), but it

has the additional right to convert to company stock on predetermined terms. For example, the loan may be for $25,000, but at the lender's option, the loan can convert into 25,000 shares of company's common stock. Some people like convertible notes because it gives them the protection of being a lender while adding the potential upside available to equity investors.

✔ **Profit participation:** Sometimes, you can raise capital by giving a right to profit participation on the sale of a certain product or line of business. For example, in exchange for $100,000 of capital to fund new software development, the company can give the investor 10 percent of all profits derived from the product's sale. This exchange is sometimes more beneficial for the company because you don't have to give the investor a percentage in the entire company nor any voting rights.

✔ **Stock options:** Many start-up companies find it desirable to grant employees stock options, allowing the employees to buy company stock at a fixed price. This incentive tool is particularly common in the Silicon Valley, and I discuss it in detail in Chapter 7.

The purpose of the federal securities laws is to protect investors. These laws require that you follow some strict rules as to the manner and sale of a stock offering and that you provide a prospectus containing material and detailed information about your company and the stock that you're offering.

Luckily, small businesses can sell stock using one of a number of exemptions from the registration requirements of the federal securities laws (see the section "Every rule has an exemption" later in this chapter for details).

Even if you don't have to register an offering, the issuance of securities remains subject to so-called *anti-fraud laws.* These laws impose liability on the company (and perhaps certain officers or directors) if the company makes an untrue statement of a material fact, omits disclosing material information to the investor, or provides misleading material information to the investor in connection with the sale of securities.

State securities laws

A company selling securities also has to worry about the securities laws of all the states in which it offers or sells the securities (sometimes referred to as *"Blue Sky" laws*).

Similar to federal law, each state's law includes a number of exemptions, but you have to jump through various hoops and make some special filings to get them.

Generally, if you qualify under SEC Rule 506 under Regulation D (check out the following section, "Every rule has an exemption"), you can obtain an exemption from the state securities registration laws. Be prepared to make some filings, though.

Every rule has an exemption

Because registered public offerings are so expensive and complicated, most start-up businesses try to take advantage of one or more of the exemptions from the federal and state registration requirements.

An important distinction for many of the exemptions is the difference between *accredited investors* and *unaccredited investors.* The government (whether state or federal) basically sees accredited investors as sophisticated enough to understand the investment's potential hazards. Accredited investors fall into several categories, primarily

- ✔ Individuals with a net worth (with or without spouse) in excess of $1 million

- ✔ A director or executive officer of the investing corporation

- ✔ Someone who had individual income in excess of $200,000 or joint income with spouse in excess of $300,000 for each of the past two calendar years and has a reasonable expectation of reaching that income level in the current year

- ✔ Any corporation, business, trust, charitable organization, or partnership not formed for the specific purpose of investing in the securities with total assets in excess of $5 million

Unaccredited investors are almost everybody else.

The following list contains some of the better exemptions for unregistered sale of securities:

- ✔ **Rule 504** allows a private company to sell up to $1 million of securities within a 12-month period. Purchasers don't have to be sophisticated, and no prescribed disclosure document exists (although you should still consider preparing a Private Placement Memorandum). Form 4-7 on the CD-ROM summarizes the contents of a Private Placement Memorandum. The company should file a Form D (Form 4-8 on the CD-ROM) with the SEC within 15 days of the first sale of a security under the offering. Form 4-9 on the CD-ROM is a transmittal letter to accompany the filing.

- ✔ **Rule 505** allows the sale of up to $5 million of securities in a 12-month period. The company can't generally solicit or advertise for investors. This rule limits the number of unaccredited investors you can have to 35. You should disclose certain specified information to the investors (unless they're all accredited), and you should file a notice on Form D with the SEC within 15 days of the first sale of securities. Form 4-9 on the CD-ROM is a transmittal letter to accompany the filing.

- ✔ **Rule 506** is the best rule to try to fall under because this rule helps exempt you from the qualification or registration requirements of state securities laws. Rule 506 has no limitation on the dollar amount of securities that you can sell, but you can't have more than 35 unaccredited investors. The company must also reasonably believe that each prospective investor (either alone or with the help of an advisor called a *purchaser representative*) has such knowledge and experience in financial and business matters that the investor can evaluate the merits and risks of the proposed investment. You should also provide a disclosure document to the prospective investors. Form D (Form 4-8 on the CD-ROM) should be filed with the SEC within 15 days of the first sale of securities. (Form 4-9 on the CD-ROM is a transmittal letter to accompany the filing.)

- ✔ **Rule 701 (Offerings to Employees)** provides for a federal exemption for privately held companies to offer stock and stock options to its employees, directors, officers, consultants, and advisors in connection with compensatory or incentive arrangements.

In order for an exemption to work, you have to follow a fair number of technical rules, which you have to prove that the company has met. You need to keep track of whom you're soliciting, whether they're qualified prospects, and to whom you're sending out Private Placement Memorandums. Check out the Control Sheet for Private Placement Memorandums (Form 4-10 on the CD-ROM), the Stock Subscription Agreement (which I describe in the section "Selling stock with a Subscription Agreement" later in this chapter) and the Stock Subscription Package (Form 4-11 on the CD-ROM) for ideas of how you can prepare proof of the compliance of your offering with these exemptions.

If you don't follow the rules to the letter, a number of bad things can happen, including possible civil and criminal penalties and the investor's right to demand his or her money back. You absolutely need the advice of a good securities lawyer.

Bolstering support with your business plan

You may need a business plan in raising funds for the business. The business plan can convey the nature of the company, its vision, its potential, the qualification of its management team, the market for the company's products, and more. But the securities laws prohibit the sale of securities through the use of any inaccurate or misleading document, even if that document is a business plan. Therefore, the business plan, when used in connection with fundraising activities, should point out the risks and the goals of the business.

For a discussion of business plans, check out Chapter 2.

Preparing a Private Placement Memorandum

A company often wants (or sometimes needs) to prepare a Private Placement Memorandum when selling stock or other securities to obtain an exemption from the securities laws. A Private Placement Memorandum discloses the material information about the company and its business — especially the risk factors associated with the investment in the company — to prospective investors.

You may not technically need the Private Placement Memorandum in very small stock offerings to a few individuals who are sophisticated and who have access to all the information they need about the company. However, a Private Placement Memorandum is a useful way to prove that the company provided all important information to investors (in case the investment goes bad and investors insist on having their money refunded).

A complete Private Placement Memorandum needs to follow several important rules, so make sure to consult with an experienced securities attorney when putting one together. The following list contains some fundamental principles to adhere to when creating a Private Placement Memorandum:

- Be certain that your statements are true.
- Don't mislead potential investors in any way.

 ✔ Don't omit any information that may affect the investor's decision.

 ✔ Lay out the risks to the potential investor.

 ✔ Provide proof of your statements.

 ✔ Don't exaggerate facts or projections.

You can make the specific contents of a Private Placement Memorandum quite detailed. Form 4-7 on the CD-ROM provides a checklist of the information required on a Private Placement Memorandum. For examples of the types of disclosures made by public companies in a *prospectus* (the public offering equivalent of a Private Placement Memorandum), check out the SEC documents contained in the online EDGAR database at www.sec.gov.

Before you go through the time and expense of preparing a full-blown Private Placement Memorandum, you may want to prepare a shorter *Pre-Offering Summary.* You can use this document to lay out the basics of your company and gauge the potential receptiveness of investors.

Form 4-12 on the CD-ROM is a sample Pre-Offering Summary for ABC, Inc.

Selling stock with a Subscription Agreement

The Subscription Agreement is an essential document for selling stock or other securities. The idea behind this document is to have the prospective investor offer to purchase securities from the company. A thorough Subscription Agreement also protects the company with numerous representations and warranties by a prospective investor.

You can also use the Subscription Agreement to get information concerning the investor's sophistication, past investment experience, income, net worth, and other relevant information. The company needs to analyze this information to determine whether the prospective investor is qualified under any applicable exemption from the securities laws. Because the company must have a reasonable basis for its decision as to whether an investor is appropriate for the company in connection with securities laws, many Subscription Agreements are tailored to provide the company with the necessary information.

The Subscription Agreement should also require that the prospective investor represent that she

 ✔ Has relied only on the information contained in the Private Placement Memorandum or other information document provided by the company

 ✔ Has the knowledge and experience necessary to evaluate the investment adequately

✔ Has had an opportunity to review any documents that she requested concerning the offering

✔ Has had prior personal or business relationships with the company, its officers, or directors; or has the business sense to protect her own interest in the transaction

✔ Realizes that the company sells the securities with an exemption from the securities laws and that she can't freely transfer these securities

A good Subscription Agreement also requires prospective investors to indemnify the company and its affiliates from and against any loss, damage, or liability due to breach of their representations or warranties contained in the Subscription Agreement.

Form 4-13 on the CD-ROM shows a sample Stock Subscription Agreement for the sale of common stock in a private company.

Romancing a Venture Capitalist

Venture capital is a widely used phrase that doesn't have an exact definition. Typically, venture capital refers to an investment fund or partnership (the "venture capitalist" or "venture fund") that focuses on investing in promising start-up and emerging companies. Venture capitalists have invested in some of today's most famous companies, including Apple, Genetech, Intel, eBay, Yahoo, and Google. Typically, this investment is in company stock (the venture capitalist gets a share in the company for the money put up).

The venture capitalist, in addition to supplying the company with money, also assists in its business planning, bringing industry knowledge to the table, as well as experience in growing businesses and expertise in taking the company public some day. The venture capitalist's primary motive is to make *a lot* of money on his investment. The track record of venture capitalists directly relates to the success they have in raising money for their partnership to invest in promising companies.

Beware — venture capitalists are interested only in businesses that can grow very BIG! So if you're a corner grocery store, sushi bar, or lemonade stand, forget it (unless you plan to grow to a chain of 500).

Preparing to meet a venture capitalist

Venture capitalists receive vast numbers of business plans and proposals from companies that want funding. If you want to stand out from the rest, you have to accomplish two things: Interest venture capitalists enough to meet with you, and knock their socks off when you do.

Here are some tips for increasing the chance that a venture capitalist pays attention to your proposal:

- Gather information about different venture capitalists (see the sidebar "Venture capital matchmaking" in this chapter).
- Prepare a top-notch business plan (see Chapter 2).
- Find a reputable third party (such as your lawyer, colleague, or accountant) to deliver your business plan or make an introduction.

When you meet with the venture capitalist, you should be prepared to communicate the following:

- You have a clear understanding of your business.
- You have a clear understanding of the hurdles facing your business.
- You have a vision for the company's growth.
- You have a sound company strategy and business plan.
- Your management team has drive and ambition.
- Your management team has relevant experience.
- Your target market is substantial and growing rapidly.
- Your business has a proprietary or differentiated product.
- Your business can realize significant gross profit margins.
- Your business has the potential to be a "home run" investment.

Form 4-14 on the CD-ROM is a sample of the type of form that venture capitalists use when deciding whether to invest in a company. Before you meet the venture capitalist, fill out this form and think about whether *you* would invest in your company.

Two things that interest venture capitalists are plans for significant growth (to at least $25 to $50 million in sales within five years) and large gross profit margins. Fast growth and high profit margins make your company an attractive acquisition target or a candidate for an *initial public offering* (IPO) of stock (acquisitions and IPOs allow the venture capitalist to turn their investment in your company into cash). If your company is limited in growth by technology or competitive factors, or if your company operates under tight profit margins, don't expect to get financing.

Venture capital matchmaking

Venture capitalists focus on particular industries and particular stages of company development. When conducting your research for venture capital sources, try to identify venture capitalists who specialize in the industry and development stage that match your company.

Industries that venture capitalists currently favor include software, biotech, medical instruments, health care, wireless, networking, computers, and the Internet.

The stages of company development that a venture capitalist may look for include:

✔ **Seed round:** The company is still a very early start-up.

✔ **First round:** The company has refined its business plan, has some of its management team in place, and is starting to develop products and sales.

✔ **Second round:** The company has made good progress on its plan, sales have started to increase, and the business is expanding.

✔ **Late stage round:** The company has done well, attacked its market, refined its product, and is now gearing up for an initial public offering or other major progress.

The following books and businesses can help you make the match:

✔ *Pratt's Guide to Venture Capital Sources* (Venture Economics)

✔ *Venture Profiles* (Venture One Corporate Headquarters, 201 Spear St., 4th floor, San Francisco, CA 94105; phone 800-677-2082; Web site www.ventureone.com)

✔ *Raising Capital For Dummies* (Wiley)

✔ *VC Experts* (www.vcexperts.com)

✔ *AllBusiness.com* (www.AllBusiness.com)

Getting to know you

Before the venture capitalist forks over cash to invest in your business, he has to get comfortable with your business and the management team.

Business due diligence

As part of getting comfortable with your company, the venture capitalist conducts *business due diligence,* meaning that he works to get an understanding of your business. This process often includes:

✔ A review of the market for the company's product

✔ A background check on the founders and key management team

✔ The company's competition

✔ Discussions with the company's key customers

✔ An analysis of financial projections for the business

✔ A review of any holes in the management team

Legal due diligence

The venture capitalist also has his lawyers conduct a *legal due diligence,* during which the lawyers check that your company doesn't have significant legal problems and that you're properly running it. You should expect to receive a Due Diligence Checklist from the venture capitalist's lawyers asking for a lot of documents and information about the company.

Responding to a Due Diligence Checklist can be time-consuming. You need to make sure that all your legal documents are in order. If they aren't, financing can be delayed or even killed. So make sure that your lawyer is experienced and knows what to expect (see the sidebar entitled "Can your lawyer handle venture capital financing?").

Here are some of the main documents that you should expect to hand over quickly:

- Key contracts
- Employment agreements
- Minutes and consents of the board of directors and shareholders
- Confidentiality and Invention Assignment Agreements with employees
- Corporate charter and bylaws
- Litigation-related documents
- Patents, copyrights, and other intellectual property-related documents

For a complete sample Due Diligence Checklist, see Form 4-15 on the CD-ROM. By reviewing and preparing the documents on this list, you can help expedite closing a deal.

Term sheets

The venture capitalist, after he is comfortable with the company and its plans, submits a *term sheet,* a summary of the proposed terms and conditions for the investment. Normally, the term sheet isn't binding. The term sheet is a serious show of interest by the venture capitalist and typically covers

- The proposed valuation that the venture capitalist places on the company
- How much the venture capitalist proposes to invest in the company and for what percentage of ownership in the company
- The form of investment (check out the section "The beginning of a beautiful relationship" later in this chapter)
- The rights to participate on the company's board
- The rights to register the venture capitalist's shares in a public offering

Can your lawyer handle venture capital financing?

You absolutely need a lawyer experienced in venture capital financings to help you get the deal done. An experienced lawyer knows what terms are standard and what terms the venture capitalist is generally willing to negotiate.

To find out if your attorney has the knowledge you need, ask her what the following terms mean:

✔ **Weighted average anti-dilution formula.** A formula that venture capitalists often insist upon to protect their investment from dwindling significantly because of any further rounds of investment in the company.

✔ **Convertible preferred stock.** The kind of stock that venture capitalists typically expect to get in your company, giving them certain preferences over other stock.

✔ **Registration rights.** Venture capitalists expect to get rights that allow them to sell their shares in a public offering.

✔ **Preemptive rights.** The venture capitalist's rights to maintain his stock percentage ownership in the company by participating in future stock sales.

✔ **Board seat rights.** The venture capitalist's right to appoint his designee or designees as members of the company's board of directors.

✔ **Co-sale rights.** The venture capitalist's right to participate in sales of stock owned by the company's founders.

A passing grade is 6 out of 6! If your lawyer doesn't know all the right answers, you need to find a more experienced lawyer.

✔ The conditions to the investment (completion of due diligence, definitive agreements in a form that the venture capitalist likes, and so on)

✔ How you plan to use the money

At this stage, the company can typically negotiate some of the key terms. You need a good lawyer to help with the intricacies of this negotiation — find one who is an expert in venture financings.

Forms 4-16 and 4-17 on the CD-ROM contain sample term sheets. With careful review, you can see the numerous rights that the venture capitalist typically expects to get.

The beginning of a beautiful relationship

After the company and the venture capitalist agree on the term sheet, the venture capitalist's attorneys usually prepare the definitive agreements reflecting the transaction. The main agreement is the *Stock Purchase Agreement,* which typically contains the following:

✔ The price of the stock that you're going to sell and number of shares that the capitalist will purchase

✔ The company's representations and warranties

The agreement's *representations and warranties* are important. Here, the company must present a truthful picture of the business's financial and operational state. A breach of the company's representations and warranties (a false or misleading statement) can lead to a real problem for the company.

✔ Various promises by the company

✔ Conditions to closing the deal

✔ A requirement to reimburse the venture capitalist's legal fees

✔ Exhibits and related agreements, which contain other rights for the venture capitalist

Most venture capital financings take the form of an agreement to sell *convertible preferred stock* to the venture capitalist. Because the stock is preferred stock, the venture capitalist gets preference over the common shareholders in the event of a liquidation or merger. Because the stock is convertible, the venture capitalist can convert the stock into common stock at his option. Certain events, such as an initial public offering (IPO) of the company, typically convert the convertible preferred stock to common stock automatically. This conversion simplifies the company's capital structure and facilitates the IPO.

The venture capitalist also typically expects to get the following rights associated with his investment:

✔ The right to elect one or more directors to the company's board of directors

✔ The right to receive various reports, financial statements, and information

✔ The right to have his stock registered for sale in a public offering at the company's cost

✔ The right to maintain his percentage share ownership in the company by participating in future stock issuances

Sometimes, the venture capitalist *stages* the investment — that is, invests some money right away and then gives additional monies as the company meets certain milestones. For the company's benefit, these milestones must be clearly defined and reasonably obtainable.

Forms on the CD-ROM

Check out the following forms that deal with raising capital for your business:

Form 4-1	**Promissory Note — Payable on Demand**	A form of note where the note holder can demand payment at any time
Form 4-2	**Promissory Note — Payable on a Designated Date**	A form of note where the principal is payable on a certain date
Form 4-3	**Summary of SBA Loan Programs**	A summary prepared by the SBA of its loan programs for small businesses
Form 4-4	**Checklist for Issuing Stock**	A sample checklist of key items to consider before issuing stock
Form 4-5	**Stock Certificate — Common Stock**	A sample certificate for common stock
Form 4-6	**Stock Certificate — Preferred Stock**	A sample certificate for preferred stock
Form 4-7	**Checklist for Contents of Private Placement Memorandums**	A checklist of items to be considered for inclusion in a Private Placement Memorandum for a securities offering
Form 4-8	**SEC Form D**	The form required by the Securities and Exchange Commission to be filed for a stock offering under SEC Regulation D
Form 4-9	**Transmittal Letter to SEC Enclosing Form D**	Cover letter to the SEC to enclose with Form D
Form 4-10	**Control Sheet for Private Placement Memorandums**	A sample sheet to keep track of the distribution of Private Placement Memorandums

(continued)

(continued)

Form 4-11	**Stock Subscription Package**	Several forms to be used in connection with larger private placement stock offerings
Form 4-12	**Pre-Offering Summary**	A summary of a company's proposed securities offering to ascertain the interest level from prospective investors
Form 4-13	**Stock Subscription Agreement**	A form of agreement for subscribing to the purchase of stock
Form 4-14	**Investment Analysis Summary Used by Venture Capitalists**	A sample form used by some venture capitalists in summarizing their analyses as to whether to invest in a company
Form 4-15	**Due Diligence Checklist**	A sample checklist of documents and information that a venture capitalist requests from a company in which it wants to invest
Form 4-16	**Short Form Venture Capital Term Sheet**	A short form sample term sheet for a venture capital investment in a company
Form 4-17	**Long Form Venture Capital Term Sheet**	A long form, annotated sample term sheet for a venture capital investment in a company
Form 4-18	**Stock Ledger and Capitalization Summary**	A sample form ledger to keep track of stock option and warrant issuances with a summary of the company's capitalization

Chapter 5

Bookkeeping and Accounting Basics

In This Chapter

▶ Understanding basic accounting principles

▶ Keeping good records

▶ Maintaining your accounting toolkit

*T*he words *bookkeeping* and *accounting* don't exactly give you a warm, fuzzy feeling. But in order to run a successful business, you have to keep good records and have a good bookkeeping and accounting system. You also need to understand the information so that you can maintain financial control of your business.

Unfortunately, not all of your record keeping can be delegated to your accountant or bookkeeper. In this chapter, I discuss some of the key forms that you need to use for basic bookkeeping and accounting. The forms focus on income statements, balance sheets, and cash flow statements (and I throw in a little advice about what records to keep, for good measure).

Choosing Your Accounting Method: Cash or Accrual

An *accounting method* is a set of rules used to determine when and how to report income and expenses in your business books and on your business income tax returns. An accounting method must consistently match income and expenses in order to clearly show your income.

Accounting software

Many retail stores and Web sites sell accounting software packages that you can use to keep records. These packages are very useful and relatively easy to use; they require very little knowledge of bookkeeping and accounting. The most popular software packages are

✔ Peachtree Accounting (from Peachtree)

✔ QuickBooks (from Intuit)

✔ Account Edge and MYOB Plus (from MYOB)

If you keep your records on a computer, you must still be able to produce legible records from the system. The IRS needs this information in printed form to determine your correct tax liability.

You can choose from two basic accounting methods:

✔ **Cash method:** You report income that you receive during the year, and you usually deduct expenses as you pay them. Service providers and construction companies typically use the cash method.

✔ **Accrual method:** You generally report income when you earn it (such as when you ship the product or perform the service), even though you may receive payment later. You deduct expenses when you incur them (such as when you receive a product or service), regardless of when you pay them. Manufacturers and retail stores that maintain inventories typically use the accrual method. *Inventories* include goods held for sale in the normal course of business, raw materials, and supplies that will physically become a part of merchandise intended for sale.

After you set up your accounting method, you must get IRS approval before you can change to another method. Changing your accounting method not only includes a change in your overall system of accounting, but also a change in the treatment of any material item.

For a detailed explanation of inventories and examples of information on getting permission to change your accounting method, see IRS Publication 538 *(Accounting Periods and Methods)* — Form 5-1 on the CD-ROM.

Keeping Records and Books

Every business should keep records, but most businesses *have to* keep certain records. You can choose any record-keeping system that's suited to your business and that clearly shows your income for your tax year. If you're involved with more than one business, you should keep a complete and separate set of records for each business.

Good records help you do the following:

- ✔ Monitor your business's progress
- ✔ Prepare your financial statements
- ✔ Identify whether receipts apply to taxable or nontaxable income
- ✔ Support the income, expenses, and credits that you report in your tax returns

Supporting documents

Purchases, sales, payroll, and other business transactions generate supporting documents, such as invoices, receipts, deposit slips, and canceled checks. These documents contain information that you need to record in your books and on your tax return. Keep your supporting documents in a safe place and organize them by year and by type of income or expense.

- ✔ **Gross receipts:** These documents refer to the income that you receive from your business. You should keep supporting documents that show the amounts and sources of your gross receipts. Examples of documents that show gross receipts include cash register tapes, bank deposit slips, receipt books, invoices, credit card charge slips, and IRS forms 1099-MISC.

- ✔ **Purchases:** You buy these items for use in production or for resale to customers. If you're a manufacturer or producer, this expenditure includes the cost of all raw materials or parts purchased for manufacture into finished products. Your supporting documents should show the amount paid and that the amount was indeed for purchases. These records help you determine the value of your inventory at year end. Examples of purchase documents include canceled checks, cash register tape receipts, credit card sales slips, and invoices.

- ✔ **Expenses:** These documents show the costs that you incur (other than purchases) to carry on your business. Your supporting documents should show the amount paid and that the amount was indeed for a business expense. Examples of expense documents include canceled checks, account statements, credit card sales slips, invoices, and petty cash slips for small cash purchases.

- ✔ **Special expenses:** Special record-keeping rules apply to travel, transportation, entertainment, and gift expenses. For more information, see IRS Publication 463 *(Travel, Entertainment, Gift, and Car Expenses)* — Form 5-2 on the CD-ROM.

- ✔ **Employment taxes:** You have to keep specific employment tax records. Check out Chapter 7 for more information on tax forms that you should maintain.

✔ **Immigration and nationalization I-9 Forms:** You need to have I-9 forms on file that back up each employee's right to work in the United States (see Form 5-3 on the CD-ROM).

✔ **Assets:** You must keep records to verify certain information about your business assets (the property that you own and use in your business) and to figure the annual depreciation and the gain or loss when you sell the assets. Purchase and sales invoices, real estate closing statements, and canceled checks are examples of documents that may show information about your assets. Your records should show:

  • When and how you acquired the asset

  • Purchase price

  • Cost of any improvements

  • Deductions taken for depreciation

  • Deductions taken for casualty losses, such as fires or storms

  • How you used the asset

  • When and how you disposed of the asset

  • Selling price

  • Expenses of sale

Recording business transactions

A good record-keeping system includes a summary of your business transactions. You ordinarily summarize business transactions in books called *journals* and *ledgers,* as follows:

✔ **Journals:** Books in which you record each business transaction shown on your supporting documents. You may have to keep separate journals for transactions that occur frequently.

✔ **Ledgers:** Books that contain the totals from all of your journals. Ledgers are organized into different accounts.

Whether you keep journals and ledgers and how you keep them depends on the type of business you're in. For example, a record-keeping system for a small business may include the following items:

✔ Business checkbook

✔ Daily Summary of Cash Receipts (Form 5-4 on the CD-ROM)

✔ Monthly Summary of Cash Receipts (Form 5-5 on the CD-ROM)

- ✔ Check Disbursements Journal (Form 5-6 on the CD-ROM)
- ✔ Depreciation Worksheet (Form 5-7 on the CD-ROM)
- ✔ Bank Reconciliation Worksheet (Form 5-8 on the CD-ROM)
- ✔ Employee Compensation Record (Form 5-9 on the CD-ROM)

Using the business checkbook

One of the first things you should do when you start a business is open a business checking account. Keep your business account separate from your personal checking account.

Consider using a checkbook that allows enough space to identify the source of deposits as business income, equity investment, or loans. You should also note the source of the deposit on the deposit slip and keep copies of all slips.

For a simple business, your business checkbook is the starting place for recording your business expenses. To effectively document business expenses, make all payments by check. If you must write a check for cash to pay a business expense, include the receipt for the cash payment in your records. If you can't get a receipt for a cash payment, note the circumstances in your records at the time of payment. Record all cash deposits into your business checking account.

Reconciling the checking account

When you receive your bank statement, make sure that the statement, your checkbook, and your account books agree. The statement balance may not agree with the balance in your checkbook and account books if the statement

- ✔ Includes bank charges that you didn't enter in your account books and subtract from your checkbook balance
- ✔ Doesn't include deposits made after the statement date or checks that didn't clear your account before the statement date

By reconciling your checking account, you

- ✔ Verify how much money you have in the account
- ✔ Make sure that your checkbook and account books reflect all bank charges and the correct balance in the checking account
- ✔ Correct any errors in your bank statement, checkbook, and account books

Use Form 5-8 on the CD-ROM to help you reconcile your checking account.

The Accounting Toolkit

As a small business owner, you should be familiar with the forms in this section of the chapter. These forms include the *Income Statement,* which you use to track your income over time; the *Balance Sheet,* which you use to look at the company's net worth at a particular time; and the *Cash Flow Statement,* which reports how much cash you have on-hand. In addition, I provide some ways to compute profit margins, and figure budgets and projections.

The Income Statement

The Income Statement figures *net income,* or the bottom line. You calculate net income by adding all revenue from your business and then subtracting all the costs and expenses of operating your business. Net income is sometimes referred to as *net profit.* Think of net income in terms of the following formula:

```
Revenue - Costs = Net Income
```

One of the most useful all-around tools for a small businessperson is the Income Statement, which you can use for projections, for tax purposes, to evaluate the company, and to interest investors. Income Statements, which cover a period of time (typically monthly, quarterly, or yearly), work best when they compare different time periods, such as 2004 versus 2003. Public companies must publish quarterly financial statements that show Income Statements from the latest quarter versus the same quarter for the previous year, as well as the same information for the year-to-date versus the previous year-to-date. To understand your business's financial condition, compare the actual results against your budget for the same period.

Income Statements can be very simple, with summaries of basic subcategories like general and administrative expenses or research and development expenses. The simplest statement includes revenues, expenses, and net income; if you just want to know net income, then a simple form probably gives you all you need. Most people need more detail, though. For income tax reporting, you need to keep track of approximately 15 different expense categories. Some expenses, like entertainment, are treated differently for tax purposes, which means that you have to keep these expenses separate.

By listing the income and expense categories that you want to see on your Income Statement, you create a *chart of accounts.* Examples of these accounts include gross sales, interest income, travel expense, rent expense, insurance expense, and repairs and maintenance. An account can be general in nature, such as automobile expenses, or you can break it down into more specific items, such as gasoline, repairs, tires, auto insurance, and so on. You can always add an account if you feel the information is valuable enough to show separately. You can also keep very detailed underlying accounts but consolidate many of them into major categories for the Income Statement.

The Income Statement for Wonderful Widgets, Inc. — shown in Form 5-10 later in this chapter (see the CD-ROM for a clean version of this form) — has 15 different accounts (a number that's sufficient for most small businesses). Form 5-11 on the CD-ROM is a Comparative Income Statement.

What investors focus on

Investors have a different focus from lenders. Lenders take much less risk and typically get a fixed rate of return, as opposed to equity investors who risk their money to share in the business's results.

Equity investors want to see the buildup in the company's value. (Lenders, on the other hand, are primarily concerned about the business's ability to repay the loan.)

An equity investor wants to know the company's current financial shape and its future prospects. Equity investors typically ask a number of questions, including

✔ How are you going to use the investment money?

✔ How much money is the business currently making?

✔ What is it expected to make in the future?

✔ How fast is the business expected to grow?

✔ What are the profit margins and are they expected to increase?

✔ Are the business's costs stable?

✔ Does the business have the necessary space?

✔ What are the business's future cash needs?

✔ Are sales accelerating?

Return on equity is one of the key measurements that an investor looks at because it tells him what the historical return has been on the money invested in the business. For example, if Wonderful Widgets had owners' equity of $100,000 at the start of 2004 and had net income of $16,100 for 2004, that's a return on equity of 16.1 percent. You can compare this return to other investment options, such as a risk-free investment in a money market account earning 1-2 percent.

Because Wonderful Widgets is a corporation, it can also express the net income in terms of *earnings per share.* This figure is the net income divided by the number of outstanding shares. The earnings per share divided by your cost per share gives you the return on your investment. Publicly traded companies frequently report their earnings in these terms.

Wonderful Widgets, Inc.
Income Statement

	Year ending	
	12-31-04	12-31-03
Gross Sales	$ 250,000	$ 195,000
Returns & Allowances	42,000	38,000
Net Revenue	208,000	157,000
Cost of Goods Sold	100,000	85,000
Gross Profit	108,000	72,000
Selling, General & Administrative		
Salaries	47,000	37,000
Payroll taxes	4,000	3,000
Employee benefits	6,000	4,500
Travel expenses	1,200	1,300
Rent expense	3,600	3,600
Advertising	1,000	3,000
Depreciation expense	3,800	3,500
Insurance expense	1,800	1,500
Office Supplies	2,200	2,000
Dues and subscriptions	800	700
Telephone	2,800	2,400
Legal and accounting services	2,500	3,500
Miscellaneous expenses	900	600
Total Selling, General & Administrative Expenses	77,600	66,600
Operating Profit	30,400	5,400
Interest Income (Expense)	(4,800)	(1,200)
Net Income before Taxes	25,600	4,200
Income Taxes	9,500	1,200
Net Income	$ 16,100	$ 3,000

Form 5-10: The Income Statement shows the company's revenues, costs, and income.

The Income Statement has a number of key components:

- **Gross sales (or gross revenues):** These figures include all operating receipts or sales of the business. *Gross* means that it's all-inclusive, without subtracting any costs. Non-operating revenue, such as interest or dividend income, should appear later in the Income Statement. Wonderful Widgets shows a line for net interest income (expense). Look at Form 5-5 to see that the interest income line item is an expense and appears after operating profit because interest income isn't considered an expense of running the business but a cost of financing the business.

- **Returns and allowances:** You subtract these items from gross revenues to arrive at net revenue. For example, a *return* is merchandise returned by the customer. This category also covers sales taxes. *Allowances* may include a discount for paying cash or for purchasing a large volume. You also include *reimbursable expenses,* costs that are simply passed on to the customer, in this category.

- **Cost of goods sold:** Costs come in two general types: *direct costs,* which are used directly to create the revenue, and *indirect costs,* which, although necessary, aren't directly involved in producing a good or service. Cost of goods sold for a manufacturer includes the costs of making the items that you sell. For a retailer, cost of goods is the cost of the inventory that you sell. For a service provider, cost of goods is the direct cost of performing the service.

- **Selling, general, and administrative expenses:** These expenses combine the costs associated with supporting the product or service. These costs are not directly related to the goods or service produced. Examples include rent, office supplies, and other overhead. Some of the more common of these expenses are shown on Wonderful Widgets' Income Statement.

- **Income taxes:** The example shown for Wonderful Widgets, Inc. provides a line item for income taxes, which means that Wonderful Widgets, Inc. is a tax-paying entity. If your business is not a tax-paying entity, then you have no need for the income tax line. For S corporations, partnerships, and LLCs, the income typically flows through to the owners, who then have to pay any income taxes.

- **Net income (or net profit):** This figure refers to the amount left after you subtract all costs and taxes from all the revenue coming in. For a small proprietor who didn't take out a salary, this amount is the earnings for the period. Normally, the more efficient a business, the more profit it makes. A business that consistently produces losses can't continue unless someone finances the losses. Comparing net income for different periods allows you to see the direction your business is taking.

The Balance Sheet

The *Balance Sheet* shows the company's financial condition as of a specific date. It shows what the business owns (its *assets*) and what the business owes (its *liabilities*). The difference between the two represents the business's equity (or net worth):

```
Assets - Liabilities = Equity
```

When preparing a Balance Sheet for the end of a period, you also generally want to show the previous period's Balance Sheet for comparison. Form 5-12 shows the Balance Sheets for Wonderful Widgets, Inc. at the end of two different years. The statement is in balance because the total assets minus the total liabilities equal the owner's equity. You can also figure *working capital,* which lenders frequently use to determine the company's ability to pay its debts or to determine the amount of cash that you can use in the short term. You can figure working capital by using the following formula:

```
Current Assets - Current Liabilities = Working Capital
```

Form 5-13 on the CD-ROM is a *Comparative Balance Sheet,* which compares the balances for two periods with increases and decreases in line items.

Assets

Assets consist of three major types: current assets, fixed assets, and other assets. Balance Sheets typically show the current assets beginning with the most liquid — cash. A Balance Sheet prepared from the account books shows the assets at their original cost. For a simple business like Wonderful Widgets, Inc., this sum comes close to showing the value of the business. However, the Balance Sheet doesn't reflect the current value for companies that have acquired many assets over a long period of time or have unrecorded intangible assets. For example, assume that a business acquired a building in 1976 for $100,000. Although the building is probably worth many times that amount today, you carry it on the Balance Sheet at its original cost.

Current assets

Current assets are those assets that you expect to convert into cash within one year. Current assets include the following:

- ✔ **Cash** includes money on hand and balances in checking and savings accounts.

- ✔ **Investments** that are shown under current assets are being held for less than a year and can readily be changed into cash. (An investment in a subsidiary is considered a long-term investment and is shown under other assets.)

Wonderful Widgets, Inc.
Balance Sheets

	12-31-04	12-31-03
Assets		
Current Assets:		
Cash	$ 10,900	$ 2,000
Investments	-	15,000
Accounts Receivable	60,000	45,000
Inventories	30,000	25,000
Prepaid expenses	5,500	5,000
Total Current Assets	106,400	92,000
Fixed Assets:		
Equipment	25,000	20,000
Furniture	8,000	7,000
Leasehold Improvements	12,000	12,000
Less Accumulated Depreciation	(10,000)	(6,200)
Net Fixed Assets	35,000	32,800
Other Assets:		
Deposits	3,000	3,000
Goodwill	10,000	11,000
Total Assets	$154,400	$138,800
Liabilities and Owner's Equity		
Current Liabilities:		
Accounts Payable	$ 9,000	$ 5,000
Accrued Wages	3,500	3,000
Current Portion of Long-Term Note	5,000	5,000
Total Current Liabilities	17,500	13,000
Long-Term Portion of Note Payable	25,000	30,000
Owner's Equity:		
Invested Capital	25,000	25,000
Accumulated Retained Earnings	86,900	70,800
Total Owner's Equity	111,900	95,800
Total Liabilities and Owner's Equity	$154,400	$138,800

Form 5-12: The Balance Sheet shows the company's assets, liabilities, and owner's equity.

- ✔ **Accounts receivable** represents money due from customers. You need to monitor the amounts due from customers closely to make sure that they don't become uncollectible, in which case you have to write them off.

- ✔ **Inventories** represent the cost of goods held for sale. Valuing inventories can become tricky because you can purchase items at different times for different amounts. Keeping track of the exact item is difficult and shortages frequently occur due to breakage, theft, and obsolescence. Cost of items that you have manufactured includes both the materials and the labor that go into their production. You also need to include items in various stages of production.

- ✔ **Prepaid expenses** are items that you've paid ahead of time (rent, insurance, or retainers for legal services, for example).

Fixed assets

Fixed assets are property, plant, and equipment items that you expect to last longer than one year. Companies usually establish a minimum dollar amount for items included in this category. A stapler may last longer than one year, but its cost is so small that you can expense it at the time of purchase much more easily. Fixed assets are often called *capital assets* or *capitalized costs.* These capitalized costs are depreciated or amortized (spread out) over the useful life of the asset.

Assume that you buy a computer for your business for $6,000 and estimate that its useful life will be three years. The depreciation is then $2,000 per year, or $167 per month. If the machine was purchased on January 1, 2004, then the accumulated depreciation is $2,000 at December 31, 2004 and $4,000 at December 31, 2005. After three years, the machine will be fully depreciated, even if you're still using it. The machine's book value is the cost minus the accumulated depreciation.

Other assets

Other assets include assets that are long term, like the deposit on a lease. Intangible assets are shown on the Balance Sheet under other assets — *goodwill* being one of the most common. Although your business may have a great deal of goodwill, it doesn't show up on your Balance Sheet unless someone has paid for it. Goodwill frequently arises when a business is purchased. *Goodwill* is the purchase price of the business in excess of the value of the tangible assets (in case you want to go goodwill hunting).

Liabilities

Liabilities are the business's debts. These debts generally fall into two categories: debts that you owe within the next year and debts that you owe beyond this year, as follows:

> ✔ **Current liabilities** are business debts that are due within one year. You should also show the portion of a long-term debt that's due within one year under current liabilities.

> ✔ **Long-term liabilities** are business debts that are due one year and beyond the date of the Balance Sheet. Examples include that portion of your real estate mortgage payable more than 12 months in the future.

Two types of liabilities that you should be familiar with are accounts payable and accrued wages. *Accounts payable* are the amounts that you owe vendors for goods or services. *Accrued wages* are the amounts owed to employees for their services performed prior to the date of the Balance Sheet. Other types of accrued expenses include interest, taxes, and insurance.

Owners' equity

Owners' equity is the business's net worth. It consists of capital that was invested in the business and accumulated earnings that have been left in the business. Invested capital can come in the form of cash or other assets transferred to the company. *Retained earnings* are the business's accumulation of profits and losses over time, and they are reduced when the owners take out money or assets in the form of dividends or a draw.

The Cash Flow Statement

The Cash Flow Statement shows you what happens to the most important asset — cash. You can have very good profits and a strong Balance Sheet but still not have money in the bank to pay your bills. The Cash Flow Statement shows you what happens to your cash over a specific period of time. Because cash flow can be so critical to the business's daily operation, you may need to follow it weekly.

The Cash Flow Statement (shown later in this chapter) is a traditional statement that I've broken down into three major categories: operating activities, investment activities, and financing activities.

Small businesses have a crucial need to know, on a day-to-day basis, how much cash they have now and are going to need in the immediate future. (See Form 5-15 for a sample weekly Cash Flow Statement Forecast for Wonderful Widgets, Inc.)

Form 5-15 shows the major entries made in Wonderful Widgets, Inc.'s checking account. By forecasting the next four weeks, the company can anticipate its cash needs. Notice in this example that the company is short cash for the first week of December, and assuming that it receives $2,500 in payment of accounts receivable during that week, it needs to come up with approximately $7,500 (shown as "other" under cash receipts). This money may be in the form of a loan from the bank or the owners; the company may possibly be able to delay some of the payments for a week.

Cash Flow Statement

	Current Period	Prior Period	Increase/ (Decrease)	Percent Change
Period Ending:	_____	_____	_____	
Cash Flows from Operating Activities	$	$		%
Net Income	_____	_____	_____	_____
Non-Cash Expenses Included in Net Income	_____	_____	_____	_____
Gain / Loss on Sale of Assets	_____	_____	_____	_____
Depreciation	_____	_____	_____	_____
Net Change in Receivables	_____	_____	_____	_____
Net Change in Payables	_____	_____	_____	_____
Net Change in Inventory	_____	_____	_____	_____
Net Change in Accrued Items	_____	_____	_____	_____
Other: _____	_____	_____	_____	_____
Other: _____	_____	_____	_____	_____
	_____	_____	_____	_____
Net Cash				
Provided by Operating Activities	$_____	$_____	$_____	$_____
Cash Flows from Investing Activities	_____	_____	_____	_____
Purchases of Capital Assets	_____	_____	_____	_____
Sales of Capital Asssets				
Loans Given	_____	_____	_____	_____
Loan Repayments				
Other: _____	_____	_____	_____	_____
Other: _____				
Other: _____	_____	_____		_____
Net Cash				
Used by Investing Activities	_____	_____	_____	_____
Cash Flows from Financing Activities	_____	_____	_____	_____
Debt Reduction	_____	_____	_____	_____
Short-Term	_____	_____	_____	_____
Non-Current	_____	_____	_____	_____
Dividends	_____	_____	_____	_____
Other: _____	_____	_____	_____	_____
Other: _____	_____	_____	_____	_____
Other: _____	_____	_____	_____	_____
Net Cash				
Used by Financing Activities	$_____	$_____	$_____	$_____
Net Increase / Decrease in Cash	$_____	$_____	$_____	$_____
Schedule of Non-Cash Investing and Financing	_____	_____	_____	_____
Purchases of Capital Assets	_____	_____	_____	_____
Loans on Capital Assets	_____	_____	_____	_____
Other: _____	_____	_____	_____	_____
Other: _____	_____	_____	_____	_____
Total Net Change	_____	_____	_____	_____

Form 5-14: A Cash Flow Statement tracks the company's cash position over time.

Cash Flow Forecast Statement

| | |-------- Actual --------| | |----------------Forecast----------------| | | |
	Nov 14	Nov 21	Nov 28	Dec 5	Dec 12	Dec 19	Dec 26
Begin Cash	5,300	5,800	2,300	1,200	1,650	650	1,150
Cash Receipts:							
A/R Collects	6,000	2,200	1,300	2,500	7,000	8,000	4,000
Other				7,500	(5,000)		
Receipts	6,000	2,200	1,300	10,000	2,000	8,000	4,000
Disbursements:							
Payroll		4,500		4,500		4,500	
Inventory A/P	3,500		2,500	2,000	2,000	2,000	2,000
Accts. Payable	2,000	1,200	900	1,500	1,000	1,000	1,000
Rent				300			
Loan payment				1,250			
Disbursements	5,500	5,700	3,400	9,550	3,000	7,500	3,000
Net cash flow	500	(3,500)	(2,200)	450	(1,000)	500	1,000
Ending Cash	**5,800**	**2,300**	**1,200**	**1,650**	**650**	**1,150**	**2,150**

Form 5-15: The Cash Flow Forecast Statement helps Wonderful Widgets, Inc. plan for its cash needs.

Computing profit margins

Managers and investors use profit margins to measure a business.

Some of the most commonly used measures on the Income Statement are *ratios of income* (either net or gross). Use the following formula and compare the ratios from one accounting period to another accounting period:

```
Ratio of Net Income = Net Income ÷ Net Revenue
```

A look at the Income Statement for Wonderful Widgets, Inc. (refer to Form 5-10) shows that net income, as a percent of net revenue, increased from 1.9 percent in 2003 to 7.7 percent in 2004. You can do the same thing to gross profit and selling and general and administrative expenses. The Income Statement shows that both of these items also improved in 2004. Comparing these figures against prior periods and also against a budget is important.

Budgets and projections

A budget helps you communicate, organize, and monitor your business. You can prepare a budget for any of the financial statements that I show you in this chapter, such as fixed assets, or you can prepare budgets for specific projects, such as product development, advertising, and so on. But most often, you prepare budgets in association with your Income Statement.

Budgets can cover any time period; however, the further into the future you go, the less reliable the numbers become. Nevertheless, long-range budgets can help you set your business strategy.

You can use your budget to

- ✔ **Set a spending target or guideline.** For example, you can forecast your net income or profit for the coming year.
- ✔ **Set an absolute maximum.** For example, you can set a budget for your advertising agency, which it can't exceed without getting approval.

A small business usually benefits most from a budget that forecasts what you expect to happen. Make realistic assumptions and avoid wishful thinking when creating your budget, and then take the following basic steps:

1. **Come up with a forecast for the sales and revenue that your business will produce.**

   This number is the most important because it drives the rest of the budget. In fact, you may want to do several budgets: a conservative one, an expected one, and an optimistic one. Doing so can help you make adjustments in your operations if conditions change.

2. **Calculate the number of employees you need to produce the goods or services.**

   Work out their expected salaries and benefits. Start with last year's actual expense numbers (unless your operation is changing a lot or is a new venture). The more detail you get into, the better understanding you have about what numbers to use.

3. **Calculate what you will spend and when you will spend it for each expense category.**

   Work out each of your anticipated expenses.

You should put the budget in the same format as the Income Statement, like in Form 5-16. This format allows you to compare actual results with the budget so that you can understand the reasons for the differences and make any necessary changes in your operations to improve your results.

Auditing financial statements

You have to make a decision about whether to have your financial statements *audited* by an independent accounting firm. Auditors review your financial statements to determine whether those statements are substantially accurate and in accordance with generally accepted accounting principals (GAAP). Prospective investors and acquirers of businesses very much want to see audited financial statements for your business.

Audited financial statements, however, cost you $5,000 to $40,000 a year, depending on the complexity of your business and whether you hire one of the "Big Four" auditors or some smaller accounting firm.

Wonderful Widgets, Inc.
20___ Quarterly Budget

	1st Qtr	2nd Qtr	3rd Qtr	4th Qtr	Total 20___
Gross Sales	$60,000	$65,000	$70,000	$65,000	$260,000
Returns & Allowances	8,000	9,000	10,000	10,000	37,000
Net Revenue	52,000	56,000	60,000	55,000	223,000
Cost of Goods Sold	25,000	26,000	28,000	26,000	105,000
Gross Profit	27,000	30,000	32,000	29,000	118,000
Selling, General & Administrative					
Salaries	11,500	12,000	13,000	13,500	50,000
Payroll taxes	1,500	1,600	1,600	1,600	6,300
Employee benefits	2,000	2,000	2,000	2,000	8,000
Travel expenses	400	300	300	300	1,300
Rent expense	900	900	900	900	3,600
Advertising	300	300	300	300	1,200
Depreciation expense	900	900	900	900	3,600
Insurance expense	500	500	500	500	2,000
Office Supplies	500	500	500	500	2,000
Dues and subscriptions	200	200	200	200	800
Telephone	900	900	900	900	600
Legal and accounting services	800	800	800	800	3,200
Miscellaneous expenses	200	200	200	200	800
Total S,G & A Expenses	20,600	21,100	22,100	22,600	86,400
Operating Profit	6,400	8,900	9,900	6,400	31,600
Interest Income (Expense)	(1,000)	(1,200)	(1,100)	(1,100)	(4,400)
Net Income before Taxes	5,400	7,700	8,800	5,300	27,200
Income Taxes	2,000	2,500	3,000	2,100	9,600
Net Income	**$ 3,400**	**$ 5,200**	**$ 5,800**	**$ 3,200**	**$17,600**

Form 5-16: The Quarterly Budget projects anticipated income and expenses.

Forms on the CD-ROM

Check out these bookkeeping forms on the CD-ROM:

Form 5-1	**IRS Publication 538**	Accounting Periods and Methods
Form 5-2	**IRS Publication 463**	Travel, Entertainment, Gift, and Car Expenses
Form 5-3	**Form I-9**	United States Custom & Immigration Services form that declares your employees resident status (required for all employees)
Form 5-4	**Daily Summary of Cash Receipts**	Form for daily cash receipts summary
Form 5-5	**Monthly Summary of Cash Receipts**	Monthly summary of cash receipts and sales tax
Form 5-6	**Check Disbursements Journal**	Journal to keep track of checks issued
Form 5-7	**Depreciation Worksheet**	Schedule to record assets and related depreciation information
Form 5-8	**Bank Reconciliation Worksheet**	Worksheet to reconcile bank statement with outstanding checks and bank charges
Form 5-9	**Employee Compensation Record**	Form to keep track of compensation owed to an employee, along with deductions
Form 5-10	**Income Statement**	Sample income statement form for figuring revenue, costs, and income
Form 5-11	**Comparative Income Statement**	Sample income statement showing comparisons over two periods
Form 5-12	**Balance Sheet**	Sample balance sheet
Form 5-13	**Comparative Balance Sheet**	Sample balance sheet showing comparisons over two periods

(continued)

(continued)

Form 5-14	**Cash Flow Statement**	Sample cash flow statement comparing two periods
Form 5-15	**Cash Flow Forecast Statement**	Bookkeeping tool that helps you anticipate future cash flows
Form 5-16	**Sample Quarterly Budget**	Budget to project anticipated quarterly income and expenses
Form 5-17	**Accounts Receivable Aging**	Sample form to keep track of accounts receivable from customers
Form 5-18	**Accounts Receivable Monthly Customer Statement**	Accounts receivable statement by customer
Form 5-19	**Delinquent Account Collection History**	Form to keep track of collection efforts for a delinquent account
Form 5-20	**Annual Summary of Expenses**	Sample annual summary of expenses by major categories
Form 5-21	**Expense Report for Meals and Entertainment**	Expense reimbursement form for employee to complete
Form 5-22	**Travel Expense Reimbursement Form**	Expense reimbursement form for travel-related expenses
Form 5-23	**Employee Attendance Record**	Form to track employee attendance and absences
Form 5-24	**Employee Monthly Time Record**	Form to keep track of an employee's monthly hours, including vacation, holiday, and overtime hours

Chapter 6

Small Business Tax Basics

In This Chapter

▶ Using the tax tools that you need for your place in the tax world

▶ Breaking down the different kinds of taxes

▶ Finding ways to save some money

▶ Asking for help

*T*axes. Yes, it's an ugly word. And the tax scheme can be awfully compli-cated. But all small business owners need to be aware of tax basics and the various filings that they have to make.

Keep in mind that this area isn't an easy one — you face federal tax filings and forms, state tax filings, local filings, sales taxes, use taxes, unemployment taxes — taxes on using the restroom can't be far behind. And you may need some professional help, too (such as an accountant, tax lawyer, or psychia-trist), to get you through the complexities.

In this chapter, I outline some important, basic tax information for small busi-nesses, especially for the early stage start-up. Read on to get a head start on some important tax issues.

Thinking about Taxes from the Ground Up

As a small business person, you can't afford *not* to think about taxes. You need to constantly keep abreast of tax law changes so that you can make pru-dent decisions that limit your tax liability. In fact, when deciding what type of business entity to set up, tax liability should be among your most important considerations.

The most important reason for thinking about taxes right from the outset is the dreaded *double tax* — where regular corporations have to pay corporate taxes on income and the company's shareholders have to pay tax on certain dividends. Double taxation means that the shareholders get a smaller part of the business's profits.

Choosing the right business entity

One of the most important tax decisions you have to make in forming a new business is choosing the most-suitable business form: corporation, S corporation, partnership, LLC, or some other form. Chapter 2 details many of the advantages and disadvantages for each type of entity.

Regular corporations (or C corporations) must pay tax on corporate income, and shareholders must also pay tax on certain dividends (these two taxes are often referred to as *double taxation*). Partnerships, LLCs, and S corporations generally have *pass-through taxation,* where the shareholders, but not the business entity, have to pay tax on the business's income. Tax issues play an important part (but aren't the sole factor) in choosing one business entity over another.

The IRS provides a lot of publications about the tax liabilities for different business forms. On the CD-ROM, pay special attention to Form 6-1, which is IRS Publication 541 *(Partnerships),* and Form 6-2, which is IRS Publication 542 *(Corporations).* Form 6-2 also contains a table that outlines corporate tax rates.

S corporations

Forming your business as an S corporation can help you by avoiding the double tax. To become an S corporation, you need to file IRS Form 2553 with the IRS by the 15th day of the third month of the tax year in which the election will apply. You may also need to file an election in the state where your business is incorporated.

You must meet a number of technical rules before you can qualify as an S corporation. (I discuss these rules in Chapter 2.) This election can mean real tax savings for many small businesses, so definitely check it out. A corporation continues to be treated as an S corporation until the status is either terminated or revoked.

Form 6-3 on the CD-ROM shows the IRS Form 2553 for electing to be an S corporation. Form 6-4 gives you a transmittal letter to send to the IRS with Form 2553.

The Tax Tool Kit

The IRS expects businesses to submit several forms, which helps it ensure that companies and individual taxpayers meet their tax obligations. Despite the current push for a new, warm-and-fuzzy IRS, I still advise you to do everything in your power not to run afoul of the tax laws. On the CD-ROM, Form 6-5, IRS Publication 594 *(Understanding the Collection Process),* outlines all the nasty things that can happen to you if you don't meet your tax obligations.

Application for a taxpayer identification number

The IRS can process your tax returns only if you have a taxpayer identification number for your business. The two most common kinds of taxpayer identification numbers are the Social Security number (SSN) for individuals and the employer identification number (EIN) for businesses.

The Social Security Administration issues a nine-digit SSN in this format: 555-44-3333. The IRS issues a nine-digit EIN in this format: 99-8888888.

Include your taxpayer identification number (SSN or EIN) on all returns or other documents that you send to the IRS. The IRS uses EINs to identify the tax accounts of employers, sole proprietors, corporations, partnerships, estates, trusts, and other entities.

You need to get an EIN if you

- Have employees
- Have a pension plan
- Operate your business as a corporation or partnership
- File any of these tax returns:
  - Employment
  - Excise
  - Alcohol, tobacco, and firearms

Apply for your EIN as soon as you form a business. You can do so by filing IRS Form SS-4 *(Application for Employer Identification Number)*. This form appears on the CD-ROM as Form 6-6 along with Form 6-7, a transmittal letter to enclose with the application. If you want more information about EINs, check out Form 6-8, IRS Publication 1915 *(Understanding Your IRS Taxpayer Identification Number)*.

Employee forms

You need to have any employees you hire fill out Form I-9 and Form W-4 on or before the first day of employment:

- **Form I-9:** The law requires you to verify that each new employee is legally eligible to work in the United States. Both you and the employee must complete the United States Customs & Immigration Service Form I-9 *(Employment Eligibility Verification)*. Form 6-9 on the CD-ROM shows Form I-9.

✔ **Form W-4:** Each employee must fill out IRS Form W-4 *(Employee's Withholding Allowance Certificate)*. You use the filing status and withholding allowances shown on this form to figure the amount of income tax to withhold from the employee's wages. You can find the W-4 as Form 6-10 on the CD-ROM.

Tax deposit coupons

You generally have to deposit employment taxes, withheld income taxes, certain excise taxes, corporate income tax, and S corporation taxes before you file your IRS tax return. You can deliver deposits with completed deposit coupons to an authorized financial institution or a Federal Reserve bank for your area — unless you make the deposits electronically (which I discuss later in this section).

To be on time, mailed deposits have to arrive at the depository by the due date. The IRS may charge you a penalty for not making deposits when due, unless you have a good reason. Most small businesses have to make monthly deposits.

Use IRS Form 8109 *(Federal Tax Deposit Coupon)* to deposit taxes. On each coupon, show the deposit amount, the type of tax, the period for which you're making a deposit, and your telephone number. Use a separate coupon for each tax and period. You must include a coupon with each deposit you make. IRS Form 8109 appears on the CD-ROM as Form 6-11.

Five to six weeks after you receive your employer identification number (EIN), the IRS sends you the coupon book. If you have a deposit due and don't have enough time to obtain a coupon book, you can get blank coupons (IRS Form 8109-B) from the IRS. You can't use photocopies of the coupons to make your deposits.

If your total deposits of Social Security, Medicare taxes, and withheld income tax during previous years exceeded $50,000, the IRS probably requires you to deposit your taxes electronically through the Electronic Federal Tax Payment System (EFTPS). Taxpayers who don't have to make deposits by EFTPS may still enroll in the system, which allows tax deposits without coupons, paper checks, or visits to an authorized depository.

For more information about how to make tax payments, see IRS Publication 15 *(Circular E, Employer's Tax Guide)*, included as Form 6-12 on the CD-ROM.

Be sure to deposit taxes on time — sizable penalties can apply if you don't. And small business owners who also act as managers can be held personally liable for withheld taxes that aren't deposited with the IRS.

Form 1099-MISC

You use Form 1099-MISC *(Miscellaneous Income)* to report certain payments that you make in your trade or business. These payments generally include

- ✔ Payments of $600 or more per year for services performed for your business by workers not treated as your employees, such as fees to attorneys, accountants, or directors
- ✔ Rent payments of $600 or more per year
- ✔ Prizes and awards of $600 or more per year, such as winnings on TV or radio shows
- ✔ Royalty payments of $10 or more per year

You also use Form 1099-MISC to report sales of $5,000 or more of consumer goods to a person for resale anywhere other than in a permanent retail establishment. You can find Form 1099-MISC on the CD-ROM as Form 6-13.

Form 8300

You file IRS Form 8300 *(Report of Cash Payments Over $10,000 Received in a Trade or Business)* if you receive more than $10,000 in cash in one transaction (or in two or more related business transactions). Cash includes U.S. and foreign coin and currency. It also includes certain monetary instruments, such as certain cashier's and traveler's checks and money orders. For more information, see IRS Publication 1544 *(Reporting Cash Payments of Over $10,000 Received in a Trade or Business),* included as Form 6-14 on the CD-ROM.

Form W-2

You file IRS Form W-2 *(Wage and Tax Statement)* to report payments to your employees, such as wages, tips, and other compensation; withheld income; Social Security; Medicare taxes; and advance earned income credit (EIC) payments. For more information on what to report on Form W-2, see the instructions that accompany that form.

IRS Form W-2 appears on the CD-ROM as Form 6-15.

A Tax for All Reasons

The type of business you operate determines what taxes you pay and how you pay them. The four general kinds of business taxes are

- Income tax
- Self-employment tax
- Employment taxes
- Excise taxes

Income tax

All businesses except partnerships must file an annual income tax return with the IRS and certain states where you conduct business. Partnerships file an *information return.* An information return is a tax filing that notifies the IRS of the partnership's activities for the year. Which form you use depends on how you've organized your business. IRS Publication 583 *(Starting a Business and Keeping Records),* included on the CD-ROM as Form 6-16, tells you which returns you may have to file.

Generally, sole proprietors, partners, and shareholders of an S corporation pay income tax by making regular estimated tax payments during the year. If you expect to owe taxes, including self-employment tax (which I discuss in the following section), of $500 or more when you file your return, you generally have to make estimated tax payments. You can use IRS Form 1040-ES *(Estimated Tax for Individuals)* to pay the tax. If you aren't required to make estimated tax payments, you can pay any tax due when you file your return.

A corporation must deposit the taxes it owes, including estimated tax payments and any balance due shown on its tax return. For information on how to make tax deposits, see the section "Tax deposit coupons" earlier in this chapter.

Self-employment tax

Self-employment tax combines Social Security and Medicare tax for individuals who work for themselves. Your self-employment tax payments contribute to your coverage under the Social Security system. Social Security coverage provides you with various retirement benefits, disability benefits, survivor benefits, and medical insurance (Medicare) benefits.

You generally pay self-employment tax if your annual net earnings from self-employment are $400 or more. You can use Schedule SE (IRS Form 1040) to figure your self-employment tax.

For more information, see IRS Publication 533 *(Self-Employment Tax),* which you can find as Form 6-17 on the CD-ROM.

Employment taxes

Employment taxes consist of the following:

- ✔ Federal income tax withholding
- ✔ Social Security and Medicare taxes
- ✔ Federal unemployment (FUTA) tax

If you have employees, check out Form 6-12 on the CD-ROM, which shows IRS Publication 15 *(Circular E, Employer's Tax Guide).* This publication explains your tax responsibilities as an employer.

You should pay particular attention to the classifications of the people who work for you: Should you treat them as employees or independent contractors for tax purposes? The label you put on them doesn't bind the IRS, and if you misclassify them, you can face some serious problems. (I discuss this issue in Chapter 10.)

Federal withholding

Businesses must withhold federal income taxes from an employee's wages. To figure how much federal income tax to withhold from each wage payment, you need the employee's Form W-4 (check out the section "Employer tax forms" earlier in this chapter) and the methods described in IRS Publication 15 *(Circular E, Employer's Tax Guide),* which is Form 6-12 on the CD-ROM.

Social Security and Medicare withholding

Social Security and Medicare taxes pay for benefits that the workers and their families receive under the Federal Insurance Contributions Act (FICA). Social Security tax pays for benefits under the old-age, survivors, and disability insurance part of FICA. Medicare tax pays for benefits under the hospital insurance part. You withhold part of these taxes from your employee's wages and you pay a matching amount yourself.

Most employers use IRS Form 941 *(Employer's Quarterly Federal Tax Return)* to report these taxes owed to the IRS. You can find this document as Form 6-18 on the CD-ROM.

Federal unemployment (FUTA) tax

The federal unemployment tax, under the Federal Unemployment Tax Act (FUTA), pays unemployment compensation to workers who lose their jobs. You report and pay FUTA tax separately from Social Security and Medicare taxes and withheld income tax. You pay FUTA tax only from your own funds. Employees don't pay this tax or have it withheld from their pay.

You report federal unemployment tax on IRS Form 940 *(Employer's Annual Federal Unemployment [FUTA] Tax Return),* which I have included as Form 6-19 on the CD-ROM. If you qualify, you can use the simpler Form 940-EZ, instead. (See IRS Publication 15 — Form 6-12 on the CD-ROM — to find out if you can use this simpler form.)

Remember, it's the FUTA tax, not the Phooey tax.

Excise taxes

If you manufacture or sell certain products, operate certain types of businesses, or use various types of equipment, facilities, or products, you may owe excise tax. Most small businesses don't fall into these categories (which include things like retail sales of heavy trucks, wagering, guns, and tobacco or alcohol products).

IRS Publication 510 *(Excise Taxes)* — Form 6-20 on the CD-ROM — provides more information on excise taxes.

Sales taxes

If your business sells retail products and your state imposes sales tax on those goods, then your business is usually responsible for collecting and paying that tax. The tax is computed on the product's sale price — not on your net profits.

As the seller of products, you are responsible for

- ✔ Properly charging and collecting the tax from the customer
- ✔ Reporting the tax amount to the appropriate state or locality in a timely manner
- ✔ Paying the tax to the appropriate state or locality in a timely manner
- ✔ Obtaining sales permits, as needed

Some states also impose a *use tax* for the use of personal property, as a complement to the sales tax. Your business is responsible for paying this tax if you conduct business in any of those states.

You can get sales tax information from the appropriate state or local government office in your area.

Penalties dead ahead!

To be sure that all taxpayers pay their fair share of taxes, the Internal Revenue Code provides penalties for those who don't file returns or pay taxes as required. The IRS can also impose criminal penalties for willful failure to file, tax evasion, or making a false statement:

✔ **Failure to file tax returns:** If you don't file your tax return by the due date, you may have to pay a penalty. The IRS bases the penalty on the amount of tax not paid by the due date.

✔ **Failure to pay tax:** If you don't pay your taxes by the due date, you have to pay a penalty for each month, or part of a month, that your taxes remain unpaid. This penalty can't be more than 25 percent of your unpaid tax.

✔ **Failure to withhold, deposit, or pay taxes:** If you don't withhold income, Social Security, or Medicare taxes from employees, or if you withhold taxes but don't deposit them or pay them to the IRS, you may be subject to a penalty on the unpaid tax, plus interest. You may also be subject to penalties if you deposit the taxes late.

✔ **Failure to file information returns:** A penalty applies if you don't file information returns by the due date, if you don't include all required information, or if you don't report information accurately.

✔ **Failure to furnish correct payee statements:** A penalty applies if you don't furnish a required statement to a payee by the required date, if you don't include all required information, or if you don't report information correctly.

✔ **Waiver of penalty:** The IRS can waive these penalties if you can show that the failures are attributable to a reasonable cause and not willful neglect.

Avoid these penalties by making sure that you have good procedures in place to accurately meet your business's tax obligations in a timely manner.

Elementary, My Dear: Deductions for Your Business

As the old cliché promises, every cloud has a silver lining. With taxes, that little ray of sunshine is deductible expenses. Knowing what is and isn't deductible can save you a lot of tax money and should affect the decisions you make as you set up your company.

Business expenses

You can normally deduct business expenses on your income tax return. According to the IRS, a business expense must be both ordinary and necessary in order to be deductible. (You may have to file a Form 1099-MISC for some expenses, as I discuss in the section "Form 1099-MISC" earlier in this chapter.)

An *ordinary* expense is one that's common and accepted in your field of business, trade, or profession. A *necessary* expense is one that's helpful and appropriate for your business, trade, or profession. An expense doesn't have to be indispensable to be considered necessary.

Examples of expenses that are normally deductible include: accounting fees, advertising, attorneys fees, commissions, employee wages, insurance, interest, mailing and delivery costs, manufacturing costs, office supplies, rent, and travel expenses.

The following list includes some expense categories of interest to start-up businesses, although you may be able to deduct many other expenses as well (also check out Publication 535, *Business Expenses* — Form 6-21 on the CD-ROM):

- ✔ **Business start-up costs:** Check out Form 6-21 on the CD-ROM (IRS Publication 535, *Business Expenses*) for details about how to deduct costs that you absorb before you open for business.

- ✔ **Depreciation:** Take a look at Form 6-22 on the CD-ROM (IRS Publication 946, *How to Depreciate Property*) for the scoop on depreciating your business equipment, which offers some potential tax benefits.

- ✔ **Business use of your home:** Look carefully at Form 6-23 on the CD-ROM (IRS Publication 587, *Business Use of Your Home — Including Use by Day Care Providers*) to see whether you meet the specific qualifications for the deduction. If you do, Form 6-24 presents the tax form for the claim, IRS Form 8829.

- ✔ **Car and truck expenses:** See Form 6-25 on the CD-ROM (IRS Publication 463, *Travel, Entertainment, Gift, and Car Expenses*) for information about the rules for claiming car and truck expenses.

- ✔ **Meal and entertainment expenses:** The IRS generally only allows your business to deduct 50 percent of your business-related meal and entertainment expenses. Check out Form 6-21 on the CD-ROM (IRS Publication 535, *Business Expenses*) for the skinny on these expenses.

Special tax benefits for shareholders of a qualified small business

To encourage investment in new ventures and small businesses, Section 1202 of the Internal Revenue Code provides a big benefit to noncorporate shareholders of a qualified small business. When a noncorporate shareholder sells stock of a qualified small business, he gets to exclude 50 percent of any long-term profits from that sale from taxable income.

You must clear a number of hurdles in order to get this tax benefit, including the following:

- **Shareholders:** A United States corporation must issue the stock to a person (not a corporation) after August 10, 1993.

- **Original issuance:** The individual trying to get the tax benefit must get the stock directly from the qualifying small business during the original issuance of the stock (generally for cash, nonstock property, or services).

- **Gross assets:** The corporation's total gross assets (all of its cash, equipment, and other assets) can't exceed $50 million until immediately after the shareholder acquires the stock.

- **Conduct of business:** The qualified small business must use at least 80 percent of its total assets (by value) actively conducting a trade or business during the term that the shareholder holds the stock.

- **Minimum time:** The stockholder must hold the stock for more than five years.

- **Maximum amount:** The maximum amount of a particular taxpayer's capital gain from stock in the corporation that is eligible for the tax benefit is the greater of $10 million or ten times the shareholder's *adjusted aggregate basis* (generally, the price paid for the stock) in the qualified small business stock sold in that year.

Although you have to jump through several hoops, you can make your business much more attractive to shareholders if the business can become a qualified small business.

Where to Go for More Help

The IRS and other government agencies offer assistance to small businesses. The following list summarizes some of the assistance available:

- **Small Business Tax Education Program:** Small business owners and other self-employed individuals can figure out business taxes through a partnership between the IRS and local organizations. Through workshops or in-depth tax courses, instructors provide training on starting a business, record keeping, preparing business tax returns, self-employment tax issues, and employment taxes. Check your telephone book for the local number of the IRS office closest to you or call 1-800-829-1040.

- **IRS tax forms and publications:** You can get forms and publications from the IRS by phone 1-800-TAX-FORM; fax 703-321-8020; and the Web site www.irs.gov.

✔ **Tax questions:** You can call the IRS with your tax questions Monday through Friday during regular business hours. Check your telephone book for the local number or call 1-800-829-1040.

✔ **Small Business Administration:** The Small Business Administration (SBA) offers training and educational programs, counseling services, financial programs, and contract assistance to small business owners. The SBA also has publications and videos on a wide range of business topics. If you want information on setting up a business from the SBA, look in your telephone directory under "U.S. Government" for the number of your local SBA office or call the small business answer desk at 1-800-8-ASK-SBA.

✔ **Other federal agencies:** Other federal agencies also release publications and pamphlets to assist small businesses. For a list of federal publications that you can buy, check out www.FedForms.gov.

Forms on the CD-ROM

Check out the large number of tax-related forms on the CD-ROM:

Form 6-1	**IRS Pub. 541**	Partnerships
Form 6-2	**IRS Pub. 542**	Corporations
Form 6-3	**IRS Form 2553**	S Corporation Election form
Form 6-4	**Transmittal Letter to IRS Enclosing S Corporation Election**	A letter to send with Form 2553
Form 6-5	**IRS Pub. 594**	The IRS Collection Process
Form 6-6	**IRS Form SS-4**	Application for Employer Identification Number
Form 6-7	**Transmittal Letter to IRS Enclosing Form SS-4**	A letter to enclose with your application for an Employer ID number
Form 6-8	**IRS Pub. 1915**	Understanding Your IRS Taxpayer Identification Number
Form 6-9	**Form I-9**	Employment Eligibility Verification
Form 6-10	**IRS Form W-4**	Employer's Withholding Allowance Certificate
Form 6-11	**IRS Form 8109**	Federal Tax Deposit Coupon

Form 6-12	**IRS Pub. 15**	Circular E, Employer's Tax Guide
Form 6-13	**IRS Form 1099-MISC**	Miscellaneous Income
Form 6-14	**IRS Pub. 1544**	Reporting Cash Payments of Over $10,000
Form 6-15	**IRS Form W-2**	Employer's Wage and Tax Statement
Form 6-16	**IRS Pub. 583**	Starting a Business and Keeping Records
Form 6-17	**IRS Pub. 533**	Self-Employment Tax
Form 6-18	**IRS Form 941**	Employer's Quarterly Federal Tax Return
Form 6-19	**IRS Form 940**	Employer's Annual Unemployment Tax Return
Form 6-20	**IRS Pub. 510**	Excise Taxes
Form 6-21	**IRS Pub. 535**	Business Expenses
Form 6-22	**IRS Pub. 946**	How to Depreciate Property
Form 6-23	**IRS Pub. 587**	Business Use of Your Home
Form 6-24	**IRS Form 8829**	Expenses for Business Use of Your Home
Form 6-25	**IRS Pub. 463**	Travel, Entertainment, Gift, and Car Expenses
Form 6-26	**IRS Form 8300**	Report of Cash Payments Over $10,000 Received in a Trade or Business
Form 6-27	**IRS Pub. 15-A**	Employer's Supplemental Tax Guide
Form 6-28	**IRS Pub. 334**	Tax Guide for Small Businesses (For Individuals Who Use Schedule C or C-EZ)
Form 6-29	**IRS Pub. 536**	Net Operating Losses
Form 6-30	**IRS Pub. 538**	Accounting Periods and Methods
Form 6-31	**IRS Pub. 560**	Retirement Plans for Small Businesses

(continued)

(continued)

Form 6-32	**IRS Pub. 1066**	Small Business Tax Workshop Workbook
Form 6-33	**IRS Pub. 1853**	Small Business Talk (an IRS publication that explains small business tax issues)
Form 6-34	**IRS Pub. 1976**	Independent Contractor or Employee?
Form 6-35	**Chart of Federal Business Tax Filings**	Summary of required federal tax filings for sole proprietorships, partnerships, and corporations
Form 6-36	**IRS Pub. 1679**	A Guide to Back-up Withholding
Form 6-37	**IRS Form W-3**	Reconciliation/Transmittal of Income and Tax Statement

Part III
Employee and Consultant Issues

The 5th Wave   By Rich Tennant

"Tell us, Walter, in your own words, why you feel you're suited for the position of goon."

In this part . . .

You can't do everything yourself. As your business grows, the people that you find and employ become more and more important to the success of your business. In this part, I give you practical advice about how to hire employees, retain and motivate them, and avoid problems with them down the road. Also, you'll find out when it makes sense to hire a consultant instead of an employee to do a particular job.

Chapter 7

Employee Hiring Tools

- -

In This Chapter

▶ Searching for that perfect employee

▶ Asking the right questions (and not asking the wrong ones)

▶ Checking your applicant's past

▶ Using the tools for hiring

- -

Good employees can be the most important ingredients in a successful business. But finding and hiring good employees can be among the most challenging aspects of running a small or growing company.

Numerous federal and state laws govern the various processes of soliciting employees, including advertising, interviewing, and hiring. If you don't follow the rules, you may find yourself as the defendant in a lawsuit over your hiring (or non-hiring) practices. Or, you may end up being stuck with a very costly and unproductive employee that you have trouble firing.

In this chapter, I give you some tips for finding and hiring employees and make suggestions about the proper paperwork to use in this area.

Finding the Cream of the Crop

Finding good employees is crucial to most businesses. The better the employees, the higher the likelihood of having a successful organization.

Similarly, bad employees can cost a business incredible amounts of time, wasted resources, and money. So it pays to take the time at the beginning to find the best candidates for the position.

Tried-and-true resources

What are the best resources for finding great candidates? Here are some ideas:

- ✔ Pay employees a bounty reward (usually $250 to $1,000) for recruiting candidates to the organization.

- ✔ Contract with employment agencies that supply permanent employees for a fee.

- ✔ Turn to headhunters or executive search firms for executive level employees (for a significant fee).

- ✔ Promote your own employees from within to fill an open position.

- ✔ Hire employees from temporary employment agencies with the possibility of hiring the employee on a permanent basis (expect to pay a fee to the temporary employment agency if you do hire permanently).

- ✔ Advertise in the classified sections of local newspapers, trade magazines, the *Wall Street Journal,* and the *National Employer's Weekly* to get your message to a large number of potential employees.

A tangled Web of resources

As companies embrace the use of the Internet, both prospective employers and employees turn more and more to the World Wide Web to identify employment candidates.

You can use the Web to find good prospects in two ways:

- ✔ **Post positions on your company's Web site.** Think about putting your open positions on your Web site. That way, prospective employees can also search your site and find out more about your company.

- ✔ **Post positions on job-related Web sites.** The Web contains a host of sites that display job postings, want ads, and résumés of prospective employees.

Job-related sites offer job openings, résumé postings, employer profiles, and career advice. One good way to find these sites is by using the Internet search engines, such as www.yahoo.com or www.google.com.

America Online also contains employment-related information. Table 7-1 lists more popular sites:

Table 7-1	Job-Related Web Sites
Web Site	*URL*
Monster	www.monster.com
Hot Jobs	www.hotjobs.com
Dice	www.dice.com
Job	www.job.com
Career Builder	www.careerbuilder.com

REMEMBER

A bundle of employment laws

Many employers are subject to laws requiring equal employment opportunity and prohibiting discrimination in employment:

✔ **Title VII of the Civil Rights Act of 1964.** Prohibits discrimination on the basis of race, color, religion, national origin, and sex. It also prohibits sex discrimination on the basis of pregnancy and sexual harassment.

✔ **The Equal Pay Act of 1963.** Prohibits employers from paying different wages to men and women who perform essentially the same work under similar working conditions.

✔ **The Age Discrimination in Employment Act (ADEA).** Prohibits discrimination against individuals who are age 40 or older. Applies to employers with 20 or more employees.

✔ **The Civil Rights Act of 1966.** Prohibits discrimination based on race or ethnic origin.

✔ **The Immigration Reform and Control Act of 1986.** Prohibits discrimination on the basis of national origin or citizenship of persons who are authorized to work in the United States.

✔ **The Americans with Disabilities Act.** Prohibits discrimination against persons with disabilities.

✔ **Other Laws.** Numerous other federal and state laws prohibit discriminatory employment practices because of an employee's bankruptcy, garnishment of wages, pregnancy, selection for jury duty, or "blowing the whistle" on illegal practices of the company.

Parlez-Vous Interview?

Most people have gone through the sweaty-palmed experience of sitting through an interview at some time. As a small business entrepreneur, you get to move over to the other side of the desk and do the interviewing. This section gives you some sample questions that can give you good information on which to base your decision and inappropriate questions that can land you in court if you don't avoid them.

Questions to ask

Form 7-1, which you can find later in this chapter, shows a list of questions that may be appropriate to ask when interviewing a prospective employee.

Questions not to ask

You probably have many questions that you want to ask a prospective employee. But certain questions can only get you in trouble (yes, you can trip over many laws in interviews). The following list contains the top ten questions that you should *not* ask:

- How old are you?
- Do you have any disabilities?
- Are you pregnant?
- Are you married with kids?
- Have you ever been arrested?
- Would you be willing to sleep with the boss?
- What is your religious affiliation?
- What is your sexual orientation?
- What ethnic background are you?
- Who played Lumpy on *Leave It to Beaver*?

So what the heck can you ask? Generally, the focus of the questions should be on the skill and experience of the candidates and the qualifications that he needs to perform the job.

**QUESTIONS TO CONSIDER
ASKING PROSPECTIVE
EMPLOYEES**

Past Jobs

- How did you get your last job?

- What were your specific responsibilities?

- What did you like about the job?

- What did you dislike about the job?

- What did you learn from the job?

- Did you run into any difficult situations? How did you handle them?

- Tell me about the types of interaction you had with other workers.

- Tell me of an accomplishment you are particularly proud of and what you did.

- What kind of supervision of other workers have you had?

- Do you have persons from your former job who would provide a professional reference?

- Why did you leave your past jobs?

- Why do you want to leave your current job?

- What is the compensation at your current job? What is your salary expectation for this position?

- Describe a typical day in your current job.

Form 7-1: Questions to consider asking prospective employees — page 1 of 3.

<u>**The New Job**</u>

- What would be your specific goals for this job?

- What experience do you have that you think will be helpful for this job?

- This job will require a lot of [describe]. Will that be a problem for you?

- This job will require interacting with [describe the types of people]. What experience do you have working with such people?

- What would you like to get from this new job?

- One requirement of this job is writing various types of reports -- e.g., weekly, monthly, projections, goals, employee evaluation, etc. What relevant experience have you had on your previous job? Do you have any writing samples you could provide us with?

- This job will require a certain amount of new client development. Have you had much experience? Tell me how you have gone about this.

<u>**Education**</u>

- What subjects did you do well in school?

- What was your major?

- Where did you attend high school, college, or post-graduate school?

- Did you work at an outside job while going to school? Describe the job.

- Are you interested in continuing your education?

- Did you have any school honors?

<u>**General Information**</u>

- What do you consider your strong points?

- What do you consider your weak points?

- What specific kind of work do you particularly enjoy doing?

- What is your long-term career objective?

Form 7-1: Questions to consider asking prospective employees — page 2 of 3.

Physical Condition

- Do you think you will be able to handle the physical aspects of this job?

- Do you currently use any illegal drugs?

- If offered a job, will you submit to a medical examination?

- This job requires medical evaluation which includes urinalysis for drug testing, etc. Do you have any objection to this?

Experience and Skills

- What special skills do you have?

- How proficient are you in using PCs?

- Are there software applications you are particularly familiar with?

Outside Activities

- What kind of job-related organizations or professional societies do you belong to (you may omit those that indicate your race, religion, color, national origin, ancestry, sex, or age)?

- How will your involvement in these activities affect your job here?

Nepotism Information

- Do you have any relatives already employed by our company? If so, who are they and what is their relationship to you?

- Do you have any relatives employed by a competitor of this company? If so, who are they and what is their relationship to you?

***

Form 7-1: Questions to consider asking prospective employees — page 3 of 3.

Checking 'Em Out

Say you think that you have interviewed the perfect person for the job. Should you extend an offer now? The answer is *no!* Before you make any definite job offer, you should perform a background and reference check on the person.

Ideally, the prospective employee signs your handy-dandy "Background Check Permission Form" (Forms 7-2 and 7-3 on the CD-ROM), which allows you to get reference information from prior employers and even do a credit check.

If you want to formally request information in writing from a prior employer, use the "Reference Check Letter" (Form 7-4 on the CD-ROM). Of course, you should make sure that the prospective employee has given you permission to do so.

You may find that past employers are reluctant to give you much information other than confirming employment, position, and salary (yes, for fear of getting sued should the company say anything bad about the former employee). And yes, your company should have the same policy with respect to your departing employees.

From a fact-checking standpoint, think about doing the following:

- ✔ **Check out school experience.** Some people lie about the degrees that they have earned or where they went to school. Definitely check out these claims.

- ✔ **Talk to the candidate's former supervisors.** If you can, try to talk to the candidate's former supervisors — they may provide much more meaningful information than that company's Human Resources Department.

- ✔ **Check for felony convictions.** For sensitive jobs, such as those in which the employee handles money, check to see if the candidate has any past felony convictions.

- ✔ **Verify past employment.** Verify that the employee worked at each of the companies listed, at the position listed, and check the dates of employment.

Remember, finding out a candidate lied about any of the above may be a tip off of bigger problems.

Hiring Tool Kit

In this section, I discuss a number of forms, letters, procedures, and agreements that can help you through the hiring process. Pay attention here — the following advice alone is worth the price of this book!

Employment applications

Think about requiring all of your prospective employees to fill out an Employment Application. An application solicits a lot of information to help you make decisions on whether or not to hire the person.

Be careful what the application contains. Some questions are illegal to ask. A good Employment Application form asks for prior work experience, special skills, educational background, and also gives consent to the company to check references.

Make sure to keep employment applications on file. The application can be helpful later if you decide to fire an employee after discovering that she lied about the information on the form.

Make sure to attach the employee's résumé to the application and keep it in your files. You may want to refer back to the résumé later if problems arise with the employee.

Form 7-5 shows a sample Employment Application form. If the applicant doesn't cut the mustard, you can send out a rejection letter similar to the sample found on Form 7-6 on the CD-ROM.

[ABC, Inc.]

Insert the name of
your company

EMPLOYMENT APPLICATION

Insert the name of
your company

[ABC, Inc.] (the "Company") is an equal opportunity/affirmative action employer. All qualified applicants will be considered without regard to age, race, color, sex, religion, nation origin, marital status, ancestry, citizenship, veteran status, sexual orientation or preference, or physical or mental disability.

Form 7-5: A sample Employment Application — page 1 of 4.

PERSONAL

Basic information from the applicant

Last Name	First	Initial	Social Security #

Other Name(s) Used	Home Telephone # ( )

Address	Business or Message # ( )

Position Applied For	Referred By	Salary Desired

Have you ever interviewed with the Company or its affiliates before? ¨Yes¨ ¨No¨	If yes, list date(s), job title(s) & location(s)
Have you ever been employed by the Company or its affiliates before? ¨Yes¨ ¨No¨	If yes, list date(s), job title(s) & location(s)
Do you have any relatives employed by the Company or its affiliates? ¨Yes¨ ¨No¨	If yes, list date(s), job title(s) & location(s)
Are you at least 18 years old? ¨Yes¨ ¨No¨	If under 18, do you have a work permit?

EDUCATION

Requests background education information

Circle Highest Grade Completed:

High School 9 10 11 12
College, Trade or Business 1 2 3 4
Graduate Studies _____

School	Address	Major Studies	Degree, Diploma, License or Certificate
High School			
College/University			
Vocational, Business, Other			
List Any Professional Designations			
Other Special Knowledge, Skills or Qualifications			

For Clerical Applicants Only:

Do you type? ¨Yes¨ ¨No¨ If yes, WPM:
Computer Skills (Hardware/Software)

Form 7-5: A sample Employment Application — page 2 of 4.

EMPLOYMENT HISTORY

Solicits detailed past employment information

List all employments for the past 10 years, starting with the most recent position. All information **must** be completed. You may attach a resume, but not in place of completing the required information.

Employed From / /	Employer Name	Supervisor Name	Starting Salary
Employed Until / /	Employer Address	Supervisor Phone #	Ending Salary
Job Title		Reason for Leaving	
Duties & Responsibilities			

Employed From / /	Employer Name	Supervisor Name	Starting Salary
Employed Until / /	Employer Address	Supervisor Phone #	Ending Salary
Job Title		Reason for Leaving	
Duties & Responsibilities			

Employed From / /	Employer Name	Supervisor Name	Starting Salary
Employed Until / /	Employer Address	Supervisor Phone #	Ending Salary
Job Title		Reason for Leaving	
Duties & Responsibilities			

Employed From / /	Employer Name	Supervisor Name	Starting Salary
Employed Until / /	Employer Address	Supervisor Phone #	Ending Salary
Job Title		Reason for Leaving	
Duties & Responsibilities			

Form 7-5: A sample Employment Application — page 3 of 4.

GENERAL

Yes   No

..   ..   May we contact your current employer for references?

..   ..   If hired, will you be able to work overtime?

..   ..   Will you be able to perform the essential job functions for the position you are applying for with or without reasonable accommodation?

..   ..   Have you ever been convicted of a crime, excluding misdemeanors and summary offenses, which has not been annulled, expunged or sealed by court? (A ¨yes¨ response does not automatically disqualify your application.)

CERTIFICATION & AUTHORIZATION

The above information is true and correct. I understand that, in the event of my employment by the Company, I shall be subject to dismissal if any information that I have given in this application is false or misleading or if I have failed to give any information herein requested, regardless of the time elapsed after discovery.

> Requires the employee to certify the accuracy of the information provided

I authorize the Company to inquire into my educational, professional and past employment history references as needed to research my qualifications for this position. I hereby give my consent to any former employer to provide employment-related information about me to the Company and will hold the Company and my former employer harmless from any claim made on the basis that such information about me was provided or that any employment decision was made on the basis of such information. I further authorize the Company to obtain any credit and consumer check.

> Authorizes reference checks

I understand that nothing in this employment application, the granting of an interview or my subsequent employment with the Company is intended to create an employment contract between myself and the Company under which my employment could be terminated only for cause. On the contrary I understand and agree that, if hired, my employment will be terminable at will and may be terminated by me or the Company at any time and for any reason. I understand that no person has any authority to enter into any agreement contrary to the foregoing.

I hereby acknowledge that I have read and agree to the above statements.

_____   _____

Signature   Date

Form 7-5: A sample Employment Application — page 4 of 4.

Offer letters

After you find the perfect employee (or at least one who satisfies your desperation standards), you are ready to make the job offer.

You can just call him over the phone and say "We want you; we have to have you; we promise you the moon if only you will grace us with your presence." Or, you can try and protect yourself from misunderstanding — and those nasty lawsuits later on — by sending a formal job offer letter like the one shown in Form 7-7.

Job offer mistakes to avoid

When you make job offers, oral or written, you need to be careful not to mislead the applicant or promise something that you can't deliver.

You need to especially avoid statements that give the applicant a false sense of security, or what the applicant may understand to be a long-term promise of employment. Avoid phrases like the following:

- ✔ "We expect you will have a long and prosperous career here."

- ✔ "You can expect your salary to increase by at least 5 percent each year."

- ✔ "After a probationary period, you will enjoy the benefits the company provides to its long-term employees."

You also want to be careful about extending different benefits to an applicant than those available to other employees. Your employees may see this action as discriminatory.

If you're going to offer the employee stock or stock options in the company, make sure that the stock only *vests,* or is earned, after some significant period of continued employment.

If you plan to offer a commission, bonus, or profit-sharing arrangement to the employee, make sure that the percentage or amount is reasonable and doesn't make the employee unprofitable for your business.

[Date]

_____
_____
_____

Re: Terms of Employment

Dear_____:

We are pleased to inform you that after careful consideration, _____(the "Company") has decided to extend this offer of employment. This letter sets forth the terms of the offer which, if you accept, will govern your employment.

Position: Duties. Your position will be_____, reporting to the _____ of the Company. Your duties and responsibilities will be designated by the Company, with an initial focus on (i)_____ and (ii) _____.

Full Time Employment. The employment term will begin on_____,_____.

Compensation. Your compensation will be $_____a year, paid twice monthly consistent with the Company's payroll practices. Your package will include participation in the health and other benefit plans of the Company's pursuant to their terms as may be amended by the Company from time to time; until the Company's health plan is adopted, your reasonable COBRA payments will be reimbursed (subject to a maximum of $_____ per month). You will be entitled to _____week's paid vacation (equivalent of____business days) for each year of full employment.

Stock Options. You will be granted options to acquire_____ shares of the Company's Common Stock, vesting_____% after one complete year of employment and_____% monthly thereafter. The options will be granted at a strike price of $_____ per share. The terms and conditions of your stock options are contained in a Stock Option Agreement of even date herewith and must be executed by you and returned to us immediately to be effective.

Employment at Will. Our employment relationship is terminable at will, which means that either you or the Company may terminate your employment at any time, and for any reason or for no reason.

Confidentiality and Invention Assignment Agreement. You will be subject to the Company's Confidentiality and Invention Assignment Agreement, which is enclosed with this letter and must be signed and returned by you before any employment relationship will be effective.

Certain Acts. During employment with the Company, you will not do anything to compete with the Company's present or contemplated business, nor will you plan or organize any competitive business activity. You will not enter into any agreement, which conflicts with your duties or obligations to the Company. You will not during your employment or within one (1) year

Form 7-7: A sample Job Offer Letter that protects the business owner — page 1 of 2.

[Date]
Page 2

after it ends, without the Company's express written consent, directly or indirectly solicit or encourage any employee, agent, independent contractor, supplier, customer, consultant or any other person or company to terminate or alter a relationship with the Company.

No Inconsistent Obligations. You represent that you are aware of no obligations legal or otherwise, inconsistent with the terms of this Agreement of with your undertaking employment with the Company. You will not disclose to the Company, or use, or induce the Company to use, any proprietary information or trade secrets of others. You represent and warrant that you have returned all proprietary and confidential information belonging to all prior employers.

Miscellaneous. Upon your acceptance, this letter will contain the entire agreement and understanding between you and the Company and supersedes any prior or contemporaneous agreements, understandings, term sheets, communications, offers, representations, warranties, or commitments by or on behalf of the Company (oral or written). The terms of your employment may in the future be amended, but only by writing and which is signed by both you and, on behalf of the Company, by a duly authorized executive officer. In making this offer, we are relying on the information you have provided us about your background and experience, including any information provided us in any Employment Application that you may have submitted to us. The language in this letter will be construed as to its fair meaning and not strictly for or against either of us. The party prevailing in any dispute between us shall be awarded reasonable attorney's fees and costs from the non-prevailing party. In the event a dispute does arise, this letter, including the validity, interpretation, construction and performance of this letter, shall be governed by and construed in accordance with the substantive laws of the State of [California or other State]. Jurisdiction for resolution of any disputes shall be solely in [City] [State].

If these terms are acceptable, please sign in the space provided below and return this letter to us. Again, we're very excited to have you join the Company.

Yours truly,

[Name]
[Title]

Agreed and Accepted:

_____
                [Name]

Form 7-7: A sample Job Offer Letter that protects the business owner — page 2 of 2.

Employment agreements

You may want some high-level employees to sign a formal Employment Agreement (or they may ask for one). A well-drafted Employment Agreement addresses the following key issues:

- ✔ The job position
- ✔ Whether the employer has the right to change the position
- ✔ The length of the agreement
- ✔ The salary, bonus, and benefits
- ✔ Whether the employee gets stock or stock options in the company (remember, the employee should earn these over time)
- ✔ When the employer can terminate the employee for good cause
- ✔ What "good cause" means
- ✔ When the employer can terminate the employee without good cause and what severance payment the employer will provide
- ✔ The employee's job responsibilities
- ✔ The employee's confidentiality obligations
- ✔ Where and how disputes will be handled

Form 7-8 (a pro-employer-oriented form that you can find later in this chapter) shows an Employment Agreement for a senior-level executive.

Confidentiality and Invention Assignment Agreements

Your employees, especially if the business is high-tech oriented, have access to a lot of the company's confidential information. You also expect your employees to come up with ideas, work product, and inventions that are useful to the business.

To make sure that your employees keep the company's proprietary information confidential, you should require them to sign a Confidentiality and Invention Assignment Agreement. This agreement deals with the confidentiality issue, but it can also provide that the ideas, work product, and inventions that the employee creates belong to the company — not to the employee.

This agreement seems fair, doesn't it? Because the company is paying the employee to produce such stuff, you want to make sure that the company has the legal right to these developments.

[Agreement with Executive Employee]

EMPLOYMENT AGREEMENT

This EMPLOYMENT AGREEMENT is entered into by and between _____ , a _____ corporation (the "Company"), and _____ , the undersigned individual ("Executive").

RECITAL

The Company and Executive desire to enter into an Employment Agreement setting forth the terms and conditions of Executive's employment with the Company.

AGREEMENT

NOW, THEREFORE, in consideration of the mutual covenants and agreements hereinafter set forth, the Company and Executive agree as follows:

1. Employment.

> Complete the proper title for the employee

(a) Term. The Company hereby employs Executive to serve as [President of the Company] [and CEO] and to serve in such additional or different position or positions as the Company may determine at its sole discretion. The term of employment shall be for a period of _____ (__) years ("Employment Period") to commence on the date hereof, unless earlier terminated as set forth herein.

> Fill in the term of the employment period

(b) Duties and Responsibilities. Executive will be reporting to [the Company's Board of Directors] [_____]. Within the limitations established by the Bylaws of the Company, the Executive shall have each and all of the duties and responsibilities of that position and such other or different duties on behalf of the Company, as may be assigned from time to time by [the Company's Board] [_____].

> State whom the employee will be reporting to

(c) Location. The initial principal location at which Executive shall perform services for the Company shall be _____.

2. Compensation.

(a) Base Salary. Executive shall be paid a base salary ("Base Salary") at the annual rate of $_____ , payable in bi-weekly installments consistent with Company's payroll practices. The annual Base Salary shall be reviewed on or before [January 1] of each year, unless Executive's employment hereunder shall have been terminated earlier pursuant to this Agreement, starting on _____ by the Board of Directors of the Company to determine if such Base Salary should be increased for the following year in recognition of services to the Company.

> This is the base salary

Form 7-8: Employment Agreement for senior-level employee — page 1 of 8.

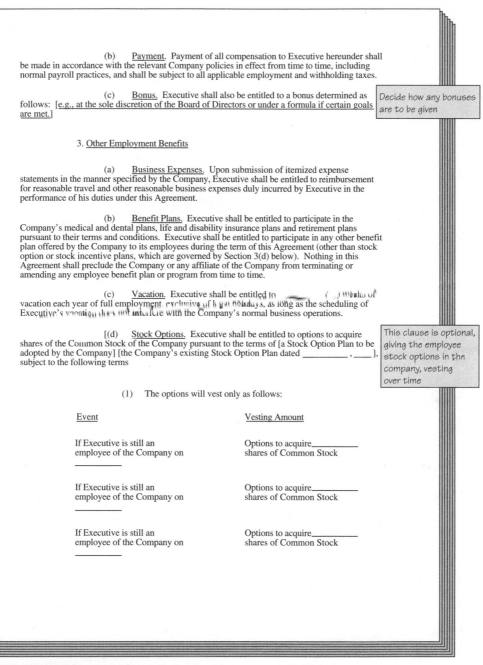

(b)   Payment. Payment of all compensation to Executive hereunder shall be made in accordance with the relevant Company policies in effect from time to time, including normal payroll practices, and shall be subject to all applicable employment and withholding taxes.

(c)   Bonus. Executive shall also be entitled to a bonus determined as follows: [e.g., at the sole discretion of the Board of Directors or under a formula if certain goals are met.]

Decide how any bonuses are to be given

3. Other Employment Benefits

(a)   Business Expenses. Upon submission of itemized expense statements in the manner specified by the Company, Executive shall be entitled to reimbursement for reasonable travel and other reasonable business expenses duly incurred by Executive in the performance of his duties under this Agreement.

(b)   Benefit Plans. Executive shall be entitled to participate in the Company's medical and dental plans, life and disability insurance plans and retirement plans pursuant to their terms and conditions. Executive shall be entitled to participate in any other benefit plan offered by the Company to its employees during the term of this Agreement (other than stock option or stock incentive plans, which are governed by Section 3(d) below). Nothing in this Agreement shall preclude the Company or any affiliate of the Company from terminating or amending any employee benefit plan or program from time to time.

(c)   Vacation. Executive shall be entitled to _____ ( ) weeks of vacation each year of full employment, exclusive of legal holidays, as long as the scheduling of Executive's vacation does not interfere with the Company's normal business operations.

[(d)   Stock Options. Executive shall be entitled to options to acquire shares of the Common Stock of the Company pursuant to the terms of [a Stock Option Plan to be adopted by the Company] [the Company's existing Stock Option Plan dated _____ , ____], subject to the following terms

This clause is optional, giving the employee stock options in the company, vesting over time

(1)   The options will vest only as follows:

Event	Vesting Amount
If Executive is still an employee of the Company on _____	Options to acquire_____ shares of Common Stock
If Executive is still an employee of the Company on _____	Options to acquire_____ shares of Common Stock
If Executive is still an employee of the Company on _____	Options to acquire_____ shares of Common Stock

Form 7-8: Employment Agreement for senior-level employee — page 2 of 8.

| If Executive is still an employee of the Company on _____ | Options to acquire_____ shares of Common Stock |
| If Executive is still an employee of the Company on _____ | Options to acquire_____ shares of Common Stock |

(2)   The exercise price for the options shall be at_____ dollar ($__) per share, as appropriately adjusted for stock splits, stock dividends, and the like.

(3)   The vested options shall be exercisable until the earlier of five (5) years after vesting or 90 days after termination of Executive's employment with the Company. No additional vesting of options shall occur after Executive's death, disability, or cessation of employment with the Company for any reason or no reason.

(4)   Issuance of the options shall be in accordance with all applicable securities laws and the other terms and conditions of the Company's Stock Option Plan and form of the Stock Option Agreement [to be adopted by the Company]].

(e)   No Other Benefits. Executive understands and acknowledges that the compensation specified in Sections 2 and 3 of this Agreement shall be in lieu of any and all other compensation, benefits and plans.

4.   Executive's Business Activities. Executive shall devote the substantial portion of his entire business time, attention and energy exclusively to the business and affairs of the Company and its affiliates, as its business and affairs now exist and as they hereafter may be changed. [Executive may serve as a member of the Board of Directors of other organizations that do not compete with the Company, and may participate in other professional, civic, governmental organizations and activities that do not materially affect his ability to carry out his duties hereunder.]

5.   Termination of Employment.

(a)   For Cause. Notwithstanding anything herein to the contrary, the Company may terminate Executive's employment hereunder for cause for any one of the following reasons: (1) conviction of a felony, any act involving moral turpitude, or a misdemeanor where imprisonment is imposed, (2) commission of any act of theft, fraud, dishonesty, or falsification of any employment or Company records, (3) improper disclosure of the Company's confidential or proprietary information, (4) any action by the Executive which has a detrimental effect on the Company's reputation or business, (5) Executive's failure or inability to perform any reasonable assigned duties after written notice from the Company of, and a reasonable opportunity to cure, such failure or inability, (6) any breach of this Agreement, which breach is not cured within ten (10) days following written notice of such breach, (7) a course of conduct amounting to gross incompetence, (8) chronic and unexcused absenteeism, (9) unlawful appropriation of a corporate opportunity, or (10) misconduct in connection with the performance of any of Executive's duties, including, without

> Allows for termination of employee for "cause" and defines "cause" broadly

Form 7-8: Employment Agreement for senior-level employee — page 3 of 8.

limitation, misappropriation of funds or property of the Company, securing or attempting to secure personally any profit in connection with any transaction entered into on behalf of the Company, misrepresentation to the Company, or any violation of law or regulations on Company premises or to which the Company is subject. Upon termination of Executive's employment with the Company for cause, the Company shall be under no further obligation to Executive, except to pay all accrued but unpaid base salary and accrued vacation to the date of termination thereof.

        (b)   <u>Without Cause.</u> The Company may terminate Executive's employment hereunder at any time without cause, provided, however, that Executive shall be entitled to severance pay in the amount of _____ (__) weeks of Base Salary in addition to accrued but unpaid Base Salary and accrued vacation, less deductions required by law, but if, and only if, Executive executes a valid and comprehensive release of any and all claims that the Executive may have against the Company in a form provided by the Company and Executive executes such form within seven (7) days of tender.

> Allows the company to fire the employee upon payment of a severance benefit

        (c)   <u>Resignation.</u> Upon termination of employment, Executive shall be deemed to have resigned from the Board of Directors of the Company if [he][she] is a director.

        (d)   <u>Cooperation.</u> After notice of termination, Executive shall cooperate with the Company, as reasonably requested by the Company, to effect a transition of Executive's responsibilities and to ensure that the Company is aware of all matters being handled by Executive.

        6.   <u>Disability of Executive.</u> The Company may terminate this Agreement without liability if Executive shall be permanently prevented from properly performing his essential duties hereunder with reasonable accommodation by reason of illness or other physical or mental incapacity for a period of more than [120] consecutive days. Upon such termination, Executive shall be entitled to all accrued but unpaid Base Salary and vacation.

        7.   <u>Death of Executive.</u> In the event of the death of Executive during the Employment Period, the Company's obligations hereunder shall automatically cease and terminate; provided, however, that within 15 days the Company shall pay to Executive's heirs or personal representatives Executive's Base Salary and accrued vacation accrued to the date of death.

        8.   <u>Confidential Information and Invention Assignments.</u> Executive [is simultaneously executing] [has executed] a Confidential Information and Invention Assignment Agreement (the "Confidential Information and Invention Assignment Agreement"). The obligations under the Confidential Information and Invention Assignment Agreement shall survive termination of this Agreement for any reason.

> Requires the employee to sign a standard Confidential Information and Invention Assignment Agreement

        9.   <u>Exclusive Employment.</u> During employment with the Company, Executive will not do anything to compete with the Company's present or contemplated business, nor will he or she plan or organize any competitive business activity. Executive will not enter into any agreement which conflicts with his duties or obligations to the Company. Executive will not during his employment or within one (1) year after it ends, without the Company's express written consent, directly or indirectly, solicit or encourage any employee, agent, independent contractor, supplier, customer, consultant or any other person or company to terminate or alter a relationship with the Company.

> Puts various limitations on the employee

Form 7-8: Employment Agreement for senior-level employee — page 4 of 8.

10.   Assignment and Transfer. Executive's rights and obligations under this Agreement shall not be transferable by assignment or otherwise, and any purported assignment, transfer or delegation thereof shall be void. This Agreement shall inure to the benefit of, and be binding upon and enforceable by, any purchaser of substantially all of Company's assets, any corporate successor to Company or any assignee thereof.

11.   No Inconsistent Obligations. Executive is aware of no obligations, legal or otherwise, inconsistent with the terms of this Agreement or with his undertaking employment with the Company. Executive will not disclose to the Company, or use, or induce the Company to use, any proprietary information or trade secrets of others. Executive represents and warrants that he or she has returned all property and confidential information belonging to all prior employers.

12.   Miscellaneous.

(a)   Attorneys' Fees. Should either party hereto, or any heir, personal representative, successor or assign of either party hereto, resort to legal proceedings in connection with this Agreement or Executive's employment with the Company, the party or parties prevailing in such legal proceedings shall be entitled, in addition to such other relief as may be granted, to recover its or their reasonable attorneys' fees and costs in such legal proceedings from the non-prevailing party or parties; provided, however, that nothing herein is intended to affect the provisions of Section 12(l).

(b)   Governing Law. This Agreement shall be governed by and construed in accordance with the laws of the State of_____without regard to conflict of law principles.

(c)   Entire Agreement. [Except with respect to the Stock Option Plan and Stock Option Agreement referenced in Section 3(d),] this Agreement, [together with the attached exhibits and the Confidential Information and Invention Assignment Agreement,] contains the entire agreement and understanding between the parties hereto and supersedes any prior or contemporaneous written or oral agreements, representations and warranties between them respecting the subject matter hereof.

(d)   Amendment. This Agreement may be amended only by a writing signed by Executive and by a duly authorized representative of the Company.

(e)   Severability. If any term, provision, covenant or condition of this Agreement, or the application thereof to any person, place or circumstance, shall be held to be invalid, unenforceable or void, the remainder of this Agreement and such term, provision, covenant or condition as applied to other persons, places and circumstances shall remain in full force and effect.

(f)   Construction. The headings and captions of this Agreement are provided for convenience only and are intended to have no effect in construing or interpreting this Agreement. The language in all parts of this Agreement shall be in all cases construed according to its fair meaning and not strictly for or against the Company or Executive.

(g)   Rights Cumulative. The rights and remedies provided by this Agreement are cumulative, and the exercise of any right or remedy by either party hereto (or by its

Form 7-8: Employment Agreement for senior-level employee — page 5 of 8.

successor), whether pursuant to this Agreement, to any other agreement, or to law, shall not preclude or waive its right to exercise any or all other rights and remedies.

(h)   Nonwaiver. No failure or neglect of either party hereto in any instance to exercise any right, power or privilege hereunder or under law shall constitute a waiver of any other right, power or privilege or of the same right, power or privilege in any other instance. All waivers by either party hereto must be contained in a written instrument signed by the party to be charged and, in the case of the Company, by an officer of the Company (other than Executive) or other person duly authorized by the Company.

(i)   Remedy for Breach; Attorneys' Fees. The parties hereto agree that, in the event of breach or threatened breach of any covenants of Executive, the damage or imminent damage to the value and the goodwill of the Company's business shall be inestimable, and that therefore any remedy at law or in damages shall be inadequate. Accordingly, the parties hereto agree that the Company shall be entitled to injunctive relief against Executive in the event of any breach or threatened breach of any of such provisions by Executive, in addition to any other relief (including damages) available to the Company under this Agreement or under law. The prevailing party in any action instituted pursuant to this Agreement shall be entitled to recover from the other party its reasonable attorneys' fees and other expenses incurred in such action.

(j)   Notices. Any notice, request, consent or approval required or permitted to be given under this Agreement or pursuant to law shall be sufficient if in writing, and if and when sent by certified or registered mail, with postage prepaid, to Executive's residence (as noted in the Company's records), or to the Company's principal office, as the case may be.

(k)   Assistance in Litigation. Executive shall, during and after termination of employment, upon reasonable notice, furnish such information and proper assistance to the Company as may reasonably be required by the Company in connection with any litigation in which it or any of its subsidiaries or affiliates is, or may become a party; provided, however, that such assistance following termination shall be furnished at mutually agreeable times and for mutually agreeable compensation.

[(l)   Arbitration. Any controversy, claim or dispute arising out of or relating to this Agreement or the employment relationship, either during the existence of the employment relationship or afterwards, between the parties hereto, their assignees, their affiliates, their attorneys, or agents, shall be settled by arbitration in [City], [State]. Such arbitration shall be conducted in accordance with the then prevailing commercial arbitration rules of the American Arbitration Association (but the arbitration shall be in front of an arbitrator appointed by JAMS/Endispute ("JAMS")), with the following exceptions if in conflict: (a) one arbitrator shall be chosen by JAMS; (b) each party to the arbitration will pay its pro rata share of the expenses and fees of the arbitrator(s), together with other expenses of the arbitration incurred or approved by the arbitrator(s); and (c) arbitration may proceed in the absence of any party if written notice (pursuant to the JAMS' rules and regulations) of the proceedings has been given to such party. The parties agree to abide by all decisions and awards rendered in such proceedings. Such decisions and awards rendered by the arbitrator shall be final and conclusive and may be entered in any court having jurisdiction thereof as a basis of judgment and of the issuance of execution for its collection. All such controversies, claims or disputes shall be settled in this manner in lieu of any action at law or equity; provided however, that nothing in this subsection shall be construed as precluding the

> This optional clause provides that disputes are to be handled by binding arbitration

Form 7-8: Employment Agreement for senior-level employee — page 6 of 8.

Company from bringing an action for injunctive relief or other equitable relief or relief under the Confidential Information and Invention Assignment Agreement. The arbitrator shall not have the right to award punitive damages, consequential damages, lost profits or speculative damages to either party. The parties shall keep confidential the existence of the claim, controversy or disputes from third parties (other than the arbitrator), and the determination thereof, unless otherwise required by law or necessary for the business of the Company. The arbitrator(s) shall be required to follow applicable law. IF FOR ANY REASON THIS ARBITRATION CLAUSE BECOMES NOT APPLICABLE, THEN EACH PARTY, TO THE FULLEST EXTENT PERMITTED BY APPLICABLE LAW, HEREBY IRREVOCABLY WAIVES ALL RIGHT TO TRIAL BY JURY AS TO ANY ISSUE RELATING HERETO IN ANY ACTION, PROCEEDING, OR COUNTERCLAIM ARISING OUT OF OR RELATING TO THIS AGREEMENT OR ANY OTHER MATTER INVOLVING THE PARTIES HERETO.]

Alternate (l):

[(l) <u>Disputes.</u> Any controversy, claim or dispute arising out of or relating to this Agreement or the employment relationship, either during the existence of the employment relationship or afterwards, between the parties hereto, their assignees, their affiliates, their attorneys, or agents, shall be litigated solely in state or federal court in [City], [State]. Each party (1) submits to the jurisdiction of such court, (2) waives the defense of an inconvenient forum, (3) agrees that valid consent to service may be made by mailing or delivery of such service to the California Secretary of State (the "Agent") or to the party at the party's last known address, if personal service delivery can not be easily effected, and (4) authorizes and directs the Agent to accept such service in the event that personal service delivery can not easily be effected. EACH PARTY, TO THE FULLEST EXTENT PERMITTED BY APPLICABLE LAW, HEREBY IRREVOCABLY WAIVES ALL RIGHT TO TRIAL BY JURY AS TO ANY ISSUE RELATING HERETO IN ANY ACTION, PROCEEDING, OR COUNTERCLAIM ARISING OUT OF OR RELATING TO THIS AGREEMENT OR ANY OTHER MATTER INVOLVING THE PARTIES HERETO.]

Page 8 contains an area to sign

Form 7-8: Employment Agreement for senior-level employee — page 7 of 8.

A good Confidentiality and Invention Assignment Agreement covers the following key points:

- The employee can't use any of the company's confidential information for her own benefit or use.

- The employee will promptly disclose to the company any inventions, ideas, discoveries, and work product related to the company's business that she makes during the period of employment.

- The company is the owner of such inventions, ideas, discoveries, and work product.

- The employee's employment with the company doesn't and can't breach any agreement or duty that the employee has with anyone else, nor can the employee disclose to the company or use on its behalf any confidential information belonging to others.

- The employee's confidentiality obligations under the agreement will continue after termination of employment.

- The agreement doesn't, by itself, represent any guarantee of continued employment.

Form 7-9 on the CD-ROM shows a sample form Employee Confidentiality and Invention Assignment Agreement.

New employee paperwork

When the new employee shows up for the first day of work, make sure that you have all of the appropriate paperwork for him to sign.

The CD-ROM includes the following paperwork for the employee to sign on the first day:

- **Employee handbook:** If you have an employee handbook, get a receipt that the employee has received and reviewed it (Form 7-10).

- **IRS Form W-4:** Each employee must complete this form for the company to determine the appropriate level of tax withholding (Form 7-11).

- **Employee benefit elections:** If your business provides employee benefit programs, such as medical insurance or pension plans, the employee should sign up and provide relevant information (identifying dependents, making required elections, and so on).

- **Confidentiality and Invention Assignment Agreement:** This agreement requires the employee to keep company information confidential (see the earlier section of the same name).

✔ **Form I-9:** The United States Customs & Immigration Service requires this form (Form 7-12). It is intended to prevent aliens from working in a place of business if they're not properly documented.

✔ **Emergency Notification:** This form advises the company of whom to contact in the event of an emergency (Form 7-13).

Forms on the CD-ROM

Check out these forms on the CD-ROM included with this book:

Form 7-1	**Questions to Consider Asking Prospective Employees**	A list of questions to consider asking prospective employees
Form 7-2	**Background Check Permission (Comprehensive)**	A form that the prospective employee signs, which gives the employer permission to check references
Form 7-3	**Background Check Permission (Simple)**	A simpler consent form from a prospective employee for the employer to perform a back-ground check
Form 7-4	**Reference Check Letter**	Letter to prior employer of pro-spective employee, requesting reference information
Form 7-5	**Employment Application for Prospective Employees**	Form for prospective employees to fill out
Form 7-6	**Rejection Letter to Applicant**	A form letter for rejecting an employee applicant
Form 7-7	**Offer Letter to Prospective Employee**	Letter providing terms of employment offer to prospec-tive employee
Form 7-8	**Employment Agreement**	Agreement for executive-level employees
Form 7-9	**Employee Confidentiality and Invention Assignment Agreement**	Agreement in which the employee agrees to keep company informa-tion confidential and to assign to the company business-related inventions developed by the employee

Form 7-10	**Employee Handbook and At Will Employee Status Acknowledgement**	A form in which the employee acknowledges receiving the employee handbook and the "at will" notice of his or her employment
Form 7-11	**IRS Form W-4**	IRS Employee's Withholding Allowance Certificate
Form 7-12	**Form I-9**	Form to be signed by the employee and required by the United States Customs & Immigration Service
Form 7-13	**Employee Emergency Notification Form**	Form that the employee fills out, identifying the person to contact in the event of an emergency
Form 7-14	**Non-Discrimination Policy**	A company policy statement prohibiting discrimination
Form 7-15	**Sexual Harassment Policy**	A company policy statement prohibiting sexual harassment
Form 7-16	**Checklist of Employment Agreement Issues from the Perspective of the Employee**	A checklist of issues for an employee to consider when negotiating an Employment Agreement

Chapter 8

Motivating and Retaining Employees

In This Chapter

▶ Showing your appreciation for your employees

▶ Using surveys to see if your workers are satisfied

▶ Giving out good employee incentives

Motivating and retaining employees is crucial to a small business's success. But the increasingly mobile workforce and the increasing demand for talented people makes retaining valuable employees a real challenge.

This chapter outlines some ideas for keeping your employees motivated and satisfied in both tangible and intangible ways.

I discuss a number of employee benefit arrangements that may make sense for your business. In particular, this chapter focuses on stock option and equity incentive arrangements as a key way to attract, retain, and motivate employees.

Motivating Employees in Good Form

You can motivate your employees in numerous creative ways. And some of these ways don't cost much in the way of money or effort!

Increasing employee job satisfaction

Despite the best intentions, many employers aren't very good at satisfying employees and keeping them from going elsewhere. But the ability to motivate and keep employees satisfied is key to a small business's success. If you find ways to make people enjoy doing their work on a daily basis, then job performance is high. If you treat your employees with respect and show that you value their input, you motivate them to do well for themselves and for the company.

The following checklist includes corporate culture ingredients that promote achievement, loyalty, and respect:

- Give employees motivating and meaningful work.

- Provide opportunities for employees to learn new skills and jobs.

- Empower employees to make the decisions necessary to obtain the results that you seek.

- Let your employees know exactly what you expect from them.

- Provide performance-review feedback to your employees at least every six months. (Check out Chapter 9 for appraisal ideas.)

- Make it clear to employees that they have real opportunities to advance within the company.

- Let valued employees know that (subject to changes in your business and in their performance) you intend for them to have a measure of job security.

- Make a special point of recognizing employees for good work.

- If possible, allow employees flexibility in their schedules with flex time, part time, and telecommuting opportunities.

Formal and informal appreciation devices

Sometimes, the best ways to motivate employees are also the easiest. After all, people usually want to do a good job but, most of all, they want to be recognized for doing a good job. And recognition can come in many forms, some of which cost little. So consider some of the following ways that you can recognize employees as a way to encourage and motivate them:

- Give informal pats on the back when an employee has done a good job.

- Offer an employee who has done an outstanding job on a project a more challenging or higher-profile project.

- Recognize an Employee of the Month and award a certificate like the one in Form 8-1.

- Recognize not only individual accomplishments, but also team accomplishments.

- Award Certificates of Appreciation for particularly outstanding performance.

CERTIFICATE OF EMPLOYEE
OF THE
MONTH
_____

This Certificate is awarded to _____[Name of Employee]_____ for his/her

election as the Employee of the Month for the month _____, 20__ for

_____[Name of Company]_____ .

_____[Name of Company]_____ sincerely appreciates and acknowledges the

efforts of _____[Name of Employee]_____ above and beyond the call of duty.

Date: _____   [Name of Company]

By: _____
                                                  President

Form 8-1: Employee of the month certificate.

Providing a flexible workplace

Increasingly, employees want flexibility in their work life. If you can provide this flexibility, you probably have a happier and more motivated work force. So what kind of flexibility policy should you consider? Here are some options, depending on the precise nature and demands of your business:

✔ **Flex time.** "Flex time" allows employees some flexibility in their work hours. For example, instead of requiring each employee to work from 9 a.m. to 5 p.m., you can grant flexibility to some employees who prefer to work 7 a.m. to 3 p.m. This option may particularly appeal to employees with young children.

✔ **Part time.** You can modify some jobs to part-time status. Indeed, you may need to use a part-time status option to keep some valued workers.

✔ **Job share.** Two people share one job. For example, two people can share one secretarial full-time position and work out between themselves the hours or days in the office. Of course, the two employees have the responsibility for covering the job at all times and for ensuring the continuity of their assignments.

✔ **Telecommuting.** Some jobs allow employees to work from home a few days a week, with computer access to the company's records and files. This option is becoming increasingly popular in technology companies.

Employee Satisfaction Surveys

Many large companies perform *Employee Satisfaction Surveys,* where employees are asked to respond to a series of questions about their employer and work environment. These surveys anticipate potential problem areas. By diligently reviewing the answers to the surveys and implementing needed changes, these companies improve employee morale.

Small businesses can also benefit from Employee Satisfaction Surveys. Here are some keys to such surveys:

✔ The employees must be able to answer anonymously so that they don't fear recriminations.

✔ The survey should ask questions that are meaningful to your particular business.

✔ The survey should ask for specific areas of improvement.

After you've tabulated the survey, you should follow up and take reasonable steps where appropriate. Communicate your desire to improve to employees. You can modify Form 8-2 (later in this chapter) for your particular business.

EMPLOYEE SATISFACTION SURVEY

This is a survey for the employees of [Name of Company]   (the "Company"). This survey is intended to give the management of the Company guidance as to improve the workplace environment. This survey is to be answered anonymously.

1. Ratings

Please give your assessment of the Company on the following matters, by circling one of the numbers from one to ten (one being awful, and ten being great)

(a) Compensation to employees   1 2 3 4 5 6 7 8 9 10

(b) Opportunity for advancement   1 2 3 4 5 6 7 8 9 10

(c) Benefits   1 2 3 4 5 6 7 8 9 10

(d) Friendly work environment   1 2 3 4 5 6 7 8 9 10

(e) Training   1 2 3 4 5 6 7 8 9 10

(f) Performance evaluation   1 2 3 4 5 6 7 8 9 10

(g) Supervision   1 2 3 4 5 6 7 8 9 10

(h) Culture   1 2 3 4 5 6 7 8 9 10

(i) Job security   1 2 3 4 5 6 7 8 9 10

(j) Flexibility in performing job   1 2 3 4 5 6 7 8 9 10

(k) Overall satisfaction with job   1 2 3 4 5 6 7 8 9 10

2. Employee Morale

(a)   How would you describe general employee morale? _____
       _____
       _____
       _____.

(b)   Do you have any specific recommendations to improve employee morale? _____
       _____
       _____
       _____.

3. Guidance

(a)   Are you given enough guidance to perform your job? _____
       _____

Form 8-2: Sample Employee Satisfaction Survey — page 1 of 3.

_____
_____.

(b)   Are you given enough feedback on your work? _____
_____
_____.

(c)   How would you change the procedure for performance appraisals? _____
_____
_____.

4. Training. What additional training of employees, if any, would you believe would be
    beneficial? _____
    _____
    _____.

5. Technology. What additional technology do you believe would be beneficial for the
    Company? _____
    _____
    _____.

6. Benefits.

    (a)   What benefits do you find valuable that the Company offers? _____
    _____
    _____.

    (b)   What additional benefits would you like to see the Company offer? _____
    _____
    _____.

7. Flexibility.

    (a)   Are you given enough flexibility to perform your job? _____
    _____.

    (b)   What additional flexibility do you think would be valuable to help you perform
            your job better? _____
    _____
    _____.

8. Supervisor.

    (a)   Are you adequately supervised? _____
    _____.

Form 8-2: Sample Employee Satisfaction Survey — page 2 of 3.

(b)   Is your supervisor fully aware of your concerns? _____
_____
_____.

(c)   How would you improve any supervisory procedures? _____
_____
_____.

9. Profitability. Do you have any suggestions to improve the profitability of the
    Company? _____
    _____
    _____.

10. Miscellaneous. Is there anything else that you believe needs change or improvement in
    the Company? _____
    _____
    _____
    _____.

Form 8-2: Sample Employee Satisfaction Survey — page 3 of 3.

Digging through the Employee Incentive Tool Kit

You have a good number of employee incentive plans available for your business — including Stock Option Plans, bonus arrangements, 401(k) plans, and profit-sharing plans. You can also think about providing some unusual perks for your employees. The following sections discuss some incentive arrangements.

Form 8-3 on the CD-ROM contains a chart of the key employee benefit plans and programs that many companies choose from.

Stock Option Plans

Stock Option Plans are an extremely popular method of attracting, motivating, and retaining employees — especially when the company can't pay high salaries. A Stock Option Plan gives the company the flexibility to award stock options to employees, officers, and consultants, allowing these people to buy stock in the company when they exercise the option.

Thousands of people have become millionaires through stock options, making these options very appealing to employees. (Microsoft has reportedly made over 1,000 employees into millionaires from stock options.)

Stock Option Plans permit employees to share in the company's success without requiring a start-up business to spend precious cash. In fact, Stock Option Plans can actually contribute capital to a company as employees pay the exercise price for their options.

The primary disadvantage of Stock Option Plans for the company is the possible dilution of other shareholders' equity when employees exercise the stock options. (As more shares are issued, a shareholder's overall percentage of interest in the company goes down.) For employees, the main disadvantage of stock options in a private company — compared to cash bonuses or greater compensation — is the lack of liquidity. Until the company creates a public market for its stock or the company is acquired, the options aren't the equivalent of cash benefits. And, if the company doesn't grow bigger and its stock doesn't become more valuable, the options may ultimately prove to be worthless.

The spectacular successes of Silicon Valley companies and the resulting economic riches of employees who held stock options have made Stock Option Plans a powerful motivational tool for employees to work for the company's long-term success.

A tale of two stock options

You can generally divide stock options under Stock Option Plans into two types: statutory (sometimes referred to as incentive stock options or ISOs) and nonstatutory.

Statutory stock options have the following key features:

- The employee doesn't have to pay tax at the time the company grants the stock option or at the time the employee exercises the option to buy the stock (although the alternative minimum tax may apply in some cases), and if the employee meets the required holding period before selling the stock, the stock sale counts as a capital gain (or loss) for tax purposes rather than as income (which is taxed at a higher rate).

- Only employees (and not independent contractors) can get statutory stock options.

- When an employee exercises his or her stock option rights for the first time in a particular year, that stock's total fair market value can't exceed $100,000. (Total fair market value is determined at the time of grant.)

- To receive the favorable tax treatment, the employee must exercise the options within three months after termination of employment.

- The stock option is not transferable.

- The *exercise price* (the price to purchase the stock underlying the option) must generally be at least 100 percent of the stock's fair market value at the time of grant.

- To be eligible for capital gains treatment on any profit, the employee must hold the stock for more than one year from the date that she exercised the stock option right and more than two years from the date that the option was granted. Otherwise, when the employee sells the stock, the IRS taxes the gain at the ordinary income tax rate, which is less favorable.

Nonstatutory stock options are options that don't qualify for the favorable tax treatment that applies to statutory stock options. Nonstatutory stock options have the following key features:

- Employees, consultants, agents, nonemployee directors, independent contractors, and other persons can receive nonstatutory stock options.

- When the stockholder exercises the option, the IRS generally taxes the option holder at ordinary income rates in an amount equal to the excess, if any, of the stock's fair market value over the option exercise price.

Getting rich on stock options

The following example shows how businesses grant stock options and how employees exercise them:

1. XYZ, Inc. hires employee John Smith.

2. As part of his employment package, XYZ grants John options to acquire 40,000 shares of XYZ's common stock at 25¢ per share (the fair market value at the time of grant).

   The options are subject to a four-year yearly vesting, which means that John has to stay employed with XYZ for one year before he gets the right to exercise 10,000 of the shares, another year for the second 10,000 shares, and so on.

   If John leaves XYZ or is fired before the end of his first year, he doesn't get any of the options.

3. After his shares are *vested* (become exercisable), John has the option to buy the stock at 25¢ per share, even if the share value has gone up dramatically.

4. After four years at XYZ, all 40,000 of his option shares are vested.

5. XYZ becomes successful and goes public. Its stock trades at $20 per share.

6. John exercises his options, and buys 40,000 shares for $10,000 ($40,000 x 25¢).

7. John turns around and sells all 40,000 shares for $800,000 (40,000 times the $20 per share price), making a nice profit of $790,000.

For example: A consultant has options to acquire 10,000 shares of stock at $1 per share. The consultant exercises that option when the stock is worth $3 per share. That tax year, the consultant has to report income of $20,000 on his tax return ($3 − $1 multiplied by 10,000). The consultant must report this income even if he doesn't sell the stock (which isn't necessarily the case with statutory stock options).

Key elements of stock options

A company needs to address a number of key issues before adopting a Stock Option Plan and issuing options. Generally, the company wants to adopt a plan that gives it maximum flexibility. Here are some of the important considerations:

✔ **Total number of shares:** The Stock Option Plan must reserve a maximum number of shares that the business can issue under the plan. You generally base this total number on what the board of directors believes is appropriate, but it typically ranges from 5 percent to 20 percent of the company's outstanding stock. Of course, you don't have to grant all options reserved for issuances.

- ✔ **Plan administration:** Although most plans appoint the board of directors as administrator, the plan should also allow the board to delegate responsibilities to a committee. The board or the committee should have broad discretion as to the optionees, the types of options granted, and other terms.

- ✔ **Vesting:** Most plans allow the company to impose vesting periods for the options — for example, the options don't become exercisable unless the employee continues to be employed with the company. The board or committee typically has a lot of room to determine appropriate vesting schedules and even waive vesting. Typically, companies set the vesting period between three and five years with a *pro rata* percentage vesting either each month or year that the optionee maintains her relationship with the company. For example, a company may have a four-year vesting period, with 25 percent vesting after each year of full employment.

- ✔ **Consideration:** The plan should give the board of directors maximum flexibility in determining how they plan to pay the exercise price, subject to applicable corporate law. So, for example, the consideration can include cash, deferred payment, or stock. A cashless feature can be particularly attractive, where the optionee can use the buildup in the value of his option (the difference between the exercise price and the stock's fair market value) as the currency to exercise the option. Public companies, however, have limitations on what they can do here.

- ✔ **Shareholder approval:** The company should generally have shareholders approve the plan, both for securities law reasons and to cement the ability to offer statutory stock options.

- ✔ **Right to terminate employment:** To prevent giving employees an implied promise of employment, the plan should clearly state that the grant of stock options doesn't guarantee any employee a continued relationship with the company.

- ✔ **Right of first refusal:** The plan (and related Stock Option Agreement) can also provide that in the event that the employee exercises the option, that shareholder grants the company a right of first refusal on transfers of those shares. Doing so allows the company to keep share ownership in the company to a limited group of shareholders.

- ✔ **Financial reports:** For securities law reasons, the plan may require that you deliver periodic financial information and reports to option holders.

- ✔ **Exercise price:** How much does the optionee have to pay for the stock when she exercises her option? Typically, the price is set at the stock's fair market value at the time that the option is granted. If the stock's value goes up, the option becomes valuable because the optionee has the right to buy the stock at the cheaper price.

✔ **Term of option:** How long does the optionee have the right to exercise the option? The Stock Option Agreement typically sets a date when the employee must exercise the option (the date is usually shortened on termination of employment or death).

✔ **Transferability restrictions:** What restrictions apply to the transfer of the option and underlying stock? Most Stock Option Agreements provide that the option is nontransferable. The agreements also state that the stock purchased by exercising the option may be subject to rights of repurchase or rights of first refusal on any potential transfers.

Profit sharing

Profit Sharing Programs are employee incentives in which the company announces that a portion of the business's profits will be set aside at year-end and distributed to the employees. To be effective, these programs need to address the following issues:

✔ **Profit threshold:** Establish a designated profit level as a goal to achieve. For example, the Profit Sharing Program may say that the program kicks in after the company has achieved at least $100,000 in profits for the year.

✔ **Percentage of profits:** Establish the percentage of profits that you plan to share with the employees and let them know in advance. For example, you may say that you will set aside 10 percent of all profits over $100,000 for the Profit Sharing Program.

✔ **Eligible participants:** Determine which employees will be eligible to participate — all employees or only certain staff members (such as the sales employees?). Or, alternatively, you may decide that although the amount of the profit sharing pool is fixed in advance, the company's management picks the recipients individually.

✔ **Continuing employment:** State that to be eligible, the employee needs to have been employed the entire year and also employed at the time that you plan to distribute the profit sharing amounts. You want to avoid giving a profit sharing award to someone whom you no longer employ.

Make sure to integrate your program into your other benefit programs so that your total benefits package is attractive and motivates employees.

Bonuses

Sometimes, the greatest motivational tool is a cash bonus for a job well done when the company has had a good year. Or consider awarding extra vacation time, extra personal leave time, or a gift. Even small, unexpected bonuses or gifts can really boost an employee's morale.

Cafeteria Plans

Cafeteria Plans are employer-sponsored benefit packages that offer employees a choice between taking cash and receiving qualified benefits (such as accident and health coverage, group-term life insurance coverage, or coverage under a dependent care program). The value of the benefits is not included in a participant's income if she chooses among the plan's benefits; however, if a participant chooses cash, you would include it in gross income as compensation. If the employee chooses qualified benefits, they are excludable as taxable income to the extent allowed by law.

Employees tend to like Cafeteria Plans because of the flexibility that they provide. For example, if one spouse is already working at another company that provides health coverage, the employee can choose to instead obtain group-term life insurance, dental, vision, or even cash.

A human resources professional or labor law attorney should design any Cafeteria Plan to make sure that it complies with all the legal requirements.

401 (k) plans

401(k) plans are retirement plans designed to encourage long-term retirement savings by employees. 401(k) plans need to meet a variety of rules contained in Section 401(k) of the Internal Revenue Code. These plans are very popular among companies and employees.

Here are the key features of such plans:

- **Employer contributions:** The employer can contribute to the plan (subject to certain limits) for the employee's benefit, and the employee doesn't have to pay immediate income tax on that contribution.

- **Employee contributions:** The employee can elect to contribute a portion of her salary to the plan, and then the employee doesn't have to pay immediate income tax on that contributed salary.

- **Investment of contributions:** The employee can choose how to invest contributed money (in stocks, bonds, and other qualifying investments, for example).

- **Tax deferral:** The taxes on the contributions and the plan's investment earnings are deferred until the employee withdraws them (generally at retirement).

- **Loan:** In some instances, a participant may be able to take a loan against the 401(k) account, and as long as the employee repays the loan before taking a distribution from the plan, the funds remain tax deferred.

> ✔ **Withdrawals:** Unless the employee is age 59½ or another exception applies (such as total disability), withdrawals by an employee may be subject to both a 10 percent penalty and regular income tax.
>
> ✔ **Rollovers:** Penalties and taxes generally don't apply if the employee changes jobs and "rolls over" his or her sums in the plan to the new employer's qualified plan that accepts rollovers. An employee can also avoid penalties and taxes in certain circumstances for rollovers into an IRA.

You can draft the nature of a 401(k) plan to accommodate certain employer needs, as long as you qualify with the appropriate tax rules.

Unusual perks

You may not want or be able to spend the money for the benefits that I discuss in this chapter. Yet, you're probably still concerned about employee morale. So how about coming up with some unusual perks for your employees, ones that don't cost an arm, a leg, and a bank loan?

Here are some ideas that other companies use:

✔ **Laundry service:** Employees can drop off their laundry at the office and have it returned the next day.

✔ **Massages:** Workers can get neck and back massages at their desks.

✔ **Car washes:** Employees can make appointments to have their cars picked up at work and washed and detailed while they work.

✔ **On-site dental visits:** A dentist can makes on-site visits to the company, and employees can make advance appointments.

✔ **Day care facilities:** Workers in many companies make use of on-site day care facilities.

✔ **Health club memberships:** Employees can get special memberships at nearby health clubs.

✔ **On-site health services:** Workers can get on-site doctor checkups, mammograms, and other health services.

✔ **Beer and pizza parties:** Beer and pizza parties are a fixture at a number of Silicon Valley companies.

✔ **Office meal delivery:** Employees working late into the night can get meal delivery services.

These perks enhance productivity and morale and provide convenience and accessibility to the employees. The cost of such perks may be worth the benefits that you gain from improved work conditions for employees — employees who are less distracted can focus more on the job at hand.

Forms on the CD-ROM

Check out the following forms dealing with motivating and retaining employees:

Form 8-1	**Certificate of Employee of the Month**	A sample certificate that you can give to an employee in appreciation of good work
Form 8-2	**Employee Satisfaction Survey**	A sample form that you can give to employees to gauge employee satisfaction
Form 8-3	**Chart of Key Employee Benefit Plans and Programs**	A chart summarizing different employee benefit plans and programs

Chapter 9

Avoiding Employee Problems

· ·

In This Chapter

▶ Setting up an employee handbook

▶ Giving appraisals before reprisals

▶ Firing employees the proper way

▶ Conducting useful exit interviews

· ·

*D*ealing with employees is a big part of running a small business. Treat employees properly, professionally, and legally, and your business is more likely to be successful.

But you can also run into many problems with respect to employees. Myriad laws are designed to protect employees; if you decide to fire an employee, you may find yourself stuck in a costly lawsuit questioning the legality of the firing.

In this chapter, I suggest ways to help you avoid employee problems — both from an ongoing operational standpoint and in the event that you do have to fire someone.

Going by the Handbook

You need to treat workers fairly and with respect. And they need to understand the rules of the workplace and the policies to which you expect them to adhere.

Maintaining good written policies helps you in the event that an unhappy employee sues you or makes a complaint to a governmental entity (such as the Equal Employment Opportunity Commission).

An employee handbook can be the central place where you lay out company policies and employee benefits and rights. Consider including descriptions of the following company policies in your employee handbook:

- ✓ Normal working hours and overtime pay
- ✓ Vacation time
- ✓ Sick days
- ✓ Use of illegal drugs or alcohol
- ✓ Sexual harassment
- ✓ Disciplinary action
- ✓ *At will employment* (the company reserves its rights to terminate employees for any reason or no reason)
- ✓ Non-discrimination
- ✓ E-mail
- ✓ Employee safety
- ✓ Internet usage

Check out the Checklist for Employee Handbooks shown in Form 9-1 on the CD-ROM.

Have each employee sign an acknowledgment and agreement form on her first day of work. This form states that the employee has read and understands your employee handbook. Make sure to keep a signed copy of this acknowledgement in the employee's personnel file.

Form 9-2 later in this chapter shows a sample Employee Handbook and At Will Employee Status Acknowledgement.

**Employee Handbook and At Will Employee Status
Acknowledgement**

The undersigned employee hereby acknowledges that he has received and read a copy of the [ABC, Inc.] Employee Handbook.

The undersigned further understands and agrees that:

1)   Additional information and policies may be implemented from time to time by [ABC, Inc.]

2)   The Employee Handbook is not an employment agreement or guarantee of employment.

3)   The employee is an "at will" employee, which means either the employee or [ABC, Inc.] may terminate the employment relationship, for any reason or for no reason.

4)   The employee's status as an at will employee can only be changed through a written agreement duly authorized and executed by the President of [ABC, Inc.] and the employee.

5)   There have been no statements, agreements, promises, representations or understandings made by any officer, employee or agent of [ABC, Inc.] inconsistent with this Acknowledgement form.

      Signature of Employee: _____
      Printed Name of Employee: _____
      Date: _____

Form 9-2: Employee Handbook and At Will Employee Status Acknowledgement.

Discrimination policy

A great number of federal and state laws prohibit various forms of discrimination against employees and prospective employees.

Your employee handbook should contain a non-discrimination policy, such as the one shown in Form 9-3 later in this chapter.

Sexual harassment policy

Your company can be held liable for sexual harassment committed by your employees, so consider adopting a sexual harassment policy and placing it in your handbook. Illegal sexual harassment occurs when one employee experiences unwelcome sexual advances, requests for sex, and other acts or statements of a sexual nature from another employee that create a hostile or abusive workplace.

Take steps to notify employees that your company doesn't tolerate sexual harassment. Your company should also do the following:

- ✔ Take reasonable steps to prevent sexual harassment: let every employee know that sexual harassment will not be tolerated and set clear boundaries for appropriate behavior.

- ✔ Investigate every complaint promptly.

- ✔ Consider disciplinary action or termination of employment for an offender.

- ✔ Take all allegations seriously.

- ✔ Establish procedures for how employees can make complaints.

- ✔ Consider an in-house seminar or training program to raise employee awareness of the issues surrounding sexual harassment.

Form 9-4 shows an example of a sexual harassment policy that you can modify to fit the particular circumstances of your business.

By adopting affirmative and reasonable steps designed to show that your business doesn't tolerate sexual harassment, three important things happen:

- ✔ The occurrence of sexual harassment decreases.

- ✔ You can try to deal with sexual harassment before it heads to litigation.

- ✔ The company can argue more effectively that it shouldn't be held liable for sexual harassment.

NON-DISCRIMINATION POLICY STATEMENT

Overall Policy

It is the policy of [ABC Inc.] (the "Company") to maintain a working environment free of all forms of unlawful discrimination. In recognition of the importance of good employee relations, all applicants are extended an equal opportunity to gain employment and all employees are extended an equal opportunity to progress in their field of endeavor.

Equal Opportunity

The Company affords equal opportunity to all employees and prospective employees without regard to race, color, sex, religion, age, marital status, disability, veteran status or national origin in the following employment practices: recruitment, hiring, placement, transfer, promotion, demotion, selection for training, layoff, termination, determination of service, rate of pay, benefit plans, compensation, and other personnel actions.

Disability

The Company will not discriminate against any employee or applicant for employment because of disability in regard to any position for which the employee or applicant for employment is qualified.

Complaint Procedure

Any individual, whether an employee or applicant for employment who believes that he or she has been discriminated against unlawfully should bring any complaint to _____ in the [Human Resources Department]. Complaints may be lodged in writing or in person. Persons who file complaints will be advised, as is appropriate, regarding any investigation, action or resolution of the problem.

Consequences

The Company will not tolerate any form of discrimination and will take appropriate disciplinary action, including possibly termination, of any person determined to have engaged in unlawful conduct under this policy.

No Retaliation

The Company will not retaliate nor discriminate against any employee or applicant because he or she has opposed any unlawful employment practice or filed a charge of employment discrimination, testified, assisted, or participated in any manner in an investigation, proceeding, or hearing related to employment practices.

* * *

Form 9-3: Non-Discrimination Policy Statement.

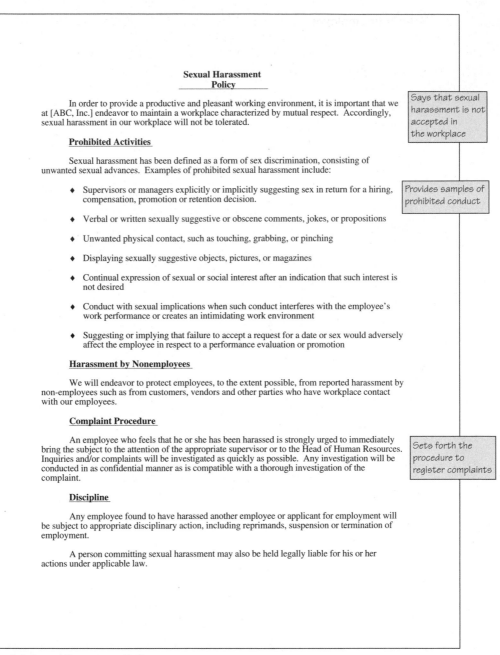

Sexual Harassment
Policy

In order to provide a productive and pleasant working environment, it is important that we at [ABC, Inc.] endeavor to maintain a workplace characterized by mutual respect. Accordingly, sexual harassment in our workplace will not be tolerated.

Says that sexual harassment is not accepted in the workplace

Prohibited Activities

Sexual harassment has been defined as a form of sex discrimination, consisting of unwanted sexual advances. Examples of prohibited sexual harassment include:

Provides samples of prohibited conduct

- ◆ Supervisors or managers explicitly or implicitly suggesting sex in return for a hiring, compensation, promotion or retention decision.

- ◆ Verbal or written sexually suggestive or obscene comments, jokes, or propositions

- ◆ Unwanted physical contact, such as touching, grabbing, or pinching

- ◆ Displaying sexually suggestive objects, pictures, or magazines

- ◆ Continual expression of sexual or social interest after an indication that such interest is not desired

- ◆ Conduct with sexual implications when such conduct interferes with the employee's work performance or creates an intimidating work environment

- ◆ Suggesting or implying that failure to accept a request for a date or sex would adversely affect the employee in respect to a performance evaluation or promotion

Harassment by Nonemployees

We will endeavor to protect employees, to the extent possible, from reported harassment by non-employees such as from customers, vendors and other parties who have workplace contact with our employees.

Complaint Procedure

An employee who feels that he or she has been harassed is strongly urged to immediately bring the subject to the attention of the appropriate supervisor or to the Head of Human Resources. Inquiries and/or complaints will be investigated as quickly as possible. Any investigation will be conducted in as confidential manner as is compatible with a thorough investigation of the complaint.

Sets forth the procedure to register complaints

Discipline

Any employee found to have harassed another employee or applicant for employment will be subject to appropriate disciplinary action, including reprimands, suspension or termination of employment.

A person committing sexual harassment may also be held legally liable for his or her actions under applicable law.

Form 9-4: Sexual Harassment Policy.

Note: Your employees can also be sexually harassed by nonemployees — such as clients, customers, vendors, and so on. Be prepared to take affirmative steps to deal with such acts.

E-Mail policy

If you provide employees with computers, consider adopting an E-Mail Policy. These rules should be clear and comprehensive. You want the employees to know that they should use e-mail only for appropriate business purposes.

Too many times, employees consider e-mail very informal and write things that can later come back to haunt the company (for example, dirty jokes to a coworker, statements of discrimination, and so on).

Here are some guidelines for what your E-Mail Policy should say:

- E-mail should at all times be professional and courteous.
- E-mail is to be used primarily or exclusively for business purposes and not for personal reasons.
- E-mail is not private or personal to the sender or recipient, and management of the company has access to all e-mail sent to or from company computers.
- All e-mail is company property.
- E-mail must not contain any illegal, libelous, or offensive statements.
- All harassing statements (sexual or otherwise) are prohibited — sex jokes are also inappropriate.
- E-mail that is deleted can still be retrieved from the company's system.
- Any violation of the company's E-Mail Policy subjects an employee to disciplinary measures or termination of employment.

Form 9-5 later in this chapter shows a sample E-Mail Policy.

Drug-free work policy

Make sure that employees know about your strong policy regarding illegal drugs. Consider including the policy statement — shown in Form 9-6 — in each new employee's first-day packet of documents to sign.

Sample E-Mail Policy

This document sets forth the policy of _____ (the "Company") with respect to e-mail. All employees who use the Company's e-mail system are required to comply with this policy statement.

> Limits use of e-mail only for company purposes

1. <u>Business Use.</u> The e-mail system is to be used solely for business purposes of the Company and not for personal purposes of the employees.

2. <u>Ownership.</u> All information and messages that are created, sent, received or stored on the Company's e-mail system is the sole property of the Company.

> States that all e-mail is the company's property

> States that the company has the right to read and monitor all e-mail

3. <u>E-mail Review.</u> All e-mail is subject to the right of the Company to monitor, access, read, disclose and use such e-mail without prior notice to the originators and recipients of such e-mail. E-mail may be monitored and read by authorized personnel for the Company for any violations of law, breaches of Company policies, communications harmful to the Company, or for any other reason.

4. <u>Prohibited Content.</u> E-mails may not contain statements or content that are libelous, offensive, harassing, illegal, derogatory, or discriminatory. Foul, inappropriate or offensive messages such as racial, sexual, or religious slurs or jokes are prohibited. Sexually explicit messages or images, cartoons or jokes are prohibited.

> Sets forth limits on what e-mail can contain

> Describes the security procedures

5. <u>Security.</u> The e-mail system is only to be used by authorized persons, and an employee must have been issued and e-mail password in order to use the system. Employees shall not disclose their codes or passwords to others and may not use someone else's code or password without express written authorization from the Company.

6. <u>No Presumption of Privacy.</u> E-mail communications should not be assumed to be private and security cannot be guaranteed. Highly confidential or sensitive information should not be sent through e-mail.

7. <u>Certain Prohibited Activities.</u> Employees may not, without the Company's express written authorization transmit trade secrets or other confidential, private or proprietary information or materials through e-mail.

8. <u>Message Retention and Creation.</u> Employees should be careful in creating e-mail. Even when a message has been deleted, it may still exist in printed version, be recreated from a back-up system, or may have been forwarded to someone else. Please note that appropriate electronic messages may need to be saved. And, the Company may be required to produce e-mail in litigation.

9. <u>Viruses.</u> Any files downloaded from e-mail received from non-Company sources must be scanned with the Company's virus detection software. Any viruses, tampering or system problems should be immediately reported to [computer systems administrator].

10. <u>Consequences of Violations.</u> Violations of this policy or other company policies may result in discipline, suspension and even termination of employment.

* * * *

> Lets the employee know that violating the policy has serious consequences

Form 9-5: A sample E-Mail Policy.

Drug-Free Workplace Policy

The following policy is required by the Drug-Free Workplace Act and complies with applicable law concerning drug use in the workplace.

1. Employees are expected and required to report to work on time and in appropriate mental and physical condition for work. It is our intent and obligation to provide a drug-free, healthful and safe work environment.

2. The unlawful manufacture, distribution, possession or use of a controlled substance on the Company's premises or while conducting the Company's business off its premises is absolutely prohibited. Violations of this policy will result in disciplinary action, up to and including termination, and may have legal consequences.

3. Employees must report any conviction under a criminal drug statute for violations occurring on or off the Company's premises while conducting company business. A report of a conviction must be made within seven (7) days after the conviction.

4. The Company recognizes drug dependency as an illness and a major health problem. The Company also recognizes drug abuse as a potential health, safety and security problem. Employees needing help in dealing with such problems are encouraged to use our employee assistance program and health insurance programs. (Further information about these programs is available from the Personnel Department.) Conscientious efforts to seek such help will not jeopardize any employee's job and will not be noted in any personal record.

I have read, understand and agree to the Company's Drug-Free Workplace Policy.

_____
Print Name

_____
Sign Name

_____
Date

Form 9-6: A sample Drug-Free Workplace Policy.

Sexual harassment 101

In recent years, a lot of employees have sued their employers, claiming sexual harassment. Actions such as the following have spurred sexual harassment suits by employees:

✔ Telling dirty jokes

✔ Making remarks that concern an employee's breasts

✔ Commenting inappropriately on an employee's outfit

✔ Asking an uninterested employee out repeatedly

✔ Suggesting that the way to advance in the company is to sleep with the supervisor

✔ Posting or circulating nude or explicitly sexual pictures

✔ Keeping pornographic Web sites on a computer terminal within view of coworkers

✔ Touching, pinching, or other physical contact that is unwelcome

Appraising Can Be Up-Raising

Employee performance appraisals are important tools for small businesses. The appraisals can be crucial in developing employees, reinforcing good performance, and pointing out areas for improvement. Appraisals provide an opportunity to formally communicate expectations for future performance.

Yet many businesses dread doing appraisals or do an inadequate job of giving them. Here are some tips for doing good performance appraisals:

✔ Convey the good and the bad concerning past performance.

✔ Set clear goals.

✔ Outline areas for improvement.

✔ Give detailed feedback — vague generalities don't help the employee.

✔ Set new goals.

✔ Establish procedures for ongoing feedback — not just once or twice a year through a formal performance appraisal process.

Good documentation — such as performance appraisals showing poor performance — is useful evidence should you get involved in a lawsuit with the employee over what you felt was a justified firing.

Form 9-7 on the CD-ROM is a sample Employee Appraisal Form.

Firing Employees

The last link in a chain of employee problems is termination. Sometimes, both the company and the employee are better off to sever the relationship. However, you need to have your ducks in a row when firing an employee, and you should also know when you run the greatest risk of being subject to a wrongful termination lawsuit. In certain cases, settling with an employee makes more sense than suffering a long, costly court battle. This section helps you find your way through these difficult issues.

Take aim . . . fire!

When can you legally fire employees? Laws and cases have become increasingly protective of employees, making this question difficult to answer. Although the *employment at will doctrine* still exists in many states (meaning that you can freely fire the employee at any time), the doctrine has many exceptions. And employees are increasingly suing managers and companies for "wrongful termination," harassment, discrimination, and other reasons.

These lawsuits can be nasty and expensive. And they can result in awful publicity for the company. Also, juries tend to sympathetic to a terminated employee.

So when can you legally fire an employee? Well, the following list gives you some reasons that generally stand up (no guarantees, though):

- ✓ **Consistent incompetence:** If the employee can't do a competent job, and if you have given the employee a reasonable opportunity to succeed, then termination is often appropriate.

- ✓ **Violation of company policy:** If you establish clear, legal, and consistent policies and if the employee clearly violates them in a meaningful way, then termination may be appropriate. Violations of anti-harassment, discrimination, or confidentiality policies are particularly actionable.

- ✓ **Repeated unexcused absenteeism or tardiness:** A company depends on its employees to show up for work and perform their jobs. Continual absences or tardiness jeopardizes the ability to complete important tasks in a timely manner. If the absenteeism or tardiness is continual and unexcused, then termination may be justified.

- ✔ **Physical violence:** If an employee commits or threatens physical violence, consider firing that person immediately. Employees are entitled to a safe work environment, and employers have a duty to take reasonable steps to provide a safe work place.

- ✔ **Drugs and alcohol:** Depending on the circumstances, being drunk or under the influence of a drug at the office may be grounds for immediate suspension or termination. Some companies now offer treatment and rehabilitation counseling as an alternative to immediate firing.

- ✔ **Illegal acts:** If you find the employee committing illegal acts, such as theft or embezzlement, immediate termination is warranted. But make sure that you know all of the facts and have heard the employee's side of the story.

- ✔ **Falsified information:** Sometimes, employees lie on their employment applications or résumés (such as claiming fake degrees or previous employment). If the falsification appears deliberate and material, termination of the employee is usually justified.

You can legally fire an employee in other instances, too. For example, if problems persist after you give an employee fair warning about job shortcomings and provide reasonable opportunity for the employee to respond, then you can usually defend firing that employee in court.

Continuing employee appraisals that show poor performance can be part of the documentation you need to prove the reasonableness of firing an employee. Check out the Employee Appraisal Form contained as Form 9-7 on the CD-ROM accompanying this book.

Ultimately, the safest approach to firing an employee is to make sure that you have a reasonable and legitimate business reason — one that you have thought out and adequately documented.

Cease fire

In a number of situations, you face greater risk of ending up in court if you fire someone. Be especially careful about these situations:

- ✔ **Prior complaints:** The employee has made prior complaints about harassment or the company doing something illegal or wrong. Or the employee has complained about safety or health conditions in the workplace. Some may see termination in these instances as wrongful retaliation. Certain laws include "whistle-blowing" protections.

- ✔ **The employee is 40 or over:** The Age Discrimination in Employment Act protects many workers who are age 40 or over from discrimination. You can't just fire someone because you think that you can replace him with a younger, cheaper employee.

✔ **The employee is a member of a protected group:** Various laws prohibit discrimination because of race, color, sex, disability, religion, or national origin. Make sure that the termination isn't a willful or deliberate attempt to discriminate against a protected person.

✔ **Employment contract:** Review any existing employment contract that you may have with the employee. And review any written policies or handbooks about how terminations can occur. This review may lead you to modify your plans or provide extra severance pay.

✔ **Inconsistent promises or statements made to the employee:** Make sure to review whether you gave the employee any promises about term of employment or how you would handle any termination. Did you make any commitments about "job security?" Employees often claim that they were promised job security or a long tenure in wrongful termination lawsuits.

✔ **Multiple layoffs:** If you find that you need to fire a number of employees at once, you have to carefully avoid any discriminatory pattern in the layoffs.

In all of these situations, you need to consult with an experienced employment attorney to help you through the potential pitfalls.

Settling up at the end

If you have a dispute with a fired employee, or if you want to avoid litigation, you may want to enter into a Settlement Agreement with the employee. Settlements can often be cheaper than protracted litigation. And a settlement can help you avoid the distractions of the potentially disruptive effect on management time and attention to litigation.

Of course, the scope of any settlement depends on an analysis of the strength of the employee's case. Your attorney can advise you of the hazards and risks that you may face if the case actually goes to trial.

What kind of payments or benefits should you consider giving the employee? Well, here are some of the more frequently requested items:

✔ Severance payment

✔ Continuation of benefits for some amount of time (if allowed under your employee benefit plans)

✔ Vesting of any unvested stock options

✔ Allowing the employee to keep her company computer, cellular phone, or other tools

✔ Payment for outplacement services

✔ A favorable reference letter for future employers (but watch out — this can come back as a problem if a future employer has problems with the employee)

✔ Reimbursement of moving or relocation expenses

Of course, if you're going to give the ex-employee some of these benefits, you should expect to get back some or all of the following in a Settlement Agreement:

✔ A release by the employee of all claims, known or unknown, that the employee may have against the company, its officers, or other employees related to the employee's employment and termination of employment

✔ An agreement that the employee will not make disparaging remarks about the company, its officers, and other employees

✔ A commitment to keep all company proprietary information confidential

✔ An agreement not to solicit any of the company's employees or customers for at least one or two years

Form 9-8, which you can find later in this chapter, shows excerpts from a sample Settlement Agreement with a terminated employee. The terminated employee agrees to release any claims against the company in exchange for a lump sum payment.

Conducting Exit Interviews

Some companies make a practice of having a formal interview with all employees who decide to leave the company (or are fired). Such an interview can serve several purposes, including the following:

✔ Finding out why the person is leaving, if voluntary

✔ Reminding the employee of his confidentiality obligations

✔ Getting feedback on company operations and policies to spot any needed areas of improvement

Form 9-9, found later in this chapter, shows a sample form that you can use to conduct an employee exit interview.

EMPLOYEE SETTLEMENT AND RELEASE AGREEMENT

This Employee Settlement and Release Agreement (the "AGREEMENT") is entered into by and between _____ ("EMPLOYEE") on the one hand and _____ ("COMPANY") on the other.

Recitals

A.   EMPLOYEE is a former employee of the COMPANY.

B.   The parties wish to resolve any claim by EMPLOYEE against the COMPANY and all other existing differences completely and amicably, without litigation. EMPLOYEE acknowledges that the payment to him under this AGREEMENT is being made for the sole purpose of avoiding the uncertainties, vexations and expense of litigation.

C.   The parties represent that they have been advised about the AGREEMENT by their respective counsel, are competent to enter into it, fully understand its terms and consequences, and enter into it knowingly and voluntarily.

Based on these recitals, the parties agree as follows:

Terms

1.   <u>No Admission.</u> This AGREEMENT is entered in connection with the compromise of disputed claims. Neither this AGREEMENT nor any action or acts taken in connection with this AGREEMENT or pursuant to it will constitute an admission by COMPANY or any other person or entity of any violation of law, nor will it constitute or be construed as an admission of any wrongdoing whatsoever. In fact, COMPANY, its officers, employees, agents and representatives specifically deny committing any unlawful act against EMPLOYEE at any time.

2.   <u>Payment.</u> Within three (3) days after execution of this AGREEMENT, and in consideration for the promises and covenants contained herein, COMPANY will cause to be delivered to counsel for EMPLOYEE a check in the amount of $_____. Except for this payment, EMPLOYEE acknowledges and agrees that he is entitled to receive no other payments, benefits, or compensation from COMPANY. EMPLOYEE represents that there are no outstanding advances or other sums due COMPANY from EMPLOYEE.

3.   <u>Tax.</u> Appropriate tax deductions shall be made by the COMPANY from the payment made under Section 2.

4.   <u>Release.</u> EMPLOYEE, on behalf of himself and his representatives, spouse, agents, heirs and assigns, releases and discharges COMPANY and COMPANY's former, current or future officers, employees, representatives, agents, fiduciaries, attorneys, directors, shareholders, insurers, predecessors, parents, affiliates, benefit plans, successors, heirs, and assigns from any and all claims, liabilities, causes of action, damages, losses, demands or obligations of every kind and nature, whether now known or unknown, suspected or unsuspected, which EMPLOYEE ever had, now has, or hereafter can, shall or may have for, upon or by reason of any act, transaction, practice, conduct, matter, cause or thing of any

> This statement says that the employee and the company want to resolve disputes between them

> States that the company is not admitting that it was at fault

> Provides for a payment to the employee

> Releases the company from liability to the employee

Form 9-8: Employee Settlement and Release Agreement — page 1 of 6.

kind whatsoever, relating to or based upon, in whole or in part, any act, transaction, practice or conduct prior to the date hereof, including but not limited to matters dealing with EMPLOYEE'S employment or termination of employment with the COMPANY, or which relate in any way to injuries or damages suffered by EMPLOYEE (knowingly or unknowingly). This release and discharge includes, but is not limited to, claims arising under federal, state and local statutory or common law, including, but not limited to, the Age Discrimination in Employment Act ("ADEA"), Title VII of the Civil Rights Act of 1964, the California Fair Employment and Housing Act, claims for wrongful discharge under any public policy or any policy of the COMPANY, claims for breach of fiduciary duty, and the laws of contract and tort; and any claim for attorney's fees. EMPLOYEE promises never to file a lawsuit or assist in or commence any action asserting any claims, losses, liabilities, demands, or obligations released hereunder.

5.   Known or Unknown Claims. The parties understand and expressly agree that this AGREEMENT extends to all claims of every nature and kind, known or unknown, suspected or unsuspected, past, present, or future, arising from or attributable to any conduct of the COMPANY and its successors, subsidiaries, and affiliates, and all their employees, owners, shareholders, agents, officers, directors, predecessors, assigns, agents, representatives, and attorneys, whether known by EMPLOYEE or whether or not EMPLOYEE believes he may have any claims, and that any and all rights granted to EMPLOYEE under Section 1542 of the California Civil Code or any analogous state law or federal law or regulations, are hereby expressly WAIVED, if applicable. Said Section 1542 of the California Civil Code reads as follows:

> A GENERAL RELEASE DOES NOT EXTEND TO CLAIMS WHICH THE CREDITOR DOES NOT KNOW OR SUSPECT TO EXIST IN HIS FAVOR AT THE TIME OF EXECUTING THE RELEASE, WHICH IF KNOWN BY HIM MUST HAVE MATERIALLY AFFECTED HIS SETTLEMENT WITH THE DEBTOR.

Releases all claims (known or unknown)

6.   Non-Disclosure. EMPLOYEE and his counsel represent that they have not disclosed the terms of this AGREEMENT to anyone other than EMPLOYEE's spouse. EMPLOYEE, his counsel and EMPLOYEE's spouse agree to keep the terms of the AGREEMENT, including the fact that a payment was made to EMPLOYEE and the amount of such payment, strictly confidential and, unless required by court order or other law, will not disclose such information without the prior written permission of the COMPANY to anyone except EMPLOYEE's attorneys or tax advisors, if any, but only after informing those persons that they too must keep the information confidential. If asked about the status of the dispute between the parties, EMPLOYEE, his counsel and EMPLOYEE's spouse may state only that "the matter has been resolved" or words to that effect, but will not otherwise disclose any information about this AGREEMENT or its terms. Because a breach of this confidentiality paragraph would cause COMPANY damages that are impracticable or too difficult to fix, in the event of such a breach, EMPLOYEE shall be liable to COMPANY for liquidated damages in the amount of $_____ for each breach, plus any attorneys' fees and costs owed pursuant to Section 13 herein and any equitable relief.

States that the employee will not disclose the terms of this agreement

7.   No Future Employment. EMPLOYEE promises not to seek employment or any other business relationship at any time in the future with COMPANY or any of its parents or affiliates and he forsakes any right to be employed or to have any other business relationship in the future with COMPANY or any of its parents or affiliates.

Form 9-8: Employee Settlement and Release Agreement — page 2 of 6.

8.   <u>No Disparagement.</u> EMPLOYEE agrees not to disparage COMPANY or any of its officers, employees, agents or representatives and will not knowingly say or do anything that would have an adverse impact on COMPANY.

> States that the employee can't disparage the company

9.   <u>References.</u> In response to any request to COMPANY from any prospective employer for an employment reference regarding EMPLOYEE, the COMPANY shall provide only EMPLOYEE's dates of employment and final job title.

> Sets forth what information is to be given to future employees

10.   <u>Further Documents.</u> Each party agrees to execute or cause their counsel to execute any additional documents and take any further action which may reasonably be required in order to consummate this Agreement or otherwise fulfill the obligations of the parties thereunder.

11.   <u>Dispute.</u> Should a dispute arise concerning this AGREEMENT or its performance, such dispute shall be resolved, at the election of the party seeking to enforce the AGREEMENT, either by court action, or by binding arbitration administered by the American Arbitration Association under its commercial dispute resolution rules. If arbitration is initiated, the arbitration shall be held in [_____City_____], [_____State_____].

12.   <u>Construction.</u> This AGREEMENT shall be construed and enforced in accordance with the laws of the State of [<u>California</u>].

> States which state law will govern

13.   <u>Attorneys' Fees.</u> Should any action be brought by any party to this AGREEMENT to enforce any provision thereof, the prevailing party shall be entitled to recover, in addition to any other relief reasonable attorneys' fees and costs and expenses of litigation or arbitration.

14.   <u>Integration.</u> This AGREEMENT constitutes an integration of the entire understanding and agreement of the parties with respect to the matters referred to in this AGREEMENT. Any representation, warranty, promise or condition, whether written or oral, between the parties with respect to the matters referred to in this AGREEMENT which is not specifically incorporated in this AGREEMENT shall not be binding upon any of the parties hereto and the parties acknowledge that they have not relied, in entering into this AGREEMENT, upon any representations, warranties, promises or conditions not specifically set forth in this AGREEMENT. No prior or contemporaneous oral or written understanding, covenant, or agreement between the parties, with respect to the matters referred to in this AGREEMENT, shall survive the execution of this AGREEMENT. Each party hereto assumes the risk of misrepresentation, concealment or mistake, and if any party should subsequently discover that any fact relied upon in entering into this AGREEMENT was untrue, or that any fact was concealed from it, or that its understanding of the facts or law was incorrect, it shall not be entitled to set aside this AGREEMENT by reason thereof. This AGREEMENT may be modified only by a written agreement executed by both parties hereto.

15.   <u>Binding Agreement.</u> The parties understand and expressly agree that this AGREEMENT shall bind and benefit (as applicable) the heirs, employees, owners, officers, shareholders, directors, subsidiaries, spouses, affiliates, successors, predecessors, agents, witnesses, attorneys, representatives, and assigns of the COMPANY and EMPLOYEE.

16.   <u>Construction.</u> The language of this AGREEMENT shall be construed as to its fair meaning and not strictly for or against either party.

Form 9-8: Employee Settlement and Release Agreement — page 3 of 6.

17.   Counterparts. This AGREEMENT may be executed in counterparts and when each party has signed and delivered at least one such counterpart, each counterpart shall be deemed an original and all counterparts taken together shall constitute one and the same AGREEMENT, which shall be binding and effective as to all parties.

18.   Headings. Headings in this AGREEMENT are for convenience of reference only and are not a part of the substance hereof.

19.   Time for Acceptance and Revocation. If required by applicable law, EMPLOYEE shall have up to 21 days from the date this Agreement is presented to EMPLOYEE to accept the terms of this AGREEMENT, although EMPLOYEE may accept it at any time within those 21 days. If required by applicable law, after acceptance, EMPLOYEE will still have an additional seven (7) days in which to revoke his acceptance. To so revoke, EMPLOYEE must send the COMPANY a written statement or revocation to be received by the COMPANY by the end of the seventh day.

> States when this agreement has to be accepted

20.   Severability. If any provision of this AGREEMENT is held to be invalid, void or unenforceable, the remaining provisions shall remain in full force and effect, except that, should paragraphs 4, 5 or 6 be held invalid, void or unenforceable, either jointly or separately, as a result of any action by EMPLOYEE, COMPANY shall be entitled to rescind the AGREEMENT and/or recover from EMPLOYEE any benefits provided to her under Section 2 above.

> Pages 5 and 6 are on the CD-ROM and contain places for the employee and the employee's counsel to sign the agreement

Form 9-8: Employee Settlement and Release Agreement — page 4 of 6 (pages 5 and 6 not shown).

Exit Interview

Date: _____

Employee's Name: _____

Department: _____

Job Title: _____

Supervisor: _____

Dates of Employment: _____

Reason for Leaving Company: _____

Get all details available

Employee Informed of Restrictions On:

_____ Solicitations of customers (if applicable)	_____ Restrictions on solicitations of employees
_____ Removing company documents	_____ Patents
_____ Confidentiality obligations	_____ Customer lists
_____ Other _____	

Remind employee of various company policies

Return of:

_____ Keys	_____ Credit Card	_____ ID card
_____ Building Pass	_____ Company Documents	
_____ Company Equipment	_____ Other Company Property	

Checklist of things to get from employee

What is your primary reason for leaving? ___ _____

_____

Do you feel you were treated fairly by the company? _____

_____

Would you consider coming back to the company? _____

_____

Were you paid an adequate salary for the work you did? _____

_____

_____

_____

Form 9-9: Employee Exit Interview — page 1 of 2.

Exit Interview
(Continued)

Do you believe management adequately recognized employee contributions? _____

_____

Did you understand company policies and the reasons for them? _____

_____

Have you observed incidences of illegal acts within the company? _____

_____

Do you feel your training was adequate? _____

_____

Were you content with your working conditions? _____

_____

Are security arrangements appropriate in the company? Could they be improved? _____

_____

Do you have any suggestions for improving employee morale? _____

_____

What was the best part of your job here? _____

_____

> Think about adding
> additional questions
> specific to your
> business

_____

Signature of Person Conducting the Interview

Form 9-9: Employee Exit Interview — page 2 of 2.

Forms on the CD-ROM

Check out the following forms dealing with employee problems on the CD-ROM accompanying this book:

Form 9-1	**Checklist for Employee Handbooks**	A checklist of items to consider including in an Employee Handbook
Form 9-2	**Employee Handbook and At Will Employee Status Acknowledgement**	A sample acknowledgment covering the Employee Handbook and At Will employment status for employees to sign
Form 9-3	**Non-Discrimination Policy**	A sample policy prohibiting unlawful discrimination in the workplace
Form 9-4	**Sexual Harassment Policy**	A sample policy giving guidance to employees and prohibiting sexual harassment
Form 9-5	**E-Mail Policy**	A sample policy concerning how employees should and should not use e-mail on company computers
Form 9-6	**Drug-Free Workplace Policy**	A sample policy — to be signed by the employee — concerning the company's policy against illegal drugs
Form 9-7	**Employee Appraisal Form**	A sample form to record an employee appraisal
Form 9-8	**Employee Settlement and Release Agreement**	A sample agreement where the employee releases any claims against the employer in exchange for some payment
Form 9-9	**Employee Exit Interview**	A sample form that you can use in connection with a departing employee

Chapter 10

Independent Contractor and Consultant Agreements

....

In This Chapter

▶ Hiring independent contractors and consultants

▶ Filing tax information for independent workers

....

As the owner of a small, growing business, you can benefit from hiring independent contractors or consultants rather than employees. You must carefully document the agreement with the independent contractor or consultant, however, to avoid some really nasty problems with the Internal Revenue Service. And if you contract with the independent contractor or consultant to develop a product, software, a book or manual, or intellectual property, you really need to document what rights you expect to retain in the end product.

In this chapter, I provide valuable forms and agreements to use when working with independent contractors and consultants. I also tell you a bit about the key business and tax issues that make these forms necessary.

Forming Relationships with Independent Contractors and Consultants

You can reap some rewards by contracting with independent contractors and consultants. Consider the following advantages:

✔ You get special expertise.

✔ You use them as needed.

✔ You save on tax contributions.

- ✔ You save on benefits.
- ✔ You have flexibility in the relationship.

But using independent contractors is not all roses and champagne. Consider the following disadvantages:

- ✔ You run the risk of tax problems.
- ✔ You may not have the same continuity in the relationship that you would have with an employee.
- ✔ You may have to pay high fees to the contractor.
- ✔ You have limited control over the contractor.
- ✔ You probably can't terminate the relationship without good cause as provided in your agreement.

Before you hire an independent contractor or consultant, you may want to get background information to determine whether he is the right person for the job. Form 10-1 on the CD-ROM offers questions that you may want to ask. If you want to check out the answers you get, have the consultant or independent contractor sign a background check form like the samples I give you in Forms 10-2 and 10-3 on the CD-ROM.

Independent Contractor Agreements

Your business must have a good form of agreement when hiring independent contractors. A good agreement covers the following:

- ✔ The services that you expect the contractor to perform
- ✔ The deadline for the services
- ✔ The specific payment terms
- ✔ The contractor's confidentiality obligations
- ✔ The fact that the contractor is performing services as *work for hire,* meaning that the company owns any end product
- ✔ The contractor's various warranties

Form 10-4, later in this chapter, gives you a good sample Independent Contractor Agreement.

INDEPENDENT CONTRACTOR AGREEMENT

This Independent Contractor Agreement (the "Agreement") is made and entered between _____ , an independent contractor hereafter referred to as "Contractor", and _____ , hereafter referred to as "Company".

In consideration of the covenants and conditions hereinafter set forth, Company and Contractor agree as follows:

1.   SERVICES

Contractor shall perform the following services for the Company (the "Work").

```
_____
_____
_____
```

> Describe the services in detail

2.   REPORTING

Contractor shall report to _____ , Contractor shall provide a weekly written report to the Company on his progress on assignments.

3.   TERM

This Agreement shall commence on _____ , 200 __ and shall expire on _____ , 200__. Contractor agrees to perform services for the Work to Company on or before the expiration of the term set forth above. The Company may terminate the use of Contractor's services at any time without cause and without further obligation to Contractor except for payment due for services prior to date of such termination. Termination of this Agreement or termination of services shall not affect the provisions under Sections 5-11, hereof, which shall survive any termination.

4.   PAYMENT

Contractor will be paid for Work performed under this Agreement as follows:

```
_____
_____
_____
```

> Describe how contractor is to be paid

Contractor will submit an invoice for the Work on _____ . Invoices shall be paid by the Company within 15 business days of receipt.

Form 10-4: A sample Independent Contractor Agreement — page 1 of 5.

5. CONFIDENTIALITY AND OWNERSHIP

Sets out provisions for confidentiality and ownership of work product

(a)   Contractor recognizes and acknowledges that the Company possesses certain confidential information that constitutes a valuable, special, and unique asset. As used herein, the term "confidential information" includes all information and materials belonging to, used by, or in the possession of the Company relating to its products, processes, services, technology, inventions, patents, ideas, contracts, financial information, developments, business strategies, pricing, current and prospective customers, marketing plans, and trade secrets of every kind and character, but shall not include (a) information that was already within the public domain at the time the information is acquired by Contractor, or (b) information that subsequently becomes public through no act or omission of the Contractor. Contractor agrees that all of the confidential information is and shall continue to be the exclusive property of the Company, whether or not prepared in whole or in part by Contractor and whether or not disclosed to or entrusted to Contractor's custody. Contractor agrees that Contractor shall not, at any time following the execution of this Agreement, use or disclose in any manner any confidential information of the Company.

(b)   To the extent any inventions, technologies, reports, memoranda, studies, writings, articles, plans, designs, specifications, exhibits, software code, or other materials prepared by Contractor in the performance of services under this Agreement include material subject to copyright protection, such materials have been specially commissioned by the Company and they shall be deemed "work for hire" as such term is defined under U.S. copyright law. To the extent any such materials do not qualify as "work for hire" under applicable law, and to the extent they include material subject to copyright, patent, trade secret, or other proprietary rights protection, Contractor hereby irrevocably and exclusively assigns to the Company, its successors, and assigns, all right, title, and interest in and to all such materials. To the extent any of Contractor rights in the same, including without limitation any moral rights, are not subject to assignment hereunder, Contractor hereby irrevocably and unconditionally waives all enforcement of such rights. Contractor shall execute and deliver such instruments and take such other actions as may be required to carry out and confirm the assignments contemplated by this paragraph and the remainder of this Agreement. All documents, magnetically or optically encoded media, and other tangible materials created by Contractor as part of its services under this Agreement shall be owned by the Company.

6. RETURN OF MATERIALS

Contractor agrees that upon termination of this Agreement, Contractor will return to the Company all drawings, blueprints, notes, memoranda, specifications, designs, writings, software, devices, documents and any other material containing or disclosing any confidential or proprietary information of the Company. Contractor will not retain any such materials.

7. WARRANTIES

States certain warranties that the contractor is to provide

Contractor warrants that:

(a)   Contractor's agreement to perform the Work pursuant to this Agreement does not violate any agreement or obligation between Contractor and a third party; and

(b)   The Work as delivered to the Company will not infringe any copyright, patent, trade secret, or other proprietary right held by any third party; and

Form 10-4: A sample Independent Contractor Agreement — page 2 of 5.

(c)   The services provided by Contractor shall be performed in a professional manner, and shall be of a high grade, nature, and quality. The services shall be performed in a timely manner and shall meet deadlines agreed between Contractor and the Company.

8.   INDEMNITY

Contractor agrees to indemnify, defend, and hold the Company and its successors, officers, directors, agents and employees harmless from any and all actions, causes of action, claims, demands, cost, liabilities, expenses and damages (including attorneys' fees) arising out of, or in connection with any breach of this Agreement by Contractor.

9.   RELATIONSHIP OF PARTIES

Contractor is an independent contractor of the Company. Nothing in this Agreement shall be construed as creating an employer-employee relationship, as a guarantee of future employment or engagement, or as a limitation upon the Company' sole discretion to terminate this Agreement at any time without cause. Contractor further agrees to be responsible for all of Contractor's federal and state taxes, withholding, social security, insurance, and other benefits. Contractor shall provide the Company with satisfactory proof of independent contractor status.

> Describes the relationship between the parties

10.   OTHER ACTIVITIES

Contractor is free to engage in other independent contracting activities, provided that Contractor does not engage in any such activities which are inconsistent with or in conflict with any provisions hereof, or that so occupy Contractor's attention as to interfere with the proper and efficient performance of Contractor's services thereunder. Contractor agrees not to induce or attempt to influence, directly or indirectly, any employee at the Company to terminate his/her employment and work for Contractor or any other person.

> Gives the contractor the right to perform other work

11.   MISCELLANEOUS

(a)   Attorneys' Fees. Should either party hereto, or any heir, personal representative, successor or assign of either party hereto, resort to legal proceedings in connection with this Agreement or Contractor's relationship with the Company, the party or parties prevailing in such legal proceedings shall be entitled, in addition to such other relief as may be granted, to recover its or their reasonable attorneys' fees and costs in such legal proceedings from the non-prevailing party or parties.

(b)   Governing Law. This Agreement shall be governed by and construed in accordance with the laws of the State of _____ without regard to conflict of law principles.

> Pick a state law

(c)   Entire Agreement. This Agreement, contains the entire agreement and understanding between the parties hereto and supersedes any prior or contemporaneous written or oral agreements, representations and warranties between them respecting the subject matter hereof.

Form 10-4: A sample Independent Contractor Agreement — page 3 of 5.

(d)   Amendment. This Agreement may be amended only by a writing signed by Contractor and by a duly authorized representative of the Company.

(e)   Severability. If any term, provision, covenant or condition of this Agreement, or the application thereof to any person, place or circumstance, shall be held to be invalid, unenforceable or void, the remainder of this Agreement and such term, provision, covenant or condition as applied to other persons, places and circumstances shall remain in full force and effect.

(f)   Construction. The headings and captions of this Agreement are provided for convenience only and are intended to have no effect in construing or interpreting this Agreement. The language in all parts of this Agreement shall be in all cases construed according to its fair meaning and not strictly for or against either party.

(g)   Rights Cumulative. The rights and remedies provided by this Agreement are cumulative, and the exercise of any right or remedy by either party hereto (or by its successor), whether pursuant to this Agreement, to any other agreement, or to law, shall not preclude or waive its right to exercise any or all other rights and remedies.

(h)   Nonwaiver. No failure or neglect of either party hereto in any instance to exercise any right, power or privilege hereunder or under law shall constitute a waiver of any other right, power or privilege or of the same right, power or privilege in any other instance. All waivers by either party hereto must be contained in a written instrument signed by the party to be charged and, in the case of the Company, by an officer of the Company or other person duly authorized by the Company.

(i)   Remedy for Breach. The parties hereto agree that, in the event of breach or threatened breach of any covenants of Contractor, the damage or imminent damage to the value and the goodwill of the Company's business shall be inestimable, and that therefore any remedy at law or in damages shall be inadequate. Accordingly, the parties hereto agree that the Company shall be entitled to injunctive relief against Contractor in the event of any breach or threatened breach of any of such provisions by Contractor, in addition to any other relief (including damages) available to the Company under this Agreement or under law.

> Gives the company the right to injunctive relief in the event of breach of contract

(j)   Notices. Any notice, request, consent or approval required or permitted to be given under this Agreement or pursuant to law shall be sufficient if in writing, and if and when sent by certified or registered mail, with postage prepaid, to Contractor's residence (as noted below), or to the Company's principal office, as the case may be.

(k)   Assistance. Contractor shall, during and after termination of services rendered, upon reasonable notice, furnish such information and proper assistance to the Company as may reasonably be required by the Company in connection with work performed by Contractor; provided, however, that such assistance following termination shall be furnished at the same level of compensation as provided in Section 2.

Form 10-4: A sample Independent Contractor Agreement — page 4 of 5.

(l)   Disputes. Any controversy, claim or dispute arising out of or relating to this Agreement or the relationship, either during the existence of the relationship or afterwards, between the parties hereto, their assignees, their affiliates, their attorneys, or agents, shall be litigated solely in state or federal court in _____, _____. Each party (1) submits to the jurisdiction of such court, (2) waives the defense of an inconvenient forum, (3) agrees that valid consent to service may be made by mailing or delivery of such service to the _____ Secretary of State (the "Agent") or to the party at the party's last known address, if personal service delivery can not be easily effected, and (4) authorizes and directs the Agent to accept such service in the event that personal service delivery can not easily be effected. EACH PARTY, TO THE FULLEST EXTENT PERMITTED BY APPLICABLE LAW, HEREBY IRREVOCABLY WAIVES ALL RIGHT TO TRIAL BY JURY AS TO ANY ISSUE RELATING HERETO IN ANY ACTION, PROCEEDING, OR COUNTERCLAIM ARISING OUT OF OR RELATING TO THIS AGREEMENT OR ANY OTHER MATTER INVOLVING THE PARTIES HERETO.

> Declares where any disputes are to be handled

> Waives jury trial in the event of a dispute

Company: Contractor:

By:_____   By:_____
                                                      [Signature]
Title:_____
                                       Name: _____
                                                         (Print)

                                       _____
                                       Social Security #

Date: _____   Address:_____

                                       _____

                                       _____

Form 10-4: A sample Independent Contractor Agreement — page 5 of 5.

Form 10-5 on the CD-ROM provides a similar agreement for consulting services.

Confidentiality and Invention Assignment Agreements

Your consultants, especially if the business is high-tech oriented, may have access to a lot of the company's confidential information. And you may expect the consultants to come up with ideas, work product, and inventions useful to your business.

In areas where you're particularly sensitive about confidentiality and the company's ownership of the product developed, you should require consultants to sign a *Confidentiality and Invention Assignment Agreement.* This agreement deals with the confidentiality issue, but it can also provide that the ideas, work product, and inventions that the consultant creates in connection with services performed for your business belong to the company (not the consultant). This agreement is more detailed and protective than the Independent Contractor Agreement that I discuss in the preceding section. You should use it with the Consulting Agreement in Form 10-5 on the CD-ROM.

A good Confidentiality and Invention Assignment Agreement covers the following key points:

- ✔ The consultant may not use any of the company's confidential information for his own benefit or use.
- ✔ The consultant should promptly disclose to the company any inventions, ideas, discoveries, and work product related to the company's business that he makes during the period of work.
- ✔ The company owns such inventions, ideas, discoveries, and work product.
- ✔ The consultant's work with the company doesn't and can't breach any agreement or duty that the consultant has with anyone else, nor will the consultant disclose to the company or use on its behalf any confidential information belonging to others.
- ✔ The consultant's confidentiality obligations under the agreement continue after termination of the relationship.

Form 10-6 in this chapter shows a sample Confidentiality and Invention Assignment Agreement for Consultants. This form is very extensive and pro-company oriented.

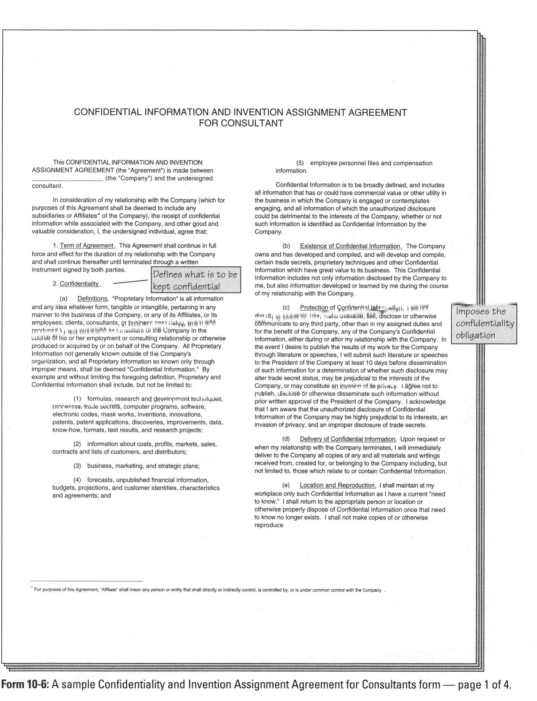

CONFIDENTIAL INFORMATION AND INVENTION ASSIGNMENT AGREEMENT FOR CONSULTANT

This CONFIDENTIAL INFORMATION AND INVENTION ASSIGNMENT AGREEMENT (the "Agreement") is made between _____ (the "Company") and the undersigned consultant.

In consideration of my relationship with the Company (which for purposes of this Agreement shall be deemed to include any subsidiaries or Affiliates* of the Company), the receipt of confidential information while associated with the Company, and other good and valuable consideration, I, the undersigned individual, agree that:

1. Term of Agreement. This Agreement shall continue in full force and effect for the duration of my relationship with the Company and shall continue thereafter until terminated through a written instrument signed by both parties.

2. Confidentiality.

> Defines what is to be kept confidential

(a) Definitions. "Proprietary Information" is all information and any idea whatever form, tangible or intangible, pertaining in any manner to the business of the Company, or any of its Affiliates, or its employees, clients, consultants, or business associates, which was produced by any employee or consultant of the Company in the course of his or her employment or consulting relationship or otherwise produced or acquired by or on behalf of the Company. All Proprietary Information not generally known outside of the Company's organization, and all Proprietary Information so known only through improper means, shall be deemed "Confidential Information." By example and without limiting the foregoing definition, Proprietary and Confidential Information shall include, but not be limited to:

(1) formulas, research and development techniques, processes, trade secrets, computer programs, software, electronic codes, mask works, inventions, innovations, patents, patent applications, discoveries, improvements, data, know-how, formats, test results, and research projects;

(2) information about costs, profits, markets, sales, contracts and lists of customers, and distributors;

(3) business, marketing, and strategic plans;

(4) forecasts, unpublished financial information, budgets, projections, and customer identities, characteristics and agreements; and

(5) employee personnel files and compensation information.

Confidential Information is to be broadly defined, and includes all information that has or could have commercial value or other utility in the business in which the Company is engaged or contemplates engaging, and all information of which the unauthorized disclosure could be detrimental to the interests of the Company, whether or not such information is identified as Confidential Information by the Company.

(b) Existence of Confidential Information. The Company owns and has developed and compiled, and will develop and compile, certain trade secrets, proprietary techniques and other Confidential Information which have great value to its business. This Confidential Information includes not only information disclosed by the Company to me, but also information developed or learned by me during the course of my relationship with the Company.

(c) Protection of Confidential Information. I will not directly or indirectly use, make available, sell, disclose or otherwise communicate to any third party, other than in my assigned duties and for the benefit of the Company, any of the Company's Confidential Information, either during or after my relationship with the Company. In the event I desire to publish the results of my work for the Company through literature or speeches, I will submit such literature or speeches to the President of the Company at least 10 days before dissemination of such information for a determination of whether such disclosure may alter trade secret status, may be prejudicial to the interests of the Company, or may constitute an invasion of its privacy. I agree not to publish, disclose or otherwise disseminate such information without prior written approval of the President of the Company. I acknowledge that I am aware that the unauthorized disclosure of Confidential Information of the Company may be highly prejudicial to its interests, an invasion of privacy, and an improper disclosure of trade secrets.

> Imposes the confidentiality obligation

(d) Delivery of Confidential Information. Upon request or when my relationship with the Company terminates, I will immediately deliver to the Company all copies of any and all materials and writings received from, created for, or belonging to the Company including, but not limited to, those which relate to or contain Confidential Information.

(e) Location and Reproduction. I shall maintain at my workplace only such Confidential Information as I have a current "need to know." I shall return to the appropriate person or location or otherwise properly dispose of Confidential Information once that need to know no longer exists. I shall not make copies of or otherwise reproduce

_____

* For purposes of this Agreement, "Affiliate" shall mean any person or entity that shall directly or indirectly control, is controlled by, or is under common control with the Company .

Form 10-6: A sample Confidentiality and Invention Assignment Agreement for Consultants form — page 1 of 4.

States that consultant will not use confidential information from someone else

Confidential Information unless there is a legitimate business need of the Company for reproduction.

(f) Prior Actions and Knowledge. I represent and warrant that from the time of my first contact with the Company I held in strict confidence all Confidential Information and have not disclosed any Confidential Information, directly or indirectly, to anyone outside the Company, or used, copied, published, or summarized any Confidential information, except to the extent otherwise permitted in this Agreement.

(g) Third-Party Information. I acknowledge that the Company has received and in the future will receive from third parties their confidential information subject to a duty on the Company's part to maintain the confidentiality of such information and to use it only for certain limited purposes. I agree that I will at all times hold all such confidential information in the strictest confidence and not to disclose or use it, except as necessary to perform my obligations hereunder and as is consistent with the Company's agreement with such third parties.

(h) Third Parties. I represent that my relationship with the Company does not and will not breach any agreements with or duties to a former employer or any other third party. I will not disclose to the Company or use on its behalf any confidential information belonging to others and I will not bring onto the premises of the Company any confidential information belonging to any such party unless consented to in writing by such party.

3. Proprietary Rights, Inventions and New Ideas.

(a) Definition. The term "Subject Ideas or Inventions" includes any and all ideas, processes, trademarks, service marks, inventions, designs, technologies, computer hardware or software, original works of authorship, formulas, discoveries, patents, copyrights, copyrightable works products, marketing and business ideas, and all improvements, know-how, data, rights, and claims related to the foregoing that, whether or not patentable, which are conceived, developed or created which: (1) relate to the Company's current or contemplated business; (2) relate to the Company's actual or demonstrably anticipated research or development; (3) result from any work performed by me for the Company; (4) involve the use of the Company's equipment, supplies, facilities or trade secrets; (5) result from or are suggested by any work done by the Company or at the Company's request, or any projects specifically assigned to me; or (6) result from my access to any of the Company's memoranda, notes, records, drawings, sketches, models, maps, customer lists, research results, data, formulae, specifications, inventions, processes, equipment or other materials (collectively, "Company Materials").

(b) Company Ownership. All right, title and interest in and to all Subject Ideas and Inventions, including but not limited to all registrable and patent rights which may subsist therein, shall be held and owned solely by the Company, and where applicable, all Subject Ideas and Inventions shall be considered works made for hire. I shall mark all Subject Ideas and Inventions with the Company's copyright or other proprietary notice as directed by the Company and shall take all actions deemed necessary by the Company to protect the Company's rights therein. In the event that the Subject Ideas and Inventions shall be deemed not to constitute works made for hire, or in the event that I should otherwise, by operation of law, be deemed to retain any rights (whether moral rights or otherwise) to any Subject Ideas and Inventions, I agree to assign to the Company, without further

Says that writings, inventions, and ideas that the consultant creates with are "work for hire" and owned by the company

consideration, my entire right, title and interest in and to each and every such Subject Idea and Invention.

(c) Disclosure. I agree to disclose promptly to the Company full details of any and all Subject Ideas and Inventions.

(d) Maintenance of Records. I agree to keep and maintain adequate and current written records of all Subject Ideas and Inventions and their development made by me (solely or jointly with others) during the term of my relationship with the Company. These records will be in the form of notes, sketches, drawings, and any other format that may be specified by the Company. These records will be available to and remain the sole property of the Company at all times.

(e) Determination of Subject Ideas and Inventions. I further agree that all information and records pertaining to any idea, process, trademark, service mark, invention, technology, computer hardware or software, original work of authorship, design, formula, discovery, patent, copyright, product, and all improvements, know-how, rights, and claims related to the foregoing ("Intellectual Property"), that I do not believe to be a Subject Idea or Invention, but that is conceived, developed, or reduced to practice by the Company (alone by me or with others) during my relationship with the Company and for one (1) year thereafter, shall be disclosed promptly by me to the Company. The Company shall examine such information to determine if in fact the Intellectual Property is a Subject Idea or Invention subject to this Agreement.

(f) Access. Because of the difficulty of establishing when any Subject Ideas or Inventions are first conceived by me, or whether it results from my access to Confidential Information or Company Materials, I agree that any Subject Idea and Invention shall, among other circumstances, be deemed to have resulted from my access to Company Materials if: (1) it grew out of or resulted from my work with the Company or is related to the business of the Company, and (2) it is made, used, sold, exploited or reduced to practice, or an application for patent, trademark, copyright or other proprietary protection is filed thereon, by me or with my significant aid, within one year after termination of my relationship with the Company.

(g) Assistance. I further agree to assist the Company in every proper way (but at the Company's expense) to obtain and from time to time enforce patents, copyrights or other rights or registrations on said Subject Ideas and Inventions in any and all countries, and to that end will execute all documents necessary:

(1) to apply for, obtain and vest in the name of the Company alone (unless the Company otherwise directs) letters patent, copyrights or other analogous protection in any country throughout the world and when so obtained or vested to renew and restore the same; and

(2) to defend any opposition proceedings in respect of such applications and any opposition proceedings or petitions or applications for revocation of such letters patent, copyright or other analogous protection; and

(3) to cooperate with the Company (but at the Company's expense) in any enforcement or infringement proceeding on such letters patent, copyright or other analogous protection.

(h) Authorization to Company. In the event the Company is unable, after reasonable effort, to secure my signature on any

Requires consultant to assist the company in protecting its rights

Form 10-6: A sample Confidentiality and Invention Assignment Agreement for Consultants form — page 2 of 4.

Imposes obligations on termination of the relationship

patent, copyright or other analogous protection relating to a Subject Idea and Invention, whether because of my physical or mental incapacity or for any other reason whatsoever, I hereby irrevocably designate and appoint the Company and its duly authorized officers and agents as my agent and attorney-in-fact, to act for and on my behalf and stead to execute and file any such application, applications or other documents and to do all other lawfully permitted acts to further the prosecution, issuance, and enforcement of letters patent, copyright or other analogous rights or protections thereon with the same legal force and effect as if executed by me. My obligation to assist the Company in obtaining and enforcing patents and copyrights for Subject Ideas and Inventions in any and all countries shall continue beyond the termination of my relationship with the Company, but the Company shall compensate me at a reasonable rate after such termination for time actually spent by me at the Company's request on such assistance.

(i)   Acknowledgement. I acknowledge that there are no currently existing ideas, processes, inventions, discoveries, marketing or business ideas or improvements which I desire to exclude from the operation of this Agreement. To the best of my knowledge, there is no other contract to assign inventions, trademarks, copyrights, ideas, processes, discoveries or other intellectual property that is now in existence between me and any other person (including any business or governmental entity).

(j)   No Use of Name. I shall not at any time use the Company's name or any the Company trademark(s) or trade name(s) in any advertising or publicity without the prior written consent of the Company.

4. Competitive Activity.

(a)   Acknowledgment. I acknowledge that the pursuit of the activities forbidden by Section 4(b) below would necessarily involve the use, disclosure or misappropriation of Confidential Information.

(b)   Prohibited Activity. To prevent the above-described disclosure, misappropriation and breach, I agree that during my relationship and for a period of one (1) year thereafter, without the Company's express written consent, I shall not, directly or indirectly, (i) employ, solicit for employment, or recommend for employment any person employed by the Company (or any Affiliate); and (ii) engage in any present or contemplated business activity that is or may be competitive with the Company (or any Affiliate) in any state where the Company conducts its business, unless I can prove that any action taken in contravention of this subsection (ii) was done without the use in any way of Confidential Information.

5. Representations and Warranties. I represent and warrant (i) that I have no obligations, legal or otherwise, inconsistent with the terms of this Agreement or with my undertaking a relationship with the Company; (ii) that the performance of the services called for by this Agreement do not and will not violate any applicable law, rule or regulation or any proprietary or other right of any third party; (iii) that I will not use in the performance of my responsibilities for the Company any confidential information or trade secrets of any other person or entity; and (iv) that I have not entered into or will enter into any agreement (whether oral or written) in conflict with this Agreement.

Limits the consultant's competitive activity

6. Termination Obligations.

(a)   Upon the termination of my relationship with the Company or promptly upon the Company's request, I shall surrender to the Company all equipment, tangible Proprietary Information, documents, books, notebooks, records, reports, notes, memoranda, drawings, sketches, models, maps, contracts, lists, computer disks (and other computer-generated files and data), any other data and records of any kind, and copies thereof (collectively, "Company Records"), created on any medium and furnished to, obtained by, or prepared by myself in the course of or incident to my relationship with the Company, that are in my possession or under my control.

(b)   My representations, warranties, and obligations contained in this Agreement shall survive the termination of my relationship with the Company.

(c)   Following any termination of my relationship with the Company, I will fully cooperate with the Company in all matters relating to my continuing obligations under this Agreement.

(d)   I hereby grant consent to notification by the Company to any of my future employers or companies I consult with about my rights and obligations under this Agreement.

(e)   Upon termination of my relationship with the Company, I will execute a Certificate acknowledging compliance with this Agreement in the form reasonably requested by the Company.

7. Injunctive Relief. I acknowledge that my failure to carry out any obligation under this Agreement, or a breach by me of any provision herein, will constitute immediate and irreparable damage to the Company, which cannot be fully and adequately compensated in money damages and which will warrant preliminary and other injunctive relief, an order for specific performance, and other equitable relief. I further agree that no bond or other security shall be required in obtaining such equitable relief and I hereby consent to the issuance of such injunction and to the ordering of specific performance. I also understand that other action may be taken and remedies enforced against me.

8. Modification. No modification of this Agreement shall be valid unless made in writing and signed by both parties.

9. Binding Effect. This Agreement shall be binding upon me, my heirs, executors, assigns and administrators and is for the benefit of the Company and its successors and assigns.

10. Governing Law. This Agreement shall be construed in accordance with, and all actions arising under or in connection therewith shall be governed by, the internal laws of the State of California (without reference to conflict of law principles).

11. Integration. This Agreement sets forth the parties' mutual rights and obligations with respect to proprietary information, prohibited competition, and intellectual property. It is intended to be the final, complete, and exclusive statement of the terms of the parties' agreements regarding these subjects. This Agreement supersedes all other prior and contemporaneous agreements and statements on these subjects, and it may not be contradicted by evidence of any prior or contemporaneous statements or agreements. To the extent that the practices, policies, or procedures of the Company, now or in the future, apply to myself and are inconsistent with the terms of this Agreement, the provisions of this Agreement shall control unless changed in writing by the Company.

Form 10-6: A sample Confidentiality and Invention Assignment Agreement for Consultants form — page 3 of 4.

States that the person is not an employee

12. Not Employment. This Agreement is not an employment agreement as I am an independent consultant. I understand that the Company may terminate my association with it at any time, with or without cause, subject to the terms of any separate written consulting agreement executed by a duly authorized officer of the Company.

13. Construction. This Agreement shall be construed as a whole, according to its fair meaning, and not in favor of or against any party. By way of example and not limitation, this Agreement shall not be construed against the party responsible for any language in this Agreement. The headings of the paragraphs hereof are inserted for convenience only, and do not constitute part of and shall not be used to interpret this Agreement.

14. Attorneys' Fees. Should either I or the Company, or any heir, personal representative, successor or permitted assign of either party, resort to legal proceedings to enforce this Agreement, the prevailing party (as defined in California statutory law) in such legal proceeding shall be awarded, in addition to such other relief as may be granted, attorneys' fees and costs incurred in connection with such proceeding.

15. Severability. If any term, provision, covenant or condition of this Agreement, or the application thereof to any person, place or circumstance, shall be held to be invalid, unenforceable or void, the remainder of this Agreement and such term, provision, covenant or condition as applied to other persons, places and circumstances shall remain in full force and effect.

16. Rights Cumulative. The rights and remedies provided by this Agreement are cumulative, and the exercise of any right or remedy by either the Company or me (or by that party's successor), whether pursuant hereto, to any other agreement, or to law, shall not preclude or waive that party's right to exercise any or all other rights and remedies. This Agreement will inure to the benefit of the Company and its successors and assigns.

17. Nonwaiver. The failure of either the Company or me, whether purposeful or otherwise, to exercise in any instance any right, power or privilege under this Agreement or under law shall not constitute a waiver of any other right, power or privilege, nor of the same right, power or privilege in any other instance. Any waiver by the Company or by me must be in writing and signed by either myself, if I am seeking to waive any of my rights under this Agreement, or by an officer of the Company (other than me) or some other person duly authorized by the Company.

18. Notices. Any notice, request, consent or approval required or permitted to be given under this Agreement or pursuant to law shall be sufficient if it is in writing, and if and when it is hand delivered or sent by regular mail, with postage prepaid, to my residence (as noted in the Company's records), or to the Company's principal office, as the case may be.

19. Agreement to Perform Necessary Acts. I agree to perform any further acts and execute and deliver any documents that may be reasonably necessary to carry out the provisions of this Agreement.

General cooperation clause

20. Assignment. This Agreement may not be assigned without the Company's prior written consent.

21. Compliance with Law. I agree to abide by all federal, state, and local laws, ordinances and regulations.

22. Acknowledgment. I acknowledge that I have had the opportunity to consult legal counsel in regard to this Agreement, that I have read and understand this Agreement, that I am fully aware of its legal effect, and that I have entered into it freely and voluntarily and based on my own judgment and not on any representations or promises other than those contained in this Agreement.

IN WITNESS WHEREOF, the undersigned have executed this Agreement as of the dates set forth below.

CAUTION: THIS AGREEMENT CREATES IMPORTANT OBLIGATIONS OF TRUST AND AFFECTS THE CONSULTANT'S RIGHTS TO INVENTIONS AND OTHER INTELLECTUAL PROPERTY THE CONSULTANT MAY DEVELOP.

Dated: _____

_____
Consultant Signature

Printed Name of Consultant: _____

[Name of Corporation]

By: _____

Name: _____

Title: _____

Allows company to recover its attorney's fees if consultant breaches this agreement

Form 10-6: A sample Confidentiality and Invention Assignment Agreement for Consultants form — page 4 of 4.

Tiptoe through the Tax Forms

Tax laws allow you to treat employees and contractors differently. In fact, decreased tax liability is one of the greatest benefits that your company can realize from using an independent contractor or consultant. You must be especially vigilant, however, to correctly fill out your forms and agreements to avoid having the IRS disagree with your assessment of a worker as an independent contractor.

Table 10-1 summarizes some key areas in which independent contractors differ from employees. Many of these issues directly affect what forms you must fill out with respect to the worker. (You can find Table 10-1 on the CD-ROM as Form 10-7.)

Table 10-1	Withholding, Benefit, and Legal Differences Between Employees and Contractors		
Employer Responsibility		**Employee**	**Independent Contractor**
Make employer contribution to Social Security		Yes	No
Make employer contribution to Medicare taxes		Yes	No
Withhold applicable taxes		Yes	No
File Form 1099-MISC with IRS if you pay the person $600 or more		No	Yes
Carry Worker's Compensation Insurance for the person		Yes	No
Contribute to unemployment insurance fund and/or tax		Yes	No
Grant employee job benefits, such as paid vacation, sick leave, holidays, and stock options		Yes	No
Pay employee for overtime		Yes	Generally no
Right to control how the worker performs the specific task for which you hire her		Generally yes	Generally no
Right to direct or control how the worker conducts the business aspects of her activities		Generally yes	Generally no

Using a contractor takes determination

Determining whether you can properly characterize a worker as an employee or an independent contractor is absolutely necessary before you enter into an independent contractor agreement. If you have the right to direct or control the specific tasks and business aspects of the worker's activities, the IRS probably considers the worker an employee, no matter what title or label you may use.

To determine whether a worker is an employee or an independent contractor, the IRS offers some guidance — IRS Publications 1976 and 1779 (Forms 10-8 and 10-9 on the CD-ROM). The following list summarizes the key factors:

- **Behavioral control:** The more independent the worker, the more likely you can classify that worker as an independent contractor. Facts that may show control over a worker include the type and degree of instructions the business gives the worker and the training the business gives the worker. Try to avoid mandating that the contractor work set hours (for example, 9 a.m. to 5 p.m.).

- **Financial control:** The more it seems that the worker is in business for himself, the more likely you can classify the worker as an independent contractor. Facts that may show this independence in financial control include the extent to which the worker has unreimbursed business expenses, the extent of the worker's own investment, the extent to which the worker makes services available to others, and the extent to which the worker can realize a profit or incur a loss.

- **Type of relationship:** The more solidly you can demonstrate a temporary relationship, the more likely that you can classify the worker as an independent contractor. Facts that may evidence your relationship include written contracts describing the relationship the parties intend to create; whether the business provides the worker with employee-type benefits, such as insurance, vacation pay, or sick pay; whether a specific end-point to the relationship exists; and the extent to which services performed by the worker provide a key aspect of the company's regular business. (The more central the work is to your regular business activity, the more likely you are to direct and control the contractor's activities.)

According to IRS rules, certain workers are automatically classified as employees; you can't treat them as independent contractors for tax purposes. These people include certain delivery drivers, certain insurance agents, workers working at their home using company-supplied materials or goods, and certain business-to-business sales people. Carefully review the IRS Web site at www.irs.gov for all these rules.

Go directly to jail: Do not pass Go or collect $200

The kooky, fun-loving people at the IRS prefer to classify workers as employees rather than independent contractors. Coincidentally, the IRS also collects more tax revenue if the worker is an employee than if the worker is an independent contractor.

The IRS requires employers to do the following for each employee (but not for each contractor):

✔ Withhold income taxes and the employee's share of Social Security and Medicare contributions

✔ Pay the employer's share of the Social Security and Medicare contributions

If the IRS determines that you should have classified a worker as an employee, rather than an independent contractor, it can assess the following penalties:

✔ Payment of federal income tax that you should have withheld from the employee

✔ Payment of Medicare contributions that you should have withheld

✔ Interest on taxes that you should have withheld

✔ A penalty for failure to properly file tax returns and pay taxes

✔ A big penalty if the IRS determines that the behavior was negligent, intentional, or fraudulent

✔ Criminal sanctions, including imprisonment and fines up to $100,000

✔ Personal liability for corporate officers, up to 100 percent of the amount that the employer should have withheld from the employee's compensation

✔ Send you to bed without supper

Okay, I assume that these horrendous penalties have your full attention. (And these are only the IRS penalties. Other government entities — such as the State Employment Department or the National Labor Relations Board — may also impose penalties.) So don't screw this up.

IRS publication 15-A (Form 10-10 on the CD-ROM) provides examples of when you can and can't classify a worker as an independent contractor.

If you want the IRS to determine whether a worker is an employee, you can file IRS Form SS-8 *(Determination of Employee Work Status for Purposes of Federal Employment Taxes and Income Tax Withholding)* with the IRS. Remember, however, that the IRS has a vested interest in classifying a worker as an employee rather than as an independent contractor.

Tax forms of the rich and famous (not poor and nameless)

The following sections tell you about two IRS forms that you need to worry about when dealing with independent contractors.

IRS Form W-9

You should require all your independent contractors to complete IRS Form W-9, which gives you information including their Social Security numbers or Employer I.D. numbers. You need this information when you make filings with the IRS. If you don't get this information, you may have to withhold taxes from the independent contractor.

Form 10-11 on the CD-ROM shows IRS Form W-9.

IRS Form 1099-MISC

If you pay an independent contractor $600 or more in a year, you need to send an IRS Form 1099-MISC at the end of the year to the IRS and to the independent contractor.

You can find IRS Form 1099-MISC included on the CD-ROM as Form 10-12.

Forms on the CD-ROM

Check out these forms on the CD-ROM:

Form 10-1	**Questions to Consider Asking Prospective Consultants of Independent Contractors**	Questions that you may find useful to ask prospective consultants or independent contractors
Form 10-2	**Background Check Permission (Simple)**	A sample simple form, to be signed by a prospective consultant or independent contractor, giving permission for a background check
Form 10-3	**Background Check Permission (Comprehensive)**	A sample comprehensive form, to be signed by a prospective consultant or independent contractor, giving permission for a background check

Form 10-4	**Independent Contractor Agreement**	A sample, pro-company-oriented Independent Contractor Agreement
Form 10-5	**Consulting Agreement**	A sample, pro-company-oriented form agreement for you to use for a consultant
Form 10-6	**Consultant Confidentiality and Invention Assignment Agreement**	A form of agreement that requires the consultant to keep company information confidential and to assign ownership of inventions and materials developed as part of the work for the company over to the company
Form 10-7	**Chart of Key Differences between Employees and Independent Contractors**	A summary chart showing the key differences in a worker being classified as an employee or independent contractor
Form 10-8	**IRS Publication 1976**	Publication that discusses classification of independent contractors versus employees
Form 10-9	**IRS Publication 1779**	Gives advice on independent contractors and employee classifications
Form 10-10	**IRS Publication 15-A**	Illustrates examples of key differences in the classification of employees and independent contractors
Form 10-11	**IRS Form W-9**	The IRS form that an independent contractor needs to sign at the beginning of the relationship
Form 10-12	**IRS Form 1099-MISC**	The IRS form that you need to file for independent contractors

Part IV
Bulletproofing Your Business

The 5th Wave
By Rich Tennant

"I just never thought to incorporate my business. Then we were hit with a massive lawsuit. Fortunately, I never lost my shirt. They also let me keep these pants, shoes, and hat."

In this part . . .

They say that you should hope for the best and expect the worst. In business, you don't necessarily have to expect the worst, but you should at least plan for it. This part gives you advice on how to create contracts that will protect your interests, how to avoid legal problems, how to protect your trademarks and trade secrets, how to avoid problems with customers, and how to negotiate a real estate lease for your business.

Chapter 11

Key Contracts

- -

In This Chapter

▶ Getting good contracts down on paper

▶ Writing a good license or distribution agreement

▶ Venturing into joint ventures

▶ Drafting effective boilerplate text

▶ Making amendments to contracts

- -

*E*very business, whether a new start-up or a large business, becomes party to a few — and in some instances many — key contracts. *Key contracts* are agreements dealing with large sums of money, such as sales agreements, leases, purchase orders, and service agreements. Some people believe that most contracts are standard or *boilerplate,* but nothing can be further from the truth You can prepare contracts in several different ways — ways that help and protect you or help and protect the other side.

A good contract can save you a lot of hassles and problems and should meet your expectations. A bad contract can lead to horrendous consequences — unexpected expenses, customer hassles, and even litigation.

In this chapter, I guide you in preparing good contracts for your business, and I discuss some important issues to consider for key contracts.

Understanding Contracts

A *contract* is the agreement between the parties, with terms and conditions, that constitutes a legal obligation. A valid contract typically requires

✔ **A meeting of the minds** between the parties defining the deal

✔ **Consideration** (something of value exchanged by each side — such as cash, a promise, goods, or services)

> ✔ **An agreement** to enter into the contract (typically evidenced by both parties signing the contract, but oral contracts can be valid, also)
>
> ✔ **Legal competence** of the parties, meaning that they're of legal age and aren't otherwise incapacitated

Contracts can come in all shapes and sizes — from preprinted form contracts, to intensely negotiated and documented agreements, to informal letters. Oral contracts can be legally binding (with certain exceptions, such as for the sale of real estate), and you can even form contracts through e-mail correspondence. However, smart small businesses rely on clear, well-drafted, written, signed contracts.

Form 11-1 later in this chapter gives you a general checklist to help you think about what you may want to include in your contract, but keep in mind that you may also need to cover other points, depending on your situation. Finally, not all of these items may be relevant or necessary for your particular situation.

The advice I give in this book is general in nature and may not apply to your particular situation. You should keep in mind the specific circumstances and language involved when you review or negotiate each contract. And you may need an experienced business lawyer to help you reach your desired goal.

Writing and Negotiating Good Contracts

How successful your business becomes depends, in an important way, on how well you draft your contracts. A well-drafted contract spells out each side's rights and obligations and protects you as much as possible. A bad contract can spell disaster.

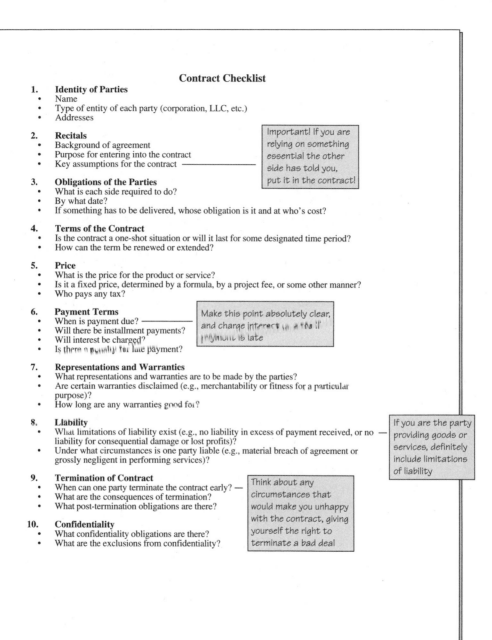

Contract Checklist

1. **Identity of Parties**
   - Name
   - Type of entity of each party (corporation, LLC, etc.)
   - Addresses

2. **Recitals**
   - Background of agreement
   - Purpose for entering into the contract
   - Key assumptions for the contract ————————

   > Important! If you are relying on something essential the other side has told you, put it in the contract!

3. **Obligations of the Parties**
   - What is each side required to do?
   - By what date?
   - If something has to be delivered, whose obligation is it and at who's cost?

4. **Terms of the Contract**
   - Is the contract a one-shot situation or will it last for some designated time period?
   - How can the term be renewed or extended?

5. **Price**
   - What is the price for the product or service?
   - Is it a fixed price, determined by a formula, by a project fee, or some other manner?
   - Who pays any tax?

6. **Payment Terms**
   - When is payment due? ——————

   > Make this point absolutely clear, and charge interest on a ten if payment is late

   - Will there be installment payments?
   - Will interest be charged?
   - Is there a penalty for late payment?

7. **Representations and Warranties**
   - What representations and warranties are to be made by the parties?
   - Are certain warranties disclaimed (e.g., merchantability or fitness for a particular purpose)?
   - How long are any warranties good for?

8. **Liability**
   - What limitations of liability exist (e.g., no liability in excess of payment received, or no — liability for consequential damage or lost profits)?
   - Under what circumstances is one party liable (e.g., material breach of agreement or grossly negligent in performing services)?

   > If you are the party providing goods or services, definitely include limitations of liability

9. **Termination of Contract**
   - When can one party terminate the contract early? —
   - What are the consequences of termination?
   - What post-termination obligations are there?

   > Think about any circumstances that would make you unhappy with the contract, giving yourself the right to terminate a bad deal

10. **Confidentiality**
    - What confidentiality obligations are there?
    - What are the exclusions from confidentiality?

Form 11-1: Contract Checklist — page 1 of 2.

11. Default
- What are the events of default?
- Does a party have a period to cure a default?
- What are the consequences of a default?

12. Disputes
- How are disputes to be handled – litigation, mediation or arbitration?
- If arbitration, what rules will govern? (e.g., JAMS/Endispute or the American Arbitration Association)
- If arbitration, how many arbitrators and how will they be picked?
- If arbitration, will there be procedures for discovery and what the arbitrator can and can't do?
- If litigation, where can or must the litigation be brought? —

> You always want to have disputes resolved in your hometown

13. Indemnification
- Is there indemnification for certain breaches or problems?
- What is the procedure required to obtain indemnification?
- Is there a cap on or exclusions from indemnification?

14. Miscellaneous
- Governing law
- Attorneys fees
- Modification of Agreement
- Notice
- Entire Agreement
- Severability
- Time of the Essence
- Survival
- Ambiguities
- Waiver
- Headings
- Necessary Acts and Further Assurances
- Execution
- Jury Trial Waivers
- Specific Performances
- Representation on Authority of Parties
- Force Majuere
- Assignment

> Don't forget these clauses — they can make or break your contract

15. Signatures
- What authority is required for one party to sign the contract (e.g., Board of Directors approval)?
- How many signatures are required?
- Are the signature blocks correct? For corporations, this is a typical appropriate signature block:

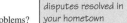

ABC, Inc.

By:_____
      John Smith, President

Form 11-1: Contract Checklist — page 2 of 2.

Here are some tips for drafting a good contract:

- ✔ **Be clear.** Make sure that the contract carefully and thoroughly describes both your responsibilities and the other side's obligations. Ambiguous language in a contract can lead to misunderstandings, delays, frustration, and litigation.

- ✔ **Be complete.** Many contracts fail because they're incomplete. You may fail to put in some important terms or expectations. Some people assume that the terms are understood and don't need to be spelled out. Wrong! Make sure that if you're relying on something important when entering into the contract (such as a promise or guarantee from the other side) that you actually include this information in the contract.

- ✔ **Look at sample contracts and forms.** The best way to start drafting a contract is to look at several sample forms that may be similar to the document you want to create. If the sample forms are any good, they alert you to issues that you may not have even thought about, and they can help to provide some good language for your contract. You can find a bunch of good sample contracts at www.AllBusiness.com.

- ✔ **Don't be too reliant on a "standard" form or sample contract.** Don't make the mistake of being too reliant on some form you may find. Often, the form doesn't really apply to your situation, may be drafted for the benefit of the wrong side, or may just stink. Most forms are simply a starting place; you need to revise them for your particular transaction.

- ✔ **Be the drafter.** A fundamental principle of contract negotiation is that you almost always want to draft the first draft. Doing so can give you a tremendous advantage in shaping the negotiations, as you can include clauses that you want and structure the deal in the way that works best for your business.

- ✔ **Make your contract look like a standard form.** Sometimes, making your contract look like a preprinted standard form (even though you may have carefully drafted it for your benefit) can help you. With word processing or desktop publishing, this task isn't hard to do, and the other side may be less inclined to negotiate if they think that your agreement is standard.

- ✔ **Be aware of legal requirements.** Certain types of provisions in a contract may be questionable, legally (such as non-competition clauses, in certain instances). You may need to put some provisions in boldface or all capital letters to make them effective. A good business lawyer can point these places out for you.

- ✔ **Use exhibits.** Sometimes, your best bet is to use *exhibits,* or addendums, to a contract. That way, you can use your base contract over and over, and you can put all the details specific to the transaction in an exhibit. Just make sure to refer to the exhibit in the main contract.

> ✔ **Have a boilerplate.** You must have good "boilerplate" or "miscella-
> neous" clauses at the end of your contract. This information may seem
> trivial, but it can end up being tremendously important in the event of
> a dispute (see the section "The Skinny on Boilerplate Text" later in this
> chapter).

Contract drafting isn't easy, but a well-drafted contract can mean the difference between making money and losing money and, ultimately, staying in
business or going out of business.

Letters of Intent

Entering into a letter of intent can be very useful for doing a particular deal. A
letter of intent allows the parties to indicate that they're seriously interested
in doing a deal and want to explore discussions further. The letter of intent
lays out the principal terms of the proposed deal to make sure that the parties involved have a meeting of the minds. For example, you may want to sign
a letter of intent to buy a business, to enter into a joint venture, or to enter
into a major contract.

Opinion is divided about the best way to write a letter of intent. One view
says that letters of intent should be short and sweet, highlighting only the
really important points. That way, the parties feel that they have momentum
towards a deal. The other view suggests that letters of intent should be relatively detailed with every major point addressed in the letter. In that way, the
parties may be less likely to encounter stumbling blocks when they try to put
together a definitive contract (and incur legal fees in doing so). The approach
you take depends on the circumstances and your personal preferences. If you
want to make sure that you have a true "meeting of the minds" for a deal,
then you should opt for the more detailed approach. If you're in a hurry and
believe that you can work out any issues that come up, then a shorter version
may work.

Here are some questions the letter of intent should attempt to answer:

> ✔ **Confidentiality:** Will you keep the on-going discussions confidential?
> What obligations does the other side have to keep the information that
> you give them confidential?
>
> ✔ **Structure:** What is the basic structure of the deal? For example, is it a joint
> venture, a sale of assets, a license, or some other type of arrangement?
>
> ✔ **Price and terms:** How much money is involved? Will the payment be in
> cash or spread out over time?
>
> ✔ **Main obligations:** What are each side's key obligations?

✔ **Closing:** By what date will the parties try to sign a definitive contract and close? Your letter can also say that if a definitive contract isn't signed by that date, then both sides are free to go elsewhere or continue discussions, at their option.

✔ **Exclusivity:** Will the negotiations between the parties be exclusive for a period of time? If you agree to exclusive negotiations, make sure that the negotiations last only for a limited period of time, such as 21 days. Agreements for exclusive negotiations can be legally binding on you.

✔ **Conditions:** What key conditions have to occur before you can execute a final agreement? For example, if the letter of intent is to buy a business, you will likely want at least two conditions — that you are satisfied with your review of the business and that you have obtained whatever financing you need to close the deal.

✔ **Binding obligations:** What obligations in the letter of intent are intended to legally bind the parties? You want to be careful here, as you don't necessarily want something in the letter to bind you to move forward on the deal. Typically, you want to say that the parties aren't bound in any way, except with respect to the confidentiality obligations.

Form 11-2, which you can find later in the chapter, gives you a sample letter of intent for the purchase of another business that illustrates some of these points.

Services Contracts

If your company is providing professional services as opposed to selling a product, you may find that you need a good *Agreement for Professional Services.* This type of agreement lays out the terms and conditions under which your business provides certain services. Examples of such services include accounting, engineering, consulting, software development, and property inspections.

Here are the key points to keep in mind when drafting or negotiating an Agreement for Professional Services:

✔ **Services to be rendered:** Clearly set forth in the contract the precise services that you plan to provide. You want to avoid broad or ambiguous language, such as "Company will provide all services necessary to make the Client's computer operations work quickly and efficiently." This type of language only leads to problems or litigation. Rather, consider language that specifically and narrowly describes what you will be actually doing, such as "Company will provide up to 50 hours of consulting time to assist Client in modifying its computer network to operate more quickly."

✔ **Fees:** Spell out the compensation that you expect to receive and when you expect to receive it. Do you expect an up-front retainer? Do you charge a lump sum for the project or by the hour? When are payments due?

[Date]

_____
_____
_____
_____

Re: Letter of Intent

Dear _____:

This letter confirms your and our mutual intentions with respect to the potential transaction described herein between _____ ("Buyer") and _____ ("Seller").

> Identitfy the prospective buyer and seller

1. **Prices and Terms**. We envisage that the principal terms of the proposed transaction would be substantially as follows:

   (a) **Business to be Acquired; Liabilities to be Assumed**. We would acquire substantially all of the assets, tangible and intangible, owned by Seller that are used in, or necessary for the conduct of, its software development business, including, without limitation: (i) the _____ software, subject to any obligations contained in disclosed license agreements and all related intellectual property; (ii) the fixed assets of Seller, (iii) any and all customer lists; and (iv) the goodwill associated therewith, all free and clear of any security interests, mortgages or other encumbrances.

   > This clause sets forth what is being purchased

   (b) **Consideration**. The aggregate consideration for the assets and business to be purchased would be $_____; provided, however, that the working capital (current assets less current liabilities) of the business to be purchased equals or exceeds $0, as shown on a closing date balance sheet prepared in accordance with generally accepted accounting principles.

   > This clause provides the amount that the buyers will pay for the business

   (c) **Due Diligence Review**. Promptly following the execution of this letter of intent, you will allow us to complete our examination of your financial, accounting and business records and the contracts and other legal documents and generally to complete due diligence. Any information obtained by us as a result thereof will be maintained by us in confidence subject to the terms of the Confidentiality Agreement executed by the parties and dated _____ (the "Confidentiality Agreement"). The parties will cooperate to complete due diligence expeditiously.

   (d) **Conduct in Ordinary Course**. In addition to the conditions discussed herein and any others to be contained in a definitive written purchase agreement (the "Purchase Agreement"), consummation of the acquisition would be subject to having conducted your business in the ordinary course during the period between the date hereof and the date of closing and there having been no material adverse change in your business, financial condition or prospects.

   > This clause says that the seller must conduct the business in the ordinary course as a condition to closing the deal

   (e) **Definitive Purchase Agreement**. All of the terms and conditions of the proposed transaction would be stated in the Purchase Agreement, to be negotiated, agreed and executed by you and us. Neither party intends to be bound by any oral or written statements or correspondence concerning the Purchase Agreement arising during the course of negotiations, notwithstanding that the same may be expressed in terms signifying a partial, preliminary or interim agreement between the parties.

   > This clause says that a full blown agreement is still necessary, as this document is only a letter of intent

Form 11-2: Letter of Intent to Purchase a Business — page 1 of 3.

(f) **Employment Agreement**. Simultaneously with the execution of the Purchase Agreement, we would enter into employment agreements with Paul Smith and John Halper on such terms and conditions as would be negotiated and agreed by them and us, including mutually agreeable provisions regarding term, base and incentive compensation, confidentiality, assignment to us of intellectual property rights in past and future work product and restrictions on competition. We would also offer employment to substantially all of Seller's employees and would expect the management team to use its reasonable best efforts to assist us to employ these individuals.

(g) **Timing**. We and you would use all reasonable efforts to complete and sign the Purchase Agreement on or before _____ and to close the transaction as promptly as practicable thereafter.

> Insert a date

2. **Expenses**. You and we will pay our respective expenses incident to this letter of intent, the Purchase Agreement and the transactions contemplated hereby and thereby.

3. **Public Announcements**. Neither you nor we will make any announcement of the proposed transaction contemplated by this letter of intent prior to the execution of the Purchase Agreement without the prior written approval of the other, which approval will not be unreasonably withheld or delayed. The foregoing shall not restrict in any respect your or our ability to communicate information concerning this letter of intent and the transactions contemplated hereby to your and our, and your and our respective affiliates', officers, directors, employees and professional advisers, and, to the extent relevant, to third parties whose consent is required in connection with the transaction contemplated by this letter of intent.

> The parties have to keep the possibility of the transaction reasonably confidential

4. **Broker's Fees**. You and we have represented to each other that no brokers or finders have been employed who would be entitled to a fee by reason of the transaction contemplated by this letter of intent.

5. **Exclusive Negotiating Rights**. In order to induce us to commit the resources, forego other potential opportunities, and incur the legal, accounting and incidental expenses necessary properly to evaluate the possibility of acquiring the assets and business described above, and to negotiate the terms of, and consummate, the transaction contemplated hereby, you agree that for a period of [45] days after the date hereof, you, your affiliates and your and their respective officers, directors, employees and agents shall not initiate, solicit, encourage, directly or indirectly, or accept any offer or proposal, regarding the possible acquisition by any person other than us, including, without limitation, by way of a purchase of shares, purchase of assets or merger, of all or any substantial part of your equity securities or assets, and shall not (other than in the ordinary course of business as heretofore conducted) provide any confidential information regarding your assets or business to any person other than us and our representatives.

> This clause gives the buyer exclusive negotiating rights to purchase the business for some period of time

6. **Miscellaneous**. This letter shall be governed by the substantive laws of the State of California without regard to conflict of law principles. This letter constitutes the entire understanding and agreement between the parties hereto and their affiliates with respect to its subject matter and supersedes all prior or contemporaneous agreements, representations, warranties and understandings of such parties (whether oral or written). No promise, inducement, representation or agreement, other than as expressly set forth herein, has been made to or by the parties hereto. This letter may be amended only by written agreement, signed by the parties to be bound by the

Form 11-2: Letter of Intent to Purchase a Business — page 2 of 3.

amendment. Evidence shall be inadmissible to show agreement by and between such parties to any term or condition contrary to or in addition to the terms and conditions contained in this letter. This letter shall be construed according to its fair meaning and not strictly for or against either party.

7. <u>**No Binding Obligation**</u>. Except for Sections 1(c) and 2 through 6, **THIS LETTER OF INTENT DOES NOT CONSTITUTE OR CREATE, AND SHALL NOT BE DEEMED TO CONSTITUTE OR CREATE, ANY LEGALLY BINDING OR ENFORCEABLE OBLIGATION ON THE PART OF EITHER PARTY TO THIS LETTER OF INTENT. NO SUCH OBLIGATION SHALL BE CREATED, EXCEPT BY THE EXECUTION AND DELIVERY OF THE PURCHASE AGREEMENT CONTAINING SUCH TERMS AND CONDITIONS OF THE PROPOSED TRANSACTION AS SHALL BE AGREED UPON BY THE PARTIES, AND THEN ONLY IN ACCORDANCE WITH THE TERMS AND CONDITIONS OF SUCH PURCHASE AGREEMENT**. The Confidentiality Agreement is hereby ratified and confirmed as a separate agreement between the parties thereto.

> This clause sets forth what is and isn't binding in this letter

If the foregoing terms and conditions are acceptable to you, please so indicate by signing the enclosed copy of this letter and returning it to the attention of the undersigned.

Very truly yours,

[Buyer]

By:_____
Title:_____

ACCEPTED AND AGREED

[Seller]

By:_____
Title:_____

Form 11-2: Letter of Intent to Purchase a Business — page 3 of 3.

- **Reimbursable costs:** If you expect the client to reimburse your out-of-pocket expenses or other costs, make sure that your contract specifically states this expectation.

- **Nonsolicitation of employees:** You should consider adding a clause that prohibits your customer from soliciting to hire away your employees who are working on the project. This clause is especially important if you have valuable, high-tech employees.

- **Late charges:** Use the contract to ensure that if the client doesn't pay your bill on time, interest begins to accrue. Typical late charges accrue at 1 to 1½ percent per month on unpaid sums.

- **Liability limitations:** Ideally, you want your contract to limit your liability in a number of ways. One typical provision says that the maximum amount of liability exposure that you have equals the amount of your fees. (After all, if your risk is greater than your fees, the job may not be worth taking.) You should also consider a clause that states that you aren't liable for consequential, punitive, or speculative damages or lost profits. Of course, various laws may limit the enforceability of such provisions, but you generally have little downside in including them in your contract.

- **Period for bringing claims:** Another way to potentially limit your liability is to limit the time period when a dissatisfied customer can bring a claim against you. For example, your contract may state that if the customer becomes aware of any problem with the services provided, then the customer has to notify you and bring a legal proceeding within six months of discovering the problem or waive the right to complain. This clause keeps someone from bringing a claim against you after your memories about the work have faded.

- **Time to perform services:** Be wary of an absolute deadline by which you must complete the services. If you don't complete the work by the deadline, what rights does the customer have? You may be in a disastrous situation if you find out that the customer can terminate the contract or withhold paying fees just because you're late finishing a project.

- **Suspension of services:** You typically want your contract to say that if you aren't paid on time, then you have the right to immediately terminate or suspend performing further services.

- **Force majeure:** This legalese clause says that if an act of God or unforeseen events (power failure, labor strike, earthquake, and so on) prevent you from doing or completing your work, your inability to perform the work is excused — at least for a reasonable time.

Form 11-3 on the CD-ROM is a sample Agreement for Professional Services.

Sales Contracts

Many small businesses sell a product and therefore need a good *Sales Contract.* The Sales Contract lays out the price, terms, and conditions for the sale of goods, equipment, or other products. The actual Sales Contract can take the form of fine print on the side of an order form or an invoice, or you can tailor it for a particular sale. The Sales Contract I discuss here can also be used instead of the Purchase Order that I discuss in the following section, except the focus here is on you as the seller as opposed to the buyer.

From your small business's perspective, you always want to start with your own form. Having your form preprinted helps it to look standard and non-negotiable. (*Note:* No standard form of Sales Contract actually exists.) As the drafter of the Sales Contract, you can make the contract more favorable to you as the seller.

Here are some important terms to address in your Sales Contract:

- **Price:** Make sure that the Sales Contract correctly states the price (often by filling in a blank space provided on the form). The Sales Contract should also spell out any discounts, installation charges, and delivery charges.

- **Price adjustments:** Consider how you may increase the prices from time to time if you're entering into a long-term contract.

- **Taxes:** Try to ensure that the purchaser is responsible for all sales taxes.

- **Payment and credit terms:** Make sure to state when payment is due. If you don't require immediate payment, consider a small discount to the purchaser if he makes payment within 10 days and a finance charge if he makes payment late (such as 30 days past due).

- **Warranties:** Decide what warranties you want to give. Ideally, you want to have limited warranties, but the competitive marketplace may require you to grant extensive warranties. Indeed, you may have one advantage over more established competitors if you offer a better warranty (one year, for example) than the current industry standard (which may be 90 days). Typical warranties state that for a designated period, the goods sold will be free from defects in workmanship and will conform to designated specifications.

- **Disclaimers:** State clearly in your Sales Contract (after you have set forth what warranties you offer) that no other warranties exist, expressed or implied, including merchantability or fitness for a particular purpose. You can usually find this disclaimer in all capital letters or boldfaced to stand out and to comply with certain provisions of the Uniform Commercial Code.

✓ **Liability limitations:** Use the Sales Contract to attempt to limit your liability under the contract. A typical clause for liability states that the seller's maximum amount of liability equals the purchase price. Make sure, too, to include a sentence that says you aren't responsible for consequential, punitive, and speculative damages or lost profits (although some laws may limit the success of the enforcement of this clause).

For a sample form of Equipment Sales Agreement, see Form 11-4 on the CD-ROM.

Purchase Orders

If you're buying products or materials from another company, you can often accomplish this purchase with a simple Purchase Order. A Purchase Order itself can be a contract. Whether you use your Purchase Order form or the seller's, consider the following points:

✓ **Complete description of goods:** Does the Purchase Order contain a complete description of the goods that you think you're buying? (This information helps you avoid misunderstandings.) Does the description include all needed parts and related items? Are you getting the latest or most updated version or model of the goods that you're purchasing?

✓ **Price:** Is the price clearly set forth? Does the purchase order include a statement that says the price sets forth the entire payment required? Be wary of hidden charges, handling fees, and delivery fees.

✓ **Delivery:** How will the seller provide the goods — will the seller deliver them, or do you pick them up? Does the seller guarantee that the goods will be ready by a certain date? Do you impose a penalty if the goods aren't ready by the designated date?

✓ **Terms:** When is payment due? Is a partial payment required in advance? Net 30 days? Payable over time?

✓ **Refund and return policy:** What refund and return rights do you have, if any? The seller wants to limit your rights. At the very least, you should get a refund or return right if the goods prove defective, don't conform to your specifications, or aren't reasonably satisfactory to you.

✓ **Tax:** How much tax must you (or the seller) pay? Who pays the tax?

✓ **Representations:** Are you buying the goods based on representations or statements from the seller or the seller's salesmen or agents? If so, make sure that the purchase order states that you're buying the goods based on those statements.

✓ **Warranties:** Do any warranties cover the goods? What do the warranties cover? How long are the warranties?

If the seller provides the Purchase Order form for you to sign, the document will undoubtedly be very one-sided (in the seller's favor). Look the purchase order over carefully and don't be afraid to make changes, even if the document is a preprinted form.

Form 11-5 on the CD-ROM gives you a sample Purchase Order to buy goods.

License Agreements

A license typically either gives you the right (and potentially the obligation) to use someone else's asset or right, or gives someone else the right to use some asset or right of yours. The *License Agreement* spells out the precise terms of those rights.

The party that gives someone use of a right or asset is known as the *licensor*. The party that receives the use of that right or asset is known as the *licensee*.

A common example of a License Agreement comes in connection with the use of software. When you buy a software product, you're buying only the right to use the software in limited ways. The License Agreement that comes along with the software sets forth these limits. Some other typical license agreements include Trade Name License, Patent License, Software License, and Copyright License.

If you're negotiating to obtain a license, or if you find yourself in the situation of providing a license for someone else, consider the following key points that the License Agreement should address:

- **Exclusivity/Nonexclusivity:** The license can be exclusive or nonexclusive. Licensors typically resist giving exclusive licenses. If the license grants exclusivity, over what areas is the license exclusive? If the license is exclusive, under what circumstances will the license convert to a nonexclusive one?

- **Term:** The License Agreement should explicitly spell out the term of the license, plus any renewal rights.

- **Payment:** The License Agreement should clearly state any upfront payments and any periodic payments that you need to maintain the license. A particular use of the license may also require an increase in payments. (For example, software licenses require greater payment as the number of users increases.)

✓ **Restrictions on use of the license:** Licensors often place a number of restrictions on use of the license, such use in certain geographic areas, or for designated purposes. (For example, a trade name licensor may grant the right to use a name, but only in a certain city.)

✓ **Infringement:** The licensee wants proof that the licensor actually owns the licensed product and that it does not infringe on the rights of third parties.

✓ **Termination:** The licensor typically defines various circumstances that allow her to terminate the License Agreement early, especially if the licensee breaches the License Agreement.

✓ **Obligation:** Licensors often impose various obligations on the licensee, such as limitations on use of the licensed materials, additional non-cash benefits that the licensor is entitled to, and other items.

✓ **Assignment and sublicense:** Depending on the agreement, the licensee may be able to assign or sublicense the license. An *assignment* typically means a transfer of all of your rights in the license, but a *sublicense* involves giving someone the right to use a portion of your rights in the license. Most License Agreements prohibit assignment or sublicensing without the licensor's approval. Licensees may want to negotiate for broader rights if they need to sublicense the product for their business.

Of course, depending on the type of license, a number of other issues arise. Check out Form 11-6 on the CD-ROM, which contains an extensive checklist of issues in dealing with Software License Agreements. Form 11-7 on the CD-ROM is a sample shrink-wrap Software License Agreement.

Joint Venture Adventures

Joint Venture Agreements typically involve two companies teaming up to develop a product, engage in research and development, start a new line of business, enter into a cooperative marketing or distribution arrangement, or some other mutually beneficial transaction.

Watch out! Joint ventures are complicated and fraught with peril. (Don't you love that phrase, "fraught with peril"? It sounds like you're jumping on the back of an alligator and riding down the Amazon River.)

You can do joint ventures in a number of ways. Both sides can set up a separate company with the two sides as shareholders. Or you can make the joint venture a contractual arrangement where the contract sets out the rights and responsibilities of the parties.

Although Joint Venture Agreements usually come with a million issues (well, at least 99), here are some key points to consider:

- ✔ **Structure:** What form will the joint venture take? A separate entity, such as a corporation, partnership, or Limited Liability Company (LLC), or just a contractual arrangement?

- ✔ **Purpose:** Does the agreement clearly set out the purpose of the joint venture? You shouldn't breeze through this step; you don't want any ambiguity here — it can sneak up and bite you from behind. You also need to make sure that the joint venture's purpose isn't so broad that it can adversely impact your core business or limit what transactions you can pursue outside of the joint venture.

- ✔ **Term:** How long will the joint venture last? Does the agreement include renewal rights? What circumstances can one party use to terminate the joint venture? You will need a "bozo" clause — that is, if your joint venture partner doesn't do what it has committed to doing (and is a bozo, to boot), then you can end the joint venture.

- ✔ **Contributions:** Does the agreement spell out each side's contributions to the joint venture? (It should.) Is each side committing a certain amount of cash? Is one side contributing some assets? What happens if the joint venture needs additional money in the future?

- ✔ **Obligations of the parties:** What will each side do? This section is especially crucial in the Joint Venture Agreement. If this information isn't clearly defined in detail, then the expectations of the parties may be different and the joint venture may be doomed to failure. (Yes, another cliché. But it's true.) For example, the contract may require one party to do "marketing," but what does marketing really entail? How many people does the party have to commit? What marketing materials do they have to prepare? What ads should they place? What minimum dollar amounts are the sides committing to for advertising? You should typically answer these types of questions in the Joint Venture Agreement.

- ✔ **Decision making:** Does the Joint Venture Agreement detail how the joint venture is going to make major and minor decisions? Do all acts relating to the joint venture need the approval of both parties, or is each joint venture partner given certain rights and latitude?

- ✔ **Dispute resolution:** If a dispute arises between the parties, how will you resolve it?

- ✔ **Employees:** Will the joint venture have separate employees, or will the parties just use their existing employees?

- ✔ **Profits:** How will you split up profits? Will one party get a priority return on the profits, or reimbursements of certain expenses, before you distribute the profits?

✓ **Special rights:** Does one party get special rights? For example, a party putting in the bulk of the cash may expect exclusive marketing rights or a license to a product developed through the joint venture.

✓ **After the joint venture ends:** What happens after the joint venture ends? Do one or both parties have rights and licenses to assets or intellectual property developed? What is the scope of such rights?

For most Joint Venture Agreements, you really do need a good lawyer to help you think through the issues and protection that you need.

For a sample of how you may structure a 50-50 joint venture into a separate joint venture corporation, check out Form 11-8 on the CD-ROM. Form 11-9 on the CD-ROM is a sample Term Sheet for Equity Investment and Strategic Alliance, which sets out the terms of the agreement between two companies.

Distribution Agreements

In many small businesses, the key to success is how well you can distribute your product. If your company's products are retail items (for example, food items, apparel, or kitchen appliances), you may want to find an experienced distributor with a great sales force and contacts. The distributor can then contract with dealers or large chains to sell your product.

The key to your relationship with the distributor is the Distribution Agreement. Although the distributor probably prefers to use its own form of Distribution Agreement (which, of course, is one-sided in the distributor's favor), consider the following key terms in the negotiations:

✓ **Territory and markets:** The contract must clearly describe the distributor's territory or business area. The contract should define the market or customer category. For example, you may want your company to handle certain major customers (like national accounts) directly and the distributor to handle other outlets. Will the territory be broad (such as the entire United States) or narrow (such as Hackensack, New Jersey)?

✓ **Exclusive versus nonexclusive:** The contract should specify whether the distributor has exclusive or nonexclusive rights to the company's products in a particular territory. But be careful here; you don't want to give exclusivity for one territory or market if you face a significant risk of lousy performance by the distributor. If you're going to give exclusive rights, consider setting sales goals that the distributor has to meet in order to maintain exclusivity.

- **Obligations of the distributor:** You must spell out the distributor's obligations. Ideally, you want a clause that says the distributor must use its "best efforts to market your products," although the distributor probably resists this phrase. So, consider setting forth in the contract the specific steps that the distributor must take (contacting all the major potential customers, appointing dealers, preparing marketing material and promotional activities, and so on).

- **Trademarks and logos:** The Distribution Agreement should prohibit the distributor from using the company's name, trademark, and logos in advertising, point of sale activities, and marketing materials except as provided in the Distribution Agreement or with the company's prior written consent. This restriction ensures that your company's goodwill, reputation, and brand name aren't hurt by the distributor's activities.

- **Product issues:** The contract needs to clearly identify the product or products that the Distribution Agreement covers. The agreement may also cover the issue of product availability and allocation of product among other distributors. The Distribution Agreement should also cover how the distributor may handle product inventory and what rights of return are available.

- **Service:** You should decide the terms for servicing the product. Will the distributor handle product servicing or warranty claims? Does the distributor have the expertise to do so? How will you compensate the distributor for servicing the product?

- **Price:** The contract needs to provide a pricing section. Generally, the price follows a schedule or the seller announces the price from time to time. The seller then typically provides an agreed discount to the distributor. You need to maintain flexibility on the price you can charge for your products.

- **Payment terms:** Practices often dictate payment terms. Ideally, you want to get an upfront deposit on a distributor's order with full payment due either 30 or 60 days after shipment. Make sure that you're comfortable with the distributor's creditworthiness.

- **Contract term and termination:** The distributor's term of the appointment and how you can terminate or renew such a term are very important issues in a Distribution Agreement. Try to get the right to terminate the contract for any reason, as long as you give at least 60 to 90 days notice. Such a termination right gives you maximum flexibility to get out of a relationship that isn't working. Also, add a provision that allows you to immediately terminate the contract if the distributor breaches its obligations or becomes bankrupt or insolvent. You must also address the potentially complicated issue of what happens after termination with respect to products, sums owed, and servicing obligations.

Distribution Agreements can be complicated. You should find out industry practice and see sample contracts from different distributors.

The Skinny on Boilerplate Text

The "boilerplate" sections usually appear at the end of the contract. Many people don't realize that the boilerplate can be crucial to a contract and isn't necessarily the same in all contracts. Indeed, boilerplate sections can be very one-sided in one way or another.

Consider some of the following key boilerplate provisions for your contracts:

- **Attorney's fees:** This clause requires that, in the event of a dispute concerning the contract between the parties, the winning party gets to recoup the attorney's fees and related costs that it racks up. If you don't have this clause, and you end up in litigation, you likely can't get your attorney's fees reimbursed — even if you win. Then again, you may not want an attorney's fees clause if the other side to a contract is a big well-funded company that would run up large legal bills.

- **Entire agreement:** This clause sets forth the principle that the contract is the final, complete, and total expression of the parties' agreement. This clause attempts to prevent a party from claiming that the deal contains other promises or terms that aren't explicitly set forth in the written contract.

- **Jurisdiction:** This clause seeks to establish exactly where you have to resolve any disputes. For example, if you're a San Francisco-based seller and the buyer is in New York, you want the contract to say that you or the buyer can bring and resolve all disputes only in San Francisco.

- **Modification of agreement:** This clause says that you may modify the contract only in writing, and all parties must sign it. You don't want someone to say that a subsequent conversation or telephone call changed the terms of your written agreement.

- **Notice:** This clause sets forth how you should give notices and other communications to the involved parties.

- **Ambiguities:** This clause says that a court or arbitrator shall interpret any ambiguous language in the contract as to its fair meaning and not strictly for or against any party.

- **Arbitration:** This clause can be tricky. In the event of a dispute between the parties, the clause requires that you resolve the dispute by binding arbitration and not litigation. Arbitration clauses can vary a great deal, and you must answer questions like who is the arbitrator, what arbitration rules you must follow, and where you will hold the arbitration.

- **Assignment:** This clause sets forth the rights or prohibitions on the contract's assignment (or "transfer"). Typically, this clause says that the contract isn't assignable, but the parties may want to allow assignment under certain circumstances. A *nonassignable contract* means that you can't transfer your rights or obligations under the contract to anyone else.

You may find other clauses appropriate to your particular situation. You need to carefully decide which ones are best for your needs and which ones you should modify or delete. Typically, the most important clauses are the "Entire Agreement," "Attorney's Fees," and "Jurisdiction" clauses.

Form 11-10 later in this chapter gives you an example of language from a number of boilerplate clauses. Consider adding the appropriate clauses to the end of your contracts.

Amending a Contract

If you want to change some of the terms after you have signed a contract, both parties have to agree to the changes. If you're making short or minor changes, you can make the changes as a separate Amendment form. If you want to make major changes, consider drafting a new contract that specifically states that the new contract supersedes and terminates the old contract.

If you go the Amendment-form route, make sure that your Amendment covers the following:

✔ The name of the earlier contract, its date, and the parties to the contract

✔ The specific changes to the contract

✔ A statement that, except as to the terms contained in the amendment, the entire original contract continues to remain in full force and effect

✔ A statement that, in the event of any conflict with the terms of the original contract, the amendment prevails

✔ Signatures by all parties to the original contract

✔ The amendment date

Form 11-11, which follows Form 11-10 later in this chapter, is a sample Amendment of a Sales Contract.

IMPORTANT BOILERPLATE PROVISIONS FOR CONTRACTS

Miscellaneous

(a)   Choice of Law. This Agreement, and any dispute arising from the relationship between the parties to this Agreement, shall be governed by *[e.g., California]* law, excluding any laws that direct the application of another jurisdiction's laws.

(b)   Attorney Fees Provision. In any litigation, arbitration, or other proceeding by which one party either seeks to enforce its rights under this Agreement (whether in contract, tort, or both) or seeks a declaration of any rights or obligations under this Agreement, the prevailing party shall be awarded its reasonable attorney fees, and costs and expenses incurred.

> Very important — this clause lets you recover your attorneys' fees if you are the prevailing party in a dispute

(c)   Notice. Any notices required or permitted to be given hereunder shall be given in writing and shall be delivered (a) in person, (b) by certified mail, postage prepaid, return receipt requested, (c) by facsimile, or (d) by a commercial overnight courier that guarantees next day delivery and provides a receipt, and such notices shall be addressed as follows:

If to _____: _____
                      _____
                      Attention:
                      Fax:

If to _____: _____
                      _____
                      Attention:
                      Fax:

or to such other address as either party may from time to time specify in writing to the other party. Any notice shall be effective only upon delivery, which for any notice given by facsimile shall mean notice which has been received by the party to whom it is sent as evidenced by confirmation slip.

(d)   Modification of Agreement. This Agreement may be supplemented, amended, or modified only by the mutual agreement of the parties. No supplement, amendment, or modification of this Agreement shall be binding unless it is in writing and signed by all parties.

> This clause says that the agreement can only be amended in writing

(e)   Entire Agreement. This Agreement and all other agreements, exhibits, and schedules referred to in this Agreement constitute(s) the final, complete, and exclusive statement of the terms of the agreement between the parties pertaining to the subject matter of this Agreement and supersedes all prior and contemporaneous understandings or agreements of the parties. This Agreement may not be contradicted by evidence of any prior or contemporaneous statements or agreements. No party has been induced to enter into this Agreement by, nor is any party relying on, any representation, understanding, agreement, commitment or warranty outside those expressly set forth in this Agreement.

> This clause says that the written agreement constitutes the entire understanding and agreement of the parties, and that no oral or other writings matter

Form 11-10: Important Boilerplate Provisions for Contracts — page 1 of 4.

(f)   Severability of Agreement. If any term or provision of this Agreement is determined to be illegal, unenforceable, or invalid in whole or in part for any reason, such illegal, unenforceable, or invalid provisions or part thereof shall be stricken from this Agreement, and such provision shall not affect the legality, enforceability, or validity of the remainder of this Agreement. If any provision or part thereof of this Agreement is stricken in accordance with the provisions of this section, then this stricken provision shall be replaced, to the extent possible, with a legal, enforceable, and valid provision that is as similar in tenor to the stricken provision as is legally possible.

This clause says that if one part of the agreement is invalid, the remaining parts still remain

(g)   Separate Writings and Exhibits. The following [*e.g., agreements, exhibits, schedules, or other separate writings*] constitute a part of this Agreement and are incorporated into this Agreement by this reference: [*List separate writings by name and date*]. Should any inconsistency exist or arise between a provision of this Agreement and a provision of any exhibit, schedule, or other incorporated writing, the provision of this Agreement shall prevail.

(h)   Time of the Essence. Time is of the essence in respect to all provisions of this Agreement that specify a time for performance; provided, however, that the foregoing shall not be construed to limit or deprive a party of the benefits of any grace or use period allowed in this Agreement.

This clause says that the time for performance under the agreement is crucial

(i)   Survival. Except as otherwise expressly provided in this Agreement, representations, warranties, and covenants contained in this Agreement, or in any instrument, certificate, exhibit, or other writing intended by the parties to be a part of this Agreement, shall survive for ___ years after the date of this Agreement.

(j)   Ambiguities. Each party and its counsel have participated fully in the review and revision of this Agreement. Any rule of construction to the effect that ambiguities are to be resolved against the drafting party shall not apply in interpreting this Agreement. The language in this Agreement shall be interpreted as to its fair meaning and not strictly for or against any party.

(k)   Waiver. No waiver of a breach, failure of any condition, or any right or remedy contained in or granted by the provisions of this Agreement shall be effective unless it is in writing and signed by the party waiving the breach, failure, right, or remedy. No waiver of any breach, failure, right, or remedy, whether or not similar, nor shall any waiver constitute a continuing waiver unless the writing so specifies.

(l)   Headings. The headings in this Agreement are included for convenience only and shall neither affect the construction or interpretation of any provision in this Agreement nor affect any of the rights or obligations of the parties to this Agreement.

Form 11-10: Important Boilerplate Provisions for Contracts — page 2 of 4.

(m) <u>Necessary Acts, Further Assurances</u>. The parties shall at their own cost and expense execute and deliver such further documents and instruments and shall take such other actions as may be reasonably required or appropriate to evidence or carry out the intent and purposes of this Agreement.

(n) <u>Execution</u>. This Agreement may be executed in counterparts and by fax.

(o) <u>Consent to Jurisdiction and Forum Selection</u>. The parties hereto agree that all actions or proceedings arising in connection with this Agreement shall be tried and litigated exclusively in the State and Federal courts located in the County of _____, State of ____. The aforementioned choice of venue is intended by the parties to be mandatory and not permissive in nature, thereby precluding the possibility of litigation between the parties with respect to or arising out of this Agreement in any jurisdiction other than that specified in this paragraph. Each party hereby waives any right it may have to assert the doctrine of forum non conveniens or similar doctrine or to object to venue with respect to any proceeding brought in accordance with this paragraph, and stipulates that the State and Federal courts located in the County of _____, State of _____ shall have in personam jurisdiction and venue over each of them for the purpose of litigating any dispute, controversy, or proceeding arising out of or related to this Agreement. Each party hereby authorizes and accepts service of process sufficient for personal jurisdiction in any action against it as contemplated by this paragraph by registered or certified mail, return receipt requested, postage prepaid, to its address for the giving of notices as set forth in this Agreement. Any final judgement rendered against a party in any action or proceeding shall be conclusive as to the subject of such final judgement and may be enforced in other jurisdictions in any manner provided by law.

> This clause says that all disputes can only be brought in the agreed upon county

(p) <u>Jury Trial Waivers</u>. To the fullest extent permitted by law, and as separately bargained-for-consideration, each party hereby waives any right to trial by jury in any action, suit, proceeding, or counterclaim of any kind arising out of or relating to this Agreement.

> This clause says that both sides are waiving a trial by jury and that any case is to be heard by a judge

(q) <u>Specific Performance</u>. The parties acknowledge that it will be impossible to measure in money the damage to them caused by any failure to comply with the covenants set forth in Section _____, that each such covenant is material, and that in the event of any such failure, the injured party will not have an adequate remedy at law or in damages. Therefore, the parties consent to the issuance of an injunction or the enforcement of other equitable remedies against them at the suit of the other, without bond or other security, to compel performance of all of the terms of Section _____, and waive the defense of the availability of relief in damages.

(r) <u>Representation on Authority of Parties/Signatories</u>. Each person signing this Agreement represents and warrants that he or she is duly authorized and has legal capacity to execute and deliver this Agreement. Each party represents and warrants to the other that the execution and delivery of the Agreement and the performance of such party's obligations hereunder have been duly authorized and that the Agreement is a valid and legal agreement binding on such party and enforceable in accordance with its terms.

(s) <u>Force Majeure</u>. No party shall be liable for any failure to perform its obligations in connection with any action described in this Agreement, if such failure results from any act of God, riot, war, civil unrest, flood, earthquake, or other cause beyond such

Form 11-10: Important Boilerplate Provisions for Contracts — page 3 of 4.

party's reasonable control (including any mechanical, electronic, or communications failure, but excluding failure caused by a party's financial condition or negligence).

(t)   Assignment.   Neither party shall voluntarily or by operation of law assign, hypothecate, give, transfer, mortgage, sublet, license, or otherwise transfer or encumber all or part of its rights, duties, or other interests in this Agreement or the proceeds thereof (collectively, "Assignment"), without the other party's prior written consent. Any attempt to make an Assignment in violation of this provision shall be a material default under this Agreement and any Assignment in violation of this provision shall be null and void.

[(u)   Arbitration.   Any controversy, claim or dispute arising out of or relating to this Agreement, shall be settled by binding arbitration in [City], [State]. Such arbitration shall be conducted in accordance with the then prevailing commercial arbitration rules of JAMS/Endispute ("JAMS"), with the following exceptions if in conflict: (a) one arbitrator shall be chosen by JAMS; (b) each party to the arbitration will pay its pro rata share of the expenses and fees of the arbitrator, together with other expenses of the arbitration incurred or approved by the arbitrator; and (c) arbitration may proceed in the absence of any party if written notice (pursuant to the JAMS' rules and regulations) of the proceedings has been given to such party. The parties agree to abide by all decisions and awards rendered in such proceedings. Such decisions and awards rendered by the arbitrator shall be final and conclusive and may be entered in any court having jurisdiction thereof as a basis of judgment and of the issuance of execution for its collection. All such controversies, claims or disputes shall be settled in this manner in lieu of any action at law or equity; [provided however, that nothing in this subsection shall be construed as precluding the bringing an action for injunctive relief or other equitable relief]. The arbitrator shall not have the right to award punitive damages or speculative damages to either party and shall not have the power to amend this Agreement. The arbitrator shall be required to follow applicable law. [IF FOR ANY REASON THIS ARBITRATION CLAUSE BECOMES NOT APPLICABLE, THEN EACH PARTY, TO THE FULLEST EXTENT PERMITTED BY APPLICABLE LAW, HEREBY IRREVOCABLY WAIVES ALL RIGHT TO TRIAL BY JURY AS TO ANY ISSUE RELATING HERETO IN ANY ACTION, PROCEEDING, OR COUNTERCLAIM ARISING OUT OF OR RELATING TO THIS AGREEMENT OR ANY OTHER MATTER INVOLVING THE PARTIES HERETO.]]

> This clause provides that disputes are to be handled by arbitration instead of litigation

Form 11-10: Important Boilerplate Provisions for Contracts — page 4 of 4.

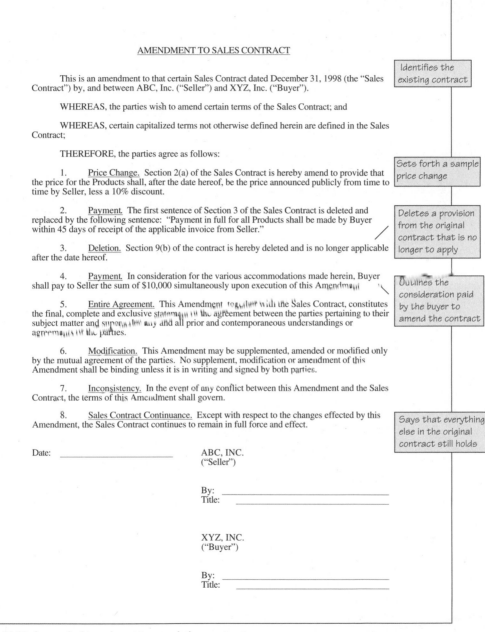

AMENDMENT TO SALES CONTRACT

This is an amendment to that certain Sales Contract dated December 31, 1998 (the "Sales Contract") by, and between ABC, Inc. ("Seller") and XYZ, Inc. ("Buyer").

WHEREAS, the parties wish to amend certain terms of the Sales Contract; and

WHEREAS, certain capitalized terms not otherwise defined herein are defined in the Sales Contract;

THEREFORE, the parties agree as follows:

1.   Price Change. Section 2(a) of the Sales Contract is hereby amend to provide that the price for the Products shall, after the date hereof, be the price announced publicly from time to time by Seller, less a 10% discount.

2.   Payment. The first sentence of Section 3 of the Sales Contract is deleted and replaced by the following sentence: "Payment in full for all Products shall be made by Buyer within 45 days of receipt of the applicable invoice from Seller."

3.   Deletion. Section 9(b) of the contract is hereby deleted and is no longer applicable after the date hereof.

4.   Payment. In consideration for the various accommodations made herein, Buyer shall pay to Seller the sum of $10,000 simultaneously upon execution of this Amendment.

5.   Entire Agreement. This Amendment together with the Sales Contract, constitutes the final, complete and exclusive statement of the agreement between the parties pertaining to their subject matter and supersedes any and all prior and contemporaneous understandings or agreements of the parties.

6.   Modification. This Amendment may be supplemented, amended or modified only by the mutual agreement of the parties. No supplement, modification or amendment of this Amendment shall be binding unless it is in writing and signed by both parties.

7.   Inconsistency. In the event of any conflict between this Amendment and the Sales Contract, the terms of this Amendment shall govern.

8.   Sales Contract Continuance. Except with respect to the changes effected by this Amendment, the Sales Contract continues to remain in full force and effect.

Date: _____   ABC, INC.
("Seller")

By: _____
Title: _____

XYZ, INC.
("Buyer")

By: _____
Title: _____

Form 11-11: A sample Amendment to an existing contract.

Forms on the CD-ROM

Check out these contract-related forms on the CD-ROM:

Form 11-1	**Contract Checklist**	A checklist of important terms to consider for contracts
Form 11-2	**Letter of Intent to Purchase a Business**	A sample letter of intent for the purchase of a business
Form 11-3	**Agreement for Professional Services**	A sample agreement for the rendering of professional services
Form 11-4	**Equipment Sales Agreement**	A sample agreement for the sale of equipment
Form 11-5	**Purchase Order**	A sample purchase order to buy goods
Form 11-6	**Checklist of Issues in Drafting and Negotiating Software License Agreements**	A checklist of issues to consider when drafting and negotiating Software License Agreements
Form 11-7	**License Agreement**	A sample shrink-wrap software license agreement
Form 11-8	**Letter of Intent for Joint Venture**	A sample letter of intent to form a 50-50 joint venture company
Form 11-9	**Term Sheet for Equity Investment and Strategic Alliance**	A sample Joint Venture Agreement
Form 11-10	**Important Boilerplate Provisions for Contracts**	Numerous, sample "boilerplate" or "miscellaneous" provisions for contracts
Form 11-11	**Amendment to Sales Contract**	A sample form of amendment to an existing Sales Contract
Form 11-12	**Bill of Sale and Assignment**	A sample simple form of Bill of Sale

Chapter 12

Legal Issues

. . . .

In This Chapter

▶ Staying clear of problems with the law

▶ Protecting personal property from business debt

▶ Delving into state and local laws

. . . .

*W*hat's a small business owner to do? You're only out to make an honest buck and maybe grow your business, but you have to stay on the right side of a kazillion laws (don't you wish you owned the domain name for www.kazillion.com?). To make things even more difficult, at least half of those kazillion laws are obscure. Failing to comply with various laws can have disastrous consequences for your business. And if you're not careful, the courts may find you personally liable for violating those laws (in addition to finding your company liable).

In this chapter, I make it my mission to give you a leg up in finding your way through this maze of red tape. I tell you about some steps that you can take to minimize your liability and your personal exposure in dealing with a number of key laws that may affect your business.

Avoiding Legal Wrangles

Listing every law that may apply to the formation and operation of a small business is almost impossible; however, you should be aware of a number of categories of law. Here is a list of the most common laws that affect your business:

✔ **Business formation laws:** See Chapter 3 for a discussion of the proper steps to take to form a corporation.

✔ **Consumer protection laws:** Various state and federal laws govern credit rules and disclosures to protect consumers from fraudulent acts, misleading advertisements, and defective products.

✔ **Contract laws:** Check out Chapter 11 for some advice on negotiating and preparing contracts, but note that state law may affect what provisions you can put in your contracts.

✔ **Employment hiring laws:** Check out the discussion of these laws in Chapter 7.

✔ **Environmental laws and regulations:** Various state and federal laws and regulations deal with issues like emissions, asbestos, hazardous waste, the discharge of water, and other items that affect the environment.

✔ **Intellectual property laws:** See Chapter 13 for a discussion of how these laws affect your business.

✔ **License and permit laws:** I discuss these laws later in this chapter, in the section "State and local business licenses."

✔ **Other employment laws:** Chapter 9 gives you ideas on how to avoid employee problems.

✔ **Securities laws:** Chapter 4 tells you how to comply with these laws when selling stock or other securities.

✔ **Tax laws:** Chapter 6 discusses some of the income tax laws, but note that you may have a variety of real property and personal property tax rules and assessments to deal with.

✔ **Zoning laws:** Local ordinances limit the use of a particular property and may regulate parking, waste disposal, signage, business that you can conduct, and so on.

Keeping good records

You have to keep good records in order to comply with various laws and to properly operate your business. So, you need to establish a system where you can file records in a way that allows you to easily and efficiently retrieve them.

You may want to consider categorizing your important business records as shown in the following list. You can combine one or more of these categories or break them down into even more categories, depending on the nature and extent of your business. Here's a good start toward organizing your business records:

✔ **Accounting and bookkeeping records:** Sales and expense information, inventory, ledgers, Income Statements, Balance Sheets, Cash Flow Statements, and other financial statements.

✔ **Bank records:** Bank statements, cancelled checks, bank reconciliations, notices from and to your bank, deposit slips, and any loan-related notices and documents.

- **Contracts:** All contracts that you have entered into, including real estate leases, equipment leases, Purchase Agreements, Sales Agreements, Joint Venture Agreements, Work for Hire Agreements, and other contracts. (See Chapter 11 for more information.)

- **Corporate records:** If your business is a corporation, these records include the Articles of Incorporation, bylaws, shareholder minutes and consents, board minutes and consents, state filings, Actions of Incorporator, and amendments to the various corporate documents. If your business is not a corporation, then you may find Partnership Agreements, LLC documents, Consents of the Owners, and similar records relevant. (See Chapters 1 and 3 for more information.)

- **Correspondence:** Letters sent by mail, certainly, but also faxes and important e-mail that you don't want to lose and do want to keep in hard copy. Include correspondence you receive and send.

- **Employee records:** Any records related to your business's employees, including completed employment applications, actual employment offer letters, employee handbooks or policies, Employment Agreements, performance appraisals, employee attendance records, employee termination letters, W-2s, and any settlement agreements with terminated employees. (See Chapters 7, 8, and 9 for more information.)

- **Business forms:** Plan to build up and maintain a host of standard forms that you use in the business. This stockpile should include your standard form of Purchase Order, Sales Agreement, offer letter to new employees, employment applications, and can include a number of the forms found on the CD-ROM.

- **Intellectual property records:** Any trademark applications, copyright filings, patent filings and patents, licenses, and Confidentiality or Non-Disclosure Agreements.

- **Marketing and advertising records:** Marketing brochures, print ads, Web banners, radio ad text, and other marketing materials.

- **Permits and licenses:** Permits, licenses, or registration forms that you need to operate the businesses, whether required under federal, state, or local law.

- **Stock records:** The company's Stock Ledger — where you record all stock and other securities transactions — copies of Stock Certificates, Options and Warrants, and copies of all securities law filings. (Check out Chapter 4 for a discussion of all of this paperwork.)

- **Tax records:** Quarterly and annual federal and state income tax filings, W-9 filings for independent contractors, records supporting tax filings, withholding tax records, and other tax related matters.

Recordkeeping can be a tedious chore, but failure to keep track of your records can cost you big-time in case of an audit or lawsuit. So start off by keeping good records in the categories that I suggest above and expand from there, if you think your business needs it.

Taking the corporate quiz: Are you legal?

You sometimes need to step back from the day-to-day grind of running a business and think about whether you're doing everything necessary to comply with the myriad laws out there. You should also think about whether you're doing enough to protect the business itself (from lawsuits filed by customers or employees, for example).

Form 12-1 shows a Small Business Legal Audit Checklist. You can use this form to help you think about some of the things that may be a problem if you don't handle them correctly. Fill out the checklist and then review it with your lawyer so that you can identify any problems and work towards solutions.

Going Down with the Ship (Not!)

You may be a big fan of the blockbuster hit *Titanic,* but if your business starts to go down, believe me, you want to be safely on the lifeboat, not clinging to the railing as the water rushes over the bow. The following sections give you tips that can help you stay above water even if you run into a few icebergs before you get your business formula down pat.

Avoiding personal liability

Your company is subject to a number of legal obligations and liabilities. Ideally, you want these liabilities to belong to the business and not run the risk that the business owners face personal exposure to business liabilities.

If you're a sole proprietorship, you can't escape that liability. But if the business is a corporation or Limited Liability Company (LLC) and you follow some basic steps, you can likely avoid the personal liability problem.

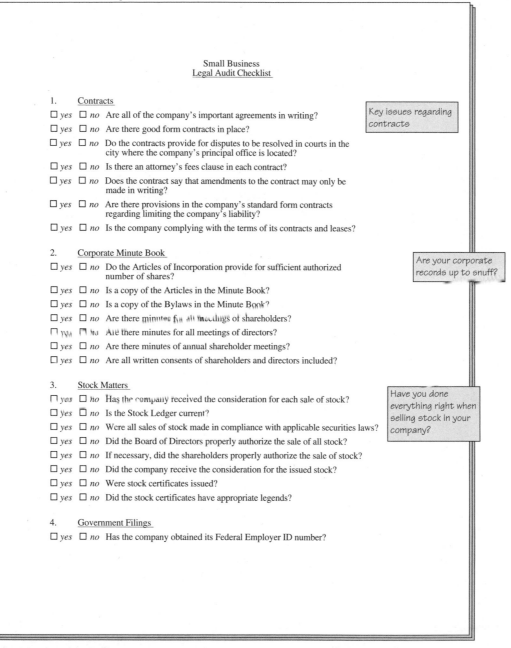

Small Business
Legal Audit Checklist

1.   Contracts

☐ *yes* ☐ *no* Are all of the company's important agreements in writing?

☐ *yes* ☐ *no* Are there good form contracts in place?

☐ *yes* ☐ *no* Do the contracts provide for disputes to be resolved in courts in the
city where the company's principal office is located?

☐ *yes* ☐ *no* Is there an attorney's fees clause in each contract?

☐ *yes* ☐ *no* Does the contract say that amendments to the contract may only be
made in writing?

☐ *yes* ☐ *no* Are there provisions in the company's standard form contracts
regarding limiting the company's liability?

☐ *yes* ☐ *no* Is the company complying with the terms of its contracts and leases?

> Key issues regarding contracts

2.   Corporate Minute Book

☐ *yes* ☐ *no* Do the Articles of Incorporation provide for sufficient authorized
number of shares?

☐ *yes* ☐ *no* Is a copy of the Articles in the Minute Book?

☐ *yes* ☐ *no* Is a copy of the Bylaws in the Minute Book?

☐ *yes* ☐ *no* Are there minutes for all meetings of shareholders?

☐ *yes* ☐ *no* Are there minutes for all meetings of directors?

☐ *yes* ☐ *no* Are there minutes of annual shareholder meetings?

☐ *yes* ☐ *no* Are all written consents of shareholders and directors included?

> Are your corporate records up to snuff?

3.   Stock Matters

☐ *yes* ☐ *no* Has the company received the consideration for each sale of stock?

☐ *yes* ☐ *no* Is the Stock Ledger current?

☐ *yes* ☐ *no* Were all sales of stock made in compliance with applicable securities laws?

☐ *yes* ☐ *no* Did the Board of Directors properly authorize the sale of all stock?

☐ *yes* ☐ *no* If necessary, did the shareholders properly authorize the sale of stock?

☐ *yes* ☐ *no* Did the company receive the consideration for the issued stock?

☐ *yes* ☐ *no* Were stock certificates issued?

☐ *yes* ☐ *no* Did the stock certificates have appropriate legends?

> Have you done everything right when selling stock in your company?

4.   Government Filings

☐ *yes* ☐ *no* Has the company obtained its Federal Employer ID number?

Form 12-1: Legal Audit Checklist — page 1 of 3.

□ *yes* □ *no* Has the company obtained its State Employer ID number?

□ *yes* □ *no* Have any required local and state licenses and permits been obtained?

□ *yes* □ *no* Has the company qualified to do business in all states it is required to?

□ *yes* □ *no* Have all annual information statements been filed with the Secretary of State? (varies from state to state)

5.   Intellectual Property Protection

□ *yes* □ *no* Have trademark registrations been obtained for company products and services?

□ *yes* □ *no* Is the "TM" or "SM" or "®" notice displayed properly on all company literature?

□ *yes* □ *no* Is a proper copyright notice put on all company copyrightable materials?

□ *yes* □ *no* Have patents been applied for company-owned inventions and discoveries?

□ *yes* □ *no* Is a trade secret protection program appropriate?

□ *yes* □ *no* Have employees signed appropriate Confidentiality and Invention Assignment Agreement?

□ *yes* □ *no* Have consultants and independent contractors signed appropriate Confidentiality and Invention Assignment Agreements?

□ *yes* □ *no* Is the company infringing the intellectual property rights of others?

□ *yes* □ *no* Is there a program in place to determine if others are violating the company's intellectual property rights?

□ *yes* □ *no* Are all needed licenses obtained?

□ *yes* □ *no* Is the company complying with all license agreements to which it is a licensee?

> Are you doing things correctly to protect your trademark, copyrights, and so on?

6.   Employment

□ *yes* □ *no* Does the Company have an "at will" employment policy in place?

□ *yes* □ *no* Do interviewers of prospective employees know what they can and can't ask?

□ *yes* □ *no* Is there a Non-Discrimination Policy in place?

□ *yes* □ *no* Is each prospective employee required to fill out a good form of Employment Application?

□ *yes* □ *no* Are employees treated fairly and evenly?

□ *yes* □ *no* Is there a Sexual Harassment Policy in place?

□ *yes* □ *no* Are job offer letters to new employees carefully drafted?

□ *yes* □ *no* Does the company have all needed forms from employees (W-2, I-9, etc.)?

> Are your employment policies in good shape?

7.   Recordkeeping

□ *yes* □ *no* Is the company keeping good records of its income and expenses?

□ *yes* □ *no* Is the company keeping track of all of its contracts?

□ *yes* □ *no* Is the company keeping track of all employee records?

> Are you keeping good records?

Form 12-1: Legal Audit Checklist — page 2 of 3.

□ *yes* □ *no* Is the company keeping track of all tax filings required?

8.   Laws. Has the company determined the applicability of the following laws to its business?

□ *yes* □ *no* Environmental laws

□ *yes* □ *no* Worker Safety laws

□ *yes* □ *no* Securities laws

□ *yes* □ *no* Consumer protection laws

□ *yes* □ *no* Advertising laws

□ *yes* □ *no* Employment laws

□ *yes* □ *no* ERISA

□ *yes* □ *no* Product liability laws

□ *yes* □ *no* Corporate laws

□ *yes* □ *no* Tax laws

□ *yes* □ *no* Commercial and Real Property laws

> Are you aware of the laws applicable to your business?

Form 12-1: Legal Audit Checklist — page 3 of 3.

A corporation can reduce the possibility that the individual shareholders are subject to liability for the corporation's obligations by following the guidelines listed below:

- ✔ **Adequate capitalization:** The corporation should ensure that it starts with a reasonable amount of money to meet its expenses and enable it to carry on its business.

- ✔ **Insurance:** The corporation should obtain insurance to cover all of its needs.

- ✔ **Formalities:** The corporation should observe all *corporate formalities,* which generally refer to treating your business as a separate entity and properly documenting the formation of the corporation, bylaws, and issuance of stock; and recording important resolutions and the minutes of shareholder and board of directors meetings. (Chapter 3 gives you a good idea of the necessary steps to take.)

- ✔ **Proper signatures:** The officers and other authorized persons should execute all letters, contracts, or other documents — signed on behalf of the corporation — in the corporation's name rather than in their individual capacity. To do so, a signature should give the corporation's name and then the officer's signature, name, and title. The signature block should generally be drafted as follows:

  XYZ, Inc.
  By: Jane Smith, President

- ✔ **No commingling:** You shouldn't commingle corporate funds with the funds of the individual shareholders or any other entity involved with the corporation. Furthermore, the corporation should maintain separate operations and records from those of other entities or subsidiaries and its shareholders.

- ✔ **Withholding:** You should make all employer withholding tax payments.

Negotiating guaranties

A number of lenders, landlords, and other creditors may insist on a personal guaranty from the company's founders or major owners before extending credit or signing a contract. A *personal guaranty* requires that the person giving the guaranty (the *guarantor*) be responsible for paying the creditor's claim in case the company doesn't pay.

Piercing the corporate veil

A corporation's creditors generally can't sue the corporation's shareholders for their personal assets (this restriction is known as *limited liability* for the shareholders). Under certain circumstances, however, creditors may be able to satisfy corporate obligations by going against shareholders' assets. Proceeding against the personal assets of the shareholders of a corporation is known as *piercing the corporate veil.*

The case law has generally permitted plaintiffs to sue for the assets of shareholders in cases of fraud or similar wrongdoing where permitting a shareholder to "hide" behind a false or flimsy corporate veil would be unfair. Although these cases aren't plentiful and usually involve bad facts (such as the shareholders totally ignoring corporate formalities), you should note that the mere incorporation of a business doesn't automatically prevent the corporation's creditors from proceeding against the assets of the shareholders, and you should take the proper steps to preserve limited liability.

Accordingly, you should treat the corporation as a separate entity — if you don't, courts may not. You should properly document transactions between the corporation and its shareholders, officers, and directors, and make sure that these transactions are fair and reasonable wherever possible (and, in any event, in accordance with applicable corporate law).

A personal guaranty exposes the guarantor's personal assets (savings, home, and so on) for repayment of the obligation. And someone can call upon the personal guaranty, even (or especially) if the company goes into bankruptcy. So obviously, if you can, avoid giving any personal guaranties.

If the other side still insists on a personal guaranty, see if you can negotiate some of the following:

- ✔ **Bigger deposit:** Ask if the creditor will forego a personal guaranty if you put up a bigger security deposit. Landlords sometimes agree to such a concept. Try to also get interest on your security deposit.

- ✔ **Limited term of guaranty:** Ask for the personal guaranty to go away after a certain period of time, as long as the company has complied with its obligations. For example, the personal guaranty may automatically terminate one year after you sign the lease with a landlord, if the company has paid rent promptly that year.

- ✔ **Limited guaranty:** Instead of having the guaranty cover all of the company's obligations, consider negotiating a maximum amount of liability — such as $25,000.

Of course, if you're the one requesting a guaranty, make sure that it's broad and enforceable. Form 12-2 on the CD-ROM contains a broad guaranty.

Checking into State and Local Laws

Unfortunately, I can't make this book cover the state laws of all 50 of these United States; that book would be the size of 16 telephone books and weigh around 70 pounds (making it difficult to take with you to the beach). The CD-ROM would be the size of a large pepperoni pizza (making it difficult to fit in that little drive). And even with a two-year head start, I'd finish about the time Halley's comet makes its next appearance (making it difficult for me to earn royalties). Instead, I point out some areas of law that you should check out yourself at the state and local level.

Getting state and local business licenses

State laws regulate many professions, businesses, and occupations, often requiring that the individual or business meet various qualifications before granting required certificates of registration, business licenses, or permits. Often, cities also require that the individual or business doing business within the city limits obtain a local business license.

States often require licensing of people or entities practicing in certain areas, including accountants, architects, bill collectors, building contractors, cosmetologists, dentists, engineers, pest control specialists, pharmacists, physicians, private investigators, psychologists, real estate agents, and technicians.

To qualify for a license for a profession or occupation, you may need to pass certain tests and have certain training or educational background. For example, real estate agents typically have to pass a test and work for a real estate broker. And most licenses are good only for a limited period of time — you have to renew them periodically. To get the renewal, you may have to take continuing education classes.

Some license laws (federal or state) require licenses or permits based on the products sold or services provided — firearms, food, gasoline, investment advice, liquor, lottery tickets, tobacco products, stocks, and trucking are just a few examples.

You can get information about the licenses and permits required for your business from a variety of sources, including the following:

- ✔ Office of Small Businesses at the state government level
- ✔ State and local Chambers of Commerce

> ✔ City government office
>
> ✔ Trade associations or professional groups
>
> ✔ Government Web sites

Registering fictitious business names

If the company plans to transact business under a name other than the one listed in its charter document (for instance, the Articles of Incorporation for a California corporation), it may have to file a fictitious business name statement with the county clerk in which the company has its principal place of business. In some places, the company may also need to publish a notification in a newspaper. Business folks commonly refer to the fictitious business name as a *d.b.a.* or *doing business as,* such as "Jones Enterprises d.b.a. American Glass & Metals."

You can typically get Fictitious Business Name Statement Forms from the county clerk's office of the county in which you intend to file, or from the newspaper that will be publishing the statement. Filing fees vary with the county or with the newspaper used for publication. Check out the instructions included within the Fictitious Business Name Statement Form.

Filing information with the state

State law may require you to file certain information forms with the Secretary of State or other governmental entity. To find out which information filings may apply in your state, contact your Secretary of State's office.

In California, for example, you must file several forms to legally set up the business. A California corporation has to file Form 1502 (Form 12-3 on the CD-ROM) within 90 days after the filing of its original Articles of Incorporation — and then periodically after that. The statement requires that you disclose the names and addresses of the company's directors and principal officers, and the address of its principal executive office or of its principal business office in California. You must also supply a general statement of the company's principal business activity and the name of its agent for service and process. You must include a filing fee with the statement; failure to file the form can result in suspension of the company's corporate powers. If you don't file the statement in a timely manner, the state can assess a penalty against the company.

Qualifying to do business in other states

You may want to consider conducting business in a state other than the one in which you organize the company. If so, you need to determine whether the company has to be qualified or registered to do business in that other state. The scope and extent of the company's activities govern whether you need such qualification.

State law in most states provides that a *foreign corporation* (that is, one created under the laws of another state) may not "do business" within the state unless it *qualifies* by making appropriate filings. For example, if you're a Delaware corporation but mainly operate in New York, you have to file to qualify to do business in New York. Here are some typical activities that require qualification in other states:

✔ Doing a substantial amount of ordinary business in the state

✔ Maintaining an active office in the state

✔ Manufacturing products in the state

Note, however, that much less significant activities may require qualification in some states.

Watch out for the state qualification requirements to legally "doing business." Although the penalties for failure to qualify vary from state to state, the following penalties may apply:

✔ A denial of the right to enforce contracts in the state courts

✔ Monetary fines on the company

✔ Monetary fines on the company's agents or officers

✔ Personal liability on the officers or agents for the acts of the company in the state

You should also consider reviewing the labor laws, taxing policies, and other business-related regulations of other states where the company plans to do business to determine whether regulations may adversely affect the company's operations in that state.

Forms on the CD-ROM

Form 12-1	**Small Business Legal Audit Checklist**	A checklist for the small business to review concerning its legal operations
Form 12-2	**Guaranty**	A pro-creditor-oriented form that guarantees performance and payment of certain obligations
Form 12-3	**Form 1502**	Statement by Domestic Stock Corporation (California)
Form 12-4	**General Power of Attorney**	A form that grants broad general powers to act on behalf of the person signing the form
Form 12-5	**Special Power of Attorney**	A form that grants specific powers to act on behalf of the person signing the form
Form 12-6	**Demand to Guarantor for Payment**	A notice to a guarantor of an obligation that the debtor is in default and that the guarantor demands payment now

Chapter 13

Protecting Your Ideas and Inventions

*M*any businesses need to protect their intellectual property. The term *intellectual property* covers a variety of rights in inventions, trade secrets, and creative works. Federal law (patents, for example) or state law (such as trade secret laws) may protect these rights.

Both the company's founders and its investors have a stake in ensuring that the company protects its intellectual property and avoids infringing the intellectual property of third parties. The company must take firm steps to achieve these goals. For example, a new company should ensure that the founders assign (or license) any existing intellectual property relevant to the new company's product. All of the company's employees and independent contractors should sign agreements that retain the company's intellectual property rights if an employee develops a new product for the company.

Silence is golden

Although the importance of intellectual property is most obvious in "high technology" businesses, intellectual property plays an important role in many other types of business. For example, Coca-Cola has two critical intellectual property assets: the formula for its soft drink and its Coca-Cola® trademark. Coca-Cola's soft drink formula has been a trade secret for over 90 years. The value of the Coca-Cola® trademark is estimated to be greater than $1 billion.

In this chapter, I discuss protecting your ideas, inventions, products, trademarks, and secrets.

Pondering Patents

The best protection you can get for a new product is a patent. A *patent* gives its inventor the right to prevent others from making, using, or selling the patented subject matter described in words in the patent's claims. A patent can be extremely valuable to an invention. For example, if you invent and get a patent on a new type of toilet seat that sings, you can prevent others from selling a singing toilet seat.

You can obtain two kinds of patent, in the words of the U.S. patent laws:

- **Utility patent:** "Any new and useful process, machine, manufacture, or composition of matter, or any new and useful improvement thereof"

- **Design patent:** "Any new, original, and ornamental design for an article of manufacture"

Here are the key issues in determining whether you can get a patent:

- You can patent only the concrete embodiment of an idea, formula, and so on for an invention.

- The invention must be new or "novel" — something different from what already exists.

- No printed publication anywhere in the world has already patented or described the invention.

- The invention must have some useful purpose (this requirement is fairly loose, but alleged perpetual motion machines are cited as examples of nonuseful inventions).

For more information on whether or not you can patent an idea, check out Form 13-1 on the CD-ROM, which covers the conditions for obtaining a patent in greater detail and Form 13-2 (also on the CD-ROM), which contains Frequently Asked Questions from the U.S. Patent and Trademark Office.

You obtain a patent in the United States by applying to the U.S. Patent and Trademark Office. This process can be complicated, take several years, and cost thousands of dollars. Generally, patent lawyers (or patent agents) who are licensed to practice before the Patent and Trademark Office must file applications. Patent lawyers can assist greatly in drafting the patent application and in further refining the scope of the invention. Generally, the patent term begins when the patent is issued and ends 20 years from the date the patent application was filed in the United States.

The government grants patents on a national basis. Consequently, a United States patent gives a business no rights in Canada or other countries. Patent laws in other countries differ significantly from those in the United States, so companies should always employ an experienced patent attorney for these matters.

Although patents can be very valuable to a company, don't expect them to lead to guaranteed riches. Few patents actually result in a financial windfall. Clever competitors can and do engineer around patent protection and bring similar products to market. Sometimes patents (which are public) provide competitors with the insight needed to make their own innovations. Remember, the first product to market isn't always the most successful. Products which combine innovation and strong marketing present companies with the greatest chance for success.

After you receive the patent, place a patent notice on or in the product, such as:

Covered by U.S. Patent #947998

If you've filed a patent application that's still pending, and if you're selling the invention, include the words *Patent Pending* on the invention. Legally, this move doesn't prevent anyone from making or selling the invention, but if a prospective competitor sees that the invention may soon have a patent, it may decide not to invest more money and resources on the product.

Legally, you can use the words *Patent Pending* on a product only if you have actually filed a patent application that's still pending.

The search for originality

After you've come up with an idea for the greatest thing since sliced bread, think about doing a patentability search before you get too excited.

A patentability search helps you determine if proceeding farther with an invention is worthwhile. This search discloses information about published articles and issued patents and helps you determine whether your invention is novel in a meaningful way. If the invention has already been covered by another patent, has been disclosed in an article, or isn't novel, then your invention may not be subject to patent protection.

A few years ago, I had a wonderful idea for a new type of headband that would work as a head massager. Thoughts of earning kazillions of dollars floated through my mind until I did a patentability search and found 15 issued patents that were all variations of my idea! I quickly moved on to the next idea.

You can do a quick search online at www.uspto.gov. A more thorough preliminary search usually costs several hundred dollars and should really be done by patent attorneys. Increasingly, online patentability search companies have been popping up. The online companies may be worth looking at for a preliminary check, but for real comfort, you need to check with a patent lawyer.

Form 13-3 on the CD-ROM contains additional information and instructions from the United States Patent and Trademark Office. If you want to buy or sell a patent, consider a Patent Assignment Agreement similar to Form 13-4, also on the CD-ROM.

Copyrights and Copycats

Almost every company creates material that is entitled to protection under copyright laws. Copyrights are usually considered to be important for book publishers or motion picture companies, but they can also be valuable for many other types of business. A copyright gives the owner the exclusive right to make copies of the work and to prepare derivative works (such as revisions) based on the copyrighted work.

Copyrights cover (get ready for a technical definition from the U.S. copyright statute) the following:

> *". . . original works for authorship fixed in any tangible medium of expression, now known or later developed, from which they can be perceived, reproduced, or otherwise communicated, either directly or with the aid of a machine or device."*

That's a mouthful, but here are some concrete examples of things that you can copyright:

- Advertising copy
- Art
- Articles
- Books
- Compilations of data
- Music
- Jewelry
- Movies
- Software

In the United States, the employer automatically owns the copyright for works that employees create "within the scope of their employment." Generally, this rule applies only to full-time employees. However, this rule doesn't exist in many foreign countries, and the company should ensure that all employees (and appropriate independent contractors) sign assignment agreements immediately after being hired.

Affix a copyright notice to all copyrightable works, such as the following:

The moment you create a work that meets the requirements for copyright protection, you automatically get a variety of copyright protections under the federal copyright statute for that work. You also obtain additional rights if you file the appropriate copyright registration form with the Copyright Office. Form 13-5 on the CD-ROM is a copyright registration form, and Form 13-6 on the CD-ROM is a sample cover letter to send with the copyright registration form.

If someone other than an employee creates a work for your company, make sure that the company owns the work's copyright. You can do so by having all parties sign a written document that spells out the agreement and includes an assignment of the copyright. The Independent Contractor Agreement (Form 13-7 on the CD-ROM) and the Consultant Confidentiality and Invention Assignment Agreement (Form 13-8 on the CD-ROM) both contain sample language, but here is a key excerpt:

To the extent any inventions, technologies, reports, memoranda, studies, writings, articles, plans, designs, specifications, exhibits, software code, or other materials prepared by Contractor in the performance of services under this Agreement include material subject to copyright protection, such materials have been specially commissioned by the Company and they shall be deemed "work for hire" as such term is defined under U.S. copyright law. To the extent any such materials do not qualify as "work for hire" under applicable law, and to the extent they include material subject to copyright, patent, trade secret, or other proprietary rights protection, Contractor hereby irrevocably and exclusively assigns to the Company, its successors, and assigns, all right, title, and interest in and to all such materials. To the extent any of Contractor rights in the same, including without limitation any moral rights, are not subject to assignment hereunder, Contractor hereby irrevocably and unconditionally waives all enforcement of such rights. Contractor shall execute and deliver such instruments and take such other actions as may be required to carry out and confirm the assignments contemplated by this paragraph and the remainder of this Agreement. All documents, magnetically or optically encoded media, and other tangible materials created by Contractor as part of its services under this Agreement shall be owned by the Company.

A contract can transfer, in whole or in part, the ownership of a copyrighted work or any of a copyright holder's rights. A Copyright Assignment (where you transfer all the rights) or a Copyright License (where you transfer only some rights) can get the job done.

Form 13-9 on the CD-ROM shows a sample Copyright Assignment Agreement, in which you transfer the assignment for the work in exchange for a certain dollar amount. The assignment includes the copyright and all other rights to the work.

Remind your employees of copyright infringement rules by posting a copy of Form 13-10 on the CD-ROM near every photocopier in your business. If you want to use someone else's copyrighted work, you should send a letter asking for her permission. Form 13-11 on the CD-ROM shows a sample of such a letter. Should someone use your copyrighted material without permission, you can send a letter like the one in Form 13-12 (which you can see later in this chapter).

Tricks of the Trademark

A *trademark right* protects the symbolic value of a word, name, symbol, or device (or a combination) that the trademark owner uses to identify or distinguish its goods from the goods of others. *Service marks,* which resemble trademarks, identify services.

The trademark (or service mark) owner can prevent others from using a "confusingly similar" mark or trade name. *Confusing similarity* is based on a comparison of the appearance of the two marks, the goods (services), and the channels of distribution for the goods (or services).

Trademarks can range from the monogram of a company's initials to more symbolic forms, such as the Morton Salt girl. Some well-known trademarks include the Coca-Cola trademark, the American Express trademark, and the IBM trademark.

You obtain rights to a trademark by actually using the mark in commerce. You don't need to register your mark to get rights in it, but federal registration does offer some advantages, which I describe in the section "Want a mark? . . . get set . . . file!" later in this chapter.

The great mark hunt

After you come up with a great name or mark for your product or service, conduct a search to determine whether your proposed name or mark may infringe on existing marks. The first place to look (which is free!) is at the U.S. Patent and Trademark Office at `www.uspto.gov`.

You can then be more comprehensive and request a search report from a search company. For a relatively small sum, these companies search the United States Patent and Trademark Office, state registers, and various business sources. They then give you a written report of their search results, which alerts you to potential problems with your proposed name or mark.

Send via certified mail [Date]

Certified Mail/Return Receipt Requested

_____
_____ Addressee
_____

Re: Infringement of Copyrighted Materials

Dear _____:

It has come to our attention that you have infringed our copyright protected work. This infringement consists of _____, which used our following copyrighted materials: _____. Your actions unlawfully misappropriates and misuses our original and creative work and deprives us of the benefits, privileges, and profits from the exclusive use of our copyrighted work.

Insert the copyrighted material that was infringed

Insert the manner in which the copyright was infringed

We have not authorized your use of our works for your commercial purposes and, therefore, as the copyright owner, we demand that you immediately cease and desist from using and from permitting any third party to use this work.

We are hereby demanding an explanation of this matter. Please contact the undersigned immediately at (____) _____-_____ so we can resolve this matter. If we do not hear from you within ten days from the date of this letter, we will be forced to pursue further action against you.

Sincerely,

[Copyright Owner]

By: _____
Title: _____

Form 13-12: Letter notifying another party of infringement of copyrighted materials.

Here are some of the Web sites that provide search services:

✔ www.nameprotect.com

✔ www.legalzoom.com

✔ www.thomson-thomson.com

✔ www.trademark-search.com

✔ www.trademark.com

Want a mark? . . . get set . . . file!

You register a proposed trademark or service mark with the United States Patent and Trademark Office. These applications permit a company to "reserve" a mark for up to four years. Trademark registration provides nationwide rights (under common law, rights are limited to the geographic area of actual use). Trademark examiners, who can be exasperating sticklers, review your application and may make you revise it several times.

Typically, you file a Trademark Application describing the proposed mark. Currently, you have to pay a $335 fee when you apply. A sample Trademark Application appears in Form 13-13 on the CD-ROM. Form 13-14 on the CD-ROM gives you a cover letter to send with the Trademark Application. You can also get additional information about the requirements for filing an application under the Basic Facts About Trademarks link on the U.S. Patent & Trademark Office Web site. See www.uspto.gov/main/trademarks.htm.

Making your mark

In coming up with a trademark or service mark for your company, remember that the best marks are those that are *fanciful, arbitrary,* or *suggestive,* as follows:

✔ **Fanciful marks** have no established current usage in any context other than one's trademarks, such as Kodak, Exxon, and Xerox. Fanciful marks are generally most distinctive.

✔ **Arbitrary marks** have an independent understood definition, but consumers don't understand it as describing or suggesting a

characteristic of the product — Arrow shirts and Camel cigarettes are examples.

✔ **Suggestive marks** suggest some characteristic of the product without actually describing the product, such as *Playboy* (the magazine), SkinVisible transparent medical tape, and Roach Motel insect traps.

✔ **Generic terms** tell people what the product is rather than where the product comes from or who sponsors it. You probably can't get these terms protected as a mark. "Light Beer" or "Lite Beer" are examples of generic terms.

Bulletproofing your marks

You can do a number of important things to protect your trademark or service mark, including the following:

- Always capitalize the first letter or all letters of the mark.

- Use ™ or ℠ with the mark if you have not yet obtained a federal mark registration.

- Always use the ® symbol next to the mark — such as American Express® — if officials have placed your mark on the federal trademark register.

- Use the mark as a proper adjective to describe your product or service, such as Xerox® copiers.

- Specifically state your ownership of the mark when you use it in ads or promotional materials: For example: Windows® is a registered trademark of Microsoft Corporation.

- Use the mark in the prescribed form with the font and colors matching those described in the federal registration.

- Educate all employees as to the proper use of marks.

- Ensure that all licensees, salespeople, and distributors use the company's marks properly.

- Be on the lookout for others using your mark without permission. Should that happen, you must take appropriate steps to stop the infringement. Be ready to take legal action because if you don't, you may lose your rights.

You can use Form 13-16 on the CD-ROM — a Trademark Assignment form — to buy or sell a trademark.

Can You Keep a Trade Secret?

A *trade secret right* allows the owner of the right to take action against anyone who breaches an agreement or confidential relationship or who steals or uses other improper means to gather secret information. Trade secrets can range from computer programs to customer lists to the formula for the Coca-Cola® soft drink.

For the most part, state law governs trade secret rights. Federal and state courts generally consider the following factors in deciding whether information constitutes a company's protectable trade secrets:

- ✔ The information's economic value (because the industry doesn't generally know the secret)

- ✔ The company's efforts to keep the information secret (both outside and within the company)

- ✔ The time and money that the company spent developing the information

- ✔ The relative commercial value of the information

- ✔ The ease or difficulty with which outsiders can independently obtain the information

You must make *reasonable efforts* to protect your trade secrets. The exact efforts vary, depending on the trade secret's nature, but some possible steps include nondisclosure agreements with employees (and other companies to whom you disclose the trade secrets), marking any lab books and other materials as confidential, and restricting access to a "need-to-know" basis.

Trade secret laws protect the owner from people who inappropriately acquire the information. However, unlike patent law, the owner has no protection from another party independently developing the same information. Most foreign countries have protection for trade secrets, but that protection is generally weaker than in the United States. Because of this difference, contracts become much more important when doing business in a foreign country.

In addition to protecting its own trade secrets, a company should be careful not to misappropriate the secrets of others. This caution is particularly important when a company hires a competitor's employee.

Speaking Confidentially . . .

Imagine this scenario: You have a great idea for a new product, business, or service, and you want to approach another company with the idea to see if they may be interested in it. How do you prevent that company from simply stealing your idea?

Ideas alone are hard to protect — unless you have a written Confidentiality Agreement (see Form 13-17 later in this chapter) with the person or company to whom you're showing your idea. The agreement provides that the recipient holds the idea in strictest confidence and uses the idea only with your explicit permission (and appropriate compensation). You must enter into this agreement *before* disclosure.

Insert your name if you are the disclosing party

CONFIDENTIALITY AGREEMENT

This CONFIDENTIALITY AGREEMENT (the "Agreement") is by and between _____ (hereinafter "Disclosing Party"), and the undersigned (hereinafter "Recipient").

WHEREAS, Recipient has requested information from Disclosing Party in connection with consideration of a possible transaction or relationship between Recipient and Disclosing Party.

WHEREAS, in the course of consideration of the possible transaction or relationship, Disclosing Party may disclose to Recipient confidential, important, and/or proprietary trade secret information concerning Disclosing Party and his/its activities.

THEREFORE, the parties agree to enter into a confidential relationship with respect to the disclosure by Disclosing Party to Recipient of certain information.

1.   Definitions. For purposes of this Agreement, "Confidential Information" shall include all information or material that has or could have commercial value or other utility in the business or prospective business of Disclosing Party. Confidential Information also includes all information of which unauthorized disclosure could be detrimental to the interests of Disclosing Party whether or not such information is identified as Confidential Information by Disclosing Party. By example and without limitation, Confidential Information includes, but is not limited to, the following: _____

Sets out what will be deemed "Confidential Information"

_____

For purposes of this Agreement, the term "Recipient" shall include Recipient, the company he or she represents, and all affiliates, subsidiaries, and related companies of Recipient. For purposes of this Agreement, the term "Representative" shall include Recipient's directors, officers, employees, agents, and financial, legal, and other advisors.

If there is something specific you want to make sure is treated confidentially, add it here

2.   Exclusions. Confidential Information does not include information that Recipient can demonstrate: (a) was in Recipient's possession prior to its being furnished to Recipient under the terms of this Agreement, provided the source of that information was not known by Recipient to be bound by a confidentiality agreement with or other continual, legal or fiduciary obligation of confidentiality to Disclosing Party; (b) is now, or hereafter becomes, through no act or failure to act on the part of Recipient, generally known to the public; (c) is rightfully obtained by Recipient from a third party, without breach of any obligation to Disclosing Party; or (d) is independently developed by Recipient without use of or reference to the Confidential Information.

These are typical exclusions from confidential information

3.   Confidentiality. Recipient and its Representatives shall not disclose any of the Confidential Information in any manner whatsoever, except as provided in paragraphs 4 and 5 of this Agreement, and shall hold and maintain the Confidential Information in strictest confidence. Recipient hereby agrees to indemnify Disclosing Party against any and all losses, damages, claims, expenses, and attorneys' fees incurred or suffered by Disclosing Party as a result of a breach of this Agreement by Recipient or its Representatives.

This is the confidentiality commitment from the other side

4.   Permitted Disclosures. Recipient may disclose Disclosing Party's Confidential Information to Recipient's responsible Representatives with a bona fide need to know such Confidential Information, but only to the extent necessary to evaluate or carry out a proposed transaction or relationship with Disclosing Party and only if such employees are advised of the confidential nature of such Confidential Information and the terms of this Agreement and are bound

Form 13-17: Confidentiality Agreement with Third Party — page 1 of 3.

by a written agreement or by a legally enforceable code of professional responsibility to protect the confidentiality of such Confidential Information.

5.   Required Disclosures. Recipient may disclose Disclosing Party's Confidential Information if and to the extent that such disclosure is required by court order, provided that Recipient provides Disclosing Party a reasonable opportunity to review the disclosure before it is made and to interpose its own objection to the disclosure.

6.   Use. Recipient and its Representatives shall use the Confidential Information solely for the purpose of evaluating a possible transaction or relationship with Disclosing Party and shall not in any way use the Confidential Information to the detriment of Disclosing Party. Nothing in this Agreement shall be construed as granting any rights to Recipient, by license or otherwise, to any of Disclosing Party's Confidential Information.

> This limits how the confidential information can be used

7.   Return of Documents. If Recipient does not proceed with the possible transaction with Disclosing Party, Recipient shall notify Disclosing Party of that decision and shall, at that time or at any time upon the request of Disclosing Party for any reason, return to Disclosing Party any and all records, notes, and other written, printed or other tangible materials in its possession pertaining to the Confidential Information immediately on the written request of Disclosing Party. The returning of materials shall not relieve Recipient from compliance with other terms and conditions of this Agreement.

8.   No Additional Agreements. Neither the holding of discussions nor the exchange of material or information shall be construed as an obligation of Disclosing Party to enter into any other agreement with Recipient or prohibit Disclosing Party from providing the same or similar information to other parties and entering into agreements with other parties. Disclosing Party reserves the right, in its sole discretion, to reject any and all proposals made by Recipient or its Representatives with regard to a transaction between Recipient and Disclosing Party and to terminate discussions and negotiations with Recipient at any time. Additional agreements of the parties, if any, shall be in writing signed by Disclosing Party and Recipient.

9.   Irreparable Harm. Recipient understands and acknowledges that any disclosure or misappropriation of any of the Confidential Information in violation of this Agreement may cause Disclosing Party irreparable harm, the amount of which may be difficult to ascertain, and therefore agrees that Disclosing Party shall have the right to apply to a court of competent jurisdiction for specific performance and/or an order restraining and enjoining any such further disclosure or breach and for such other relief as Disclosing Party shall deem appropriate. Such right of Disclosing Party is to be in addition to the remedies otherwise available to Disclosing Party at law or in equity. Such right of Disclosing Party is to be in addition to the remedies otherwise available to Disclosing Party at law or in equity. Recipient expressly waives the defense that a remedy in damages will be adequate and any requirement in an action for specific performance or injunction for the posting of a bond by Disclosing Party.

> Gives you a right to seek an injunction if the agreement is breached

10.   Survival. This Agreement shall continue in full force and effect at all times.

11.   Successors and Assigns. This Agreement and each party's obligations hereunder shall be binding on the representatives, assigns, and successors of such party and shall inure to the benefit of the assigns and successors of such party; provided, however, that the rights and obligations of Recipient hereunder are not assignable.

12.   Governing Law. This Agreement shall be governed by and construed in accordance with the laws of the State of [State]. The parties hereby irrevocably consent to the jurisdiction of the state and federal courts located in [City], [State], in any action arising out of or relating to this Agreement, and waive any other venue to which either party might be entitled by

> Put in where you would like any disputes to be handled

Form 13-17: Confidentiality Agreement with Third Party — page 2 of 3.

domicile or otherwise.

13.   Attorney's Fees. If any action at law or in equity is brought to enforce or interpret the provisions of this Agreement, the prevailing party in such action shall be awarded its attorneys' fees and costs incurred.

14.   Counterparts and Right. This Agreement may be signed in counterparts, which together shall constitute one agreement. The person signing on behalf of Recipient represents that he or she has the right and power to execute this Agreement.

15.   Entire Agreement. This Agreement expresses the full and complete understanding of the parties with respect to the subject matter hereof and supersedes all prior or contemporaneous proposals, agreements, representations and understandings, whether written or oral, with respect to the subject matter. This Agreement is not, however, to limit any rights that Disclosing Party may have under trade secret, copyright, patent or other laws that may be available to Disclosing Party. This Agreement may not be amended or modified except in writing signed by each of the parties to the Agreement. This Agreement shall be construed as to its fair meaning and not strictly for or against either party. The headings hereof are descriptive only and not to be construed in interpreting the provisions hereof.

Date: _____

_____ ("Disclosing Party")

By: _____

Title: _____

_____ ("Recipient")

By: _____

Title: _____

Form 13-17: Confidentiality Agreement with Third Party — page 3 of 3.

Forms on the CD-ROM

Check out the following forms on the CD-ROM related to protecting your intellectual property:

Form 13-1	**Novelty and Other Conditions for Obtaining a Patent**	U.S. Patent and Trademark Office summary of various conditions for obtaining a patent
Form 13-2	**General Information Concerning Patents**	Covers patents, from the U.S. Patent and Trademark Office
Form 13-3	**Application for a Patent**	U.S. Patent and Trademark Office summary concerning applying for a patent
Form 13-4	**Patent Assignment**	An agreement for assigning a patent
Form 13-5	**Copyright Registration**	Form to register copyrightable literary works with the Copyright Office
Form 13-6	**Cover Letter to Copyright Office**	Sample letter to the Copyright Office enclosing a Copyright Registration form
Form 13-7	**Independent Contractor Agreement**	Sample contract with an independent contractor that's skewed in the company's favor
Form 13-8	**Invention Assignment Agreement**	Comprehensive agreement between the company and a consultant protecting the company's intellectual property rights
Form 13-9	**Copyright Assignment**	An agreement for assigning a copyright
Form 13-10	**Copyright Compliance — Photocopying Policy**	A policy statement to post near the company's copy machines, reminding users of issues in complying with the copyright laws
Form 13-11	**Permission Request to Use Copyrighted Material**	A sample letter requesting the right to use copyrighted material

Form 13-12	**Notice of Infringement of Copyrighted Work**	A sample letter notifying another party that they have infringed on your copyrighted work
Form 13-13	**Trademark Registration**	A Trademark Registration application from the U.S. Patent and Trademark Office
Form 13-14	**Cover Letter to Patent and Trademark Office**	Sample letter to U.S. Patent and Trademark Office to send with Trademark Registration form
Form 13-15	**Trademark FAQs**	Frequently Asked Questions about trademarks, from the U.S. Patent and Trademark Office
Form 13-16	**Trademark Assignment**	An agreement for assigning a trademark
Form 13-17	**Confidentiality Agreement With Third Party**	An agreement where the recipient agrees to keep confidential an idea or product presented by the disclosing party
Form 13-18	**Trade Name License Agreement**	A license granting the right to use a trade name
Form 13-19	**Mutual Non-Disclosure Agreement (Short Form)**	An agreement allowing two companies to exchange confidential agreement with mutual protection obligations

Chapter 14

Avoiding Customer Problems

. . . .

In This Chapter

▶ Establishing payment terms

▶ Offering incentives

▶ Understanding warranties

▶ Extending credit while reducing your risk

▶ Playing hardball when you have to

. . . .

*U*nfortunately, at one time or another, your small business is likely to have problems with its customers — like not being paid for the product or service that you've provided. In this chapter, I give you tips for avoiding some common customer problems. I also offer suggestions for handling problems if they do happen.

Doing Preventative Maintenance

The best way to handle customer problems is to avoid them in the first place. The information in this section can't ensure that your customers sing your praises hither and yon, but if you apply it properly, you may have better luck getting paid on time and limiting your potential liability.

Setting up a customer payment policy

From the beginning, you need to implement clear-cut payment policies with your customers. A clear-cut policy prevents misunderstandings and lets the customer know when you expect payment. If you aren't getting cash up front, all your contracts and invoices should clearly state when payment is due and what happens if the customer pays late. You can make it look something like the following:

Customer Payment Policy. All payments must be received by ABC, Inc. within 30 days of the date of an invoice. Any payments received after said date will be subject to a late interest fee of one-and-one-half percent (1½%) per month. The customer shall also be responsible for all attorneys' fees, court costs, and related expenses incurred in the event that payment is not timely made and proceedings are brought by ABC, Inc. to collect sums owed.

Giving an early payment discount

You can improve your cash flow and cut down on delinquent payments by offering a discount for early payment. Consider adding the following clause (or one similar to it) to your invoices and contracts:

Early Payment Discount. The Customer shall be entitled to receive a discount on the bill of two percent (2%) of the face amount of the bill. In order to receive this discount, ABC, Inc. must receive full payment within ten (10) days of the date of this invoice.

Handing out warranties

Warranties are statements or promises made about a particular product. Warranties can take a variety of shapes, and you don't even have to label them "warranties" to find yourself in a legal obligation. You also don't necessarily have to include warranties in your contract — statements that you make in product literature or advertisements may constitute legally enforceable warranties. If you breach the warranty, the buyer may hold you legally liable.

Warranties can be express or implied, written or oral. *Expressed warranties* are direct statements, such as "This computer is new" or "This DVD has eight hours of video." No one expressly states *implied warranties,* but the customer can reasonably infer them (that the product does what it should do, for example).

A variety of laws are designed to protect people buying consumer products. You can find information on some of them at www.AllBusiness.com. These laws impact your potential liability for defective products and your ability to limit your liability. Here's some practical advice for complying with these laws:

- ✔ **Advertisements:** Be careful about what you say in your advertisements and product literature. Don't make exaggerated claims or claims that you can't easily back up.

- ✔ **Limited warranties:** If you're going to give a warranty for the product, label it a *Limited Warranty.* Full warranties generally give the customer broad protection if a problem arises with the product. In your contract (or in a document included with the product), you need to specifically list what your Limited Warranty involves. Go over things like the term of the warranty, what the warranty covers, and situations when the warranty no longer applies.

✔ **Limit customer remedies:** Use your Limited Warranty to restrict customer remedies for breach of the warranty. You should have the option to either refund the purchase price or to repair or replace the product.

✔ **Disclaim other warranties:** Disclaim all other warranties, either express or implied, as part of your Limited Warranty. You should typically put these disclaimers in bold capitalized letters.

✔ **Liability limitations:** State that you aren't liable for special, incidental, consequential, or various other damages, and that, should someone hold you liable, your maximum liability is equal to the price the customer paid for the product.

Form 14-1 later in this chapter shows a sample Limited Warranty (drafted for a software product) that encompasses these concepts.

Giving Credit Where Credit's Due

In many lines of business, making your customers' purchase of your product or service as easy as possible can make the difference between a company that's holding on and a company that's prospering. But you don't have to give away the farm. This section tells you about forms that give you the best chance of getting your money after extending credit.

Preparing to extend credit

If you're going to extend any significant credit to a customer (other than accepting a credit card, in which case the credit card company takes care of this stuff), consider taking some or all of the following steps:

✔ **Have customers fill out a Credit Application:** A Credit Application solicits important information about the customer's background, such as

  • How the customer operates (individual, corporation, partnership, or sole proprietorship)

  • The trade that the customer is in

  • References (from other companies that extend credit to the customer and regularly receive payment on time from that customer)

  • Bank references

Form 14-2, which follows Form 14-1, shows a sample Credit Application.

Limited Warranty

LIMITED WARRANTY.   ABC, Inc.   (the "Company") warrants that (a) its _____ Software (the "Software") will perform substantially in accordance with the accompanying written materials for a period of ninety (90) days from the date of receipt and (b) that the medium on which the Software is contained will be free from physical defects in materials and workmanship normal use and service for a period of one (1) year. In the event applicable law imposes any under implied warranties, the implied warranty period is limited to ninety (90) days from the date of receipt. Some jurisdictions do not allow such limitations on duration of an implied warranty, so the above limitation may not apply to you.

CUSTOMER REMEDIES. The Company's and its suppliers' entire liability and your exclusive remedy shall be, at the Company's option, either (a) return of the price paid for the Software, or (b) repair or replacement of the Software that does not meet this Limited Warranty and which is returned to the Company with a copy of your receipt. This Limited Warranty is void if failure of the Software has resulted from accident, abuse, or misapplication. Any replacement Software will be warranted for the remainder of the original warranty period or thirty (30) days, whichever is longer.

NO OTHER WARRANTIES. TO THE MAXIMUM EXTENT PERMITTED BY APPLICABLE LAW, THE COMPANY AND ITS SUPPLIERS DISCLAIM ALL OTHER WARRANTIES, EITHER EXPRESS OR IMPLIED, INCLUDING, BUT NOT LIMITED TO IMPLIED WARRANTIES OF MERCHANTABILITY AND FITNESS FOR A PARTICULAR PURPOSE, WITH REGARD TO THE SOFTWARE AND ANY RELATED OR ACCOMPANYING WRITTEN MATERIALS. THIS LIMITED WARRANTY GIVES YOU SPECIFIC LEGAL RIGHTS. YOU MAY HAVE OTHER RIGHTS WHICH VARY FROM JURISDICTION TO JURISDICTION.

NO LIABILITY FOR DAMAGES. IN NO EVENT SHALL THE COMPANY OR ITS SUPPLIERS BE LIABLE FOR ANY DAMAGES WHATSOEVER (INCLUDING WITHOUT LIMITATION, SPECIAL, INCIDENTAL, CONSEQUENTIAL, OR INDIRECT DAMAGES FOR PERSONAL INJURY, LOSS OF BUSINESS PROFITS, BUSINESS INTERRUPTION, LOSS OF BUSINESS INFORMATION, OR ANY OTHER PECUNIARY LOSS) ARISING OUT OF THE USE OF OR INABILITY TO USE THIS PRODUCT, EVEN IF THE COMPANY HAS BEEN ADVISED OF THE POSSIBILITY OF SUCH DAMAGES. IN ANY CASE, THE COMPANY'S AND ITS SUPPLIERS' ENTIRE LIABILITY UNDER ANY PROVISION OF THIS AGREEMENT SHALL BE LIMITED TO THE AMOUNT ACTUALLY PAID BY YOU FOR THE SOFTWARE. BECAUSE SOME JURISDICTIONS DO NOT ALLOW THE EXCLUSION OR LIMITATION OF LIABILITY FOR CONSEQUENTIAL OR INCIDENTAL DAMAGES, THE ABOVE LIMITATION MAY NOT APPLY TO YOU.

Describes the limited warranty

Limits the customer's remedies in the event of breach of the warranty

Disclaims other warranties

Form 14-1: This Limited Warranty for a software product protects the software vendor.

CREDIT APPLICATION

The undersigned is applying for credit with _____ (the "Company") and agrees to abide by the terms and conditions of the Company's standard contract.

1. Company Name
and Address   _____

   _____

   _____

2. Phone (   ) _____   Fax (   ) _____

3. Federal Tax ID or Social Security No. _____

4. Type of Business _____   No. of Employees _____

5. Date Business Established _____

6. Types of Products You Will Purchase _____

7. Amount of Credit Requested $ _____

8. Check which is applicable to you:

   ☐ Corporation   ☐ General Partnership   ☐ Limited Partnership

   ☐ LLC   ☐ Sole Proprietorship   ☐ Other : _____

9. State where your company was organized : _____

10. Have you or any of your affiliates ever had credit with us before or purchased from us before? Yes ___ No ___

    If yes, under what name? _____

11. Name or title of persons authorized to act on your behalf : _____

12. Trade References

    Reference #1 Name and Address : _____

    _____

    _____

    Phone (   ) _____

    Reference #2 Name and Address : _____

    _____

    _____

    Phone (   ) _____

Form 14-2: A sample Credit Application — page 1 of 2.

Reference #3 Name and Address : _____

_____

_____

Phone ( ) _____

13. Bank References

Bank #1 Account # _____ Phone ( ) _____

Contact Person _____

Name of Bank _____

Address _____

Bank #2 Account # _____ Phone ( ) _____

Contact Person _____

Name of Bank _____

Address _____

14. Financial Information about your Company :

Assets : $ _____

Liabilities: $ _____

Approximate Annual
Net Income: $ _____

15. Have you or your officers or affiliates ever filed a petition in bankruptcy? _____

16. Are you subject to any litigation? _____ If so, describe here : _____

_____

_____

17. Are you current in meeting your other financial obligations? _____

We declare that the above information is true, correct and complete and is given to induce the Company to extend credit. We authorize the Company to make such credit investigation as the Company sees fit, including contacting the above trade references and banks and obtaining credit reports. We authorize all trade references, banks and credit reporting agencies to disclose to the Company any and all information concerning the financial and credit history of my company and myself:

I have read the terms and conditions stated below and agree to all of those terms and conditions

Name of Company _____

Authorized Signature : _____

> Various terms and conditions are
> included on Form 14-2 on the CD-ROM

Form 14-2: A sample Credit Application — page 2 of 2.

✔ **Run a credit check:** Consider obtaining a credit report from a credit rating agency, such as TRW, Dun & Bradstreet, or Equifax. To get information on individuals, you need their consent to do a search (you can include a request for consent in the Credit Application). You typically need the individual's name, city, Social Security number, and (if the name is common) date of birth. After you get the credit report, review it carefully to determine the customer's payment history.

✔ **Require a customer guarantee:** If the customer is a company with minimal assets, request that the owners personally guarantee the company's obligations. Then make sure that the person giving the guarantee has some assets to back up the guarantee.

✔ **Have the customer sign a security agreement:** Take a security interest in the goods if you're selling them on credit and if they're expensive. A security interest provides you with the benefit that, if the customer doesn't pay, you can sell or take back the goods (as opposed to being simply one of the customer's unsecured creditors).

In order to do this, you need the customer to sign a Security Agreement and UCC Financing Statement covering the goods. You can typically get the UCC Financing Statement from the office of your Secretary of State. Officials then file the statement in the appropriate public office, such as the Secretary of State or County recorder (depending on your state's requirements). Also, your business lawyer can provide you with the relevant forms.

Reducing the risk of nonpayment

Unless your customer pays you in cash at the time of the sale, you'll probably encounter a number of situations with a high risk of nonpayment. And for a small business, nonpayment can seriously impact profits and cash flow!

So here are some tips to reduce the risk of nonpayment:

✔ Send out bills as promptly as possible.

✔ Make sure that your bills clearly identify the goods or services rendered, the dates purchased, and any other relevant information.

✔ Send follow-up reminders of past due notices immediately, with a big "Past Due" stamp on the cover of the notice.

✔ Daily, monitor payments that are due. Forms 14-3 (Accounts Receivable Aging) and 14-4 (Accounts Receivable Monthly Customer Statement), which appear later in this chapter, can help you keep track of overdue payments.

✔ Telephone the customer or accounts payable department and ask what you can do to speed up payment.

Accounts Receivable Aging

Customer Name	Contact	Phone	Total Amount	0-30 Days	61-90 Days	Over 90 Days
Total			$	$	$	$

Form 14-3: An Accounts Receivable Aging form.

Accounts Receivable Monthly Customer Statement

Customer Name: _____

Customer Address: _____

_____

_____

Credit Limit: _____

Invoice Number	Invoice Date	Product or Service Description	0-30 Days $	31-60 Days $	61-90 Days $	Over 90 Days $
Total Balance Due:						

Form 14-4: An Accounts Receivable Monthly Customer Statement.

✔ Have a set of demand letters ready to send when payment becomes overdue (see the section "Getting Your Money the Hard Way" later in this chapter).

✔ Consider compromising the amount owed or extending the time for payment if the customer has financial problems. If you do agree to extend time, insist on a periodic payment plan.

✔ Respond promptly, in writing, if the customer disputes the amount owed. Otherwise, you can lose some rights under various credit laws. If you decide to settle over a disputed amount, consider using Form 14-5 on the CD-ROM (Settlement of Disputed Amount).

✔ Consider stopping any future sales to the customer unless that customer pays the bill or the two of you reach a compromise. Also, consider cash payment on delivery as a condition to any new sale.

No matter what steps you choose to take, remember to be courteous and professional. Just make sure to keep on top of the problem before it escalates.

Credit laws

A fair number of laws regulate the extension of credit and debt collections practices (primarily the extension of credit to individuals). The laws are both federal and state, and they mandate various disclosures and procedures that you have to follow. The following list gives you a summary of some (but by no means all) of the key laws:

✔ **Truth in Lending Act.** The federal Truth in Lending Act requires you to disclose credit terms to people who apply for credit with your business, including monthly finance charge, annual percentage interest rate, payment due dates, the total sale price with all charges, and late payment charges and policies.

✔ **Equal Credit Opportunity Act.** This statute prohibits discrimination against a credit applicant on the basis of race, color, religion, national origin, age, sex, or marital status.

✔ **The Fair Credit Billing Act.** This statute lists your responsibilities if a customer claims that your bill or invoice is mistaken. The customer must notify you of the alleged error within 60 days of the date that you mailed the first bill, and you have to respond within 30 days after receiving the notice from the customer. Then you have to conduct a reasonable review of the situation and either notify the customer — within 90 days of receipt of the customer's letter — as to why the bill is correct or you must correct the error. If you don't follow this procedure, you can be liable for various penalties and fines under this law and state variations of this law.

✔ **Fair debt collection laws.** Many states have laws regulating collection practices that they deem harassing or unfair, including writing or calling the debtor so often as to be harassing, threatening criminal action against the debtor, using obscene language, and calling the debtor at unreasonable hours.

Dealing with debtors can be tricky because of the many laws that protect them. Make sure that you have checked out your state laws before you wade into the waters.

Getting Your Money the Hard Way

Sometimes, you have to resort to tougher measures to get payment from your customer. This section provides you with some tools to wrench your just payment from deadbeat customers.

Mailing out collection letters

As part of your forms arsenal, you should have several form letters ready to send out when a customer's account becomes past due. The letters can be increasingly firm. You can find some samples in Forms 14-6, 14-7, and 14-8 later in this chapter.

Getting your attorney to send letters

If your calls and letters haven't worked, consider having your attorney send a letter demanding payment. The customer may view the request more seriously when it comes from an attorney and, consequently, may be more inclined to pay.

Form 14-9, which follows Form 14-8 later in this chapter, shows you a sample attorney letter demanding payment. You can revise this form to fit your circumstances and have your attorney put it on his or her letterhead to send. By doing so, you may save yourself some legal fees because the attorney doesn't have to prepare this form.

Relying on collection agencies

Collection agencies specialize at tracking down and extracting payment from overdue debtors. You typically use collection agencies as a last resort (except for suing the customer in court) because these agencies keep a large percentage of what they collect for themselves. Remember, too, that using a collection agency may alienate the customer (but then again, who wants customers who don't pay their debts?).

[LETTERHEAD]

[Date]

_____
_____
_____

Re: <u>Courtesy Reminder of Late Payment</u>

Dear _____ :

Your payment of $[*amount*] pursuant to our invoice dated _____, 200__ has not arrived by the date required. We are sure that this is an oversight and ask that you please send it today in the enclosed self-addressed envelope. If we are forced to spend time collecting overdue accounts receivable, we will not be able to offer our valued clients, such as yourselves, our current prices.

If you have already sent your payment to us, please accept our thanks. If you have any questions, please feel free to call the undersigned at (__) _____.

Sincerely,

[Company]

By:_____
Title:_____

Form 14-6: Courtesy reminder of late payment.

[LETTERHEAD]

[Date]

_____
_____
_____

Re: <u>Demand for Payment</u>

Dear _____ :

        Our numerous attempts to resolve your long overdue account have not been successful. As you know, your overdue balance now equals $_____(which includes interest on the overdue account).

        Your failure to make payment on your account may prompt us to take legal action to collect the account immediately. We are hopeful that you will act promptly and forward payment of the outstanding amounts as quickly as possible, but in no event later than_____. 20___. Interest will continue to accrue on this past due account. If you have any questions, please call the undersigned immediately at (__)_____.

Sincerely,

[Company]

By:_____
Title: _____

Form 14-7: A firm demand for overdue payment.

[LETTERHEAD]

[Date]

<u>Certified Mail</u>

_____

_____

_____

Re: <u>Final Demand for Payment</u>

Dear_____:

Despite our efforts to resolve your past due account, payment on this account has still not been made.

We are informing you that this is your final notice and last opportunity to make payment.

Unless we have your check for $_____ within the next five (5) days, we shall immediately commence legal action against you. If the matter goes that far, you will also be liable for all attorneys' fees and court costs. Such an action may also adversely affect your credit rating.

If you have any questions or wish to discuss this matter, please call the undersigned immediately at (__)_____ .

Sincerely,

[Company]

By: _____

Title: _____

Form 14-8: A strongly worded final demand letter for overdue payment.

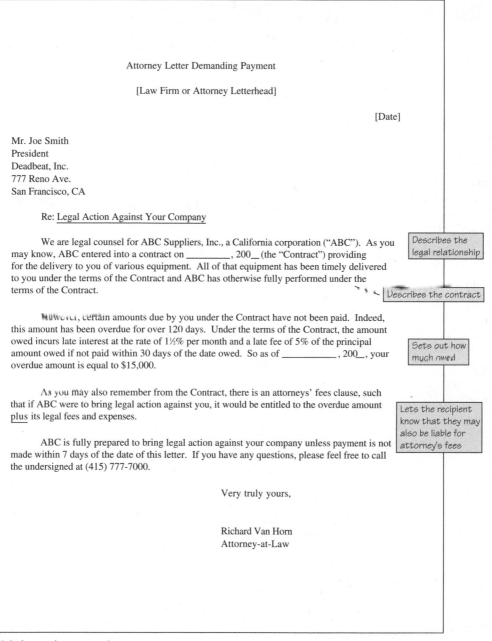

Attorney Letter Demanding Payment

[Law Firm or Attorney Letterhead]

[Date]

Mr. Joe Smith
President
Deadbeat, Inc.
777 Reno Ave.
San Francisco, CA

Re: Legal Action Against Your Company

We are legal counsel for ABC Suppliers, Inc., a California corporation ("ABC"). As you may know, ABC entered into a contract on _____, 200__ (the "Contract") providing for the delivery to you of various equipment. All of that equipment has been timely delivered to you under the terms of the Contract and ABC has otherwise fully performed under the terms of the Contract.

Describes the legal relationship

Describes the contract

However, certain amounts due by you under the Contract have not been paid. Indeed, this amount has been overdue for over 120 days. Under the terms of the Contract, the amount owed incurs late interest at the rate of 1½% per month and a late fee of 5% of the principal amount owed if not paid within 30 days of the date owed. So as of _____, 200__, your overdue amount is equal to $15,000.

Sets out how much owed

As you may also remember from the Contract, there is an attorneys' fees clause, such that if ABC were to bring legal action against you, it would be entitled to the overdue amount plus its legal fees and expenses.

Lets the recipient know that they may also be liable for attorney's fees

ABC is fully prepared to bring legal action against your company unless payment is not made within 7 days of the date of this letter. If you have any questions, please feel free to call the undersigned at (415) 777-7000.

Very truly yours,

Richard Van Horn
Attorney-at-Law

Form 14-9: A sample attorney letter.

Forms on the CD-ROM

Check out the following forms on the CD-ROM dealing with customer problems:

Form 14-1	**Limited Warranty**	A form of Limited Warranty for a software product, with various disclaimers and limitations of liability
Form 14-2	**Credit Application**	An application that a prospective customer should fill out prior to your granting the customer credit
Form 14-3	**Accounts Receivable Aging**	A sample accounting report to keep track of aging of all accounts-receivables
Form 14-4	**Accounts Receivable Monthly Customer Statement**	A sample report to keep track of accounts receivable status by customer
Form 14-5	**Settlement of Disputed Account**	An agreement to compromise on disputed amounts owed
Form 14-6	**Courtesy Reminder of Late Payment**	A sample letter courteously reminding the customer that payment is overdue
Form 14-7	**Demand for Payment**	A letter demanding payment on an overdue account
Form 14-8	**Final Demand for Payment**	A letter more forcefully demanding payment and labeled a "final demand"
Form 14-9	**Attorney Letter Demanding Payment**	A form of letter from an attorney demanding overdue payment
Form 14-10	**Delinquent Account Collection History**	A log to keep track of efforts to collect overdue accounts
Form 14-11	**Notice of Dishonored Check**	A notice to a customer that the customer's check has bounced

Chapter 15

Real Estate Leases
for Your Business

In This Chapter

▶ Negotiating rent

▶ Determining use of the premises

▶ Keeping your options open

▶ Looking at key negotiation issues

▶ Making an offer

Most small businesses need to lease space. And as your business grows, you need to add additional space. A lease agreement constitutes a significant financial commitment for your business, yet many people blindly sign leases that bind their business for many years without any meaningful attempt to negotiate the terms of the lease.

In this chapter, I tell you what to look out for when signing a lease and what you should try to negotiate in a good lease. However, you may also want to have an experienced real estate attorney review the lease before you sign it.

Negotiating an Office Lease

When you find a great space for the business and are ready to lease, the landlord typically hands you a preprinted agreement that looks (for all the world) like a standard form. The landlord probably calls this document the *standard lease,* as if the perfect form of a lease agreement had been chiseled in stone eons ago.

Lease gotchas

Landlords often hand you a form lease that contains gotchas. *Gotchas,* a highly technical term, are provisions that may cost you a lot of money or headaches in ways that you didn't plan. Your best bet is to try and negotiate them out of the lease.

Here are some classic gotchas:

✔ The landlord's right to pass increased operating costs in the building on to the tenant without limitation (resulting in increased rent payable by the tenant)

✔ The tenant's obligation to pay any increased taxes as a result of the landlord selling the building

✔ The landlord's right to terminate your lease early for his convenience

✔ A disclaimer about the building and the services provided to tenants

✔ Severe limitations or prohibitions on subletting your space (you may need to sublet space if your business shrinks)

✔ A requirement of personal guarantees or payment of the rent from the company's owners

---

Pay attention here: This form is undoubtedly totally one-sided in favor of the landlord. No standard lease exists. And regardless of whether the form looks standard or preprinted, don't be afraid to carefully review and negotiate the lease.

Your ability to negotiate changes to an office lease depends on how much leverage you have. Are other companies vying for the space? Has the space been vacant for a long time? Are you willing to pay a good rent? Face it: If Microsoft and General Motors are about to engage in a bidding war for the same prime space that you're interested in, all of your negotiating skills mean *zilch* (zero, in technical legal terms).

Assuming that you do have some leverage, the following sections detail the key provisions of an office lease.

Form 15-1, which you can find later in this chapter, shows a checklist of issues to consider when negotiating an office lease.

CHECKLIST FOR OFFICE LEASES

1. **Space**
   (a) What is the rentable square footage?
   (b) What is the usable square footage?
   (c) Is rent based on usable or rentable square footage?
   (d) Verify square footage number provided by the landloard.

2. **Permitted Uses of the Premises**
   (a) What uses of the premises are permitted?
   (b) Is the permitted use clause broad enough for possible changes in the business?
   (c) Is the permitted use clause broad enough for potential assignments or subleases?
   (d) Can the use clause be drafted to include "any lawful purposes"?
   (e) Can uses be changed with landlord's consent, which consent can't be unreasonably withheld or delayed?

3. **Primary lease term**
   (a) What is the commencement date of the lease?
   (b) What happens if the space is not ready on the commencement date? Is there rent abatement, monetary damages, right to cancel the lease, or other remedies specified?
   (c) What is the termination date?
   (d) Does the landlord have the right to terminate early without a cause?
   (e) Does the tenant have the right to terminate early by payment of a fee?

4. **Rentals**
   (a) What is the base rent for the primary term?
   (b) Are there escalating clauses?
   (c) Are there cost of living increases?
   (d) Is there a cap on any rent increases?
   (e) Is there a reasonable grace period and written notice before a late charge is imposed?

5. **Common area maintenance, HVAC, and Operating costs**
   (a) What does the tenent have to contribute for common area maintenance, ventilating, heating, air conditioning, and other building operation costs?
   (b) Is there a cap?
   (c) Can the amount be increased each year?
   (d) Real estate taxes and other impositions:
       (i) Does the tenant have to pay a portion of the real estate taxes?
       (ii) What increases over base year are allowed?
       (iii) Is there a cap on tax increases?
       (iv) Does the tenant have to pay increased taxes that may occur on sale of the building?
   (e) Are there any special provisions or exeptions on the payment of these expenses?
   (f) When is payment due?

Form 15-1: The office lease checklist. (Page 1 of 4)

      (g)   What detailed reports does the landlord have to provide the tenant showing the actual expenses?

      (h)   What audit rights does the tenant have to review the landlord's books and records?

      (i)   Are there provisions made for weekend and holiday service? What are the charges?

      (j)   Does the tenant have a remedy for service interruption?

6.   **Tenant Improvements**

      (a)   What tenant improvements will be necessary?

      (b)   What is the cost?

      (c)   How much time will it take to complete teh tenant improvements?

      (d)   Will the landlord contribute to the cost for the tenant improvements?

      (e)   What approvals will be necessary?

      (f)   What permits will be necessary?

      (g)   Does the landlord or the tenant own any improvements?

7.   **Repairs and replacements**

      (a)   What responsibility does the tenant have for repairs or replacements?

      (b)   What reponsibility does the landlord have for repairs or replacements?

      (c)   At the end of the tenancy, is tenant's obligation to return the premises in same condition at the beginning of tenancy, excluding (1) orginary wear and tear, (2) damage by fire and other unavoidable casualty, and (3) alterations previously approved by landlord?

8.   **Utilities**

      (a)   Direct supply or individually metered?

      (b)   Method of computing payment?

9.   **Assignment and subletting:**

      (a)   Is the landlord's written approval required?

      (b)   What standard is there for approval? absolute discretion? reasonable approval?

      (c)   Does the landlord have the right to cancel the lease if notified of a proposed assignment of sublease?

      (d)   If the assignment or sublet is at a higher price than the base rent, who keeps the excess? or what split is there?

      (e)   Can the lease be assigned to affiliates of the tenant without landlord approval?

      (f)   Can the landlord terminate the lease if the stock ownership of the tenant changes?

10.   **Subordinating and attornment:**

      (a)   All present or future mortgages?

      (b)   Execution of estoppel certificates required?

      (c)   Tenant agrees to attorn to landlords successor in interest?

11.   **Destruction:**

      (a)   Is there a right of cancellation for the tenant in the event of destruction?

Form 15-1: The office lease checklist. (Page 2 of 4)

    (b)   What obligation does the landlord have to rebuild?

    (c)   Does the tenant share in any proceeds from insurance?

12. **Indemnity and Disclaimer:**
    (a)   Indemnity mutual or tenant only?
    (b)   Waiver of claims mutual or tenant only?
    (c)   Waiver of subrogation?
    (d)   Landlord liability limited to interest in property?

13. **Default:**
    (a)   Does the tenant have a cure period after notice of a breach?
    (b)   What remedies are available for breach?

14. **Landlord's warranties:**
    (a)   Quiet enjoyment of premises by the tenant?
    (b)   First class services?
    (c)   Security building?
    (d)   Ownership of building?

15. **Option to renew:**
    (a)   Does the tenant have the option to renew the lease?
    (b)   How long is the renewel option?
    (c)   How far in advance must the option be exercised?
    (d)   How is rent determined for the renewal period?

16. **Right of first offer for additional space**
    (a)   What is the scope of any right of first offer or first refusal?
    (b)   How is rent determined?
    (c)   How long does the tenant have before exercising the right?

17. **Security Deposit**
    (a)   What is the amount?
    (b)   Can it be a letter of credit?
    (c)   Is there interest on the security deposit?
    (d)   Does the lease provide for the return of the tenant's security deposit within a set number of days after termination of the lease?

18. **Guaranty:**
    (a)   Is a personal guarantee required?
    (b)   When does the quarantee terminate?

19. **Mortgages:**
    (a)   Can any mortgages adversely affect the tenant's rights if foreclosed upon?

20. **Free rent:**
    (a)   Will the landlord grant a free rent period?
    (b)   When does it have to be returned (e.g., on breach of lease)?

21. **Are there any peculiar landlord obligations that should be included?**

Form 15-1: The office lease checklist. (Page 3 of 4)

22. **Compliance With Law:**
    (a) Does landlord warrant that the premises are in compliance with applicable law?
    (b) If tenant is obligated to comply with applicable law, does it exclude matters that should more properly be the responsibility of the landlord (e.g., asbestos problems, disability access)?
    (c) Is landlord obligated to comply with all laws applicable to its control of the building?

23. **Insurance:**
    (a) What insurance is the tenant required to maintain?
    (b) What insurance is the landlord required to maintain?
    (c) Has the tenant's insurance agent reviewed the insurance requirements in the lease?

24. **Rules and Regulations**
    (a) Are there specific rules and regulations in existence?
    (b) Can the rules be changed without approval of tenant?
    (c) Is the landlord required to enforce the rules and regulations against other tenants?
    (d) Are there any rules that interfere with the expected operations of the tenant?

25. **Rights of Entry:**
    (a) Exclusive of emergencies, what notice must the landlord give in advance for entry into the tenant's premises?
    (b) Are there any restrictions on landlord interfering with tenant's business in showing the premises to buyers, lenders or prospective tenant's?

26. **Signage:**
    (a) What signage is the tenant allowed to put in or about the building and premises?

27. **Parking:**
    (a) How many parking spaces will be allowed to the tenant?
    (b) At what cost?

Form 15-1: The office lease checklist. (Page 4 of 4)

Rent

You need to do a cost analysis between buildings to properly estimate your business's future rental costs.

Any analysis of a given space's desirability typically begins with the fixed rent that the landlord quotes you. But you have to evaluate this starting point in light of other factors. For example, landlords may quote a monthly lease rate of $2 per square foot, typically meaning *rentable* square footage. The actual *usable* square footage of the premises is the space that you actually can use for your business operations.

Usable square footage is less than rentable square footage because it deducts common areas, such as public corridors, elevators, lobbies, and bathrooms, from the overall calculation. So, to compare apples to apples, you have to know the exact *usable* square footage of each space you're considering.

The structure of the lease payments may also be important. For example, a start-up business without much capital may want two or three months of free rent at the beginning of the lease, with a lower rental for the first year and increasing rentals for the second and third years.

When analyzing the cost of space, you must also take into account other operating costs that the landlord may pass on to you, the tenant. Some leases require the tenant to pay for all cleaning, building security, air-conditioning, maintenance, and so on (a so-called *Triple Net Lease*). And some leases require the landlord to provide and pay for basic services, while the tenant pays a proportionate share of any cost increases that the landlord incurs for such services over the initial base year of the lease.

Keep in mind that different buildings have different costs, and landlords may charge for services in a different manner. So the types and amounts of the costs that the landlord passes on to the tenant can have a big impact on the economics of a lease.

Negotiating permitted uses

The lease typically has a section that sets forth the permitted uses of the leased space.

Making this permitted use clause as broad as possible works to your advantage as the tenant, even if you initially have a narrow intended purpose.

Because your business may grow and your plans may change, you want the flexibility to use the space in any reasonable, legal manner.

Also, a narrow permitted use clause can often serve as a restriction on your ability to assign or sublet the space.

So what's the best permitted use clause? See if you can get the landlord to agree to something like the following:

> Tenant is permitted to use the premises for any legal purpose or business.

If the landlord doesn't go for that, at least spell out all of your expected or potential uses.

You may also want to take a look at Form 15-2 on the CD-ROM — an Addendum to Real Estate Lease that benefits the tenant.

Working out the term of the lease

The length of the lease has a significant impact on the rental rate. Landlords typically like longer term leases and are more willing to make concessions for such leases. With a long lease, the landlord enjoys the financial security of a regular rental stream over a number of years. And the landlord can avoid the hassle and expense of re-leasing the space.

From the tenant's side, a long term lease has both benefits and risks. The benefit is knowing that you have the premises available at a predictable cost for the long term. The risk is that the company may outgrow the space, may need less space as its business contracts, or is locked into paying what turns out to be above-market rent if demand for rentals subsequently declines.

If you can get it, the best of all worlds is a shorter term lease with renewal options. You're usually much better off getting a 2-year lease with four 2-year renewal options rather than getting stuck in a 10-year lease.

Escalating rent

Fixed rent over longer term leases is relatively rare, because landlords often try to build in rent escalation provisions.

Sometimes, landlords insist on annual increases based upon the percentage increases in the Consumer Price Index (CPI). If you're confronted with such a request, do two things to make rent increases manageable:

- ✔ Try to arrange that the CPI doesn't kick in for at least 2 years.

- ✔ Try to get a cap on the amount of each year's increase (for example, no more than a 3 percent increase in any year).

Here's a sample clause for putting those two things to work:

> Any rent increases under this Lease shall commence no earlier than two (2) years after the date of the commencement of this Lease. The maximum amount that the rent may be increased in any one year (starting in the third year of this Lease) shall be three percent (3%) over the beginning base rent under this Lease.

If you have to live with a rent escalation clause, consider a predetermined fixed amount, like

- ✔ $2,000 a month for the first year

- ✔ $2,200 a month for the second year

- ✔ $2,400 a month thereafter

Such a provision gives you more predictability in planning your business.

Make sure that your business plan projections adequately reflect such increases.

Operating costs

The starting point for determining your operating costs is identifying what services the landlord provides, what services the tenant must get directly, and who bears the cost. The following are typical costs for office space:

- ✔ Heating, ventilating, and air conditioning (commonly referred to as HVAC)

- ✔ Cleaning and janitorial services

- ✔ Electricity

- ✔ Repairs

- ✔ Security

If the landlord is charging you separately for such services, try to negotiate a fixed fee or cap on the amount.

If the landlord pays for basic services but charges you for increases in the cost of rendering those services, ask the landlord how he's calculating that increase. For example, some landlords may figure the base year for calculating the starting point of costs as one in which the building isn't fully occupied (heat not necessarily fully on, not all lights in use, and so on). In this case, your company's moving in naturally causes cost increases. Get the landlord to count the base-year costs as if the building were fully occupied and operational.

Landlords often try to get tenants to pay for increases in property taxes on the building. Watch out for this trick because if the property has been held for a long time before being sold, the value of the property may be significantly higher after the sale for property tax purposes. The end result is a higher property tax that you may be stuck paying. Tell the landlord that having to pay for such an increase isn't fair to you.

Landlords also try to throw in items as operating expenses that should really be capital expenses (and thus not properly chargeable to a tenant). So make sure that the definition of operating expenses that you may be liable for doesn't include capital improvements, financing charges, and other capital costs.

In addition, some landlords charge extra for services supplied other than on "business days" or "after hours." So look at this clause carefully and try to limit charges for extra services to those situations that are truly extraordinary and don't happen on a regular basis. A start-up business may find this point particularly important, where workers often spend nights and weekends working.

The operating costs section of your base can mean big, unexpected costs, so carefully anticipate the problems!

Allowing for tenant improvements and alterations

Most form leases provide that the tenant can't make any alterations or improvements to the premises without the landlord's consent. Those provisions are typically too restrictive for the tenant, and you should attempt to negotiate changes. For example, try to get the right to make non-structural changes or changes costing less than $5,000 without the need to obtain the landlord's consent.

Before you can occupy the space, you may need to make some improvements or alterations to the premises to make it appropriate for your business needs.

Here are some key questions to answer about the initial tenant improvements and alterations:

> ✔ What is the scope of changes?
>
> ✔ What is the cost?
>
> ✔ How much time do you need to complete the improvements?
>
> ✔ What permits or approvals do you need?
>
> ✔ Will the landlord help pay for the improvements?
>
> ✔ Who owns the improvements after the lease is terminated?

Try to get a clause stating that you're allowed to remove any trade fixtures and alterations that you pay for, provided that you repair any damages to the premises.

If you anticipate the need to make alterations or improvements in the future, the lease should provide that you may make them with the landlord's consent, but that the landlord can't unreasonably withhold or delay that consent.

Also, be aware of the clause that says you have to return the premises in their original condition at the end of the lease. Try to negotiate a clause that states the following:

> The premises will be returned to the Landlord at the end of the tenancy in the same condition as at the beginning of the tenancy, excluding (1) ordinary wear and tear, (2) damage by fire and unavoidable casualty not the fault of the Tenant, and (3) alterations previously approved by the Landlord.

Setting up rules about assignment and subletting

The assignment and subletting clause of the lease can prove to be a very important provision. *Assignment* generally refers to transferring the lease totally to someone else. *Subletting* typically means leasing a portion of your space to someone else or for a period shorter than the original lease. Typically, the landlord's lease form states that the tenant may not assign or sublet the lease without the landlord's prior consent, with such consent to be granted or withheld at the landlord's sole discretion.

You should attempt to modify such a clause in several ways. The ideal change provides that an assignment or sublease requires the landlord's consent, but that the landlord can't unreasonably withhold or delay that consent. (A landlord probably won't give you the total right to assign or sublease without some kind of approval procedure.)

If the landlord does give you a reasonableness standard on your proposed assignment or sublease, she may insist upon *a recapture right.* The landlord may want to recapture the space for her own use or re-leasing. This condition is generally acceptable to you as the tenant, as long as the landlord pays you any profit that you expect to make on the assignment or sublease.

If an assignment or subletting comes with potential profit, then the landlord typically expects to share in that profit. Often, the split is 50-50, but make sure to recoup any expenses that you incur in getting an assignee or subtenant before a profit split.

A start-up tenant should also negotiate enough flexibility in the assignment and subletting clause to allow for mergers, reorganizations, and share ownership changes.

See if you can freely assign and sublet the lease to the company's subsidiaries and affiliates.

Be particularly leery of a clause that says the landlord can deem a change in more than 50 percent of the company's stock ownership an assignment that is prohibited without the landlord's approval. A prohibited assignment can result in the landlord terminating a favorable lease. As the company grows and new people invest in the company, you can inadvertently trigger this clause.

On the CD-ROM, you can find a sample Assignment of Lease (Form 15-3) and a sample Real Estate Sublease (Form 15-4).

Figuring out renewal options

Because you don't know your company's future space needs, renewal options for the lease can help you out a lot. But some landlords may be reluctant to grant such options because doing so limits their flexibility to market the space to prospective tenants.

If you can get a renewal option, try to get the option rent at a fixed predetermined rental. Try to avoid the options based on "fair market rent" at the option term.

Here are the key issues for renewal options:

  ✔ How many option terms can you get?

  ✔ How long is each option term?

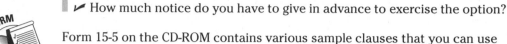

✔ What rent does the landlord charge for the option term?

✔ How much notice do you have to give in advance to exercise the option?

Form 15-5 on the CD-ROM contains various sample clauses that you can use for a renewal option in a lease.

Option to expand

The right to expand into additional or adjoining space in a building can be very valuable. After all, you're planning to have your business grow, aren't you?

These expansion options have several variations. First, you can have a fixed expansion option, where the tenant has a defined period of time in which to exercise the option. Here is an example of this type of option:

> Tenant shall have the right to occupy that certain space adjacent to its existing leased space, of approximately 1,000 square feet, for an additional monthly rent of $500. Tenant must exercise this expansion option within 120 days of the date of this Lease by giving written notice to Landlord. In that event, all other terms of this Lease shall apply to this expansion space.

Form 15-6 on the CD-ROM is a sample letter offering to expand space in a building that you lease.

Alternatively, the tenant can have a *Right of First Offer* on any space that becomes available in the building. The landlord under this alternative has to first present any space available to the tenant before marketing it to third parties.

Finally, you can try for a *Right of First Refusal* on space. That obligates the landlord to bring to you first any deals that he's willing to sign with third parties for space in the building and allow you to match the deal and pre-empt the third party.

Any expansion option can help you, so try to get what you can.

Looking into security deposits

The landlord typically requires you to post a security deposit for performance of your lease obligations. This security deposit is generally equal to one or two month's rent, but a landlord may insist on more if the company is new or financially unstable.

From the tenant's perspective, try to get the following:

✔ Interest on the security deposit

✔ A reduction in the amount of the security deposit if the tenant pays the rent on time for at least a year

✔ A provision that says the landlord must return the security deposit within 15 days of the termination of the tenancy

Try to obtain the clauses above in an amendment to the landlord's lease. Form 15-7 on the CD-ROM is a sample Lease Amendment that you can use.

Some landlords may insist on a personal guarantee from the business founders if the potential tenant is a corporation or other entity. Try to avoid this situation — it puts your personal, as well as business, assets at risk.

Reviewing the rules and regulations of the building

Landlords often have separate rules and regulations that apply to the building. These rules may contain a number of restrictions and limitations as to what you can do in the building.

Make sure to review these rules and regulations before you sign the lease, and try to get your lease to include the following:

✔ The terms of the lease govern if any inconsistencies arise between your lease and the landlord's rules and regulations.

✔ The rules must be reasonable, and the landlord can't adopt any new rules that aren't reasonable.

✔ The landlord will enforce these rules against all of the building's tenants.

And of course, if some of the rules and regulations are problematic for your business, make sure that your lease gives you the needed waiver or flexibility.

Offering an Offer Letter

Okay, so say that you've found some space that looks ideal for the business. How do you begin negotiations? Well, you can submit an *Offer Letter* to the landlord, laying out the terms that you find acceptable. From there, you can commence the negotiations and move to a definitive lease. Form 15-8 later in this chapter shows a sample Offer Letter.

Letter Announcing New Terms

[Letterhead]

[Date]

Re: Offer to Lease Space in Your Building

Dear_____:

        We have now reviewed your property at [address] (the "Property") and are quite interested in leasing space in the property. We beleive we would be excellent tenants and are prepared to consummate a lease as soon as possible.

        As a way to commence our discussions, let us lay out some of the key terms which we believe would be acceptable to us:

Leased Premises: The_____floor at the Property, consisting of
                                     approximately_____ square feet

Commencement Date of Lease: _____ . 20___

Length of Lease: _____years

Monthly Rent: $_____ for the first____ ___years of the Lease. $_____
                                     for the remaining years of the Lease.

Utilities: All utilities to be paid for by the Lessee, except for

                                     _____ .

Parking: Lessee to have_____ parking spaces in the building.

Use of Lease Premises: General office use and/or any other legal use.

Improvements: Lessor to make the following improvements to the Lease
                                     Premises prior to Lessee's occupancy:_____
                                     _____ .

Right to Renew: Lessee to have the right to renew the Lease for an
                                     additional_____ years, for $_____per month rent.

Form 15-8: A letter offering lease terms. (Page 1 of 2)

[Landlord]
[Date]
Page 2

Taxes: All taxes on the property shall be payable by Lessor.

Assignment & Subletting: The Leased Premises shall not be assigned or sublet
                                  without the consent of Lessor, which consent shall not be
                                  unreasonably withheld or delayed.

Security Deposit: $ _____

Form of Lease: To be mutually agreed upon between Lessor and Lessee.

      We are happy to discuss any of these terms and look forward to a long and mutually beneficial relationship. So that you may appreciate how responsible of a tenant we would be, I enclosed some background information on our company.

      Let us set up a meeting to discuss this as soon as possible.

              Very truly yours,

Enclosure

Form 15-8: A letter offering lease terms. (Page 2 of 2)

Forms on the CD-ROM

Form 15-1	**Checklist for Office Leases**	A checklist of issues to look out for in analyzing office leases
Form 15-2	**Addendum to Real Estate Lease (For the Benefit of the Tenant)**	A sample Addendum designed to give some protections and benefits to the tenant from the standard form of lease provided by the landlord
Form 15-3	**Assignment of Lease**	A form of assignment of lease by a tenant
Form 15-4	**Office Sublease**	A sample office sublease
Form 15-5	**Option to Renew Real Estate Lease**	Sample provisions to add to a real estate lease granting the tenant a right to renew the lease at the end of the term
Form 15-6	**Option to Expand Space Leased in a Building**	A sample provision for a tenant to expand a lease to include additional space in the building
Form 15-7	**Amendment to Lease**	Form used to amend a lease
Form 15-8	**Offer to Lease Space**	A sample letter offering to lease space
Form 15-9	**Option to Purchase**	A sample provision giving the tenant the option to buy the property being leased
Form 15-10	**Consent by Lessor to Assignment of Lease**	A consent by the landlord to the assignment of a lease
Form 15-11	**Consent by Lessor to Sublease**	A consent by a landlord to a proposed sublease
Form 15-12	**Demand for Rent**	A sample letter firmly demanding rent payment from a tenant
Form 15-13	**Notice of Change in Rent**	A sample letter notifying a tenant of an impending rent change

Part V
Spreading the Word

The 5th Wave   By Rich Tennant

"There you go Mr. Mellman. As agreed, every bird I sell over the next 12 months will be trained to say, 'Hello', 'Pretty bird', and 'Mellman's Carpet World'. Some of the birds have trouble with the word, 'carpet'. It comes out 'crapet'. That gonna be a problem?"

In this part . . .

After your business is safely off the ground, you need to get the word out. A little publicity just won't do — your market needs to hear about your company as often as possible. The more people hear positive things about your company, the more they will feel positively toward it. In this part, I tell you the ins and outs of two of the most cost-effective methods of gaining your market's mindshare: the Web and the press.

Chapter 16

Web Sites, Your Business, and You

In This Chapter
▶ Finding and registering an Internet domain name
▶ Negotiating Web Site Development Contracts
▶ Peeking into the Web site legal kit

*B*usinesses of every size are embracing the World Wide Web. Consumers have spent enormous amounts of money buying goods and services online, and this spending will only increase. Even companies that aren't ready to sell goods and services through the Web are putting up Web sites as a way to provide the public with information about the company.

However, when establishing a business Web site, you face a number of legal, business, intellectual property, and contractual issues. In this chapter, I navigate you through some of the trapdoors so that you can properly establish your Web site.

Determining a Domain Name

In order to establish your business Web site, you need to get a *domain name* that no one else has taken. Your domain name is your address on the Web.

The domain name has two parts. The first is the top-level domain (such as .com, .org, .edu, and so on). The second part identifies the site's name (IBM, Intel, and so on). So, for example, Microsoft's domain name is microsoft.com.

What's the Web about, Alfie?

I'm not going to bore you with a lot of technical stuff. You can find hundreds — if not thousands — of books and articles about geeky Web stuff.

Suffice it to say, the Internet is a bunch of connected computers. The World Wide Web is the portion of the Internet that allows you to view graphics, text, and even listen to audio.

For your purposes, the Web gives you the opportunity to let millions of people access information about your company and to advertise your goods and services.

So what do all those endings mean? Here's a list of the major ones and what they generally represent:

- `.com`: Businesses
- `.edu`: Educational institutions
- `.gov`: Government offices
- `.mil`: Military sites
- `.net`: Networking organizations
- `.org`: Organizations that don't fall into any of the above categories (such as `www.salvationarmy.org`)

Sites in countries other than the U.S. typically have a two-letter zone, such as `.fr` for France or `.au` for Australia.

Because each domain name has to be unique, you must check to make sure that the name you want hasn't been taken. You may find this experience frustrating because many domain names have already been registered.

Running a check on an e-brilliant name

Say that you have come up with a brilliant domain name for your business — how about `eBrilliant.com`?

You can use a variety of Web sites to quickly and easily check whether a domain name is available, including:

> ✔ www.NetworkSolutions.com
>
> ✔ www.Register.com
>
> ✔ www.GoDaddy.com

Some Web sites allow you to simultaneously check other extensions related to your desired name (such as www.eBrilliant.net). If someone else already owns the name, you can find out who and get his or her contact information (in case you want to see if that person may be interested in selling the name).

Registering a domain name

After you've found an available name, you can register to buy it online in a manner of minutes. Any site that allows you to search for a domain name typically also allows you to purchase that name.

The registration fee for a domain name can vary, but you typically have to pay $35 for the first year. You then have to pay a yearly renewal fee to keep the name. Renewal fees depend on which company you initially registered with, but you can also change registrars (although you have to deal with some paperwork). Yearly renewal fees typically range from $8.95 a year to $35 a year. You have to make sure to pay the renewal fee, otherwise you lose the right to use the domain name (but the registrars usually bug you numerous times to remind you to pay the renewal fee).

To actually put up a Web site, you need a hosting service for your site. The company you initially register the name with can give you various options for hosting services. The web hosting business has a lot of competitors, so you can also do a Web search on www.Google.com and www.Yahoo.com to find numerous choices.

Buying a domain name from an existing holder

Sometimes, you decide on the perfect domain name for your business, but someone else owns it. What do you do? Well, first, go to their Web site and check out what they have. If they have some elaborate Web site that looks like it has taken a lot of time and energy to build, they probably won't sell the name cheaply (or sell at all).

If you still want the domain name, you can contact the person and offer to buy the name. You can find out contact information for domain name holders by checking out the WHOIS link on www.networksolutions.com.

If you reach an agreement on price with the domain name holder, you should draft a short form of agreement that covers the following points:

- ✔ The current holder is transferring the name to you, as well as all right, title, and interest associated with the name.

- ✔ The name has no liens, encumbrances, or security interests.

- ✔ The holder will sign all necessary paperwork and cooperate to transfer the domain name on the records of Network Solutions.

You can check out a good sample Domain Name Purchase Agreement (and purchase it in a downloadable format) from www.AllBusiness.com.

The seller also has to sign and notarize a Domain Name Change Agreement, which you can find at www.networksolutions.com. Make sure that the seller does this official stuff before you give full payment because, without this signed agreement, you can't change the ownership over to you on the records of the Network Solutions.

Of domains and trademarks

Registering a domain name doesn't give you any trademark rights to that name, but domain names and trademark rights can overlap. Trademarks aim to prevent confusion between familiar words, symbols, and distinctive combinations used in a commercial manner. A company may choose not to register every name associated with its products as a domain name. However, that name may still qualify as a trademark because the consumer associates it with that company. Consequently, the ownership and use of domain names have caused some disputes.

Being master of your domain name

Thinking of an unused domain name can be a frustrating process. Here are a few tips:

- ✔ Avoid common names — someone has likely taken them already.

- ✔ Keep your name simple so users can easily remember it.

- ✔ Do a trademark search on the name.

- ✔ Look for domain names that someone already owns but has up for sale, such as those at www.GreatDomains.com.

Chapter 16: Web Sites, Your Business, and You **303**

Hiring someone to develop your Web site

Unless computers are your stock in trade, you're likely to prefer that someone else develop your Web site. Web site development companies have sprung up like mushrooms in the last few years. They all promise to get your Web site up and running, but their price varies from $1,000 to $100,000, depending on the bells and whistles that you want.

Follow these tips to find the right developer for you:

✔ Review a number of commercial Web sites. Sites often list the developer and include a link to the developer's Web site.

✔ Ask your business associates who they have used and what experience they had.

✔ Check newspaper and magazine listings — many developers advertise their services.

In your registration application, you certify that using the proposed domain name won't interfere with or infringe the right of any third party in any jurisdiction, with respect to trademark or any other intellectual property right. You also have to agree to give up a domain name if a competing claimant presents evidence that the granted domain name is identical to a valid and subsisting trademark or service mark owned by someone else

Before you spend a lot of time creating your Web site, consider hiring an experienced search organization to perform a domain name and related trademark search. Check out Chapter 13 for the details on these searches.

You can find the official Trademark Registration form on Form 16-1 on the CD-ROM. This form lets you register with the Patent and Trademark Office (PTO). Form 16-2 on the CD-ROM shows a sample cover letter to the PTO.

The Web Site Development Contract

Unless you happen to be a techie-type person or have nothing better to do with your time than to try to understand Web design and HTML, you should consider contracting with a Web site developer to create your site. Finding the right Web developer isn't always easy (see the sidebar "Hiring someone to develop your Web site"), but, when you do, make sure that you have that person sign a well-prepared contract. These contracts can cover many issues; here are key things that your contract should contain:

- ✔ You're hiring the Web site developer as an independent contractor performing a "work for hire" service under the Copyright Act. (See the discussion in Chapter 10 on independent contractors.)

- ✔ Your company solely owns all screens, graphics, domain names, and content, as well as the site's look and feel. You also own all underlying software, object code, digital programming, source code, and the like developed for you.

- ✔ The developer represents that he won't knowingly infringe upon or violate anyone's copyright or other intellectual property rights when developing the site.

- ✔ You and the developer agree to a timetable and budget for the site's completion, including specific payment milestones.

- ✔ You can produce a change order regarding the site's specifications; the change order doesn't result in exorbitant extra costs or delays.

- ✔ You will receive documentation and source code for all software associated with the site from the developer in a timely manner.

- ✔ You have the right to reject the work if it doesn't meet designated specifications. The contract should also spell out your correction options if you reject the work.

- ✔ You state the site's anticipated functionality and technological requirements.

- ✔ You charge the developer with the duty of fixing any bugs and failed links (include the maximum time for correction).

Form 16-3 on the CD-ROM (and shown later in this chapter) gives you a complete checklist of issues to cover in your Web Site Development Agreement.

Carefully and continuously review your Web site. Make sure that you charge a knowledgeable employee with routinely monitoring and updating the site.

Checklist of Issues for Web Site Development Contracts

Many companies contract out the development of their Web sites to third party developers. Companies should ensure that the contract with the Web site developer address several key areas, including ownership and intellectual property rights, the development process, functionality of the end product, problems that may arise and corrective measures required to be undertaken, covenents of the developer, confidentiality, and other provisions. The following is a checklist of issues.

A.   **Ownership and Intellectual Property Issues.** The development agreement should clearly address the issue of ownership of and intellectual property issues related to the content, screens, software, and information developed. The agreement can address:

- That the Web site developer is an independent contractor performing a work for hire service under the Copyright act;

- That all screens, graphics, domain names, content and the look-and-feel of the site developed shall be owned solely by the company, together with all underlying software, object code, digital programming, source code, and the like;

- Provisions addressing whether the developer retains rights to use any materials or software it gains from its creation of the Web site;

- That all intellectual property developed in connection with the site will be owned solely by the company;

- That the developer in developing the site, will not infringe or violate the copyright and other intellectual property rights of third parties;

- That the developer is bundling or using any prior intellectual property that it owns and of which it wishes to keep ownership, that the company will receive a perpetual, irrevocable, worldwide, royalty free transferable license to the same;

- Which party is responsible for securing various rights, licenses, clearances, and other permissions related to works, graphics or other copyrighted materials to be used or otherwise incorporated in the Web site; and

- That a copyright notice will be displayed on designated parts of the company's site.

B.   **The Development Process.** The development agreement can address various issues associated with the development of the site, progress payments, and acceptance precedures. Such provisions could address:

- A timetable and budget for completion of the site, including specific payment milestones as progress is made on site development;

Form 16-3: Checklist of Issues for Web Site Development Contracts, page 1 of 4.

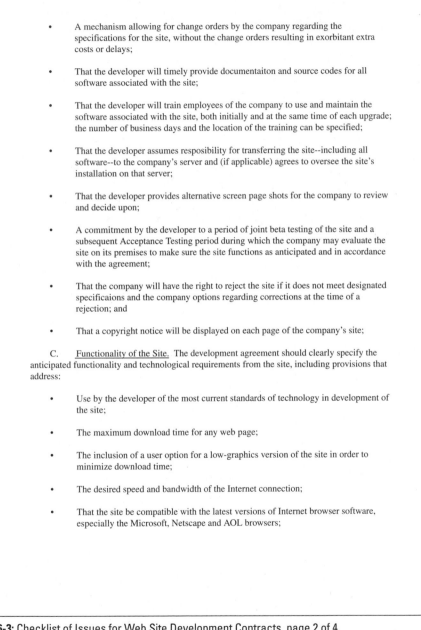

- A mechanism allowing for change orders by the company regarding the specifications for the site, without the change orders resulting in exorbitant extra costs or delays;

- That the developer will timely provide documentaiton and source codes for all software associated with the site;

- That the developer will train employees of the company to use and maintain the software associated with the site, both initially and at the same time of each upgrade; the number of business days and the location of the training can be specified;

- That the developer assumes resposibility for transferring the site--including all software--to the company's server and (if applicable) agrees to oversee the site's installation on that server;

- That the developer provides alternative screen page shots for the company to review and decide upon;

- A commitment by the developer to a period of joint beta testing of the site and a subsequent Acceptance Testing period during which the company may evaluate the site on its premises to make sure the site functions as anticipated and in accordance with the agreement;

- That the company will have the right to reject the site if it does not meet designated specificaions and the company options regarding corrections at the time of a rejection; and

- That a copyright notice will be displayed on each page of the company's site;

C.   Functionality of the Site. The development agreement should clearly specify the anticipated functionality and technological requirements from the site, including provisions that address:

- Use by the developer of the most current standards of technology in development of the site;

- The maximum download time for any web page;

- The inclusion of a user option for a low-graphics version of the site in order to minimize download time;

- The desired speed and bandwidth of the Internet connection;

- That the site be compatible with the latest versions of Internet browser software, especially the Microsoft, Netscape and AOL browsers;

Form 16-3: Checklist of Issues for Web Site Development Contracts, page 2 of 4.

- That the site will be funcitoning 24 hours a day, seven days a week, except for schedules maintenance/downtime;

- The number of users that will be able to simultaneously access the site as well as response time for users requests;;

- How the site will be properly integrated with the company's intranet or other data server structure;

- That additions, corrections or modifications to the site may be made by the company without interference with site operations;

- The security safegaurds, procedures and firewalls that the site must contain;

- The expected functionality of online credit verification and acceptance procedures; and

- The scope and procedure for the company being able to easily access, records, and compile information about the sites users and customers.

D.   Problems and Corrective Measures. The development agreement should address the problems that may arise and the developer's duty to promptly correct such problems, including:

- The developer's duty to fix any bugs and failed links, including maximum time for correction;

- The revision of the site to comply with the functionality specifications;

- Any particular warranties or disclaimers by the developer;

- That the developer agrees to ensure that the software for the site is free of any viruses or disabling devices; and

- The rights of the company for termination of the agreement and the liability of the developer upon such termination.

E.   Covenants of the Developer. The development agreement may impose a variety of additional duties on the developer, such as:

- That the developer will, if requested by the company, publish information about the site with a mutually agreeable set of search engines and direcitons;

- That the developer will not during the site development or thereafter use the company's trademarks, service marks or logos, except with the company's express written approval;

Form 16-3: Checklist of Issues for Web Site Development Contracts, page 3 of 4.

- That the developer will not use its service affiliation with the company for its own promotional purposes without prior written consent;

- That the developer will compy with all applicable laws in connection with its activities; and

- That the developer will maintain satisfactory insurance and will provide proof of its policies.

F.   Confidentiality. The company will want to obligate the developer to keep all confidential or proprietary information that it learns about the company or its customers strictly confidential, and not use such information other than in conneciton with the developer's obligations under the development agreement. The agreement may also require that the developer's employees and consultants working on the site development project execute a Confidentiality and Invention Assignment Agreement. This agreement may also address the issue of whether the developer is permitted to subcontract portions of the development project.

G.   Miscellaneous. As in any good contract, the following types of claused shoyuld be considered for the development agreement:

- That in the event of a dispute, the prevailing party will be entitled to recoup its attorney's fees and costs;

- Whether disputes will be handled by litigation or arbitration;

- What governing law will govern and wher eany disputes must be brought;

- That the contract contains the complete and entire understanding and agreement of the parties;

- That the agreement can only be amended in writing; and

- That the agreement is not assignable by the developer.

Form 16-3: Checklist of Issues for Web Site Development Contracts, page 4 of 4.

The Web Site Legal Kit

Conducting business in cyberspace doesn't mean that you don't have to worry about real-world liability issues. This section provides important sample language and contracts that provide you some protection if you use them on your Web site.

Online Contract

If you plan to sell products or services through your Web site, you need to prepare and include an Online Contract (sometimes called a Terms of Use Agreement) on your site.

An *Online Contract* is like a normal customer contract — it describes the terms and conditions for the sale of your product or service. However, unlike traditional contracts, the customer doesn't have to provide a formal signature. Typically, the customer registers with the site or starts the process of purchasing, and then the site directs her to the Online Contract. Before the customer can purchase anything, she has to accept or agree to the contract's terms (usually by clicking an "accept" button).

Carefully craft your contract to protect the company from liability and address the key terms and conditions for the provision of goods or services. Display the contract conspicuously and make it readily available to customers. Ideally, each page on the site (or at least key portions of the site) should have language stating that the Online Contract governs use of the site or the purchase of goods and services through the site. Make sure that you also always provide a *hyperlink* (those underlined thingies that whoosh you off to other Web pages) to the full contract.

Post at your own peril

Although you may be tempted to include all kinds of information on your site, be careful what you post. Following are some common mistakes:

✔ Posting someone else's copyrighted information or other materials

✔ Posting sensitive company information, including any trade secrets

✔ Posting information that you don't want a competitor to see (remember, anyone can access your site)

✔ Posting content that is lewd, libelous, or obscene

✔ Posting out-of-date information

✔ Posting information that someone can use against you in any litigation

When a customer agrees to the terms of the Online Contract, make sure that you have a procedure in place to create and store records of that agreement.

A well-drafted Online Contract answers a number of key questions that protect the seller:

- ✔ Are there any limitations on the type of goods or services sold?

- ✔ Is the product being sold "as is"?

- ✔ Do the goods or service come with any limited warranties? If not, do you have a disclaimer of any express or implied warranties?

- ✔ What is the refund policy?

- ✔ Does the contract limit the company's liability if something goes wrong?

- ✔ Where should a customer bring any disputes? (Ideally, he can bring disputes only in the company's hometown.)

- ✔ What is your privacy policy?

- ✔ Does the contract have all the necessary boilerplate clauses? (Check out Chapter 11 for a discussion of boilerplate clauses.)

- ✔ Do you have a clause that requires binding arbitration for any disputes?

Form 16-4 on the CD-ROM provides a sample Online Contract.

Terms of Use Agreement references

Make sure that your online customers know of your terms for selling goods or providing information. You can do so by adding the following to the bottom of your Web site's key pages:

The use of this site, and the terms and conditions for the sale of any goods and services, is governed by our Terms of Use Agreement. By using this site you acknowledge that you have read the Terms of Use Agreement and the disclaimers and caveats contained in this site, and that you accept and will be bound by the terms thereof.

Link the disclaimer to the full text of the Terms of Use Agreement.

Copyright notices

Make sure that you place a notice of copyright on your site. The following gives you some sample language for the notice (see Form 16-5 on the CD-ROM):

Copyright ©2005 by ABC, Inc. All the text, graphics, audio, design, software, and other works are the copyrighted works of ABC, Inc. All Rights Reserved. Any redistribution or reproduction of any materials herein is strictly prohibited.

Web site information disclaimers

A good Web site includes a strong disclaimer regarding the accuracy of information posted on the Web site. After all, you don't want someone suing you because you didn't get something quite right on your site. Although a disclaimer can't guarantee protection, it can certainly help.

Form 16-6, shown on the following page, is a sample disclaimer of the information on your Web site. (Sometimes this disclaimer is part of your Terms of Use Agreement.)

Forms 16-7 and 16-8 on the CD-ROM give you additional disclaimers.

Hyperlink disclaimers

If you provide a link from your site to another site, consider adding a *hyperlink disclaimer*. This disclaimer warns visitors that you don't guarantee or endorse the linked sites. You may want to format it like this example:

This site contains links to other Internet sites. Such links are not endorsements of any products or services in such sites, and no information in such site has been endorsed or approved by XYZ, Inc.

Hyperlink disclaimers are on Form 16-9 of the CD-ROM.

Sample Online Disclaimers
Regarding Information

THE INFORMATION FROM OR THROUGH THIS SITE IS PROVIDED "AS-IS," "AS AVAILABLE," AND ALL WARRANTIES, EXPRESS OR IMPLIED, ARE DISCLAIMED (INCLUDING BUT NOT LIMITED TO THE DISCLAIMER OF ANY IMPLIED WARRANTIES OF MERCHANTABILITY AND FITNESS FOR A PARTICULAR PURPOSE). THE INFORMATION MAY CONTAIN ERRORS, PROBLEMS OR OTHER LIMITATIONS. OUR SOLE AND ENTIRE MAXIMUM LIABILITY FOR ANY INACCURATE INFORMATION, FOR ANY REASON, AND USER'S SOLE AND EXCLUSIVE REMEDY FOR ANY CAUSE WHATSOEVER, SHALL BE LIMITED TO THE AMOUNT PAID BY THE CUSTOMER FOR THE INFORMATION RECEIVED (IF ANY). WE ARE NOT LIABLE FOR ANY INDIRECT, SPECIAL, INCIDENTAL, OR CONSEQUENTIAL DAMAGES (INCLUDING DAMAGES FOR LOSS OF BUSINESS, LOSS OF PROFITS, LITIGATION, OR THE LIKE). WHETHER BASED ON BREACH OF CONTRACT, BREACH OF WARRANTY, TORT (INCLUDING NEGLIGENCE), PRODUCT LIABILITY OR OTHERWISE, EVEN IF ADVISED OF THE POSSIBILITY OF SUCH DAMAGE. THE LIMITATIONS OF DAMAGES SET FORTH ABOVE ARE FUNDAMENTAL ELEMENTS OF THE BASIS OF THE BARGAIN BETWEEN US AND YOU. WE WOULD NOT PROVIDE THIS SITE AND INFORMATION WITHOUT SUCH LIMITATIONS. NO REPRESENTATIONS, WARRANTIES OR GUARANTEES WHATSOEVER ARE MADE AS TO THE ACCURACY, ADEQUACY, RELIABILITY, CURRENTNESS, COMPLETENESS, SUITABILITY OR APPLICABILITY OF THE INFORMATION TO A PARTICULAR SITUATION.

All responsibility and liability for any damages caused by viruses contained within the electronic files of this site are disclaimed.

All terms and conditions with respect to this site is governed by a <u>Terms of Service Agreement</u>.

> Sets out that the information is "as is," with no guarantees

> Tries to limit your potential liability

> The underlined text should then hyperlink to the language of the Terms of Service Agreement

Form 16-6: A sample online disclaimer regarding information.

Forms on the CD-ROM

Check out the forms on the CD-ROM that deal with your business and the Web:

Form 16-1	**Trademark Registration Form**	An official document for registering a trademark with the U.S. Patent and Trademark Office
Form 16-2	**Cover Letter**	Cover letter for the Trademark Registration Form
Form 16-3	**Checklist of Issues for Web Site Development Contracts**	A checklist of issues to review when negotiating and drafting a Web Site Development Contract
Form 16-4	**Sample Online Contract**	A sample Online Contract for the sale of goods through a Web site
Form 16-5	**Sample Copyright and Trademark Protection Notice**	A sample copyright and trademark notice to include on a Web site
Form 16-6	**Sample Online Disclaimer Regarding Information**	A sample disclaimer for information posted on a Web site
Form 16-7	**Sample Disclosure Regarding Products**	A sample disclaimer that concerns the products sold on a commercial Web site
Form 16-8	**Sample Online Disclosure Regarding Online Contracts**	A sample disclosure that notifies Web site visitors of the terms and conditions involved in the sale of a product or service; the disclosure includes a link to the terms and conditions
Form 16-9	**Sample Online Disclaimers About Hyperlinks**	Sample disclaimers concerning hyperlinks to other sites

Chapter 17

Press Releases and Dealing with the Press

In This Chapter

▶ Understanding the ins and outs of press releases

▶ Writing press releases

▶ Getting your press release noticed

*I*n today's Information Age, you can almost immediately disseminate infor-mation and publicity about your business, product, service, or news by dialing a phone, sending a fax, or clicking a mouse.

The key to favorable media coverage is knowing whom to target and how to effectively and efficiently get the word out. The more specific you are with the press, the better your chances for favorable coverage. In this chapter, I discuss preparing and distributing press releases and dealing with the press.

Drafting Good Press Releases

Press releases are documents that contain summary information about a topic, business, event, or person. You distribute press releases to journalists, newspapers, magazines, and other news media. To attract the media's atten-tion, make the information in the press release as media-friendly as you can. Reporters expect most press releases to follow the same general format, regardless of whether you send the press release via conventional mail, as a fax, or by e-mail. Although you should follow the standard format, concen-trate on making your content as interesting and newsworthy as possible.

First things first

The press's awesome power is also a Pandora's Box. One article in a highly visible publication like *Fortune* magazine or even your local newspaper may seem like a business's dream. But if the author or reporter has a negative opinion of your product, then bad publicity may quickly ensue.

The adage that "any coverage is good coverage" is not a statement to do business by. Just talk to the PR folks at a well-known fast food chain after an E. coli outbreak.

A well-written press release may result in several favorable developments, such as

- Tremendous free publicity for your company (such as when an article is published in the newspaper or trade publication)
- Interest from customers who may not have been aware of your company
- Interest from potential investors or strategic partners
- Opportunities to explain, correct, or clarify your point of view

Getting the keys to a press release

Reporters get tons of press releases every day. Some grab their attention, provide the right information in the right format, and become stories. Others just find their way to the trash bin, and you don't want your press release to languish alongside pencil shavings and leftover tuna salad.

Your press release needs to cover the basic information: who, what, when, where, why, and how. Tell the media who you are, what you're announcing, and why they should care. (*Remember:* Less is more.) Always include the following information:

- Contact name and phone (critical!)
- Web site address
- Release time (immediate release or release upon a specified date)
- Headline
- Dateline (what city the story originates from)

When writing a press release, begin with the major news angle that you want to promote and then elaborate with three to five paragraphs. Use several third-party quotes (from customers or industry experts, for example). End your press release with three pound signs (###) or the number 30 (written –30–), which is shorthand for "the end." You should center these symbols under the last line of text.

Before you send out the release, make sure that your top management, any users, and other cited parties review and clear the text. And don't forget to check your spelling — reporters can be real sticklers for spelling and grammar.

Every time you use your mailing list, verify that it's up-to-date, accurate, and reflects the target readership for this particular release.

Delivering press releases

After you prepare a great press release, consider sending it to the following places:

- Local newspapers
- Magazines and newsletters that focus on your industry
- Specialized business newspapers (such as the *San Francisco Business Times,* if you happen to be doing business in the San Francisco area)
- Local radio stations that cover business news
- Local television shows that cover business topics

If you can, always send the press release to a specific reporter or editor. Spend a little time and effort contacting various organizations to confirm the most logical recipient's correct name and title (and verify the spelling, while you're at it). Most media outlets list their phone numbers in the Yellow Pages.

You can send your press releases in a variety of ways:

- **Regular mail:** Sending press releases by regular mail is pretty old-fashioned. If your material is time sensitive, regular mail may take too long to get to the right person in the media organization.

- **Fax:** Faxes have plusses and minuses, but many businesses now commonly use them to disseminate press releases. On the plus side, you can send the press release immediately and get it to the correct person fairly quickly. However — here's the minus — reporters are sometimes inundated with faxes, and yours may be lost in the shuffle.

✔ **E-mail:** Businesses often send press releases by e-mail. But don't send it all across the country — many journalists consider it *spam* (junk e-mail that they don't want). If you do send your release by e-mail, make the subject line succinct and compelling. You can frequently obtain e-mail addresses by calling the media outlet or going to the publication's Web site.

Use all three methods — regular mail, fax, and e-mail — to send your press releases to the really key people.

Checking Out Some Sample Press Releases

You may want to consider creating a press release for any landmark event, such as

✔ **Major developments:** When you make an acquisition, enter into a strategic alliance, or land a significant contract, you may want to let others know. The sample press release on Form 17-1 on the CD-ROM announces a major development that affects the company. The sample on Form 17-2 on the CD-ROM announces a company milestone.

✔ **Employee promotion:** When you promote an employee to a significant position, an announcement can be good for your company and boost employee morale and visibility. Form 17-3 on the CD-ROM gives you a sample press release that announces an employee promotion.

✔ **Hiring of key employee:** Telling the press about a new hire for an important position can lead to increased attention on your company. Check out Form 17-4 later in this chapter.

✔ **New product or service:** Always issue a press release if you develop a new product or service. After all, a little free publicity never hurt anyone's business. Form 17-5, which you can see later in this chapter, shows a sample press release that announces a new product. The sample press releases on Forms 17-6 and 17-7 on the CD-ROM announce new services.

Press Release -- Hiring of Key Employees

For Immediate Release

Contact:

Jan Harrison
Great Restaurants, Inc.
Phone: (415) 985-2000
Fax: (415) 985-2001
E-mail: jharrison@greatrestaurants.com.

> The name and vital information of the contact person at the company

Chicago, Illinois (November 1, 2004) -- Great Restaurants, Inc., the owner of the chain of Smokehouse Restaurants, announced the hiring of Ken Graham as Chief Financial Officer. He will be responsible for all financial and accounting functions for the company.

> Describes who was hired

"We are lucky to have someone of Ken's background and expertise come on board," said Allan Rezzler, President of Great Restaurants. "Ken will be a perfect fit for us, as we rapidly grow our business." "We plan to open 10 more restaurants in the coming two years," said Mr. Rezzler.

Ken was the Treasurer with Parmesan Restaurants, Inc. for four years, and before that Corporate Controller for Chophouse Restaurants, Inc.

Ken earned a B.S. from Stanford University in Accounting, graduating Phi Beta Kappa. He is a certified public accountant and a member of the American Institute of Certified Public Accountants.

> Background of employee

Great Restaurants, Inc. is the owner of the popular Smokehouse Restaurant chain. Its chain of restaurants is known for their great service and high quality grilled foods. The company employs 150 people in the greater Chicago area and has won numerous local awards for its food and service. The company's web site at www.greatrestaurants.com contains additional information.

> Summary information about the company

###

Form 17-4: A sample press release that announces the hiring of a key employee.

Press Release – New Product

For Immediate Release

Contact: Richard Anderson
            Catchy Software Inc.
            Phone: (415)771-8000
            Fax: (415) 771-8001
            Email: randerson@catchysoftware.com

> The name and vital information of the contact at the company

New Software for Small Businesses

San Francisco, California (November 30, 2004) -- Catchy Software Inc., the makers of the Biz Success™ suite of software products, today introduced Biz LegalAdvisor™, a new software product aimed at giving start-up and emerging businesses high quality forms and legal advice.

> Put the most pertinent information first

Biz LegalAdvisor™ combines a comprehensive package of forms, checklists and agreements with explanations and guides. The software provides guidelines and forms for almost any legal matter encountered by small businesses -- from issues relating to employment to stock sales to intellectual property.

> Describes the new product

"This is a cutting edge product far superior to anything in the marketplace," said Richard Anderson, the President of Catchy Software Inc.

> Quote from the president

More than 900,000 new business are started each year. "With Biz LegalAdvisor™, many business owners and entrepreneurs will now be able to avoid legal pitfalls and save thousands of dollars in legal fees," said Richard Anderson.

Catchy Software Inc. is a San Francisco based software company whose mission is to provide software products to start-up and emerging businesses that are comprehensive, useful and of high quality. The company has 35 employees and has successfully developed other business software. More information can be obtained by visiting the company's Web site at www.catchysoftware.com.

> Summary information about the company

###

Form 17-5: A sample press release that announces a new software product.

Meeting the Press

In order to get your story covered, you generally have to pitch your idea to a reporter or editor. Unfortunately, from the reporter's point of view, your fascinating story may be just another competitor for time or space in a humdrum working day. So, you have to do two things — identify the players and make the story idea compelling.

Image is key, and the public often takes the media's perception as reality. Remember that the media is pivotal in providing coverage that shows your company in a positive light.

Knowing the key players

If you really want to know who the key media contacts are in a particular area, take a look at the industry magazines and write down the person's name from the masthead. Get the staffer's e-mail addresses from the masthead or the publication's Web site. Take down the names of contributors and contributing editors (freelancers), together with any listed e-mail addresses. Checking out these magazines costs you little, and you can be sure that you're accurate.

One reporter may do a better job covering your particular type of business, or may tend to be more open to new stories. Find out who's covering what's hot and what's not in your industry.

Pay attention to the angle of the stories. Anyone who covers your competition is a potential publicity target. Although you want the coverage of a larger media outlet, don't ignore the benefits of a smaller and more local angle. Regional coverage is easier to get and can reach more appropriate venues.

Getting the reporter's attention

To receive media coverage, you have to get the reporter's attention. You want to make sure that the story idea sounds exciting, has a broad appeal, and is appealing to the medium (such as TV, newspaper, or trade journal). Different mediums do require different tactics, but every idea and every story needs a hook. Concentrate on writing human interest stories, profiles (people, products, companies, or causes), and trends. Use action-packed words and terms that directly and clearly describe your concept.

TIP

Writing press releases

I can't guarantee you media coverage, but I can tell you eight things to do when dealing with the press:

✔ Be sure that your news is appropriate to the reporter or editor. (Don't send real estate news to the lifestyle editor, for example.)

✔ Put the press release's focus at the top of the page.

✔ Be clear about the product or company.

✔ Include basic information, such as contact or reference information.

✔ Be straightforward, avoiding corporate double-talk and slick advertising terms.

✔ Provide an obvious audience connection or interest.

✔ Be truthful.

✔ Be patient — wait for the reporter to call you.

Planning and timing gets your story noticed. Every news-gathering organization adheres to a time schedule known as a *media calendar*. This calendar helps the reporters and editors plan future stories. Knowing how these publications establish deadlines is half the battle. The easier you make it for the reporter or editor to cover your story, the better your chances to gain press coverage.

Here's a breakdown of the major forms of media calendars that you may have to deal with:

✔ **Daily print reporters** write feature articles up to a month in advance, so send out releases with time-dated material a month prior to expected publication.

✔ **Monthly publication journalists** close their editorial content about two months in advance of the issue date. If you want a story to run in May, submit the idea in March.

✔ **Radio, television, and electronic journalists** run short but timely stories based on breaking news. Given the dynamic nature of these mediums, be prepared to give an interview or a demonstration when they call.

Establishing a media relations policy

If your business consists of more than a few people, think about establishing a Media Relations Policy for all employees to follow. The policy tells employees how to handle inquiries and discussions with the media.

You can make your Media Relations Policy short and sweet, such as the sample that appears in Form 17-8 later in this chapter.

Media Relations Policy

It is important that inquiries by the media in relation to our company be handled in accordance with the following policy:

All inquiries should be referred to _____ (the "Spokesperson"). As the Company's chief spokesperson, the Spokesperson will respond directly or designate another party to serve as spokesperson. The Spokesperson also will direct the process by which a response is determined or position taken. If the Spokesperson is not available, inquiries should be referred to the _____.

This policy covers all forms of responses to the media, including "off the record" and anonymous statements.

Form 17-8: A sample Media Relations Policy.

Off the record?

Is anything you say to a member of the press *really* off the record? The safest answer is *no*. Remember Connie Chung's infamous interview with Newt Gingrich's elderly mother when she said, "Just between you and me, Mrs. Gingrich, what do you think about First Lady Hillary Clinton?" Much to everyone's surprise (including then House Speaker Newt Gingrich), millions of viewers heard the national broadcast of his mother's less-than-flattering comments.

First and foremost is the issue of trust — do you have a good working relationship with the reporter? If you have any doubts, then consider everything you say to be "on the record," even if the reporter assures you otherwise. Ask yourself if you can afford for the information to be made public. If the answer is *yes,* then proceed to offer extraneous, yet important, information that may help the reporter understand your story a little better.

And always, always confirm with the reporter that your comments are off the record *before* you make the statements. Reporters don't give you "do overs." Unless you specifically state in advance that the reporter shouldn't use the comments, everything, and I mean *everything,* is fair game.

Forms on the CD-ROM

Check out these forms on the CD-ROM related to dealing with the media:

Form 17-1	**Press Release — Major Development**	A sample press release that announces a major development that affects the company
Form 17-2	**Press Release — Web Site Milestone**	A sample press release that announces a milestone for a Web-based business
Form 17-3	**Press Release — Promotion of Employee**	A sample press release that announces an existing employee's promotion to a key position
Form 17-4	**Press Release — Hiring of Key Employees**	A sample press release that announces the hiring of a new, senior-level employee
Form 17-5	**Press Release — New Product**	A sample press release that announces a new product
Form 17-6	**Press Release — New Service**	A sample press release that announces a new service
Form 17-7	**Press Release — New Web-Based Service**	A sample press release that announces a new, Web-based service
Form 17-8	**Media Relations Policy**	A sample company policy statement that you should distribute to employees or include in the employee handbook concerning response to media inquiries

Part VI
The Part of Tens

The 5th Wave   By Rich Tennant

SPAM KING
MASS EMAIL MARKETING
A Limited Canker on the Butt
of Society Partnership

In this part . . .

I love top ten lists — and this part is chock-full of top ten lists to help you with your business. You'll find ten tips to help your business become more successful and ten Web sites that are useful resources for small businesses. I round out this part with a list of publications that are winners for small business owners.

Chapter 18

Ten Ideas to Make Your Business More Successful

● ●

In This Chapter

▶ Getting ideas from all kinds of places

▶ Making your business look good

● ●

Sometimes, small businesses get in a rut. They don't step back and plan for the future or come up with creative ideas for improving the business. This chapter presents ten ideas that may work wonders for your business. (Or at least get your own creative juices flowing.)

Team Up with Another Company

Consider a joint venture or strategic alliance with another company. These ventures or alliances can be broad (such as a joint venture to develop a new product or technology) or simple (such as an agreement to co-advertise a product or service). The most logical strategic partners are companies in related industries, but on occasion, you may want to include competitors in that list. Strategic alliances offer the following benefits:

✔ Access to capital

✔ Access to international markets

✔ Access to new distribution channels

✔ Access to new or existing products

✔ Access to new technology

✔ Enhanced ability to compete

✔ Enhanced credibility

✔ Reduced cost and uncertainty

Get Advice

Because you can't possibly know everything you need to make your business successful, get advice from as many sources as you can. Talk to your lawyer, accountant, and banker. Ask questions of entrepreneurs who have survived some of the same problems that you face. If they're willing, your competitors can provide particularly valuable advice. Who knows — you may end up in some kind of strategic alliance with them.

One way to get systematic advice is to set up a Board of Advisors. Include people with different experience and backgrounds on your board. Have regular meetings (once a month or so) during which you bounce questions and ideas off board members. People may be more willing to take on this task because it generally involves far less responsibility and liability than being on a Board of Directors. (Make sure to give them some incentive for participating, such as stock options or a small fee.)

Send Gifts to Your Key Customers

Successful businesses build up goodwill. If your company has some key customers, consider sending the main contact a present as a show of appreciation. This present doesn't have to be a Ferrari or a Picasso — just some small token that says you value their business. Just think how you would feel if one of your suppliers did that. Wouldn't you be more likely to give that supplier a preference in future dealings?

Consider giving the following items as gifts:

- Desk clock
- Gift certificate for two to a classy restaurant
- Nice wine or champagne
- Tickets to a hot show or sporting event
- A gift tailored to the recipient's hobby

Seek Financing When You Don't Need It

If your business is doing well, you may — mistakenly — not see any pressing need to obtain more bank financing or equity funding. But the best time to seek financing is when you *don't* need it. You aren't forced into a corner and you don't risk cash-flow problems if you have adequate credit.

Consider going to a lender to establish a credit line and soliciting venture capitalists or other investors for an equity investment in your company, even if you don't need the financial boost right now. Banks and investors are more inclined to approve your business for loans when that business is doing well. And you're in a better bargaining position because you have absolutely no pressing need to obtain the financing.

Try Different Ideas

Successful businesses try a lot of different things — using different advertisements, adding new products, and improving old products. By trying new things, you can obtain increased flexibility and find better approaches to your business.

Encourage new ideas from employees and customers. Don't be afraid to try out the new ideas, especially if the cost isn't outrageous. Who knows? Maybe your next idea will be the equivalent of the hula hoop, the semiconductor chip, or penicillin. Well, maybe not. But hopefully the next idea at least keeps you excited about the business.

Motivate and Reward Employees

You absolutely have to reward and motivate employees to make your business successful. By failing to motivate and reward employees, you risk losing your best workers.

You can motivate and reward employees in many ways. Of course, raises, bonuses, and perks are always effective, but people also want to be recognized and encouraged for good performance. So make sure that you continually recognize your employee's achievements.

For true motivation, consider including employees in a stock option or profit sharing plan. The history of Silicon Valley success stories shows that you can make these plans into tremendous motivational tools.

Research Your Competition

You need information about your competitors to make good competitive decisions and to help you develop and market your products and services. So, start and continue to get as much information as you can about your competitors and their products. Information sources include the following:

- ✔ Advertisements
- ✔ Annual reports
- ✔ Customers who have bought from or been solicited by competitors
- ✔ News clipping services
- ✔ Newspaper and trade magazine articles
- ✔ Product literature
- ✔ The World Wide Web

Review all the information that you can get and keep it in an organized file. It may come in handy later.

Get Favorable Publicity

Publicity or a favorable article about your company can generate some amazing results. Good publicity may generate new customers, interest potential investors in your company, and even raise your visibility to potential employees and strategic partners. Create some press releases that spotlight something interesting about your company, or pitch a story to a local newspaper. Visibility can lead to great, unexpected rewards!

Ask Your Employees

Ask your employees to submit two suggestions a week to improve your business. In many cases, the people doing a job have the best ideas for improving it. And by showing that you're willing to pay attention to what workers have to offer, you improve the likelihood of motivating and keeping good employees. Asking employees for their opinions and involving them in decisions can lead to happier employees and a more profitable business.

Build a Great Company Web Site

Even small businesses can profit from having a great Web site. And, with the incredible growth of professional Web site development companies, Web sites have become very easy to build and maintain. Think of a Web site as an additional way to market your company and its products or services. Put your *URL* (Web site address) in all your advertisements and marketing literature. Just make sure that you keep your site interesting, informative, and up-to-date! Check out other Web sites to find the look and feel that appeals to you.

Chapter 19

Ten Great Web Sites for Small Businesses

In This Chapter

▶ Checking out the Web for business resources

▶ Getting a helping hand from the government

▶ Reading the paper online

▶ Banking on the Web

*E*verybody's talking about the World Wide Web and how it helps small businesses obtain information that was formerly available only to larger competitors. If you're not sure where you're surfing, however, cyberspace quickly deteriorates into a time sinkhole. This chapter provides you with a map and a compass to get you started in the right direction. I list ten Web sites that may come in handy for your small business. Check out each one and then bookmark them all for frequent, easy access. I've done the searching; all you have to do is surf the Net.

AllBusiness

www.AllBusiness.com

This premier site for small and growing businesses and entrepreneurs contains advice on

- ✔ Starting a business
- ✔ Incorporation
- ✔ Sales & marketing
- ✔ Internet & technology

- Legal
- Employment and consulting
- Finance & accounting

The site also contains

- A comprehensive set of downloadable sample contracts, letters of intent, business letters, and checklists
- Business and research directories
- Services and products of interest to small businesses
- Questions and answers
- Business guides
- A Platinum Program providing special offers, savings, and discounts

Business Week

www.businessweek.com

The online site for *Business Week* magazine contains a number articles in the current issue of *Business Week,* articles from past issues, information on the latest bank loan and CD rates, software reviews for business, discussions of Web sites, and more. The site is well designed, searchable, and has many articles that relate to the financing and operations of particular companies.

The site also contains an interactive buying guide for purchasing computers, complete with computer reviews and rankings. The Quotes and Portfolio section provides a personal-portfolio stock tracker, historical stock information, and more. *Business Week* allows free Web site access to subscribers of its magazine, but nonsubscribers must pay an annual access fee.

The Small Business Administration

www.sba.gov

The Small Business Administration Web site is huge. The site map alone lists 25 areas, each with several pages, forms, and services. Definitely plan to check out the Financing Your Business page, which describes all the different ways that the SBA can help you secure business funding. You can also find references to various small business laws and regulations on this site.

The SBA goes out of its way to connect small businesses with a wide range of services, including links and descriptions of various non-SBA resources — both federal and state. The site boasts a large list of shareware, which you can download from the site. This site also provides information on the Electronic Federal Tax Payment System (EFTPS) and includes a searchable database of business cards submitted by small companies across the country. For once, the government actually helps you expand your company.

The Internal Revenue Service

www.irs.gov

Granted, you don't want to contact the IRS unless you absolutely have to. But on those occasions when you do, the Web offers you a way to get in touch with the IRS without leaving home or being put on hold. This site isn't just a repository for IRS forms and publications: It provides access to advice concerning taxpayer rights, electronic payment services, and the addresses of all the IRS service centers and offices. You can even join an e-mail list for updates on various IRS regulations and changes to forms.

You may also want to check out the Tax Info for Business section. This page contains the Business Tax Kit — which provides the IRS forms applicable to small businesses — as well as answers to questions, links to other non-tax Web sites, tax calendars, and other services. You can use the IRS Web site to find the site for your state's taxation agency. Just link to the Federation of Tax Administrators home page (or find it yourself at www.taxadmin.org/fta), find your state, and use that link to go to the site.

Entrepreneur

www.entrepreneur.com

Entrepreneur.com's tagline is "Solutions for Growing Businesses." The site, the online version of *Entrepreneur* magazine, is divided into the following major categories:

- Start-ups
- HomeBiz
- Franchise
- Business Opportunities
- Money

- Marketing
- Management
- E-Biz
- Technology

The site contains a number of useful articles, books, how-to guides, franchise listings, research services, and tools. Although not as useful as www. AllBusiness.com, it does provide some helpful guidance.

CBS Marketwatch

www.marketwatch.com

The CBS Marketwatch site can really help you get insights and up-to-date coverage of the stock market and public companies. The site has the following major sections:

- Markets
- Personal Finance
- My Portfolio
- Newsletters & Research
- Investor Tools
- TV & Radio
- Trading Strategies
- Retirement Weekly

The site also offers a free service that sends you periodic e-mail alerts on the stock market and the economy. A variety of columnists provide solid insight on the markets and Internet and technology stocks. The site gives you a valuable source for keeping up with the markets.

American Express — Small Business

www.americanexpress.com

The American Express site provides a large amount of useful small business information. The Business Planning and Resources library offers information and useful tools. You can obtain personal answers from a leading small business expert in the advice section, under "Small Business."

If you visit regularly, you may notice frequently updated tips and guest columns concerning use of the Web, trade shows, promoting your business, credit options, and other important information for small businesses. And, of course, the site details how American Express can help your small business.

Newspaper Web Sites

```
www.nytimes.com

www.latimes.com

www.wsj.com
```

Most major newspapers now post an electronic edition on the Internet. The electronic versions provide the same news and articles available in their print counterparts. You can also access the newspapers' classified, subscription, and advertising departments. Most of these newspapers offer some sort of automatic, electronic delivery. You choose the kinds of information you want delivered, and each day, the paper sends you the news stories that you choose over the Internet. Although some newspapers charge you for these services, currently the *L.A. Times* and *New York Times* offer free registration. The *Wall Street Journal Online* requires a subscription payment for access to the full online newspaper.

Even without electronic delivery, newspapers online can give you a great convenient resource. Try researching your clients through the city newspaper of your next out-of-town sales call. The Internet sure beats microfiche at the library or calling every newsstand for a week-old paper.

Wells Fargo

```
www.wellsfargo.com
```

I picked Wells Fargo's Web site because of how that company uses the Web to do business. Most banks now have Web sites; however, those sites mainly act as advertisements for the bank's services, along with some basic information on the economy or money markets. Generally, bank sites allow you to familiarize yourself with what your bank offers without reading little pamphlets or talking to a loan officer.

The Wells Fargo Web site offers extensive online banking services. Many banks specially develop their online banking services for small businesses. In a home-based company, or in a company with only a few employees, the advantages of computer banking are obvious. Online banking is clearly the trend for the future; eventually, all banks will offer some type of online banking, especially as more people become convinced of the security protections that bank Web sites offer. If your bank doesn't yet offer online banking, take a minute to browse Wells Fargo's services. By doing so, you at least know what services to request from your bank when it does start online banking.

The Wells Fargo site also provides information about payroll services, retirement plans, and other benefit plans.

Yahoo!

www.yahoo.com

Yahoo! is an incredibly popular site (probably because it's friendly to Web beginners). Yahoo! is very easy to use, and it has several channels that you use to narrow the amount of information that you search. Yahoo! also contains several non-search areas. In fact, Yahoo! is as much an online information resource as it is a search engine.

One of the things that makes Yahoo! especially helpful to small businesses is the Finance channel. As you delve into subchannels, Yahoo! gives you extensive links to business-oriented sites, each with a one or two line synopsis. These links can help you find the Web site that you need without resorting to the search engine.

Advertisers pay Yahoo! to run promotions or place advertisements at the site, which means that you can use most of it for free.

Chapter 20

(Almost) Ten Great Publications for Small Businesses

In This Chapter

▶ Checking out business periodicals

▶ Looking into some great books for small businesses

The Wall Street Journal

The Wall Street Journal is an absolutely indispensable daily business paper. This newspaper has in-depth coverage of breaking business, finance, and stock market news. The paper includes special summaries and forecasts of federal and state tax developments once a week. Although it often covers large, publicly held companies, *The Wall Street Journal* often contains articles on small, privately held companies, venture capital developments, and important legal and business issues for small businesses.

The Wall Street Journal, 200 Burnett Road, Chicopee, MA 01020; phone 800-JOURNAL; Web site www.wsj.com.

Inc.

Inc. bills itself as "The Magazine for Growing Companies." The magazine profiles up-and-coming companies, frequently featuring success stories. A variety of articles cover entrepreneurship, payroll, motivating employees, marketing, strategic planning, and financial statements. Regular features also include case studies, questions and answers, technology guides, and profiles.

Inc. Magazine, 375 Lexington Avenue, New York, NY 10017; phone 212-499-2000; Web site www.inc.com.

Business Week

Business Week is an extremely informative and broad-based publication. It contains numerous articles, summaries, profiles, commentary, and analysis of international markets, economic trends, government outlook, science and technology, marketing, people, legal affairs, information technology, small business, public company developments, the stock market, banking and financing transactions, and much more. The weekly magazine is well written with broad coverage of interest to entrepreneurs and many types of businesses.

Business Week, P.O. Box 506, Hightstown, NJ 08520-9493; phone 800-635-1200; Web site www.businessweek.com.

Entrepreneur

Entrepreneur describes itself as providing "Solutions for Growing Businesses." The monthly magazine contains many articles on entrepreneurial companies. The articles tend to be both easy to read and interesting, with a variety of pictures and graphics. Regular columns include topics on tax, financing, tech toys, franchising, small business jobs, Web sites, and more. You may find the marketing and management tips particularly useful. The magazine also has a great number of advertisements that target products and services for small businesses.

Entrepreneur Media, Inc., 2445 McCabe Way, Irvine, CA 92614; phone 949-261-2325; Web site www.entrepreneur.com.

Fortune

Fortune is a sophisticated magazine that tracks national and international business trends. Each issue contains a number of features on companies in the news, plus in-depth analysis on industry trends and trendsetters. Although a great many of the stories involve public companies (AT&T, Microsoft, and TCI, for example), much of the analysis and industry discussion can help small businesses. Special sections include "Techno File," "Smart Managing," and "Investing."

Fortune, Time & Life Building, Rockefeller Center, New York, NY 10020; phone 800-621-8000; Web site www.fortune.com.

Fast Company

Fast Company is an interesting magazine that provides insights on how people cope with life and work in the new economy. In past issues, its feature articles have covered customer service, strategic decisions, leadership, reengineering, career, marketing and branding, innovation, Internet and technologies, and other topics. Interesting regular columns include "Action Items," "Fast Companies," "Insights," and "Reader's Choice Books." The magazine also has stories on fast-growing companies.

Fast Company, 375 Lexington Avenue, New York, NY 10017; phone 820-542-6029; Web site www.fastcompany.com.

Forbes

Forbes is a very comprehensive business publication with interesting articles, insights, polls, and feature stories. Its broad coverage includes business, the markets, technology, careers, compensation, personal finance, networking, entrepreneurship, retirement strategies, investment advice, and more.

Forbes is also well-known for feature articles, such as the "200 Best Small Companies," the "World's Richest People," and the "Best Paid CEOs." Its focus on small business and e-commerce is particularly good.

Forbes, 28 West 23rd St., 11th Floor, New York, New York, 10010; phone 212-366-8900; Web site www.forbes.com.

Built to Last: Successful Habits of Visionary Companies

Built to Last, by James C. Collins and Jerry I. Porras (Harper Business), is an interesting and readable analysis of visionary companies. The authors studied a number of leading companies in direct comparison to their competitors to find out how the truly exceptional companies differ from other companies. The authors have filled the book with hundreds of specific examples and concepts, including fun ones such as "Big Hairy Audacious Goals." Entrepreneurs, executive officers, and managers can find practical insight into management principles, quality orientation, marketing, and the benefits of core values. In the book, the authors debunk a number of management myths and identify characteristics of truly visionary companies.

Business Contracts Kit For Dummies

This book, which I wrote (and Wiley publishes), provides a great discussion of how to draft and negotiate business contracts. The types of contracts covered include

- ✔ Confidentiality Agreements
- ✔ License Agreements
- ✔ Employment Agreements
- ✔ Letters of Intent
- ✔ Consulting Agreements
- ✔ Stock Purchase Agreements
- ✔ Sales & Service Agreements

Appendix

What's on the CD-ROM

• •

▶ System requirements

▶ Using the CD

▶ What you'll find on the CD

▶ Troubleshooting

• •

*T*he *Small Business Kit For Dummies,* 2nd Edition CD-ROM includes more than 200 sample forms and agreements to use in your business. You'll find a lot of what you need to start, finance, grow, and market your business.

System Requirements

Make sure that your computer meets the minimum system requirements in the following list. If your computer doesn't match up to these requirements, you may experience problems in using the contents of the CD:

- ✔ A PC with a 300 MHz+ Pentium II or faster processor or a Macintosh Power 500MHz G3 processor.

- ✔ Microsoft Windows 98 SE, 2000, or XP, or OS X 10.2.6.

- ✔ At least 96MB of RAM installed on your computer. For best performance, we recommend at least 128MB of RAM installed.

- ✔ A CD-ROM drive.

If you need more information on the basics, check out these books published by Wiley Publishing, Inc.: *PCs For Dummies,* 9th Edition, by Dan Gookin; *Macs For Dummies,* 8th Edition, by David Pogue; *iMac For Dummies,* 3rd Edition, by David Pogue; *Mac OS X For Dummies,* 3rd Edition, by Bob LeVitus; or *Windows 98 For Dummies, Windows 2000 Professional For Dummies,* or *Windows XP For Dummies,* all by Andy Rathbone.

Using the CD

Follow these steps to access the software on the book's CD:

1. **Insert the CD into your computer's CD-ROM drive.**

2. **The interface launches.**

   Note for Windows Users: If you have autorun disabled, click Start⇨ Run. In the dialog box that appears, type D:\start.exe. Replace D with the proper letter if your CD-ROM drive uses a different letter. (If you don't know the letter, see how your CD-ROM drive is listed under My Computer.) Click OK.

   Note for Mac Users: The CD icon will appear on your desktop, double-click the icon to open the CD and double-click the "Start" icon.

3. **An agreement with respect to the book and CD-ROM appears.**

   Read through the agreement, and then click the Accept button if you want to use the CD. After you click Accept, the License Agreement window won't bother you again.

4. **The CD interface appears.**

   The interface coordinates installing the programs and running the demos. The interface basically enables you to click a button or two to make things happen.

Adobe Reader

For Mac OS X 10.2; Windows 98, NT, 2000, Me, or XP.

Some forms are included on the CD in Adobe's Portable Document Format (PDF), and Adobe Reader allows you to view it on your computer.

Forms, Forms, and More Forms

The forms on the CD-ROM come in two distinct flavors:

- ✔ Word documents. You can modify these forms to fit your personal business needs.

- ✔ Adobe Acrobat (PDF) files. Some files (such as IRS forms and publications) can only be seen if you install the Adobe Reader. You cannot modify these forms, but you can print them out.

Table A-1 summarizes the forms and agreements on the CD-ROM.

Table A-1	Forms at a Glance	
Form Number	*Form Name*	*Description*
Form 1-1	**Comparison Chart for Different Business Entities**	A chart showing the key features of partnerships, corporations, and other business entities
Form 1-2	**Checklist for Drafting General Partnership Agreements**	A checklist of items to consider when drafting a General Partnership Agreement
Form 1-3	**Checklist for Drafting Limited Partnership Agreements**	A checklist of items to consider when drafting a Limited Partnership Agreement
Form 1-4	**Checklist for Formation of a Corporation**	A checklist of items to consider when forming a corporation
Form 1-5	**S Corporation Election Form (Form 2553)**	The IRS Form to elect S corporation status
Form 1-6	**Transmittal Letter to the IRS Enclosing S Corporation Election Form**	A sample letter to the IRS for use when sending the S corporation election
Form 1-7	**Checklist for Drafting LLC Operating Agreements**	A checklist of items to consider when drafting an LLC Operating Agreement
Form 2-1	**Sample Business Plan Cover Page**	Sample cover page for a business plan (includes a confidentiality blurb)
Form 2-2	**Sample Executive Summary for Business Plan**	A sample business plan executive summary for a software company
Form 2-3	**Sample Projections for Business Plan**	Several sample financial forecasts for a business plan
Form 2-4	**Sample Short Form Business Plan**	A sample condensed business plan for a consumer product company
Form 3-1	**Checklist for Formation of a California Corporation**	A checklist of issues to consider when forming a California corporation

(continued)

Table A-1 *(continued)*

Form Number	Form Name	Description
Form 3-2	**Guide to Operation of Newly Formed California Corporation**	A comprehensive guide and discussion for forming a California corporation
Form 3-3C	**Articles of Incorporation (California Corporation)**	Sample Articles to be filed with the California Secretary of State for forming the corporation
Form 3-3D	**Certificate of Incorporation (Delaware Corporation)**	Sample Certificate of Incorporation to be filed with the Delaware Secretary of State necessary for forming the corporation
Form 3-4C	**Transmittal Letter Enclosing Articles of Incorporation to the California Secretary of State**	A sample letter to send to the California Secretary of State enclosing the Articles of Incorporation
Form 3-4D	**Transmittal Letter Enclosing Certificate of Incorporation to the Delaware Secretary of State**	A sample letter forwarding the Certificate of Incorporation for filing with the Delaware Secretary of State's office
Form 3-5C	**Action of Incorporator (California Corporation)**	A form where the incorporator appoints initial directors for a California corporation
Form 3-5D	**Action of Incorporator (Delaware Corporation)**	A form where the incorporator appoints initial directors for a Delaware corporation
Form 3-6C	**Bylaws (California Corporation)**	Sample form bylaws for a California corporation
Form 3-6D	**Bylaws (Delaware Corporation)**	Sample form bylaws for a Delaware corporation
Form 3-7C	**Action by Unanimous Written Consent of the Board of Directors in Lieu of Organizational Meeting (California Corporation)**	A form of written consent of the board of directors of a California corporation adopting various important organizational resolutions
Form 3-7D	**Action by Unanimous Written Consent of the Board of Directors in Lieu of Organizational Meeting (Delaware Corporation)**	A form of written consent of the board of directors of a Delaware corporation adopting various important organizational resolutions

Form Number	Form Name	Description
Form 3-8	**Notice of Meeting of the Board of Directors**	A form of written notification of a board of directors meeting
Form 3-9	**Declaration of Mailing Notice of Board Meeting**	A sample form for the corporate records showing that proper notice was given for a board of directors meeting
Form 3-10	**Waiver of Notice and Consent to Holding Meeting of Board of Directors**	A form for the board of directors to sign waiving requirement of a written notice for a meeting
Form 3-11	**Action by Unanimous Written Consent of the Board of Directors**	Template for actions by unanimous written consent rather than at a meeting
Form 3-12	**Minutes of Meeting of the Board of Directors**	Template for recording the actions taken at a board of directors meeting
Form 3-13	**Board Resolution Approving Agreement**	Sample resolution to be approved by a board of directors approving the corporation entering into an agreement
Form 3-14	**Board Resolution Approving Borrowing**	Sample resolution to be approved by a board of directors approving the corporation making a certain borrowing
Form 3-15	**Board Resolution Approving Sale of Common Stock**	Sample resolution to be approved by a board of directors approving the sale of stock by the corporation
Form 3-16	**Board Resolution Approving a Stock Option Plan**	Sample resolution to be approved by a board of directors approving a Stock Option Plan
Form 3-17	**Board Resolution Approving Grant of Stock Options**	Sample resolution to be approved by a board of directors approving the grant of designated stock options to particular individuals
Form 3-18	**Board Resolution Approving Amendment of Bylaws**	Sample resolution to be approved by a board of directors approving amendment of the corporate bylaws

(continued)

Table A-1 *(continued)*

Form Number	Form Name	Description
Form 3-19	**Board Resolution Approving Amendment to Articles of Incorporation**	Sample resolution to be approved by a board of directors approving amendment of the Articles of Incorporation
Form 3-20	**Board Resolution Approving an Employment Agreement**	Sample resolution to be approved by a board of directors approving execution of an employment agreement with a senior-level employee
Form 3-21	**Board Resolution Appointing Officers**	Sample resolution to be approved by a board of directors appointing officers to the corporation
Form 3-22	**Board Resolution Approving an Acquisition**	Sample resolution to be approved by a board of directors approving the acquisition of a business
Form 3-23	**Board Resolution Approving Dividends**	Sample resolution to be approved by a board of directors approving declaring dividends to be distributed to the shareholders
Form 3-24	**Board Resolution Approving Establishing a Committee of the Board**	Sample resolution to be approved by a board of directors that establishes a precisely-named committee of the board
Form 3-25	**Board Resolution Approving Accountants**	Sample resolution to be approved by a board of directors appointing accountants for the corporation
Form 3-26	**Board Resolution Approving a Stock Split**	Sample resolution to be approved by a board of directors approving a stock split
Form 3-27	**Board Resolution Approving a Lease**	Sample resolution to be approved by a board of directors approving the corporation entering into a lease
Form 3-28	**Board Resolution Approving Purchase of Property**	Sample resolution to be approved by a board of directors approving the purchase of a particular property

Form Number	Form Name	Description
Form 3-29	**Board Resolution Approving Sale of Series A Preferred Stock**	Sample resolution to be approved by a board of directors approving the offer and sale of Series A preferred stock of the corporation
Form 3-30	**Board Resolution Approving S Corporation Election**	Sample resolution to be approved by a board of directors approving the corporation electing to be taxed as an S corporation
Form 3-31	**Board Resolution Regarding Annual Shareholders Meeting**	Sample resolution to be approved by a board of directors establishing the date of the annual meeting of the shareholders and other related matters
Form 3-32	**Board Resolution Regarding Qualification to Do Business**	Sample resolution to be approved by a board of directors authorizing the corporation to qualify to do business in appropriate states
Form 3-33C	**Action by Written Consent of Shareholders (California Corporation)**	A form of written consent for initial actions or documents to be approved by the shareholders
Form 3-33D	**Action by Written Consent of Stockholders (Delaware Corporation)**	A form of written consent for initial actions or documents to be approved by the stockholders
Form 3-34	**Notice of Annual Meeting of Shareholders**	A notice to be sent to shareholders of a corporation informing them of the date and place of the Annual Meeting of Shareholders
Form 3-35	**Declaration of Mailing Notice of Shareholder Meeting**	A form for the Secretary or Assistant Secretary of a corporation to complete and sign, declaring that a form of Notice of Shareholder Meeting in the form was attached and sent to all shareholders
Form 3-36	**Notice of Special Meeting of Shareholders**	A form to be sent to the shareholders notifying them of the date, time, and purpose of a special meeting of the shareholders

(continued)

Table A-1 *(continued)*

Form Number	Form Name	Description
Form 3-37	**Waiver of Notice and Consent to Holding Meeting of Shareholders**	A form of waiver, to be signed by the shareholders, consenting to a meeting of the shareholders without notice required by the corporation's bylaws
Form 3-38	**Action by Written Consent of Shareholders**	A template for action to be taken by the written consent of the shareholders of a corporation, in place of action taken at a meeting
Form 3-39	**Minutes of Meeting of Shareholders**	A template for minutes of a shareholders meeting of a corporation
Form 3-40	**Shareholder Resolution Appointing Directors**	A sample shareholders resolution for appointing the directors of a corporation
Form 3-41	**Shareholder Resolution Confirming Accountants**	A sample shareholders resolution confirming and approving the designation of accountants of the corporation
Form 3-42	**Shareholder Resolution Approving Amendment of Bylaws**	A sample shareholders resolution for approval of the amendment of the corporate bylaws
Form 3-43	**Shareholder Resolution Approving Amendment of Articles of Incorporation**	A sample shareholders resolution for approval of the amendment of the Articles of Incorporation
Form 3-44	**Shareholder Resolution Approving an Acquisition**	A sample shareholders resolution for approving the acquisition of a business
Form 3-45	**Shareholder Resolution Approving a Stock Option Plan**	A sample shareholders resolution for approving a Stock Option Plan
Form 3-46	**Shareholder Resolution Approving an Agreement**	A sample shareholders resolution for approving the corporation entering into an agreement
Form 3-47	**Shareholder Resolution Approving Sale of Stock**	A sample shareholders resolution for approving the sale of Common Stock by the corporation

Form Number	Form Name	Description
Form 3-48	**Shareholder Resolution Approving Increasing the Size of the Board**	A sample shareholders resolution for approving an amendment to the corporate bylaws to increase the size of the board of directors and to elect new directors for the new seats
Form 3-49	**Shareholder Resolution Appointing Director to Fill Vacancy**	A sample shareholders resolution for appointing a new director to fill a vacant seat on the corporation's board of directors
Form 3-50	**California Form 1502 (Statement by Domestic Stock Corporation)**	The form that the California Secretary of State requires new California corporations to fill out
Form 3-51	**Transmittal Letter to California Secretary of State Enclosing Form 1502**	A transmittal letter enclosing Form 1502
Form 3-52	**California Form 25102(f) (Notice to California Department of Corporations)**	The form that can be filed with the California Department of Corporations in connection with the issue of private placement stock
Form 3-53	**Transmittal Letter to California Department of Corporations Enclosing Form 25102(f)**	A sample letter forwarding the Form 25102(f) to the California Department of Corporations
Form 3-54	**California S Corporation Election Form**	The form to be filed with the California Franchise Tax Board to elect to be taxed as an S corporation
Form 3-55	**Transmittal Letter to Franchise Tax Board Enclosing S Corporation Election Form**	A sample letter forwarding the California S corporation election form to the California Franchise Tax Board
Form 3-56	**Stock Certificate – Common Stock**	Sample Common Stock certificate for a privately held company
Form 3-57	**Stock Certificate – Preferred Stock**	Sample Preferred Stock certificate for a privately held company

(continued)

Table A-1 *(continued)*

Form Number	Form Name	Description
Form 3-58	**Stock Ledger and Capitalization Summary**	A sample form to be used to keep track of the issue of stock, preferred stock, options, and warrants
Form 3-59C	**Right of First Refusal Agreement (California Corporation)**	A sample agreement where the shareholders have to offer a California corporation a right of first refusal on any transfer of their shares
Form 3-59D	**Right of First Refusal Agreement (Delaware Corporation)**	A sample agreement where the shareholders have to offer a Delaware corporation a right of first refusal on any transfer of their shares
Form 4-1	**Promissory Note – Payable on Demand**	A form of note where the note holder can demand payment at any time
Form 4-2	**Promissory Note – Payable on a designated Date**	A form of note where the principle is payable on a certain date
Form 4-3	**Summary of SBA Loan Programs**	A summary prepared by the SBA of its loan programs for small businesses
Form 4-4	**Checklist for Issuing Stock**	A sample checklist of key items to consider before issuing stock
Form 4-5	**Stock Certificate – Common Stock**	A sample certificate for common stock
Form 4-6	**Stock Certificate – Preferred Stock**	A sample certificate for preferred stock
Form 4-7	**Checklist for Contents of Private Placement Memorandums**	A checklist of items to be considered for inclusion in a Private Placement Memorandum for a securities offering
Form 4-8	**SEC Form D**	The form required by the Securities and Exchange Commission to be filed for a stock offering under SEC Regulation D

Form Number	Form Name	Description
Form 4-9	**Transmittal Letter to SEC Enclosing Form D**	Cover letter to the SEC to enclose with Form D
Form 4-10	**Control Sheet for Private Placement Memorandums**	A sample sheet to keep track of the distribution of Private Placement Memorandums
Form 4-11	**Stock Subscription Package**	Several forms to be used in connection with larger private placement stock offerings
Form 4-12	**Pre-Offering Summary**	A summary of a company's proposed securities offering to ascertain the interest level from prospective investors
Form 4-13	**Stock Subscription Agreement**	A form of agreement for subscribing to the purchase of stock
Form 4-14	**Investment Analysis Summary Used by Venture Capitalists**	A sample form used by some venture capitalists in summarizing their analyses as to whether to invest in a company
Form 4-15	**Due Diligence Checklist**	A sample checklist of documents and information that a venture capitalist requests from a company in which it is interested in investing
Form 4-16	**Short Form Venture Capital Term Sheet**	A sample short form term sheet for a venture capital investment in a company
Form 4-17	**Long Form Venture Capital Term Sheet**	A long form, annotated sample term sheet for a venture capital investment in a company
Form 4-18	**Stock Ledger and Capitalization Summary**	A sample form ledger to keep track of stock option and warrant issuances with a summary of the company's capitalization
Form 5-1	**IRS Publication 538**	Accounting Periods and Methods
Form 5-2	**IRS Publication 463**	Travel, Entertainment, Gift, and Expenses

(continued)

Table A-1 *(continued)*

Form Number	Form Name	Description
Form 5-3	**Form I-9**	United States Customs & Immigration Services form that declares your employees resident status (required for all employers)
Form 5-4	**Daily Summary of Cash Receipts**	Form for daily cash receipts summary
Form 5-5	**Monthly Summary of Cash Receipts**	Monthly summary of cash receipts and sales tax
Form 5-6	**Check Disbursement Journal**	Journal to keep track of checks issued
Form 5-7	**Depreciation Work Sheet**	Schedule to record assets and related depreciation information
Form 5-8	**Bank Reconciliation Worksheet**	Worksheet to reconcile bank statement with outstanding checks and bank charges
Form 5-9	**Employee Compensation Record**	Form to keep track of compensation owed to employees, along with deductions
Form 5-10	**Income Statement**	Sample income statement form for figuring revenue, costs, and income
Form 5-11	**Comparative Income Statement**	Sample income statement showing comparisons over two periods
Form 5-12	**Balance Sheet**	Sample balance sheet
Form 5-13	**Comparative Balance Sheet**	Sample balance sheet showing comparisons over two periods
Form 5-14	**Cash Flow Statement**	Sample cash flow statement comparing two periods
Form 5-15	**Cash Flow Forecast Statement**	Bookkeeping tool that helps you anticipate cash flow
Form 5-16	**Sample Quarterly Budget**	Budget to project anticipated quarterly income and expenses
Form 5-17	**Accounts Receivable Aging**	Sample form to keep track of accounts receivable from customers

Form Number	Form Name	Description
Form 5-18	**Accounts Receivable Monthly Customer Statement**	Accounts receivable statement by customer
Form 5-19	**Delinquent Account Collection History**	Form to keep track of collection efforts for a delinquent account
Form 5-20	**Annual Summary of Expenses**	Sample annual summary of expenses by major categories
Form 5-21	**Expense Report for Meals and Entertainment**	Expense reimbursement form for employee to complete
Form 5-22	**Travel Expense Reimbursement Form**	Expense reimbursement form for travel-related expenses
Form 5-23	**Employee Attendance Record**	Form to track employee attendance and absences
Form 5-24	**Employee Monthly Time Record**	Form to keep track of employee's monthly hours, including vacation, holiday, and overtime hours
Form 6-1	**IRS Pub. 541**	Partnerships
Form 6-2	**IRS Pub. 542**	Corporations
Form 6-3	**IRS Form 2553**	S Corporation Election form
Form 6-4	**Transmittal Letter to IRS Enclosing S Corporation Election**	A letter to send with Form 2553
Form 6-5	**IRS Pub. 594**	The IRS Collection Process
Form 6-6	**IRS Form SS-4**	Application for Employer Identification Number
Form 6-7	**Transmittal Letter to IRS Enclosing Form SS-4**	A letter to enclose with your application for an Employer ID number
Form 6-8	**IRS Pub. 1915**	Understanding Your IRS Taxpayer Identification Number
Form 6-9	**Form I-9**	Employment Eligibility Verification
Form 6-10	**IRS Form W-4**	Employer's Withholding Allowance Certificate

(continued)

Table A-1 *(continued)*

Form Number	Form Name	Description
Form 6-11	**IRS Form 8109B**	Federal Tax Deposit Coupon
Form 6-12	**IRS Pub. 15**	Circular E, Employer's Tax Guide
Form 6-13	**IRS Form 1099-MISC**	Miscellaneous Income
Form 6-14	**IRS Pub. 1544**	Reporting cash payments of over $10,000
Form 6-15	**IRS Form W-2**	Employer's Wage and Tax Statement
Form 6-16	**IRS Pub. 583**	Starting a Business and Keeping Records
Form 6-17	**IRS Pub. 533**	Self-Employment Tax
Form 6-18	**IRS Form 941**	Employer's Quarterly Federal Tax Return
Form 6-19	**IRS Form 940**	Employer's Annual Unemployment Tax Return
Form 6-20	**IRS Pub. 510**	Excise Taxes
Form 6-21	**IRS Pub. 535**	Business Expenses
Form 6-22	**IRS Pub. 946**	How to Depreciate Property
Form 6-23	**IRS Pub. 587**	Business Use of Your Home
Form 6-24	**IRS Form 8829**	Expenses for Business Use of Your Home
Form 6-25	**IRS Pub. 463**	Travel, Entertainment, Gift, and Car Expenses
Form 6-26	**IRS Form 8300**	Report of Cash Payments Over $10,000 Received in a Trade or Business
Form 6-27	**IRS Pub. 15-A**	Employer's Supplemental Tax Guide
Form 6-28	**IRS Pub. 334**	Tax Guide for Small Businesses (For Individuals Who use Schedule C or C-EZ)
Form 6-29	**IRS Pub. 536**	Net Operating Losses
Form 6-30	**IRS Pub. 538**	Accounting Periods and Methods

Form Number	Form Name	Description
Form 6-31	**IRS Pub. 560**	Retirement Plans for Small Businesses
Form 6-32	**IRS Pub. 1066**	Small Business Tax Workshop Workbook
Form 6-33	**IRS Pub. 1853**	Small Business Talk (an IRS publication that explains small business tax issues)
Form 6-34	**IRS Pub. 1976**	Independent Contractor or Employee?
Form 6-35	**Chart of Federal Business Tax Filings**	Summary of required federal tax filings for sole proprietorships, partnerships, and corporations
Form 6-36	**IRS Pub. 1679**	A Guide to Backup Withholding
Form 6-37	**IRS Form W-3**	Reconciliation/Transmittal of Income and Tax Statement
Form 7-1	**Questions to Consider Asking Prospective Employees**	A list of questions to consider asking prospective employees
Form 7-2	**Background Check Permission (Comprehensive)**	A form that the prospective employee signs, which gives the employer permission to check references
Form 7-3	**Background Check Permission (Simple)**	A simple consent form from a prospective employee for the employer to perform a background check
Form 7-4	**Reference Check Letter**	Letter to prior employer of prospective employee, requesting reference information
Form 7-5	**Employment Application for Prospective Employees**	Form for prospective employees to fill out
Form 7-6	**Rejection Letter to Applicant**	A form letter for rejecting an employee applicant
Form 7-7	**Offer Letter to Prospective Employee**	Letter providing terms of employment offer to prospective employee

(continued)

Table A-1 *(continued)*

Form Number	Form Name	Description
Form 7-8	**Employment Agreement**	Agreement for executive-level employees
Form 7-9	**Employee Confidentiality and Invention Assignment Agreement**	Agreement in which the employee agrees to keep company information confidential and to assign to the company business-related inventions developed by the employee
Form 7-10	**Employee Handbook and At Will Employee Status Acknowledgement**	A form in which the employee acknowledges receiving the employee handbook and the "at will" notice of his or her employment
Form 7-11	**IRS Form W-4**	IRS Employee's Withholding Allowance Certificate
Form 7-12	**Form I-9**	Form to be signed by the employee and required by the United States Customs & Immigration Service
Form 7-13	**Employee Emergency Notification Form**	Form the employee fills out, identifying the person to contact in the event of an emergency
Form 7-14	**Non-Discrimination Policy**	A company policy statement prohibiting discrimination
Form 7-15	**Sexual Harassment Policy**	A company policy statement prohibiting sexual harassment
Form 7-16	**Checklist of Employment Agreement Issues From the Perspective of the Employee**	A checklist of issues for an employee to consider when negotiating an Employment Agreement
Form 8-1	**Certificate of Employee of the Month**	A sample certificate to be given to an employee in appreciation of good work
Form 8-2	**Employee Satisfaction Survey**	A sample form to be given to employees to gauge employee satisfaction

Form Number	Form Name	Description
Form 8-3	**Chart of Key Employee Benefit Plans and Programs**	A chart summarizing different employee benefit plans and programs
Form 9-1	**Checklist for Employee Handbooks**	A checklist of items to consider including in an Employee Handbook
Form 9-2	**Employee Handbook and At Will Employee Status Acknowledgement**	A sample acknowledgement covering the Employee Handbook and At Will employment status for employees to sign
Form 9-3	**Non-Discrimination Policy**	A sample policy prohibiting discrimination in the workplace
Form 9-4	**Sexual Harassment Policy**	A sample policy giving guidance to employees and prohibiting sexual harassment
Form 9-5	**E-Mail Policy**	A sample policy concerning how e-mail should and should not be used on company computers
Form 9-6	**Drug-Free Workplace Policy**	A sample policy, to be signed by the employee, concerning the company's policy against drugs
Form 9-7	**Employee Appraisal Form**	A sample form to be used to record an employee appraisal
Form 9-8	**Employee Settlement and Release Agreement**	A sample agreement where the employee releases any claims against the employer in exchange for some payment
Form 9-9	**Employee Exit Interview**	A sample form to be used in connection with a departing employee
Form 10-1	**Questions to Consider Asking Prospective Consultants or Independent Contractors**	Questions that may be useful to ask prospective consultants or independent contractors
Form 10-2	**Background Check Permission (Simple)**	A sample simple form, to be signed by a prospective consultant or independent contractor, giving permission for a background check

(continued)

Table A-1 *(continued)*

Form Number	Form Name	Description
Form 10-3	**Background Check Permission (Comprehensive)**	A sample comprehensive form, to be signed by a prospective consultant or independent contractor, giving permission for a background check
Form 10-4	**Independent Contractor Agreement**	A sample pro-company-oriented Independent Contractor Agreement
Form 10-5	**Consulting Agreement**	A sample pro-company-oriented form agreement to be used for a consultant
Form 10-6	**Consultant Confidentiality and Invention Assignment Agreement**	A form of agreement that requires the consultant to keep company information confidential and to assign ownership of inventions and materials developed as part of the work for the company over to the company
Form 10-7	**Chart of Key Differences between Employees and Independent Contractors**	A summary chart showing key differences in a worker being classified as an employee or independent contractor
Form 10-8	**IRS Publication 1976**	Publication that discusses classification of independent contractors versus employees
Form 10-9	**IRS Publication 1779**	Gives advice on independent contractors and employees designation
Form 10-10	**IRS Publication 15-A**	Illustrative examples of key differences in classification of employees and independent contractors
Form 10-11	**IRS Form W-9**	The IRS form to be signed by an independent contractor at the beginning of the relationship
Form 10-12	**IRS Form 1099-MISC**	The IRS form to be filed for independent contractors
Form 11-1	**Contract Checklist**	A checklist of important terms to consider for contracts

Form Number	Form Name	Description
Form 11-2	**Letter of Intent to Purchase a Business**	A sample letter of intent for the purchase of a business
Form 11-3	**Agreement for Professional Services**	A sample agreement for the rendering of professional services
Form 11-4	**Equipment Sales Agreement**	A sample agreement for the sale of equipment
Form 11-5	**Purchase Order**	A sample purchase order to buy goods
Form 11-6	**Checklist of Issues in Drafting and Negotiating Software License Agreements**	A checklist of issues to consider when drafting and negotiating Software License Agreements
Form 11-7	**License Agreement**	A sample shrink-wrap software license agreement
Form 11-8	**Letter of Intent for Joint Venture**	A sample letter of intent to form a 50-50 joint venture company
Form 11-9	**Term Sheet for Equity Investment and Strategic Alliance**	A sample Joint Venture Agreement
Form 11-10	**Important Boilerplate Provisions for Contracts**	Numerous sample "boilerplate" or "miscellaneous" provisions for contracts
Form 11-11	**Amendment to Sales Contract**	A sample form of amendment to an existing Sales Contract
Form 11-12	**Bill of Sale and Assignment**	A sample simple form of Bill of Sale
Form 12-1	**Small Business Legal Audit Checklist**	A checklist for the small business to review concerning its legal operations
Form 12-2	**Guaranty**	A pro-creditor-oriented form that guarantees performance and payment of certain obligations
Form 12-3	**Form 1502**	Statement by Domestic Stock Corporation (California)
Form 12-4	**General Power of Attorney**	A form that grants broad general powers to act on behalf of the person signing the form

(continued)

Table A-1 *(continued)*

Form Number	Form Name	Description
Form 12-5	**Special Power of Attorney**	A form that grants specific powers to act on behalf of the person signing the form
Form 12-6	**Demand to Guarantor for Payment**	A notice to a guarantor of an obligation that the debtor is in default and payment is now being demanded from the guarantor
Form 13-1	**Novelty and Other Conditions for Obtaining a Patent**	U.S. Patent and Trademark Office summary of various conditions for obtaining a patent
Form 13-2	**General Information Concerning Patents**	Covers patents, from the U.S. Patent and Trademark Office
Form 13-3	**List of Patent Application Forms**	U.S. Patent and Trademark Office summary of forms for applying for a patent. Forms are available at www.uspto.gov.
Form 13-4	**Patent Assignment**	An agreement for assigning a patent
Form 13-5	**Copyright Registration**	Form to register copyrightable literary works with the Copyright Office
Form 13-6	**Cover Letter to Copyright Office**	Sample letter to the Copyright Office enclosing a Copyright Registration form
Form 13-7	**Independent Contractor Agreement**	Sample contract with an independent contractor that's skewed in the company's favor
Form 13-8	**Invention Assignment Agreement**	Comprehensive agreement between the company and a consultant protecting the company's intellectual property rights
Form 13-9	**Copyright Assignment**	An agreement for assigning a copyright
Form 13-10	**Copyright Compliance – Photocopying Policy**	A policy statement to post near the company's photocopy machines, reminding users of issues in complying with the copyright laws

Form Number	Form Name	Description
Form 13-11	**Permission Request to Use Copyrighted Material**	A sample letter requesting the right to use copyrighted materials
Form 13-12	**Notice of Infringement of Copyrighted Work**	A sample letter notifying another party that they have infringed on your copyrighted work
Form 13-13	**Trademark Registration**	A Trademark registration application from the U.S. Patent and Trademark Office
Form 13-14	**Cover Letter to U.S. Patent and Trademark Office**	Sample letter to U.S. Patent and Trademark Office to send with Trademark registration form
Form 13-15	**Trademark FAQs**	Frequently Asked Questions about trademarks from the U.S. Patent and Trademark Office
Form 13-16	**Trademark Assignment**	An agreement for assigning a trademark
Form 13-17	**Confidentiality Agreement with Third Party**	An agreement where the recipient agrees to keep confidential a idea or product presented by the disclosing party
Form 13-18	**Trade Name License Agreement**	A license granting the right to use a trade name
Form 13-19	**Mutual Non-Disclosure Agreement (Short Form)**	An agreement allowing two companies to exchange confidential agreement and mutual protection obligations
Form 14-1	**Limited Warranty**	A form of Limited Warranty for a software product, with various disclaimers and limitations of liability
Form 14-2	**Credit Application**	An application to be filled out by a prospective customer prior to granting the customer credit
Form 14-3	**Accounts Receivable Aging**	A sample accounting report to keep track of aging of all accounts-receivables

(continued)

Table A-1 *(continued)*

Form Number	Form Name	Description
Form 14-4	**Accounts Receivable Monthly Customer Statement**	A sample report to keep track of aging of accounts receivables status by customer
Form 14-5	**Settlement of Disputed Account**	An agreement to compromise on disputed accounts owed
Form 14-6	**Courtesy Reminder of Late Payment**	A sample letter courteously reminding the customer that payment is overdue
Form 14-7	**Demand for Payment**	A letter demanding payment on an overdue account
Form 14-8	**Final Demand for Payment**	A letter more forcefully demanding payment and labeled a "final demand"
Form 14-9	**Attorney Letter Demanding Payment**	A form of letter from an attorney demanding overdue payment
Form 14-10	**Delinquent Account Collection History**	A log to keep track of efforts to collect overdue accounts
Form 14-11	**Notice of Dishonored Check**	A notice to a customer that the customer's check has bounced
Form 15-1	**Checklist for Office Leases**	A checklist of issues to look out for in analyzing office leases
Form 15-2	**Addendum to Real Estate Lease (For the Benefit of the Tenant)**	A sample Addendum designed to give some protections and benefits to the tenant from the standard form of lease provided by the landlord
Form 15-3	**Assignment of Lease**	A form of assignment of lease by a tenant
Form 15-4	**Office Sublease**	A sample office sublease
Form 15-5	**Option to Renew Real Estate Lease**	Sample provisions to add to a real estate lease granting the tenant a right to renew the lease at the end of the term

Form Number	Form Name	Description
Form 15-6	**Option to Expand Space Leased in a Building**	A sample provision for a tenant to expand a lease to include additional space in the building
Form 15-7	**Amendment to Lease**	Form used to amend a lease
Form 15-8	**Offer to Lease Space**	A sample letter offering to lease space
Form 15-9	**Option to Purchase**	A sample provision giving the tenant the option to buy the property being leased
Form 15-10	**Consent by Lessor to Assignment of Lease**	A consent by the landlord to the assignment of a lease
Form 15-11	**Consent by Lessor to Sublease**	A consent by a landlord to a proposed sublease
Form 15-12	**Demand for Rent**	A sample letter firmly demanding rent payment from a tenant
Form 15-13	**Notice of Change in Rent**	A sample letter notifying a tenant of an impending rent change
Form 16-1	**Trademark Registration Form**	An official document for registering a trademark with the Patent and Trademark Office
Form 16-2	**Cover Letter**	Cover letter for the Trademark Registration Form
Form 16-3	**Checklist of Issues for Web Site Development Contracts**	A checklist of issues to review when negotiating and drafting a Web Site Development Contract
Form 16-4	**Sample Online Contract**	A sample Online contract for the sale of goods through a Web site
Form 16-5	**Sample Copyright and trademark Protection Notice**	A sample copyright and trademark notice to be included in a Web site
Form 16-6	**Sample Online Disclaimer Regarding Information**	A sample disclaimer for information posted on a Web site
Form 16-7	**Sample Online Disclaimer Reference**	A sample disclaimer that concerns the use of a commercial Web site

(continued)

Table A-1 *(continued)*

Form Number	Form Name	Description
Form 16-8	**Sample Online Disclosure Regarding Online Contract**	A sample disclosure that notifies Web site visitors of the terms and conditions involved in the sale of a product or service; the disclosure includes a link to the terms and conditions
Form 16-9	**Sample Online Disclaimers Re: Hyperlinks**	Sample disclaimers regarding hyperlinks to other sites
Form 17-1	**Press Release – Major Development**	A sample press release that announces a major development that affects the company
Form 17-2	**Press Release – Web Site Milestone**	A sample press release that announces a milestone for a Web-based business
Form 17-3	**Press Release – Promotion of Employee**	A sample press release that announces an existing employee's promotion to a key position
Form 17-4	**Press Release – Hiring of Key Employee**	A sample press release that announces the hiring of a new senior-level employee
Form 17-5	**Press Release – New Product**	A sample press release that announces a new product
Form 17-6	**Press Release – New Service**	A sample press release that announces a new service
Form 17-7	**Press Release – New Web-Based Service**	A sample press release that announces a new, Web-based service
Form 17-8	**Media Relations Policy**	A sample company policy statement to be distributed to employees or included in the employee handbook concerning response to media inquiries

Troubleshooting CD Problems

We tried our best to compile programs that work on most computers with the minimum system requirements. Alas, your computer may differ, and some programs may not work properly, for some reason.

The two likeliest problems are that you don't have enough memory (RAM) for the programs that you want to use or that you have other programs running that are affecting the installation or running of a program. If you get an error message such as `Not enough memory` or `Setup cannot continue`, try one or more of the following suggestions and then try using the software again:

- ✔ **Turn off any antivirus software running on your computer.** Installation programs sometimes mimic virus activity and may make your computer incorrectly believe that it's being infected by a virus. You undoubtedly want to turn your antivirus software back on when you're finished installing the software.

- ✔ **Close all running programs.** (If necessary, this may even include closing the CD interface and running a product's installation program directly from Windows Explorer or the Macintosh Finder.) The more programs you have running, the less memory is available to other programs. Installation programs typically update files and programs; so if you keep other programs running, installation may not work properly.

- ✔ **Have your local computer store add more RAM to your computer.** This option is, admittedly, a drastic and somewhat expensive step. However, if you have a Windows PC or a Power Macintosh, adding more memory can really help the speed of your computer and allow more programs to run at the same time.

If you still have trouble with the CD, please call Wiley Product Technical Support at 800-762-2974 (outside the United States, call 1-317-572-3994) or via our Web site at `www.wiley.com/techsupport`. Wiley provides technical support only for installation and other general quality-control items; for technical support on the applications themselves, consult the program's vendor or author.

To place additional orders or to request information about other Wiley products, please call 800-225-5945.

Index

●●●

• A •

absenteeism, 175
accounting forms
  Balance Sheet, 94–97
  Cash Flow Statement, 97–99
  Income Statement, 90–93
accounting method, 85–86
Accounting Periods and Methods
    (IRS Form 538), 86
accounts payable, 97
accounts receivable, 96
Accounts Receivable Aging form, 269, 270
Accounts Receivable Monthly Customer
    Statement form, 269, 271
accredited investor, 73
accrual method of accounting, 86
accrued wages, 97
Action by Written Consent of Stockholders
    (Form 3-33C), 51
Action of Incorporator, 44, 46
Addendum to Real Estate Lease (Form
    15-2), 286
Adobe Reader, 342
advice, getting, 328
Age Discrimination in Employment Act,
    123, 176
Agreement for Professional Services,
    213, 217
alcohol use at work, 176
AllBusiness Web site, 331–332
alliance, strategic, 327
allowance, 93
amending contract, 226, 231
American Express–Small Business Web
    site, 334–335
Americans with Disabilities Act, 123
angel investor, 69
anti-dilution right, 71
anti-fraud laws, 73

application
  for credit, 265, 267–269
  for employment, 129–133
  false information, giving on, 176
*Application for Employer Identification
    Number* (IRS Form SS-4), 107
arbitrary mark, 254
arbitration clause in contract, 225, 230
Articles of Incorporation, 43–44, 45
assets
  current, 94, 96
  documents supporting, 88
  fixed, 96
  overview of, 94
assignment
  of lease, 289–290
  of license, 221
assignment clause in contract, 225, 230
Assignment of Lease (Form 15-3), 290
assumptions underlying financial
    forecast, 34
at will employment, 166, 167, 175
attorney
  advice from, getting, 328
  checking with, 2
  contract and, 208
  Joint Venture Agreement and, 223
  letter demanding payment and, 273, 277
  loan and, 65
  patent and, 248–249
  real estate lease and, 279
  venture capital financing and, 81
attorney's fees clause in contract, 225, 227
auditing of financial statement, 101

• B •

background check, 128
balance sheet, 33, 94–97
Bank Reconciliation Worksheet, 89

bank records, 234
basis, 18
binding obligation
  Distribution Agreement and, 224
  Joint Venture Agreement, 222
  letter of intent and, 213
  License Agreement, 221
Blue Sky laws, 73
Board of Advisors, 328
board of directors
  fiduciary relationship and, 49
  initial actions by, 49–50
  ongoing actions by, 50
  responsibility of, 48–49
  Stock Option Plan and, 159
board seat right, 81
boilerplate clause in contract, 212, 225–226,
    227–230
bonus, cash, 160
bookkeeping
  accounting method, 85–86
  accounting software, 86
  Balance Sheet, 94–97
  business checkbook, 89
  Cash Flow Statement, 97–99
  Income Statement, 90–93
  journal and ledger, 88
  record-keeping system, 86–87, 234
  supporting documents, 87–88
borrowing money
  negotiating terms for, 64–65
  overview of, 64
  promissory note, 66
  from Small Business Administration,
    66, 68
break-even analysis, 33
budget, 100–101, 102
*Built to Last: Successful Habits of Visionary
    Companies* (James Collins and Jerry
    Porras), 339
business concepts, general, Web site for, 2
Business Contracts Kit For Dummies
    (Richard D. Harroch), 340
business due diligence, 79
business entity
  comparison chart for, 10–11
  corporation, 16–18

  Limited Liability Company (LLC), 19–20
  overview of, 9
  partnership, 12–15
  sole proprietorship, 12
  tax issues and, 106
Business Expenses (IRS Publication 535), 114
business plan
  company description, 29
  competition section, 32
  cover page, 26, 27
  description of, 23
  executive summary, 26, 28, 29
  financial section, 33–34, 35
  functions of, 24
  information excluded from, 24
  management section, 30–31
  market section, 31
  marketing section, 32
  mini, writing, 36, 37–39
  product section, 30
  raising capital and, 75
  reviews of, 34
  samples of, Web sites for, 24
  standard format for, 25–26
  tips for, 25
  writing, 23–24
Business Plans For Dummies (Paul Tiffany
    and Steven Peterson), 33
business transaction, recording, 88–89
*Business Use of Your Home–Including Use by
    Day Care Providers* (IRS Publication
    587), 114
Business Week (magazine), 338
Business Week Web site, 332
buying domain name from existing holder,
    301–302
bylaws, 46

• C •

C corporation, 16–17
Cafeteria Plans, 161
California, incorporating in, 43, 45
candidate for job, interviewing, 124–127
capital asset, 96

capital, raising
  borrowing, 64–68
  business plan and, 75
  financing, seeking when not needed, 328–329
  leasing equipment and, 68–69
  principles about, 63
  stock, selling, 69–77
  venture capital, 77–82
capitalizing corporation, 51–53
car expenses, 114
cash flow projection, 33
Cash Flow Statement, 97–99
cash method of accounting, 86
CBS Marketwatch Web site, 334
CD-ROM
  system requirements for, 341
  troubleshooting, 365
  using, 342
CD-ROM forms
  Action by Written Consent of Stockholders (3-33C), 51
  Action of Incorporator (3-5C and 3-5D), 46
  Addendum to Real Estate Lease (15-2), 286
  Agreement for Professional Services (11-3), 217
  Assignment of Lease (15-3), 290
  background check (10-2 and 10-3), 188
  Background Check Permission (7-2 and 7-3), 128
  Bank Reconciliation Worksheet (5-8), 89
  benefit plan chart (8-3), 156
  board minutes or consents (3-8 to 3-32), 50
  broad guaranty (12-2), 241
  business entities (1-1), 9
  bylaws (3-6C and 3-6D), 46
  California incorporation (3-1 and 3-2), 43
  Check Disbursements Journal (5-6), 89
  Checklist for Employee Handbooks (9-1), 166
  checklist for Software License Agreement (11-6), 221
  Comparative Balance Sheet (5-13), 94
  Confidentiality and Invention Assignment Agreement (7-9 and 13-8), 145, 251

Consulting Agreement (10-5), 194
Control Sheet for Private Placement Memorandums (4-10), 74
Copyright Assignment Agreement (13-9), 251
copyright infringement rules (13-10), 252
copyright registration (13-5), 251
copyright registration cover letter (13-6), 251
corporation checklist (1-4), 16
corporation securities and tax issues (3-50 to 3-55), 51
Daily Summary of Cash Receipts (5-4), 88
Depreciation Worksheet (5-7), 89
Due Diligence Checklist (4-15), 80
emergency notification (7-13), 146
Employee Appraisal (9-7), 175
Employee Compensation Record (5-9), 89
employee handbook receipt (7-10), 145
Equipment Sales Agreement (11-4), 219
evaluating independent contractor or consultant (10-1), 188
FAQ from U.S. Patent and Trademark Office (13-2), 248
format of, 342
hyperlink disclaimer (16-9), 311
Independent Contractor Agreement (13-7), 251
I-9 (5-3, 6-9, and 7-12), 88, 107, 145
IRS Form 538 (5-1), 86
IRS Form 940 (6-19), 112
IRS Form 941 (6-18), 111
IRS Form 1099-MISC (6-13 and 10-12), 109, 202
IRS Form 2553 (1-5 and 6-3), 19, 106
IRS Form 2553 transmittal letter (6-3), 106
IRS Form 8109 (6-11), 108
IRS Form 8829 (6-24), 114
IRS Form SS-4 (6-6), 107
IRS Form SS-4 transmittal letter (6-7), 107
IRS Form W-2 (6-15), 109
IRS Form W-4 (6-10 and 7-11), 108, 145
IRS Form W-9 (10-11), 202
IRS Publication 15 (6-12), 108, 111
IRS Publication 15-A (10-10), 201
IRS Publication 463 (5-2 and 6-25), 87, 114

CD-ROM forms *(continued)*
  IRS Publication 510 (6-20), 112
  IRS Publication 533 (6-17), 111
  IRS Publication 535 (6-21), 114
  IRS Publication 541 (6-1), 106
  IRS Publication 542 (6-2), 106
  IRS Publication 583 (6-16), 110
  IRS Publication 587 (6-23), 114
  IRS Publication 594 (6-5), 106
  IRS Publication 946 (6-22), 114
  IRS Publication 1544 (6-14), 109
  IRS Publication 1779 (10-9), 200
  IRS Publication 1915 (6-8), 107
  IRS Publication 1976 (10-8), 200
  IRS transmittal for S corporation filing
    (1-6), 19
  joint venture agreement (11-8), 223
  Lease Amendment (15-7), 292
  letter offering to expand space in leased
    building (15-6), 291
  letter requesting permission to use
    copyrighted work (13-11), 252
  letter to send after using copyrighted
    work (13-12), 252
  Limited Partnership Agreement checklist
    (1-3), 15
  Monthly Summary of Cash Receipts
    (5-4), 88
  Online Contract (16-4), 310
  online copyright notice (16-5), 311
  Operating Agreement checklist (1-7), 20
  organizational board resolutions (3-7C
    and 3-7D), 50
  Partnership Agreement checklist (1-2), 14
  Patent Assignment Agreement (13-4), 250
  patent, conditions for obtaining (13-1), 248
  Pre-Offering Summary (4-12), 76
  press releases (17-1, 17-2, 17-3, 17-6, and
    17-7), 318
  Private Placement Memorandum
    checklist (4-7), 76
  promissory note (4-1 and 4-2), 66
  Purchase Order (11-5), 220
  Real Estate Sublease (15-4), 290
  Reference Check Letter (7-4), 128

rejection letter (7-6), 129
Right of First Refusal Agreement
    (3-59C and 3-59D), 52
SBA loan programs (4-3), 68
Settlement of Disputed Amount
    (14-5), 272
Software License Agreement (11-7), 221
stock certificate (3-56 and 3-57), 52
stock ledger (3-58), 52
Stock Subscription Agreement (4-13), 77
Stock Subscription Package (4-11), 74
term sheet (4-17), 81
Term Sheet for Equity Investment and
    Strategic Alliance (11-9), 223
Trademark Application (13-13), 254
Trademark Application cover letter
    (13-14), 254
Trademark Assignment (13-16), 255
Trademark Registration (16-1), 303
U.S. Patent and Trademark Office cover
    letter (16-2), 303
venture capitalist (4-14), 78
Web Site Development Agreement
    (16-3), 304
Web site disclaimers (16-7 and 16-8), 311
Withholding, Benefit, and Legal
    Differences Between Employees and
    Contractors (10-7), 199
Certificate of Appreciation, 150–151
Certificate of Incorporation, 43–44
chart of accounts, 90–91
Check Disbursements Journal, 89
checkbook, business, 89
checking account, reconciling, 89
Checklist for Employee Handbooks
    (Form 9-1), 166
Circular E, Employer's Tax Guide
    (IRS Publication 15), 108, 111
Civil Rights Act of 1966, 123
clarity of contract, 211
Coca-Cola, 247
collateral for loan, 65
collection agency, using, 273
collection letter, sending, 273
Collins, James, *Built to Last: Successful
    Habits of Visionary Companies*, 339

commingling of assets, 240
common stock, 71
Comparative Balance Sheet (Form 5-13), 94
competition, researching, 329–330
competition section (business plan), 32
competitive advantage, describing in
    business plan, 30, 32
completeness of contract, 211
Confidentiality Agreement, 256–259
Confidentiality and Invention Assignment
    Agreement
  consultant or contractor and, 194–198
  copyright and, 251
  hiring and, 137, 145
"confusingly similar" trademark, 252
consultant
  Confidentiality and Invention Assignment
    Agreement, 194–198
  copyright and, 251
  forming relationship with, 187–188
Consulting Agreement (Form 10-5), 194
Consumer Price Index (CPI), rent based on,
    286–287
consumer protection laws, 233
contract. *See also* leasing
  Agreement for Professional Services,
    213, 217
  amending, 226, 231
  boilerplate sections of, 225–226, 227–230
  checklist for, 209–210
  for conducting business online, 309–310
  deadline and services, 217
  Distribution Agreement, 223–224
  with employee, 177
  Joint Venture Agreement, 221–223
  letters of intent, 212–213, 214–216
  License Agreement, 220–221
  Purchase Order, 219–220
  requirements of, 207–208
  Sales Contract, 218–219
  for Web site development, 303–308
  writing, 208, 211–212
Control Sheet for Private Placement
    Memorandums (Form 4-10), 74
convertible note, 72
convertible preferred stock, 81, 82

copyright
  overview of, 250–251, 253
  Web site and, 309, 311
Copyright Assignment Agreement
    (Form 13-9), 251
corporate formalities, 240
corporate records, 235
corporation. *See also* shareholders
  Action of Incorporator, 44, 46
  Articles of Incorporation, 43–44, 45
  benefits of, 236, 240
  board of directors, 48–50, 159
  bylaws, 46
  C type, 16–17
  capitalizing, 51–53
  cost of forming, 47–48
  forming, 41, 48
  minute book, 47
  name for, choosing, 41–42
  overview of, 16, 41
  S type, 18–19, 106
  state of, choosing, 43
Corporations (IRS Publication 542), 106
correspondence, 235
co-sale right, 81
cosigner for loan, 65
cost
  of goods sold, 93
  of incorporation, 47–48
  of operating expenses in real estate lease,
    287–288
cover page (business plan), 26, 27
CPI (Consumer Price Index), rent based on,
    286–287
creative ideas to improve business
  advice, getting, 328
  build Web site, 330
  financing, seeking when not needed,
    328–329
  gifts, giving to key customers, 328
  publicity, getting favorable, 330
  researching competition, 329–330
  rewarding employees, 329
  seeking and trying, 329
  suggestions, soliciting employees for, 330
  teaming up with another company, 327

credit
  application for, 265, 267–269
  legal issues, 272
  overview of, 265
Credit Application, 265, 267–268
CSC (registered agent), 44
CT Corporation, 44
current assets, 94, 96
current liability, 97
customers. *See also* credit
  collection letters or agency, 273
  early payment discount for, 264
  gifts for, 328
  payment policy for, 263–264
  reducing risk of nonpayment by, 269–272
  warranty and, 264–265

• *D* •

Daily Summary of Cash Receipts, 88
d.b.a. (doing business as), 12, 243
deadline and services contract, 217
debtor, dealing with, 272
deduction for business expense, 113–114
default of loan, 65
Delaware, incorporating in, 43
demand note, 66
depreciation, 114
Depreciation Worksheet, 89
design patent, 248
Determination of Employee Work Status for Purposes of Federal Employment Taxes and Income Tax Withholding (IRS Form SS-8), 201
developer for Web site, contracting with, 303–308
direct cost, 93
disclaimer
  in Sales Contract, 218
  on Web site, 311, 312
discrimination
  in employment, laws prohibiting, 123
  protected group and, 177
dispute over payment owed, 272
Distribution Agreement, 223–224

documentation and performance appraisal, 174
documents, supporting, 87–88
domain name
  buying from existing holder, 301–302
  description of, 299–300
  registering, 301
  searching on, 300–301
  trademark and, 302–303
double taxation, 16, 105, 106
drug use at work, 176
drug-free work policy, 171, 173
due date for loan, 64
Due Diligence Checklist, 80

• *E* •

early payment discount, 264
earnings per share, 91
EIN (employer identification number), 107
Electronic Federal Tax Payment System (EFTPS), 108
e-mail policy, 171, 172
e-mailing press release, 318
emergency notification form, 146
Employee Appraisal (Form 9-7), 175
Employee Compensation Record, 89
Employee Handbook, 165–166
employee records, 235
Employee Satisfaction Survey, 152–155
employee tax forms, 107–108
employees. *See also* motivating employees
  announcing in press release, 319
  background and reference checks of, 128
  candidate, interviewing, 124–127
  commitment of, 31
  exit interview, 178, 183–184
  finding good, 121–123
  firing, 175–178
  hiring practices, 121
  independent contractor compared to, 199, 201
  nondisclosure agreement, 256
  nonsolicitation of, 217
  offer letter, 134–136

paperwork to fill out on first day, 145–146, 166, 167

performance appraisal, 174

retaining, 149–150, 152, 156–160

rewarding, 329

soliciting for suggestions, 330

workers automatically classified as employees, 200

Employee's Withholding Allowance Certificate (IRS Form W-4), 108, 145

employer identification number (EIN), 107

Employer's Annual Federal Unemployment (FUTA) Tax Return (IRS Form 940), 112

Employer's Quarterly Federal Tax Return (IRS Form 941), 111

Employment Agreement, 137, 138–144

Employment Application, 129–133

employment laws, 123

employment taxes

overview of, 111–112

records of, 87

encouraging new ideas, 329

entertainment expenses, 114

entire agreement clause in contract, 225

Entrepreneur (magazine), 338

Entrepreneur Web site, 333–334

environmental laws, 234

Equal Credit Opportunity Act, 272

Equal Pay Act of 1963, 123

equipment, leasing, 68–69

Equipment Sales Agreement (Form 11-4), 219

equity investor, 91

Estimated Tax for Individuals (IRS Form 1040-ES), 110

excise tax, 112

Excise Taxes (IRS Publication 510), 112

exclusivity

Distribution Agreement and, 223

letter of intent and, 213

License Agreement and, 220

executive summary (business plan), 26, 28, 29

exercise price, 157, 158, 159

exhibit to contract, 211

exit interview, 178, 183–184

expenses

documents supporting, 87

as tax deduction, 113–114

Expenses for Business Use of Your Home, (IRS From 8829), 114

• **F** •

failure of small business, 23

Fair Credit Billing Act, 272

false information, giving on application, 176

fanciful mark, 254

Fast Company (magazine), 339

faxing press release, 317

Federal Insurance Contributions Act (FICA), 111

Federal Tax Deposit Coupon (IRS Form 8109), 108

federal unemployment tax (FUTA), 111

federal withholding, 111

feedback, performance-review, 150

FICA (Federal Insurance Contributions Act), 111

fictitious name certificate, 12, 243

fiduciary relationship

of board members, 49

description of, 13, 15

filing information with state, 243

financial section (business plan), 33–34

financing, seeking when not needed, 328–329

finding good employees, 121–123

firing employees

exit interview, 178, 183–184

legal reasons for, 175–176

risks of, 176–177

Settlement Agreement, 177–178, 179–182

fixed asset, 96

flexible workplace, 152

Forbes (magazine), 339

force majeure, 217, 229–230

forecast, 101

foreign corporation, 244

forms. *See* CD-ROM forms; IRS Forms

Fortune (magazine), 338
401(k) plan, 161–162
FUTA (federal unemployment tax), 111

• *G* •

general partnership, 13–14
gifts, giving to key customers, 328
goodwill, 96
grace period for loan payment, 65
gross receipts, 87
gross sales (gross revenues), 93
guarantor for loan, 65
guaranty, negotiating, 240–241

• *H* •

Harroch, Richard D., *Business Contracts Kit For Dummies*, 340
hiring practices
  application for employment, 129–133
  Confidentiality and Invention Assignment Agreement, 137, 145
  Employee Handbook, 165–166
  Employment Agreement, 137, 138–144
  offer letter, 134–136
  overview of, 121
  paperwork filled out on first day, 145–146, 166, 167
home, business use of, 114
hosting service for Web site, 301
How to Depreciate Property (IRS Publication 946), 114
hyperlink, 309
hyperlink disclaimer, 311

• *I* •

identifying key media players, 321
illegal act, 176
image, 321
immigration and nationalization I-9 form, 88, 107, 145
Immigration Reform and Control Act of 1986, 123

improving business. *See* creative ideas to improve business
Inc. (magazine), 337
income projection, 33, 35
Income Statement
  budget and, 100–101, 102
  overview of, 90–93
  ratios of income, 100
income taxes, 93, 110
incompetence, 175
incorporator, 44, 46
indemnification, 46
independent contractor
  agreement with, 188–194
  characteristics of, 200
  Confidentiality and Invention Assignment Agreement, 194–198
  copyright and, 251
  employee compared to, 199, 201
  forming relationship with, 187–188
  tax forms for, 202
Independent Contractor Agreement (Form 13-7), 251
indirect cost, 93
information return, 110
infringement of copyrighted materials, 253
I-9 (immigration and nationalization) form, 88, 107, 145
initial public offering (IPO), 78
intangible asset, 96
intellectual property
  Confidentiality Agreement, 256–259
  copyright and, 250–251
  overview of, 247
  patent and, 248–250
  trade secret right, 255–256
  trademark, 252–255
intellectual property records, 235
interest rate for loan, 64–65
Internal Revenue Code
  Section 401(k), 161
  Section 1202, 114–115
Internal Revenue Service (IRS) Web site, 115, 333
interviewing job candidate, 124–127

inventory, 86, 96
investors
  accredited versus unaccredited, 73
  financing, seeking when not needed,
    328–329
  Income Statement and, 91
  Subscription Agreement, 76–77
  types of, 69
IPO (initial public offering), 78
IRS Forms
  538, *Accounting Periods and Methods*, 86
  940, *Employer's Annual Federal
    Unemployment (FUTA) Tax Return*, 112
  941, *Employer's Quarterly Federal Tax
    Return*, 111
  1040-ES, *Estimated Tax for Individuals*, 110
  1099-MISC, *Miscellaneous Income*, 109
  independent contractor and, 202
  2553, *S Corporation Election Form*,
    18, 19, 106
  8109, *Federal Tax Deposit Coupon*, 108
  8300, *Report of Cash Payments Over
    $10,000 Received in a Trade or
    Business*, 109
  8829, *Expenses for Business Use of Your
    Home*, 114
  SS-4, *Application for Employer
    Identification Number*, 107
  SS-8, *Determination of Employee Work
    Status for Purposes of Federal
    Employment Taxes and Income Tax
    Withholding*, 201
  W-2, *Wage and Tax Statement*, 109
  W-4, *Employee's Withholding Allowance
    Certificate*, 108, 145
  W-9, 202
IRS (Internal Revenue Service). *See also*
    Internal Revenue Code
  accounting method and, 86
  penalties for nonpayment of taxes, 113
  Web site, 115, 333
IRS penalties
  for late payment of taxes, 108, 109
  for nonpayment of taxes, 113
IRS Publications
  15, *Circular E, Employer's Tax Guide*,
    108, 111

  15-A, *Employers Supplemental Tax
    Guide*, 201
  463, *Travel, Entertainment, Gift, and Car
    Expenses*, 87, 114
  510, *Excise Taxes*, 112
  533, *Self-Employment Tax*, 111
  535, *Business Expenses*, 114
  541, *Partnerships*, 106
  542, *Corporations*, 106
  583, *Starting a Business and Keeping
    Records*, 110
  587, *Business Use of Your Home–Including
    Use by Day Care Providers*, 114
  594, *Understanding the Collection Process*,
    106
  946, *How to Depreciate Property*, 114
  1544, *Reporting Cash Payments Over
    $10,000 Received in a Trade or
    Business*, 109
  1779, advice on independent contractor
    and employee designation, 200
  1915, *Understanding Your IRS Taxpayer
    Identification Number*, 107
  1976, classifying independent contractors
    versus employees, 200
issuing stock, 52, 69–70

• *J* •

job share, 152
joint venture, 327
Joint Venture Agreement, 221–223
journal, 88
jurisdiction clause in contract, 225, 229

• *K* •

key contract, 207. *See also* contract

• *L* •

L.A. Times Web site, 335
lawyer
  advice from, getting, 328
  checking with, 2
  contract and, 208

lawyer *(continued)*
  Joint Venture Agreement and, 223
  letter demanding payment and, 273, 277
  loan and, 65
  patent and, 248–249
  real estate lease and, 279
  venture capital financing and, 81
Lease Amendment (Form 15-7), 292
leasing
  assignment and subletting, 289–290
  equipment, 68–69
  expansion options, 291
  "gotchas" and, 280
  improvements and alterations to office
    space, 288–289
  offer letter, 292–294
  office space, 279–284
  operating costs and, 287–288
  permitted uses and, 285–286
  renewal options, 290–291
  rent and, 285
  rules and regulations for building and, 292
  security deposit, 291–292
  working out term of, 286
ledger, 88
Legal A 'it Checklist, 236, 237–239
legal due diligence, 80
legal entity
  comparison chart for, 10–11
  corporation, 16–18
  Limited Liability Company (LLC), 19–20
  overview of, 9
  partnership, 12–15
  sole proprietorship, 12
  tax issues and, 106
legal issues. *See also* intellectual property;
    specific laws
  common, affecting business, 233–234
  in contract, 211
  credit, 272
  filing information with state, 243
  Legal Audit Checklist, 236, 237–239
  licenses and permits, 242–243
  negotiating guaranties, 240–241
  overview of, 233
  patent, 249
  personal liability, avoiding, 236, 240

  qualifying to do business in other
    state, 244
  record-keeping and, 234–236
  registering fictitious business name, 243
  state and local laws, 242–244
  warranty, 264–265, 266
  Web site business, conducting, 309–312
letters
  from attorney demanding payment,
    273, 277
  collection, sending, 273
  copyright registration cover letter
    (Form 13-6), 251
  demanding payment, 275, 276
  of intent, 212–213, 214–216
  IRS Form 2553 transmittal (Form 6-3), 106
  IRS Form SS-4 transmittal (Form 6-7), 107
  job offer, 134–136
  Offer Letter for real estate, 292–294
  offering to expand space in leased
    building (Form 15-6), 291
  Reference Check (Form 7-4), 128
  rejecting job applicant (Form 7-6), 129
  reminding customer of late payment, 274
  requesting permission to use copyrighted
    work (13-11), 252
  to send after using copyrighted work
    (13-12), 252
  Trademark Application cover letter
    (Form 13-14), 254
  U.S. Patent and Trademark Office cover
    letter (Form 16-2), 303
liabilities, 94, 96–97
liability issues
  C corporation, 17
  corporation, 16, 41
  general partnership, 13
  Limited Liability Company (LLC), 19, 20
  Limited Liability Partnership (LLP), 15
  limited partnership, 14
  personal, avoiding, 236, 240
  Sales Contract and, 219
  service contract, 217
  shareholders and, 241
  sole proprietorship, 12
  warranty and, 265
License Agreement, 220–221

license, business, state and local, 242–243
licensee, 220
licensor, 220
Limited Liability Company (LLC), 19–20
Limited Liability Partnership (LLP), 15
limited partnership, 14–15
Limited Partnership Agreement checklist
    (Form 1-3), 15
limited warranty, 264–265, 266
loan
  against 401(k) plan, 161
  negotiating terms of, 64–65
  overview of, 64
  promissory note, 66
  from Small Business Administration,
    66, 68
local press coverage, 321
logo, 224
long-term liability, 97
Low Doc program, 66

• *M* •

mailing list, updating, 317
mailing press release, 317
management section (business plan), 30–31
manufacturing plan, 30
market section (business plan), 31
marketing section (business plan), 32
meal expenses, 114
media. *See also* press release
  key players, identifying, 321
  publicity, getting favorable, 330
  reporter's attention, getting, 321–322
  trust and "off the record" comments, 323
media calendar, 322
media relations policy, 322–323
Medicare tax, 110, 111
Microsoft, 156
mini business plan
  sample of, 37–39
  writing, 36
minute book, 47
Miscellaneous Income (IRS Form 1099-MISC)
  independent contractor and, 202
  overview of, 109

modification of agreement clause in
    contract, 225, 227
monitoring Web site, 304
Monthly Summary of Cash Receipts, 88
motivating employees
  appreciation devices, 150–151
  bonus, cash, 160
  Cafeteria Plans, 161
  Employee Satisfaction Survey, 152–155
  401(k) plan, 161–162
  overview of, 149–150
  perks, 162–163
  Profit Sharing Program, 160
  Stock Option Plans, 156–160
  success and, 329

• *N* •

name for corporation, choosing, 41–42
necessary expense, 114
negotiating
  guaranties, 240–241
  office lease, 279–284
  rent for office space, 285
  terms for loan, 64–65
net income, 90, 93
net profit, 90
New York Times Web site, 335
nondisclosure agreement, 256
non-discrimination policy, 168, 169
nonsolicitation of employees, 217
nonstatutory stock options, 157–158

• *O* •

offer letter, 134–136
office space
  assignment and subletting, 289–290
  expansion options and lease, 291
  improvements and alterations to, 288–289
  negotiating lease for, 279–284
  offer letter, 292–294
  operating costs for, 287–288
  permitted uses for, 285–286
  renewing lease for, 290–291
  rent for, 285

office space *(continued)*
  rules and regulations for building, 292
  security deposit, 291–292
  working out term of lease for, 286
Online Contract, 309–310
Operating Agreement, 19
Operating Agreement checklist
    (Form 1-7), 20
ordinary expense, 114
owners' equity, 97

• P •

partnership
  general, 13–14
  limited, 14–15
  Limited Liability, 15
  overview of, 12
Partnership Agreement, 13
Partnership Agreement checklist
    (Form 1-2), 14
Partnerships (IRS Publication 541), 106
part-time work, 152
pass-through entity, 15
pass-through taxation, 106
patent, 248–250
Patent Assignment Agreement
    (Form 13-4), 250
Patent Pending, 249
payment policy for customers, 263–264
penalties (IRS)
  for late payment of taxes, 108, 109
  for nonpayment of taxes, 113
performance appraisal, 174
permitted use clause in lease contract, 285
personal guaranty, negotiating, 240–241
personal liability, avoiding, 236, 240
personnel. *See* employees
Peterson, Steven, *Business Plans For
    Dummies*, 33
piercing corporate veil, 241
placement agent, 69
planning, importance of, 23. *See also*
    business plan
policies, written
  collecting in handbook, 165–166
  customer payment, 263–264

drug-free work, 171, 173
e-mail, 171, 172
media relations, 322–323
non-discrimination, 168, 169
refund and return, 219
sexual harassment, 168, 170–171
violation of, 175
Porras, Jerry, *Built to Last: Successful Habits
    of Visionary Companies*, 339
posting position on Web site, 122
preemptive right, 81
preferred stock, 17, 71
Pre-Offering Summary, 76
prepaid expense, 96
prepayment of loan, 65
press release
  creating, 330
  delivering, 317–318
  drafting, 315–316
  events to announce in, 318
  hiring of key employees example, 319
  information to include in, 316–317
  new product example, 320
  writing, 322
Private Placement Memorandum, 75–76
pro rata share, 16
product, announcing in press release, 320
product section (business plan), 30
profit margin, computing, 100
profit participation, 72
Profit Sharing Program, 160
Projected Income Statement, 35
projections, 101
promissory note, 66, 67, 72
property tax increases and rent
    amount, 288
prospectus, 76
protecting intellectual property
  Confidentiality Agreement, 256–259
  copyright, 250–251
  overview of, 247
  with patent, 248–250
  trade secret right, 255–256
  trademark, 252–255
Purchase Order, 219–220
purchases, documents supporting, 87

• Q •

qualifying to do business in other state, 244

• R •

raising capital
  borrowing, 64–68
  business plan and, 75
  financing, seeking when not needed,
    328–329
  leasing equipment and, 68–69
  principles about, 63
  stock, selling, 69–77
  venture capital, 77–82
ratios of income, 100
real estate
  assignment and subletting, 289–290
  expansion options and lease, 291
  improvements and alterations to, 288–289
  negotiating lease for, 279–284
  offer letter, 292–294
  operating costs for, 287–288
  permitted uses for, 285–286
  renewing lease for, 290 291
  rent for, 285
  rules and regulations for building, 292
  security deposit, 291–292
  working out term of lease for, 286
Real Estate Sublease (Form 15-4), 290
recapture right, 290
recognizing employees, 150–151
reconciling checking account, 89
record-keeping system
  business checkbook, 89
  categories for, 234–236
  journal and ledger, 88
  overview of, 86–87
  supporting documents, 87–88
redemption right, 71
reference check, 128
refund and return policy, 219
regional press coverage, 321
registered agent, 44
registered trademark, 255

registering
  domain name, 301
  fictitious business name, 243
registration right, 81
reimbursable expense, 93
rent for office space
  fixed versus escalating, 286–287
  negotiating, 285
Report of Cash Payments Over $10,000
    Received in a Trade or Business
    (IRS Form 8300), 109
reporter
  getting attention of, 321–322
  trust and "off the record" comments, 323
Reporting Cash Payments Over $10,000
    Received in a Trade or Business
    (IRS Publication 1544), 109
representation, 219
researching competition, 329–330
resources. *See also* Web sites
  on competition, 329–330
  computers, 341
  for finding good employees, 122
  licenses and permits, 242–243
  publications, 337–339
  tax issues, 115–116
  venture capital, 79
retained earnings, 97
retaining employee
  with flexible workplace, 152
  satisfaction with job, increasing, 150
  Stock Option Plans, 156–160
return, 93
return on equity, 91
rewarding employees, 329
Right of First Offer, 291
Right of First Refusal, 159, 291
Right of First Refusal Agreement, 52
rollover of 401(k) plan, 162

• S •

S corporation
  overview of, 18–19
  tax issues and, 106

S Corporation Election Form (IRS Form 2553), 18, 19, 106
Sales Contract
  Amendment to, 231
  overview of, 218–219
sales tax, 112
satisfaction of employees, increasing, 150
SBA (Small Business Administration)
  loan from, 64, 66, 68
  resources of, 116
  Web site, 68, 332–333
search engine, 42
searching. *See also* finding good employees
  business names, 42
  domain names, 300–301
  patents, 249
  trademarks, 252
  for venture capital, 79
Secretary of State, checking business name
    with, 42
Securities and Exchange Commission
    (SEC), 71, 76
securities law
  limited partnership and, 15
  overview of, 71–75
security agreement, 269
security deposit on leased space, 291–292
security, issuing, 52
seeking new idea, 329
self-employment tax, 110–111
Self-Employment Tax (IRS Publication
    533), 111
service mark, 42, 252
services contract, 213, 217
Settlement Agreement, 177–178, 179–182
Settlement of Disputed Amount (Form
    14-5), 272
sexual harassment, 174
sexual harassment policy, 168, 170–171
shareholders
  actions by, 50–51
  corporation and, 16, 17, 18
  description of, 48
  limited liability for, 241
  of qualified small business, tax benefits
    for, 114–115
  size of board and, 49

signature block, 240
Small Business Administration (SBA)
  loan from, 64, 66, 68
  resources of, 116
  Web site, 68, 332–333
Small Business Tax Education Program, 115
Social Security
  coverage, 110
  withholding, 111
Social Security number (SSN), 107
software
  accounting, 86
  License Agreement for, 220
sole proprietorship, 12
special expense, documents supporting, 87
SSN (Social Security number), 107
staging investment, 82
"standard" contract, 211
"standard" lease, 279–280
Starting a Business and Keeping Records
    (IRS Publication 583), 110
start-up business, expense categories
    for, 114
state of incorporation, choosing, 43
statutory stock option, 157
stock. *See also* securities law
  IPO (initial public offering), 78
  issuing, 52, 69–70
  Private Placement Memorandum, 75–76
  Subscription Agreement, 76–77
  types of, 71
stock ledger, 52, 53
stock option, 72
Stock Option Plan
  elements of, 158–160
  overview of, 156
  types of, 157–158
Stock Purchase Agreement, 81–82
stock records, 235
Stock Subscription Agreement
    (Form 4-13), 77
Stock Subscription Package (Form 4-11), 74
strategic partnership, 69
subletting leased space, 289–290
sublicense, 221

Subscription Agreement, 76–77
suggestions, soliciting from employees, 330
suggestive mark, 254
system requirements for using
    CD-ROM, 341

• T •

tardiness, 175
tax deposit coupon, 108–109
tax issues
  benefits for shareholders of qualified
      small business, 114–115
  C corporation, 18
  corporation, 16
  deposit coupons, 108–109
  employee forms, 107–108
  employee versus independent contractor,
      199, 201
  employment tax records, 87
  employment taxes, 111–112
  excise tax, 112
  general partnership, 14
  identification number, 107
  income taxes, 93, 110
  legal entity and, 106
  Limited Liability Company (LLC), 20
  Limited Liability Partnership (LLP), 15
  limited partnership and, 15
  overview of, 105
  penalties for late payment, 108, 109
  penalties for nonpayment, 113
  property tax increases and rent
      amount, 288
  resources, 115–116
  S corporation and, 106
  sales tax, 112
  self-employment tax, 110–111
  sole proprietorship, 12
tax records, 235
teaming up with another company, 327
telecommuting, 152
term sheet, 80–81
Term Sheet for Equity Investment and
    Strategic Alliance (Form 11-9), 223

terminating employee
  exit interview, 178, 183–184
  legal reasons for, 175–176
  risks of, 176–177
  Settlement Agreement, 177–178, 179–182
Terms of Use Agreement, 310
Tiffany, Paul, *Business Plans For
    Dummies*, 33
Title VII of Civil Rights Act of 1964, 123
top-level domain, 299–300
trade secret, 309
trade secret right, 255–256
trademark
  business name and, 42
  Distribution Agreement and, 224
  domain name and, 302–303
  obtaining, 252–255
Trademark Application cover letter (Form
    13-14), 254
Trademark Application (Form 13-13), 254
Trademark Assignment (Form 13-16), 255
Trademark Registration (Form 16-1), 303
transferability issues
  copyright, 251
  general partnership, 14
  Limited Liability Company (LLC), 20
  limited partnership and, 15
  sole proprietorship, 12
  stock, 17
  Stock Option Plan, 160
*Travel, Entertainment, Gift, and Car
    Expenses* (IRS Publication 463), 87, 114
Triple Net Lease, 285
troubleshooting CD-ROM, 365
truck expenses, 114
Truth in Lending Act, 272

• U •

UCC Financing Statement, 269
Understanding the Collection Process
    (IRS Publication 594), 106
*Understanding Your IRS Taxpayer
    Identification Number* (IRS Publication
    1915), 107
updating Web site, 304

U.S. Patent and Trademark Office, 248, 254
use tax, 112
usury laws, 64–65
utility patent, 248

• *V* •

venture capitalist
  business due diligence, 79
  description of, 69, 77
  legal due diligence, 80
  preparing for meeting with, 78
  searching for, 79
  staging investment, 82
  Stock Purchase Agreement, 81–82
  term sheet, 80–81
vesting period and Stock Option Plan, 159
violence by employee, 176

• *W* •

Wage and Tax Statement (IRS Form W-2), 109
The Wall Street Journal (newspaper), 337
Wall Street Journal Online, 335
warrant, 72
warranty
  expressed versus implied, 264
  laws regarding, 264–265
  Purchase Order and, 219
  Sales Contract and, 218
Web Site Development Agreement
    (Form 16-3), 304
Web sites. *See also* domain name
  AllBusiness, 331–332
  American Express–Small Business,
    334–335
  business concepts, general, 2
  business plan samples, 24
  Business Week, 332
  CBS Marketwatch, 334
  contract for development of, 303–308
  copyright and, 309, 311
  domain name holder, finding, 302
  domain name search, 301

Entrepreneur, 333–334
  federal publications, 116
  hiring developer for, 303
  hosting service, 301
  information disclaimers, 311, 312
  IRS, 115
  job-related, 122–123
  monitoring and updating, 304
  newspapers, 335
  posting positions on, 122
  registered agent, 44
  search engines, 42
  SEC (Securities and Exchange
    Commission), 76
  selling product or service through,
    309–310
  Small Business Administration,
    68, 332–333
  success and, 330
  Terms of Use Agreement, 310
  trademark search, 254
  U.S. Patent and Trademark Office, 249, 254
  venture capital, 79
  Wells Fargo, 335–336
  Wiley Product Technical Support, 365
  Yahoo!, 336
weighted average anti-dilution formula, 81
Wells Fargo Web site, 335–336
whistle-blowing protection, 176
Wiley Product Technical Support, 365
withdrawal from 401(k) plan, 162
working capital, 94
workplace, flexible, 152
World Wide Web, 300
writing business plan, 23–24

• *Y* •

Yahoo! Web site, 336

• *Z* •

zoning laws, 234

Wiley Publishing, Inc.
End-User License Agreement

5. **Limited Warranty.**

   (a) WPI warrants that the Software and Software Media are free from defects in materials and workmanship under normal use for a period of sixty (60) days from the date of purchase of this Book. If WPI receives notification within the warranty period of defects in materials or workmanship, WPI will replace the defective Software Media.

   (b) WPI AND THE AUTHOR(S) OF THE BOOK DISCLAIM ALL OTHER WARRANTIES, EXPRESS OR IMPLIED, INCLUDING WITHOUT LIMITATION IMPLIED WARRANTIES OF MERCHANTABILITY AND FITNESS FOR A PARTICULAR PURPOSE, WITH RESPECT TO THE SOFTWARE, THE PROGRAMS, THE SOURCE CODE CONTAINED THEREIN, AND/OR THE TECHNIQUES DESCRIBED IN THIS BOOK. WPI DOES NOT WARRANT THAT THE FUNCTIONS CONTAINED IN THE SOFTWARE WILL MEET YOUR REQUIRE-MENTS OR THAT THE OPERATION OF THE SOFTWARE WILL BE ERROR FREE.

   (c) This limited warranty gives you specific legal rights, and you may have other rights that vary from jurisdiction to jurisdiction.

6. **Remedies.**

   (a) WPI's entire liability and your exclusive remedy for defects in materials and workmanship shall be limited to replacement of the Software Media, which may be returned to WPI with a copy of your receipt at the following address: Software Media Fulfillment Department, Attn.: *Small Business Kit For Dummies, 2nd Edition,* Wiley Publishing, Inc., 10475 Crosspoint Blvd., Indianapolis, IN 46256, or call 1-800-762-2974. Please allow four to six weeks for delivery. This Limited Warranty is void if failure of the Software Media has resulted from accident, abuse, or misapplication. Any replacement Software Media will be warranted for the remainder of the original warranty period or thirty (30) days, whichever is longer.

   (b) In no event shall WPI or the author be liable for any damages whatsoever (including without limitation damages for loss of business profits, business interruption, loss of business information, or any other pecuniary loss) arising from the use of or inability to use the Book or the Software, even if WPI has been advised of the possibility of such damages.

   (c) Because some jurisdictions do not allow the exclusion or limitation of liability for consequential or incidental damages, the above limitation or exclusion may not apply to you.

7. **U.S. Government Restricted Rights.** Use, duplication, or disclosure of the Software for or on behalf of the United States of America, its agencies and/or instrumentalities "U.S. Government" is subject to restrictions as stated in paragraph (c)(1)(ii) of the Rights in Technical Data and Computer Software clause of DFARS 252.227-7013, or subparagraphs (c) (1) and (2) of the Commercial Computer Software - Restricted Rights clause at FAR 52.227-19, and in similar clauses in the NASA FAR supplement, as applicable.

8. **General.** This Agreement constitutes the entire understanding of the parties and revokes and supersedes all prior agreements, oral or written, between them and may not be modified or amended except in a writing signed by both parties hereto that specifically refers to this Agreement. This Agreement shall take precedence over any other documents that may be in conflict herewith. If any one or more provisions contained in this Agreement are held by any court or tribunal to be invalid, illegal, or otherwise unenforceable, each and every other provision shall remain in full force and effect.

Agreement With Respect to the
Small Business Kit For Dummies, 2nd Edition
Book and Accompanying Software

READ THIS. You should carefully read these terms and conditions before buying the *Small Business Kit For Dummies, 2nd Edition* (the "Book") and opening the software packet(s) included with the Book. This is an agreement ("Agreement") between you, Wiley Publishing, Inc. ("Publisher") and the author of the Book ("Author"). By buying the Book and/or opening the accompanying software packet(s), you acknowledge that you have read, understand and accept the following terms and conditions. If you do not agree and do not want to be bound by such terms and conditions, promptly return the Book and the unopened software packet(s) to the place you obtained them for a full refund.

1. **License Grant.** Subject to the terms of this Agreement, Publisher grants to you (either an individual or entity) a nonexclusive, revocable, non-transferable, non-sublicenseable license to use the Book and one copy of the enclosed software program(s) (collectively, the "Software") solely for your own personal or business purposes. You may use the Software solely on a single computer (whether a standard computer or a workstation component of a multi-user network). The Software is in use on a computer when it is loaded into temporary memory (RAM) or installed into permanent memory (hard disk, CD-ROM, or other storage device). Author reserves all rights not expressly granted herein.

2. **Restrictions.**

    (a) You may only (i) make one copy of the Software for backup or archival purposes, or (ii) transfer the Software to a single hard disk, provided that you keep the original for backup or archival purposes. You may not (i) rent or lease the Software, (ii) copy or reproduce the Software through a LAN or other network system or through any computer subscriber system or bulletin-board system, or (iii) modify, adapt, or create derivative works based on the Software. You may not reverse engineer, decompile, or disassemble the Software.

    (b) Your license for the Book and the Software and any text, graphics, information, materials or documents (collectively defined as "Content and Materials") therein are subject to the following additional restrictions and prohibitions on use: You may not (i) copy, print (except for the express limited purpose permitted by Section 1 above), republish, display, distribute, transmit, sell, rent, lease, loan or otherwise make available in any form or by any means all or any portion of the Book or any Content and Materials; (ii) use the Book, Software or any materials obtained therefrom to develop, or use as a component of, any information, storage and retrieval system, database, information base, or similar resource (in any media now existing or hereafter developed), that is offered for commercial distribution of any kind, including through sale, license, lease, rental, subscription, or any other commercial distribution mechanism; (iii) create compilations or derivative works of any Content and Materials from the Book or the Software; (iv) use any Content and Materials from the Book or the Software in any manner that may infringe any copyright, intellectual property right, proprietary right, or property right of Publisher, Author or any third parties; (v) remove, change or obscure any copyright notice or other proprietary notice or terms of use contained in the Book or the Software; (vi) make any portion of the Book or the Software available through any timesharing system, service bureau, the Internet or any other technology now existing or developed in the future; (vii) use the Book or the Software in a manner that violates any state or federal laws; and (viii) export or re-export the Software or any portion thereof in violation of the export control laws or regulations of the United States.

3. **Copyright.** The content, organization, graphics, design, compilation, magnetic translation, digital conversion and other matters related to the Book and the Software are protected under applicable copyrights, trademarks and other proprietary (including but not limited to intellectual property) rights. The copying, redistribution, use or publication by you of any such matters, except as allowed by Section 1 above, is strictly prohibited. You do not acquire ownership rights to any content, document or other materials contained in the Book or the Software. No claim is made to any government-issued forms, agreements or other content. The copyright to all of the contents in the Book and the forms, agreement and checklists in the Software are owned by the Author.

4. **Forms, Agreements & Documents.** The Software and the Book contain sample forms, agreements, checklists, business documents and legal documents (collectively, "Documents"). All Documents are provided on a non-exclusive license basis only for your personal one-time use for non-commercial purposes, without any right to re-license, sublicense, distribute, assign or transfer such license. Documents are provided without any representations or warranties, express or implied, as to their suitability, legal effect, completeness, currentness, accuracy, and/or appropriateness. THE DOCUMENTS ARE PROVIDED "AS IS", "AS AVAILABLE", AND WITH "ALL FAULTS", AND THE PUBLISHER AND THE AUTHOR DISCLAIM ANY WARRANTIES, INCLUDING BUT NOT LIMITED TO THE WARRANTIES OF MERCHANTABILITY AND FITNESS FOR A PARTICULAR PURPOSE. The Documents may be inappropriate for your particular circumstances. Furthermore, state laws may require different or additional provisions to ensure the desired result. You should consult with legal counsel to determine the appropriate legal or business documents necessary for your particular transactions, as the Documents are only samples and may not be applicable to a particular situation. Some Documents are public domain forms or available from public records, but you should check to see if any newer or updated versions have been issued.

5. **No Legal Advice or Attorney-Client Relationship**. Information contained on or made available from the Book or the Software is not intended to and does not constitute legal advice, recommendations, mediation or counseling under any circumstance and no attorney-client relationship is formed. No warranty or guarantee is made as to the accurateness, completeness, adequacy or currentness of the information contained in the Book or the Software. Your use of information on the Book or the Software is entirely at your own risk.

6. **Indemnification.** You agree to indemnify, defend and hold the Publisher and the Author and their partners, agents, officers, directors, employees, subcontractors, successors, assigns, third party suppliers of information and documents, product and service providers, and affiliates (collectively, "Affiliated Parties") harmless from any liability, loss, claim and expense related to your breach of this Agreement.

7. **Disclaimer.** THE INFORMATION, CONTENT AND DOCUMENTS FROM OR THROUGH THE BOOK OR THE SOFTWARE ARE PROVIDED "AS-IS," "AS AVAILABLE," WITH "ALL FAULTS", AND ALL WARRANTIES, EXPRESS OR IMPLIED, ARE DISCLAIMED (INCLUDING BUT NOT LIMITED TO THE DISCLAIMER OF ANY IMPLIED WARRANTIES OF MERCHANTABILITY AND FITNESS FOR A PARTICULAR PURPOSE). THE SOFTWARE MAY CONTAIN BUGS, ERRORS, PROBLEMS OR OTHER LIMITATIONS. THE PUBLISHER, AUTHOR AND THEIR AFFILIATED PARTIES HAVE NO LIABILITY WHATSOEVER FOR YOUR USE OF THE BOOK AND/OR SOFTWARE, EXCEPT AS PROVIDED IN SECTION 8(b). IN PARTICULAR, BUT NOT AS A LIMITATION THEREOF, THE PUBLISHER, AUTHOR AND THEIR AFFILIATED PARTIES ARE NOT LIABLE FOR ANY INDIRECT, SPECIAL, INCIDENTAL OR CONSEQUENTIAL DAMAGES (INCLUDING, BUT NOT LIMITED TO, DAMAGES FOR LOSS OF BUSINESS, LOSS OF PROFITS, LITIGATION, OR THE LIKE), WHETHER BASED ON BREACH OF CONTRACT, BREACH OF WARRANTY, TORT (INCLUDING NEGLIGENCE), PRODUCT LIABILITY OR OTHERWISE, EVEN IF ADVISED OF THE POSSIBILITY OF SUCH DAMAGES. THE NEGATION AND LIMITATION OF DAMAGES SET FORTH ABOVE ARE FUNDAMENTAL ELEMENTS OF THE BASIS OF THE BARGAIN BETWEEN PUBLISHER, AUTHOR

AND YOU. THE BOOK AND THE SOFTWARE WOULD NOT BE PROVIDED WITHOUT SUCH LIMITATIONS. NOTHING IN THE BOOK OR THE SOFTWARE SHALL CREATE ANY WARRANTY, REPRESENTATION OR GUARANTEE NOT EXPRESSLY STATED IN THIS AGREEMENT.

ALL RESPONSIBILITY OR LIABILITY FOR ANY DAMAGES CAUSED BY VIRUSES CONTAINED WITHIN THE SOFTWARE IS DISCLAIMED.

8. **Limitation of Liability.**

   (a) The Author, Publisher and any Affiliated Party shall not be liable for any loss, injury, claim, liability, or damage of any kind resulting in any way from (a) any errors in or omissions from the Book and/or the Software, or (b) your use of the Book and/or the Software.

   (b) THE AGGREGATE LIABILITY OF THE PUBLISHER, THE AUTHOR AND THE AFFILIATED PARTIES IN CONNECTION WITH ANY CLAIM ARISING OUT OF OR RELATING TO THE BOOK AND/OR THE SOFTWARE SHALL NOT EXCEED THE COST OF THE BOOK AND THAT AMOUNT SHALL BE IN LIEU OF ALL OTHER REMEDIES WHICH YOU MAY HAVE AGAINST THE AUTHOR, THE PUBLISHER AND ANY AFFILIATED PARTY. YOU AGREE TO LOOK SOLELY TO THE PUBLISHER FOR ANY CLAIMS ASSOCIATED WITH THE BOOK AND/OR THE SOFTWARE.

9. **Miscellaneous.** This Agreement shall be treated as though it were executed and performed in San Francisco, California, and shall be governed by and construed in accordance with the laws of the State of California (without regard to conflict of law principles). Any cause of action by you with respect to the Book and the Software must be instituted within one (1) year after the cause of action arose or be forever waived and barred. All actions shall be subject to the limitations set forth in Section 7 and Section 8. The language in this Agreement shall be interpreted as to its fair meaning and not strictly for or against any party. Any rule of construction to the effect that ambiguities are to be resolved against the drafting party shall not apply in interpreting this Agreement. If any provision of this agreement is held illegal, invalid or unenforceable for any reason, that provision shall be enforced to the maximum extent permissible, and the other provisions of this Agreement shall remain in full force and effect. If any provision of this Agreement is held illegal, invalid or unenforceable, it shall be replaced, to the extent possible, with a legal, valid, and unenforceable provision that is similar in tenor to the illegal, invalid, or unenforceable provision as is legally possible. To the extent that anything in or associated with the Book or the Software is in conflict or inconsistent with this Agreement, this Agreement shall take precedence. The Publisher's or Author's failure to enforce any provision of this Agreement shall not be deemed a waiver of such provision nor of the right to enforce such provision. The title, headings and captions of this Agreement are provided for convenience only and shall have no effect on the construction of the terms of this Agreement.

10. **Arbitration.** Any legal controversy or legal claim arising out of or relating to this Agreement, the Book or the Software shall be settled solely by confidential binding arbitration in accordance with the commercial arbitration rules of JAMS, before one arbitrator. Any such controversy or claim shall be arbitrated on an individual basis, and shall not be consolidated in any arbitration with any claim or controversy of any other party. The arbitration shall be conducted in San Francisco, California. Each party shall bear its own attorneys' fees. Each party shall bear one-half of the arbitration fees and costs incurred through JAMS. The arbitrator shall not have the right to award punitive damages or speculative damages to either party and shall not have the power to amend this Agreement. The arbitrator shall be required to follow applicable law. IF FOR ANY REASON THIS ARBITRATION CLAUSE BECOMES INAPPLICABLE, THEN EACH PARTY, TO THE FULLEST EXTENT PERMITTED BY APPLICABLE LAW, HEREBY IRREVOCABLY WAIVES ALL RIGHT TO TRIAL BY JURY AS TO ANY ISSUE RELATING HERETO IN ANY ACTIONS, PROCEEDINGS, OR COUNTERCLAIM ARISING OUT OF OR RELATING TO THIS AGREEMENT, THE BOOK AND/OR THE SOFTWARE.

11. **U.S. Government Restricted Rights.** Use, duplication or disclosure of the Software by the U.S. Government is subject to restrictions stated in paragraph (c)(1)(ii) of the Rights in Technical Data and Computer Software clause of DFARS 252.227-7013, and in subparagraphs (a) through (d) of the Commercial Computer-Restricted Rights clause at FAR 52.227-19, and in similar clauses in the NASA FAR supplement, when applicable.

DO NOT BUY THE BOOK OR USE THE SOFTWARE UNLESS YOU UNDERSTAND AND AGREE WITH THE FOREGOING AGREEMENT.

*****

FOR DUMMIES®

The easy way to get more done and have more fun

PERSONAL FINANCE & BUSINESS

Investing FOR DUMMIES
0-7645-2431-3

Home Buying FOR DUMMIES
0-7645-5331-3

Grant Writing FOR DUMMIES
0-7645-5307-0

Also available:

Accounting For Dummies
(0-7645-5314-3)

Business Plans Kit For Dummies
(0-7645-5365-8)

Managing For Dummies
(1-5688-4858-7)

Mutual Funds For Dummies
(0-7645-5329-1)

QuickBooks All-in-One Desk Reference For Dummies
(0-7645-1963-8)

Resumes For Dummies
(0-7645-5471-9)

Small Business Kit For Dummies
(0-7645-5093-4)

Starting an eBay Business For Dummies
(0-7645-1547-0)

Taxes For Dummies 2003
(0-7645-5475-1)

HOME, GARDEN, FOOD & WINE

Feng Shui FOR DUMMIES
0-7645-5295-3

Gardening FOR DUMMIES
0-7645-5130-2

Cooking FOR DUMMIES
0-7645-5250-3

Also available:

Bartending For Dummies
(0-7645-5051-9)

Christmas Cooking For Dummies
(0-7645-5407-7)

Cookies For Dummies
(0-7645-5390-9)

Diabetes Cookbook For Dummies
(0-7645-5230-9)

Grilling For Dummies
(0-7645-5076-4)

Home Maintenance For Dummies
(0-7645-5215-5)

Slow Cookers For Dummies
(0-7645-5240-6)

Wine For Dummies
(0-7645-5114-0)

FITNESS, SPORTS, HOBBIES & PETS

Fitness FOR DUMMIES
0-7645-5167-1

Golf FOR DUMMIES
0-7645-5146-9

Guitar FOR DUMMIES
0-7645-5106-X

Also available:

Cats For Dummies
(0-7645-5275-9)

Chess For Dummies
(0-7645-5003-9)

Dog Training For Dummies
(0-7645-5286-4)

Labrador Retrievers For Dummies
(0-7645-5281-3)

Martial Arts For Dummies
(0-7645-5358-5)

Piano For Dummies
(0-7645-5105-1)

Pilates For Dummies
(0-7645-5397-6)

Power Yoga For Dummies
(0-7645-5342-9)

Puppies For Dummies
(0-7645-5255-4)

Quilting For Dummies
(0-7645-5118-3)

Rock Guitar For Dummies
(0-7645-5356-9)

Weight Training For Dummies
(0-7645-5168-X)

Available wherever books are sold.
Go to www.dummies.com or call 1-877-762-2974 to order direct

WILEY

FOR DUMMIES®

A world of resources to help you grow

TRAVEL

Italy
0-7645-5453-0

Hawaii
0-7645-5438-7

Walt Disney World & Orlando
0-7645-5444-1

Also available:

America's National Parks For Dummies
(0-7645-6204-5)

Caribbean For Dummies
(0-7645-5445-X)

Cruise Vacations For Dummies 2003
(0-7645-5459-X)

Europe For Dummies
(0-7645-5456-5)

Ireland For Dummies
(0-7645-6199-5)

France For Dummies
(0-7645-6292-4)

Las Vegas For Dummies
(0-7645-5448-4)

London For Dummies
(0-7645-5416-6)

Mexico's Beach Resorts For Dummies
(0-7645-6262-2)

Paris For Dummies
(0-7645-5494-8)

RV Vacations For Dummies
(0-7645-5443-3)

EDUCATION & TEST PREPARATION

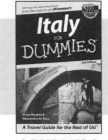

Spanish
0-7645-5194-9

Algebra
0-7645-5325-9

U.S. History
0-7645-5249-X

Also available:

The ACT For Dummies
(0-7645-5210-4)

Chemistry For Dummies
(0-7645-5430-1)

English Grammar For Dummies
(0-7645-5322-4)

French For Dummies
(0-7645-5193-0)

GMAT For Dummies
(0-7645-5251-1)

Inglés Para Dummies
(0-7645-5427-1)

Italian For Dummies
(0-7645-5196-5)

Research Papers For Dummies
(0-7645-5426-3)

SAT I For Dummies
(0-7645-5472-7)

U.S. History For Dummies
(0-7645-5249-X)

World History For Dummies
(0-7645-5242-2)

HEALTH, SELF-HELP & SPIRITUALITY

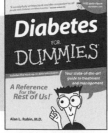

Diabetes
0-7645-5154-X

Sex
0-7645-5302-X

Parenting
0-7645-5418-2

Also available:

The Bible For Dummies
(0-7645-5296-1)

Controlling Cholesterol For Dummies
(0-7645-5440-9)

Dating For Dummies
(0-7645-5072-1)

Dieting For Dummies
(0-7645-5126-4)

High Blood Pressure For Dummies
(0-7645-5424-7)

Judaism For Dummies
(0-7645-5299-6)

Menopause For Dummies
(0-7645-5458-1)

Nutrition For Dummies
(0-7645-5180-9)

Potty Training For Dummies
(0-7645-5417-4)

Pregnancy For Dummies
(0-7645-5074-8)

Rekindling Romance For Dummies
(0-7645-5303-8)

Religion For Dummies
(0-7645-5264-3)

FOR DUMMIES®

Plain-English solutions for everyday challenges

HOME & BUSINESS COMPUTER BASICS

0-7645-0838-5

0-7645-1663-9

0-7645-1548-9

Also available:

Excel 2002 All-in-One Desk Reference For Dummies (0-7645-1794-5)

Office XP 9-in-1 Desk Reference For Dummies (0-7645-0819-9)

PCs All-in-One Desk Reference For Dummies (0-7645-0791-5)

Troubleshooting Your PC For Dummies (0-7645-1669-8)

Upgrading & Fixing PCs For Dummies (0-7645-1665-5)

Windows XP For Dummies (0-7645-0893-8)

Windows XP For Dummies Quick Reference (0-7645-0897-0)

Word 2002 For Dummies (0-7645-0839-3)

INTERNET & DIGITAL MEDIA

0-7645-0894-6

0-7645-1642-6

0-7645-1664-7

Also available:

CD and DVD Recording For Dummies (0-7645-1627-2)

Digital Photography All-in-One Desk Reference For Dummies (0-7645-1800-3)

eBay For Dummies (0-7645-1642-6)

Genealogy Online For Dummies (0-7645-0807-5)

Internet All-in-One Desk Reference For Dummies (0-7645-1659-0)

Internet For Dummies Quick Reference (0-7645-1645-0)

Internet Privacy For Dummies (0-7645-0846-6)

Paint Shop Pro For Dummies (0-7645-2440-2)

Photo Retouching & Restoration For Dummies (0-7645-1662-0)

Photoshop Elements For Dummies (0-7645-1675-2)

Scanners For Dummies (0-7645-0783-4)

Get smart! Visit www.dummies.com

- **Find listings of even more Dummies titles**
- **Browse online articles, excerpts, and how-to's**
- **Sign up for daily or weekly e-mail tips**
- **Check out Dummies fitness videos and other products**
- **Order from our online bookstore**

Available wherever books are sold. Go to www.dummies.com or call 1-877-762-2974 to order direct